For Marian, Gabriella, Joshua, and Michael

Contents

List of Tables and Figures

Tables

Figures

Preface to the Fourth Edition

The third edition of this book was written about four years ago, when François Mitterrand was already in his second term as president and the Socialist party was still in full control of French national affairs. Since then, the Socialists have been disavowed in regional, local, and parliamentary elections; a new conservative government has been installed, and thus another round of "cohabitation" has begun. The modernization and globalization of the French economy continued as the country became more tightly interconnected with the European Union. At the same time, unemployment grew apace and the social-protection mechanisms became overloaded. As a result, governmental authorities began to examine the limits of the welfare state, and the public became increasingly disgruntled with its leaders and the political parties that had brought them forward. This disaffection expressed itself in a growing "dealignment" from traditional political parties and the rise of smaller formations oriented toward limited issues and in periodic mass demonstrations focusing on problems of education, immigration, employment, and crime. Nevertheless, there was a deepening consensus about the nature of the regime and the stability it embodied. The institutions of that regime continued to remain in place; however, there were a number of changes, by means of formal constitutional amendments, legislative enactments, and pattern modifications, that brought France into line with European Union norms and that provided for a better institutional balance, especially in the relationship between the executive and the legislature.

The continuities and changes are reflected in this edition. The chapter arrangement has been retained; the approach of this book remains unambiguously institutional but is marked by attention to the historical background and evolution of institutions and to the behavior of individuals who use (or abuse) them. The treatment of the political party system has been updated; much of its detail has been kept, both to show its inherent complexity and to indicate the incessant changes in the parties' internal and external relationships and the interplay of events, ideologies, and personalities. The discussion of the executive and of public policy has been brought up to date as well; and the treatment of parliament, administration, the judiciary, and civil liberties has been extended to account for new developments. Several themes—constitutional reform, public attitudes, education, economic policy, and the European Union—are treated in more than one place. I have tried to furnish illustrative examples of policies and actions and cite a variety of viewpoints, some of them in the text and others in the notes. Many of the tables, figures, and survey data have been redone and new ones have been added. The notes and references are numerous and wide-ranging, but I do not pretend that they are exhaustive. Much of the material is taken from public documents, monographs, and the periodical press. This has been supplemented by information I gleaned from French and American colleagues and friends as well as by insights I was able to gather at close range in 1991–1992 as a visiting professor at the Institut d'Etudes Politiques of the University of Grenoble.

For whatever merit this study possesses, I owe thanks to many people. Some have read individual chapters and commented on specific details; others have discussed certain themes with me and provided critiques, clarifications, and suggestions; and still others helped me unwittingly in the sense that I have learned much from their writings. I wish to express my gratitude in particular to the following: François d'Arcy, Jacques Coeuillet, Maurice Croisat, Julius W. Friend, Paul Godt, Pierre Martin, Vincent Hoffmann-Martinot, Dominique Labbé, Jean-Luc Parodi, Françoise Praderie, Jean-Louis Quermonne, Philippe Roqueplo, Jean Tournon, and Georges Zeller. To this list I must add the late Douglas Ashford, for our discussions enriched my understanding of problems and processes of French public policy. I also want to record my indebtedness to three anonymous reviewers of the previous edition, who provided overall appraisals and made useful suggestions for improvement. Furthermore, I want to thank the following individuals who read the entire manuscript for the present edition and whose helpful comments and advice I tried valiantly to follow:

Frank R. Baumgartner, Texas A&M University
Mary-Jane Deeb, The American University
Ronald Francisco, University of Kansas
John T. S. Keeler, University of Washington
Arthur B. Gunlicks, University of Richmond
Gordon Tolle, South Dakota State University

I must not fail to signal my appreciation of Owen Lancer and David Shapiro of Longman Publishing Group for their encouragement, their professionalism, and their patience, and the copy editor, Claire Caterer, for her meticulousness. Last but not least, I thank my wife, Marian, who has shared my experiences in France and, in many ways, the making of this book. For all errors of fact, interpretation, and omission I alone continue to remain responsible.

William Safran

chapter 1

France: The Historical and Constitutional Background

An observer of France is struck by the importance of politics to most of its citizens and by the controversies surrounding the meaning of political developments. Since the revolution of 1789, whose bicentennial was celebrated a few years ago, there have been many changes of regime, accompanied by changes in social structure, public attitudes, and political style. These changes have been interpreted in various ways. To some, they are steps in a continual climb toward freedom, equality, reason, and prosperity; to others, they are deplored as signifying the abandonment of order and authority; to still others, the changes have occurred at too slow a pace, so that France has lagged behind some of its neighbors. Fundamental disagreements about the ideal political system and anxieties about the country's future have in the past been reflected in polarized political parties, arguments about the constitution, and, often enough, street fights, general strikes, and rebellions. Yet the majority of French men and women have shared a highly developed sense of national identity and an immense pride in their country, the beauty of its landscape, its long history, the glory of its monarchs, the military exploits of its generals, its global diplomatic role, its intellectual and artistic achievements, the variety of its cuisine, the spread of its language, and the influence of its political ideas.

At the same time, the French have been increasingly concerned about the loss of their uniqueness, which has been challenged by the internationalization and popularization of their national culture, the spread of American influence on their language and mores, and the growing irrelevance of many of their ideologies. Nothing has been more unsettling to the French than the question of how France can protect its national character and its independence while at the same time becoming part of an increasingly integrated European Union.

1

France is the third largest country in Europe (after Russia and Ukraine), its boundaries having been more or less fixed some two centuries ago. It achieved national unity earlier than did Germany or Italy; it was the first important European country to produce a revolution, to commit itself to republican rule, and to export its democratic ideals to foreign countries. Its great natural wealth, once measured in agricultural terms, led to relative economic self-sufficiency and inward-looking tendencies, whereas its universalist principles and its military power contributed to its international outlook. It is a country in which revolutionary mythologies persisted alongside social and economic traditionalism and in which the apparent disorder in politics contrasted with orderly and relatively rigid patterns of culture in general: the geometric layout of Paris and other cities, the neoclassical architecture, the formal gardens, the stylized drama, a strictly codified etiquette, uniform school curricula, and the continuing attempts by the authorities to exert formal control over the purity of the French language.[1]

Historically, France owes much to Julius Caesar. Survivals of the Roman conquest are obvious: the Romance language, the Roman law, the mixed racial stock (Latin grafted onto the indigenous Celtic and Germanic), and the French toleration (at least in principle) of different races. The movement toward centralization of the various autonomous provinces was gradual and occurred essentially from about A.D. 1000 to the sixteenth century.

Geographically, France is far from a uniform country. There are mountainous areas, such as the Alps, the Jura, and the Vosges in the east, the Pyrenees in the south, and the Auvergne (Massif Central) in the south-center. In the south, there is the subtropical vegetation typical of the Mediterranean; around Paris and its surrounding regions, there are forested areas and extensive wheat fields; in the west, the flat coastal Vendée fronts on the Atlantic Ocean; and the flatlands of the northwest spill over into Belgian Flanders. The French like to point to these diverse features, in addition to the moderate climate and the fertility of the soil, and to relate them to the development of national pride, the hexagonal symmetry of the country's map, and the peculiar mix of national and local orientations.

France is at least as complex as the United States and as diverse geographically and culturally. It is noteworthy that the two countries share many features, regardless of differences in historical development. To name just a few common traits: (1) the belief that a constitution does not "evolve" organically but is the result of rational choice—a belief reflected in the United States in the founders' conviction that a political experiment could be started from scratch and that previous political formulas could be rejected *in toto,* and in France, in the politics, culture, and religion of reason, which shortly after the revolution of 1789 led to the temporary "abolition" of God, the Christian calendar, and traditional social institutions; (2) the principle of popular sovereignty, that is, the axiom that governmental powers are derived from the people; (3) a commitment to the principle of equal rights for all; (4) a persistent localism in politics; and (5) a commitment to equal representation and to a public and secular educational system for the masses.

THE LEGACY OF THE REVOLUTION

Five of France's eleven political systems since 1789 have been republics. The remainder comprised three monarchies, two empires, and one fascist puppet state. Each republic has given France new institutions and patterns, which were at least partly incorporated into succeeding regimes. The First Republic (1792 to 1799) proclaimed the notion of popular sovereignty, produced the Declaration of the Rights of Man and the Citizen, reduced the power of the Catholic church, and inaugurated the secular age in politics. During the Second Republic (1848 to 1852), universal male suffrage was introduced, and a plebiscitary element—the election of the president by popular vote—was injected into French political life. During the Third Republic (1875 to 1940), the church was formally disestablished, the executive branch was weakened and made responsible to a parliament that asserted its supremacy, and the French nation, it seemed, was decisively converted to republicanism.

Still, many innovations introduced during the old monarchical system (the *ancien régime*) and many pre-republican social patterns persisted well into the twentieth century. The monarchical centralization of administration, introduced by Cardinal de Richelieu, Mazarin, and Colbert during the seventeenth century, continued to the present republic with only minor modifications, and the pre-eminence of Paris, secured by the Bourbon rulers, still informs French political, economic, and cultural life. The old social and legal distinctions between the nobility and the middle class that had marked the *ancien régime* gave way, but they were replaced by almost equally pronounced distinctions between the bourgeoisie and the working class. The French republic, whatever its latest constitutional expression, continued to be adorned with several monarchist glosses: the glorification of French kings and of the royal and martial tradition in the history books, the châteaux, and museums; the refurbishing of old buildings and neighborhoods in the name of art or cultural continuity; and the nostalgia for a national hero.

Just as popular dissatisfactions with existing monarchies expressed themselves in periodic uprisings that culminated in republican experiments, republics were inevitably overlaid with reactionary institutions and ideologies. The attempt in 1789 to moderate the absolute rule of the Bourbon dynasty ended with its abolition. The revolutionary republic that replaced it was in turn replaced by the Reign of Terror, a directory, and, finally, a consulate. This last gave way to the First Empire of Napoleon Bonaparte (who had been first consul) in 1804. When that empire collapsed, largely from external causes, the French regime returned to Bourbon rule with the accession of Louis XVIII to the throne in 1814. That regime retained, at least in theory, some of Napoleon's accomplishments: the establishment of a merit-based civil service, the abolition of feudal tax obligations, and a system of codified laws. The Charter of 1814 provided a framework for a constitutional monarchy on the English model. The charter called for religious freedom, the sanctity of property, procedural safeguards against arrest, equality before the law, and some participation in the legislative process by a bicameral parliament.

But when Charles X ascended to the throne in 1824, monarchical rule became increasingly arbitrary. The subsequent replacement of the Bourbon king by Louis-Philippe (of the House of Orléans) after the Revolution of July 1830 was intended to provide a better opportunity for the development of constitutional rule. As if to underline its republican spirit, the "July Monarchy" used as its symbol not the fleur-de-lis of the Bourbons but the tricolor flag of the revolution of 1789. Censorship was abolished; equality before the law was guaranteed; extraordinary courts were forbidden; trial by jury was instituted; and the Parliament was granted more significant lawmaking responsibilities. But that regime too was a disappointment, for Parliament continued to be disregarded, opposition leaders were arrested, and political liberty did not flourish.

In 1848, the French revolted again and instituted the Second Republic. The Constitution of (November) 1848 was a remarkably democratic and modern document, especially because its social provisions foreshadowed the constitutions of twentieth-century welfare states. The one plebiscitary feature of the Constitution—the provision for the direct election of the president—was soon injudiciously used by the French people when they voted for Louis Napoleon, the nephew of the great emperor, as president and elected an Assembly with a monarchist major-ity—and when, three years later, they acquiesced in the establishment of the Second Empire under Napoleon III.

The Second Empire was, in theory, a republican or "popular" empire in the sense that it was inaugurated by a plebiscite. The Constitution of January 1852, on which it was based, confirmed "the great principles proclaimed in 1789." The chief executive was "responsible to the French people" (rather than to God), and legislative power was to be exercised collectively by the president,[2] the Senate, and the Chamber of Deputies. The Senate was appointed by Napoleon III, but the Chamber was elected on the basis of universal manhood suffrage. However, legislative initiative rested with the president (later emperor), and ministers were responsible to him rather than to Parliament. The republican features of the Constitution were progressively subverted by imperial interference in legislative elections, the persecution of opposition candidates, and the requirement of an oath of imperial support and allegiance for all deputies. To counteract growing popular disenchantment—perhaps boredom—with the regime after 1860, Napoleon III made halfhearted attempts to liberalize it by increasing the power of the Parliament, which even obtained the right of legislative initiative. But it was too late, because the defeat of France at the hands of the Prussians in 1870 discredited and disorganized the Second Empire, and a rebellion in Paris hastened its demise.

The regime that followed the Second Empire was a republic by default. The National Assembly that was hurriedly elected in 1871 to provide a government capable of negotiating peace with Bismarck's Germany did not want a republic at all: More than 400 of its 650 deputies were monarchists. But since the Assembly could not agree on which of the three dynasties (Bourbon, Orléans, Bonaparte) should be called upon to provide a king, the precise nature of the regime was left unsettled. The Assembly adopted a skeleton constitution that dealt merely with "the organization of public powers"—the executive and legislature—and the relationship between them. This constitution contained neither a preamble nor a bill of rights. The first provisional president, Adolphe Thiers, who had served as a minister in several preceding monarchical regimes, had become convinced that "a republic divides us least." His successor, Marshal Mac-Mahon, was a conservative, a clericalist, and a monarchist. The question of the regime was tentatively and surreptitiously settled in 1875, when the Parliament adopted—by a one-vote majority—an amendment providing that "the president of the *Republic* shall be elected by a plurality of votes of the Senate and the Chamber of Deputies meeting in joint session."[3]

The "provisional" Third Republic was to last 65 years, and the political patterns established in it were to influence succeeding republican regimes. There was a popularly elected Chamber of Deputies, juxtaposed to a Senate dominated by indirectly elected, relatively aged, and conservative representatives of rural communes. The cabinet, though appointed by the president, was collectively responsible to Parliament, which could oust it by a vote of censure. The president, elected for seven years, was not "responsible" in that his acts had to be countersigned by a minister. But he did have the power to dissolve the Chamber (after consulting the Senate).

The conflict between the legislature and the executive was never fully resolved, at least in formal constitutional terms, and was to lead to several crises. The first and most important of these was the episode of May 16, 1877, when President Mac-Mahon ousted a republican prime minister with whom he did not get along (in spite of the latter's solid support in the Chamber of Deputies), appointed a monarchist in his stead, and dissolved Parliament. The newly elected Chamber was even more solidly republican (or "leftist," in the context of that period) than its predecessor; and when, early in 1879, the Senate too was brought under the control of the republicans, Mac-Mahon saw himself as effectively repudiated and resigned. Nearly all presidents who succeeded him were deliberately selected on the basis of their lack of ambition. The presidential dissolution power atrophied, and the chief of state became a figurehead, like an English monarch, rather than an active decision maker. In fact, of the 14 presidents of the Third Republic, only 6 served full 7-year terms.[4] The Third Republic became a parliamentary regime that proved durable but very unstable, with the legislature recklessly overturning cabinets at an average rate of once every eight months.

While in Britain a gradually evolving democracy and parliamentary supremacy could accommodate itself easily to the retention of traditional institutions and patterns, such as the Crown, the House of Lords, the established church, and the acceptance of a deferential and hierarchical social order, the French, with their Cartesian intellectualism,[5] were unable to compromise among clashing political norms. "Republicanism" was grudgingly accepted, but its precise meaning was subject to disagreement. Its dominant expression was Jacobinism, which could be traced back to a belief (espoused by Rousseau as well as the men of the Reign of Terror) in a direct democracy that excluded all intermediaries or mediating structures, such as political parties, interest groups, and local governments; in egalitarianism and anticlericalism (opposition to the [Catholic] church, particularly its political role); and in the supremacy of the state as the embodiment of the "general will" (or the public interest). And yet the Paris Commune of 1871,[6] the first French egalitarian (or "socialist") uprising, was mercilessly crushed by the bourgeoisie that led the new republic. Despite the distrust of institutions that would interpose themselves between people and government, the role of the Senate, an indirectly elected body, became very important. A commitment to the republic did not necessarily mean the acceptance of a particular manifestation of it: The government was hated, although the state was depended on by various sectors of society that expected protection and subvention.

Nor did the commitment to the republic resolve a deep-seated disagreement about political values. This dissensus stemmed from the confusion of three strains coexisting in French political culture: rationalism, historicism, and hero worship. The rationalistic spirit has been reflected in recurring attempts to elevate a particular set of abstract principles and to construct a "logical" political system on their basis.[7] This attitude was personified by Abbé Siéyès, who, after the revolution of 1789, wrote several draft constitutions based on his principles of an "indivisible popular sovereignty" and a "just representation"—principles first embodied in the Constitution of 1791. Historicism implies the belief that a political system cannot be constructed from logical blueprints; it is a reaction to, and an evolution from, a nation's collective experiences, which do not always follow rational patterns. In order to "explain" their political positions, many French citizens used to refer, without more specific identification, to "the 18th Brumaire" (of 1799, when Napoleon instituted his coup d'état); "the July Monarchy" (of 1830); "the Affair of May 16" (1877); "the episode of May 13" (the revolt of the French officers in Algeria in 1958); and "the May Events" (of 1968)—as if the references were clearly understood by all French schoolchildren. Moreover, all French political attitudes are said to be shaped by the revolution of 1789. The republicans have considered themselves the true heirs of the revolution because they trace their own faith in a secular and parliamentary government to the years following that great event. The moderates believed that the revolution established, once and for all, the political ascendancy of the bourgeoisie. Leftists considered it their task to "complete" the revolution by adding economic rights to the political rights already gained, thereby achieving "liberty, equality, and fraternity"; and the political Right saw the revolution as a mistake to be rectified. The hero-worshipping French are essentially antirationalist and historicist. The belief that institutions are run by people and are therefore corruptible is coupled with the belief that there are individuals who are untainted by corruption and who must be called upon to rectify the evils of the "system" and to advance national unity. The French have always had numerous historical models for such heroes.

The remembrance of these heroes and the revolt against reason explain why the Third Republic was confronted with repeated eruptions of traditionalism, Bonapartism, monarchism, and fascism. In 1886, General Boulanger, a "man on horseback," was encouraged by antirepublican and clericalist forces to institute a coup d'état, and he might have succeeded had he not lost his nerve. The Dreyfus Affair, in which militarism, monarchism, clericalism, and anti-Semitism, abetted by a corrupt judiciary, colluded in the pressing of trumped-up espionage charges against a Jewish military officer, occurred in the 1890s; it divided France into two hostile camps and almost destroyed the republic. A century has passed since that affair began, but it is still evoked as a reminder of how hatred and injustice can undermine democracy. In the 1920s and 1930s, the *Action française*, the *Croix de feu*, and other extreme nationalist and antidemocratic movements challenged the legitimacy of the regime. Yet the Third Republic survived all these challenges. In the first decade of the twentieth century, the church was separated from the state, and the regime was on solid enough foundations to emerge intact from the experience of World War I. Parliament had asserted its supremacy, at least in theory, and much progress was achieved despite chronic cabinet instability and legislative immobility; and when the Popular Front, a left-wing coalition under Léon Blum in 1936, attempted to institute far-reaching social reforms, it seemed that the egalitarian aspect of republicanism would finally be taken into account.

The Third Republic—so far, the longest-lasting regime since 1789—ended with the fall of Paris to the invading German armies in the summer of 1940. Whether the Vichy regime that followed was constituted legally or not; whether the republic could have survived if France had not been defeated; whether the political institutions had been so subverted from within by apathy, defeatism, or antidemocratic sentiment that France's ability to fight Germany was destroyed— all these are questions not susceptible to clear answers, even after a half century.[8] France has only gradually been freeing itself from a Vichy guilt complex stemming from the fact that many of its citizens collaborated with the Nazi regime, in particular with its persecution of the Jews, and the country has been reexamining the Occupation period objectively in fiction, nonfiction, and films.[9]

THE RISE AND FALL OF THE FOURTH REPUBLIC

When France was liberated in 1944, monarchism was dead. A new spirit of unity had been forged during the Resistance, and there was general agreement that the republic should be continued or renewed. Most Catholics had become republican, and their party, the Popular Republican Movement (*Mouvement républicain populaire*—MRP) had emerged from the Resistance as the largest party. The Communist Party too was considered respectable and patriotic. An unprecedented leftist majority, composed of the MRP, the Socialists, and the Communists, participated in the first postwar government coalition and agreed on the need to establish a progressive, welfare-oriented republic.

Nevertheless, there was disagreement about the *form* of that republic. The Communists and Socialists favored a strong unicameral legislature and a weak executive. The first-draft constitution that embodied these ideas was, however, rejected in a popular referendum held in May 1946. A second-draft constitution provided for bicameralism. This constitution, which inaugurated the Fourth Republic, was ratified by a bare plurality of the French people: Only 60 percent of the electorate participated in the referendum, and of these only two-thirds voted yes. The Communists remained unenthusiastic about the Constitution, for they opposed a second parliamentary chamber. The most vocal opposition came from General Charles de Gaulle, the wartime leader of the Free French and the head of the provisional government that had been formed after the liberation. The general and his supporters were convinced that the constitution was foredoomed to failure because of its imperfections (chief among these being the absence of a strong executive). They started a vigorous campaign against the document, a campaign that gave rise to the Rally of the French People (*Rassemblement du peuple français*—RPF), the first Gaullist mass movement.

There were indeed many structural weaknesses in the Fourth Republic Constitution. The Assembly was given too much power, while the role of the Council of the Republic, a pale copy of the Third Republic Senate, was ill defined and ambiguous. The dual executive was reminiscent of the Third Republic: The president, elected by Parliament, was a mere figurehead; and the prime minister, the real decision maker, was chosen by and responsible to the legislature. The prime minister theoretically possessed dissolution power, but he exercised that power only once.

The Assembly remained sensitive about its constitutionally defined legislative supremacy, but in the absence of coherent and stable majorities, that chamber could not fully play its role. Because of its inability or unwillingness to make unpleasant decisions, it delegated legislative or decree powers to cabinets (in violation of the Constitution) only to oust them once decisions had been made. Cabinet instability was aggravated by the ambitions of numerous politicians who considered themselves of ministerial caliber (*ministrables*) and were eager for cabinet posts.

Any postmortem of the Fourth Republic is of course incomplete if one disregards the accomplishments of that regime. It instituted the first national modernization plan for the economy and thereby helped bring prosperity to France. It initiated extensive social legislation, including paid vacations for all workers,[10] comprehensive medical insurance, and subsidies to families with children. It started France on the road to decolonization and committed the nation to participation in the European Coal and Steel Community and, subsequently, the Common Market.

To be sure, there were policy failures, foremost among them the failure to reform the tax system, to provide adequate wages to industrial workers, and to reduce significantly the gap between the rich and the poor. It is possible that these problems might have been resolved and the imperfections of the Constitution transcended by political practice had it not been for the colonial question, the frustration of the military and the scarcity of strong leaders capable of dealing with these issues.

Members of the military, in particular, brought up with the historical memories (or myths) of a glorious national army, had in their lifetimes experienced mainly defeats: the fall of France in 1940, the defeat at Dien Bien Phu in Indochina in 1954, the Suez misadventure of 1956, and a continuing inability to pacify the rebels in North Africa. Just as German officers had blamed the "politicians" for the defeat of Germany in 1918, so the French generals had tried to assign the blame for their lack of military victories to the politicians and the republic that had brought these men forward.

The final years and months of the Fourth Republic saw a rapid succession of "prosystem" (i.e., essentially centrist) governments that were, however, unable to deal with the problem of Algeria (whose indigenous population was fighting to free itself from French colonial rule) and, as it turned out, to save the regime. The French Parliament had made a few last-ditch attempts to eliminate certain constitutional difficulties. In 1954, the Constitution had been amended to make the investiture of prime ministers easier—and thus to make deadlocks less likely—by requiring a relative (or simple) rather than an absolute majority. In March 1958, in order to reduce the scope of irresponsible behavior on the part of deputies, a reform was instituted that forbade backbenchers to introduce bills resulting in an increase of public expenditure. In addition, the Assembly sharply limited its own power to oust a cabinet by a vote of censure.[11] But these reforms came too late. Moreover, General de Gaulle, who had "saved" the honor of France in the past, waited in his country home at Colombey-les-deux-Eglises for the opportunity to act as the savior of his nation once more.

In April 1958, the resident military in Algeria established—in a manner reminiscent of 1793—a Committee of Public Safety. Its demand for the return of de Gaulle to power was echoed by the general's political supporters on the mainland of France. In May, the president of the Republic, René Coty, sent a letter to de Gaulle exploring the possibility of the general's return. De Gaulle promptly held a press conference in which he announced his "availability" and began to take steps to form a government. The coup de grâce of the Fourth Republic was finally delivered by President Coty when he (somewhat belatedly) informed Parliament that he had asked the general to form a government and that he would resign if the formation of such a government were prevented.[12]

THE SOURCES AND NATURE OF
THE FIFTH REPUBLIC CONSTITUTION

On June 1, 1958, de Gaulle was formally invested as prime minister by the Assembly and empowered by the latter to undertake a revision of the Constitution. The Fifth Republic Constitution, which was written in record time, is an eclectic document that incorporates monarchical, plebiscitary, and traditional republican features (see Table 1.1), in addition to specifically Gaullist innovations.[13]

In modern French political history, there have been two conflicting constitutional theories: the Rousseauist theory of complete popular sovereignty, as enunciated in the *Social Contract*,[14] and the doctrine of a "mixed government." According to Rousseau's theory, a truly democratic constitution is based on the principle that all political sovereignty rests inalienably with the people, who can

TABLE 1.1   Fifth Republic features and their precedents

Feature of the Fifth Republic Constitution	Precedent or Model
Popular election of president (amendment: 1962; first election: 1965)	Constitution of 1848 (Second Republic)
Seven-year term of president	Fourth Republic
Power to appoint prime minister without prior parliamentary consultation	Second Republic
Presidential dissolution power	Third Republic (until 1879)
Presidential lawmaking (by decree)	Second Republic
Economic and Social Council	Third and Fourth Republics
Referenda or plebiscites for constitutional amendments	1802 (Napoleon Bonaparte made consul for life)
	1852 (Napoleon III vested with imperial powers)
Limit of Parliament's budget-making powers	End of Fourth Republic
President as "co-initiator" of legislation	Second and Third Republics
President as negotiator of treaties	Second and Third Republics
Plebiscitary appeal to the people	Constitution of 1852 (Napoleon III)
Constitution adopted by referendum	Year I (1792) Year III (1795) Year VIII (1799) Fourth Republic (1946)
Incompatibility of cabinet office with parliamentary mandate	Constitution of 1791 (constitutional monarchy)

delegate decision-making power only imperfectly, if at all, to a legislature. The second constitutional principle envisages a balanced mixture of executive, legislative, and judicial institutions, all of which derive equally from the people and are therefore "coordinate" (but not as separate from each other as Montesquieu had envisaged them in his *Spirit of the Laws*[15]). The Rousseauist doctrine was reflected in the "Jacobin" Constitution of 1792, which gave unlimited power to a constituent assembly as the best possible articulator of the "general will," and in the Fourth Republic's grant of legislative supremacy to the National Assembly. The doctrine of a mixed government was embodied generally in monarchist regimes (e.g., the constitutions of 1791, 1814, and 1830): In these, the principle of popular sovereignty was reaffirmed but was institutionally reflected only in an elected lower house. That chamber, rather than being the sole decision maker, had to act in "concert" with a nonelective king and a chamber of the nobility.[16] To some extent, the idea of a mixed government was embodied in the scanty constitutional articles of the Third Republic, which granted legislative power to the Assembly but gave the executive the power to appoint ministers and to dissolve Parliament.

The Fifth Republic Constitution, on the face of it, adheres neither to the Jacobin principle nor to that of a "mixed" system. The very order of the constitutional provisions—sovereignty, the president, the government, Parliament—implies an enhanced position for the executive, and the provisions detailing the power of the legislature seem to render that branch neither supreme nor even coordinate.

The president's powers—to preside over the cabinet, to appoint the prime minister, and to dissolve the legislature—are basically Third Republic features, though after the May 16 episode, these powers had eroded. The provision for the independent (and later direct) election of the president is reminiscent of the Second Republic, whereas the incompatibility of cabinet office and parliamentary mandate is a feature found in both the monarchical Constitution of 1791 and the Second Empire Constitution. The extralegislative election of the president, his power to introduce measures through his ministers, and his power to appoint the prime minister (and, in effect, the cabinet) without prior parliamentary consultation were based on provisions found in the Constitution of the Second Republic (1848); and the president's appeal to the people was based on the Constitution of 1852. The president's power to negotiate treaties and to dissolve Parliament, the constitution of the Senate and its relatively equal position vis-à-vis the Assembly, and the omission of a clearly stipulated set of provisions regarding civil liberties are all features reminiscent of the Third Republic's Constitutional Laws of 1875. The Fourth Republic too is heavily reflected in the provisions of the Fifth, notably with respect to the following: the seven-year term of the president; his power to send messages to Parliament and to ask that body to reconsider bills it has passed; the election of senators by an electoral college of local politicians; provisions concerning martial law and the establishment of an Economic and Social Council; and, of course, an Assembly chosen by universal suffrage.

The specifically "Gaullist" aspects of the Constitution are not easy to determine because the sources of Gaullism are diverse and its nature is intertwined with Bonapartism. In his Bayeux speech of June 16, 1946, de Gaulle, while publicly opposing the first draft of a constitution for the Fourth Republic, had proposed a system of separation of powers; an indirectly elected Senate in which, in conformity with corporatist tradition, socioeconomic and professional sectors would be represented; and a chief executive who would be "above parties"[17] and would select his prime minister and preside over the cabinet. Some of the Gaullist notions of government had been espoused by Michel Debré and René Capitant (a "left-wing" Gaullist), who suggested the shortening of the sessions of a parliament that would operate within the framework of enumerated powers.

The central feature of the Fifth Republic Constitution, a strong, quasi-monarchical executive, is considered to be the most Gaullist of the innovations, because the general, in his memoirs and public utterances, had consistently advocated it. However, one should keep in mind that de Gaulle merely embraced a constitutional preference that was a recurrent theme in France. The restoration of a genuine monarchy became unthinkable in that country long ago, but the glorification of kings and the association of national greatness with monarchical regimes are still emphasized in its public schools. Moreover, most of the French regimes after 1789, including republics, have been adorned (or encumbered) with certain monarchist elements. The Constitution of the Year III (1795) empowered the executive to appoint and dismiss ministers; the Charter of 1814 gave the king extensive legislative powers; the laws of 1830 reaffirmed the royal veto power; the Constitution of the Second Republic (1848) provided for a relatively weak president who was still entitled to convoke the Assembly for special sessions, introduce bills, and negotiate treaties; the Constitution of 1852 (put into effect after the coup d'état by Napoleon III) granted most legislative and other powers to the executive; and the Constitutional Law of 1875 (Third Republic) gave legislative initiative both to the president and to the chambers, and granted the president the power to appoint ministers.

In the course of the Third Republic, the Parliament had asserted its supremacy at the expense of the president, whose legislative, appointive, and dissolution powers had gradually atrophied. Parliamentary supremacy and presidential weakness had become republican constitutional norms, which were embodied in the Fourth Republic Constitution of 1946. But throughout the Third and Fourth Republics, the "myth" of an authoritarian president had persisted and had been propagated by various movements and individuals who (like General Boulanger in the 1880s) had viewed Parliament as ill suited to express the general will. Reflecting a growing hostility to deputies for their alleged selfishness and incompetence, numerous proposals to strengthen the presidency were made in the early part of the twentieth century.[18]

Immediately after World War II, the overreaction to Marshal Pétain's authoritarianism was so widespread that few Frenchmen seriously thought that a strong executive was feasible in a republican regime or would accept the idea of either the people or an electoral college replacing Parliament as the instrument for selecting the executive. Between 1941 and 1943 even Michel Debré, who was later to become the orthodox Gaullist par excellence, had written essays and letters in which he expressed opposition to a popularly elected president and opposed a presidential regime altogether because he feared that France would be governed by a general on the basis of proclamations.[19]

Nonetheless, at various times throughout the postwar period, especially during the last few years of the Fourth Republic, notions of presidentialism were disseminated not only by de Gaulle himself but also by Socialists, Christian Democrats, and others.[20] The president came to be viewed as an ideal person to hold the overseas territories and France together—perhaps following the example of Britain, where the queen was the focal point of cohesion for the Commonwealth. After 1956, many elements of the intellectual Left and Right favored the direct election of the president (following the U.S. model).[21] Others proposed the direct election of the prime minister,[22] but this alternative was not held out as a serious possibility for France because of its chronic multiparty tendencies and imperfect party discipline. As we have seen, some reforms had been instituted between 1954 and 1958 to strengthen the executive vis-à-vis Parliament, but these reforms had not been effective or credible because they had not been endorsed by the people.

The plebiscitary features of the Fifth Republic Constitution, introduced by the Gaullists in order to weaken parliamentary and other intermediaries and to strengthen the president, were not Gaullist innovations. One aspect of plebiscitarism, popular ratification of the constitution, has had a particularly hallowed place in French constitutional history: The constitutions of 1792, 1795, 1799, and 1946 had all been submitted to the people. But the same is true of the *invalidation of republican rule* and its replacement by authoritarian and Bonapartist regimes: The naming of Napoleon I as consul for life in 1802, the establishment of the Bonapartist hereditary line in 1804, and the investiture of Napoleon III as emperor in 1852 had all been approved by plebiscite.[23] Even where clear French precedents do not exist, certain Fifth Republic features are not entirely novel in that they probably drew upon foreign examples. Thus the authors of Article 16 (emergency powers) must have based their work partly on Article 48 of the Weimar Constitution, and the use of referenda for ordinary legislation may have been based on the examples of Switzerland and contemporary Italy.

The Fifth Republic does, however, represent a sharp break with the Fourth Republic because its Constitution tilts power decisively on the side of the executive and because it mirrors the political doctrines and institutional preferences of one man. Furthermore, the circumstances surrounding its establishment are in many ways different from those of earlier French republics, which were attempts to reconstitute republican regimes after authoritarian experiences. The First Republic was the consequence of a rebellion against the monarchs of the *ancien régime*; the Second Republic followed the revolution of 1848 and the deposition of the July Monarchy; the Third Republic was a reaction to the military failures of Napoleon III as well as to the bloody suppression of the Paris Commune; and the Fourth Republic was both a reaction to the Vichy regime and an attempt to restore the democratic antebellum status quo.

The Fifth Republic, in contrast, was not a reaction to the authoritarianism of an earlier regime. Therefore, to many observers *at that time* it did not represent a step forward in republican terms: Insofar as republicanism was equated with the elevation of Parliament at the expense of a powerful executive, the Fifth Republic was considered institutionally retrogressive. Yet much of the Fifth Republic Constitution—in particular its executive-administrative character—can be explained by the fact that the new regime was historically opportune (i.e., fitted into a cyclical pattern of French constitutional development). According to Dorothy Pickles, modern French political history has been divided into three-part cycles, each beginning with a moderate monarch, followed by a liberalized ("republican") regime, and ending in a conservative reaction (see Table 1.2). But whereas the conservative reactions to the Republic of 1792, the July Monarchy, and the Third Republic after the 1880s had been institutionally reflected in empires or dictatorships, the response to the parliamentary excesses of the Fourth Republic was a regime in which many republican features were retained. These features (as we shall see later) lent themselves easily enough to democratic interpretation.

Nonetheless, the Fifth Republic Constitution contains more innovations than its immediate predecessor. First, there is the notion of presidential *arbitrage*: The president is responsible for both observing and interpreting the Constitution.

TABLE 1.2 Political cycles and regimes

Modern Monarchy	Liberalization	Conservative Reaction
Constitutional monarchy of 1791	Republic of 1792	Dictatorial government of 1795
		First Empire, 1804
Restoration of 1815	July Monarchy, 1830	Second Empire
Early Third Republic, 1870–1879	Third Republic from presidency of Jules Grévy	Vichy Regime
———	Fourth Republic	Fifth Republic (1958–1981)
———	Fifth Republic (1981–?)	

SOURCE: Based on Dorothy Pickles, *The Fifth French Republic*, 3d ed. (New York: Praeger, 1965), pp. 3–5.

Second, the Fifth Republic Constitution limits the length of parliamentary sessions, reduces the number and the power of legislative committees, and streamlines the budgetary process in a way that leaves it essentially an executive matter. Third, it contains a specific mention of political parties, including a stipulation (also found in the constitutions of Italy and the German Federal Republic) that political parties "must respect the principles of national sovereignty and democracy."[24] Fourth, it provides a sharing of legislative power among the executive, the legislature, and the people and for that reason differentiates among organic laws, ordinary laws, regulations and decrees, and referenda (see Chapter 7). A fifth feature is the double responsibility of the prime minister to the president and to Parliament. Finally, Article 16 (discussed more fully in Chapter 6) gives the president discretionary power to act in case the constitutionally established institutions do not function normally.

One might even argue that the Fifth Republic is unique because, unlike other republics, it was inaugurated in a somewhat unconstitutional manner. After investing de Gaulle as prime minister of a (provisional) government, the Fourth Republic Parliament granted that government the power to change the Constitution, in violation of Article 90 of the Fourth Republic Constitution (then still in effect), which provided that constitutional amendments could be initiated only in Parliament. Hence one prominent anti-Gaullist argued that the installation of the Fifth Republic was a coup d'état that had only a thin veneer of legality.[25] Indeed, the law of June 3, 1958, which empowered the government to draw up a new constitution, could be considered almost as "unconstitutional"—and therefore as "illegal"—as the law of July 10, 1940, by which the Chamber of Deputies of the Third Republic had ceded all power (including the power to set aside the Constitution) "to the Government of the Republic, under the authority and signature of Marshal Pétain."[26] This does not mean that the Gaullist regime should be compared to the Vichy regime, because the Fifth Republic Constitution, unlike Pétain's "French State," was endorsed in a popular referendum and therefore legitimated. Indeed, if one attaches a quantitative element to the criterion of popular endorsement, one may even argue that the Fifth Republic Constitution (which was approved by 80 percent of the electorate) was more "legitimate" than its immediate predecessor (which had been endorsed by only about 40 percent of registered voters). It remains true that in France, popular sovereignty is the source of a republican constitution, just as it is in Britain, where parliamentary enactments or cabinet actions that have the consequence of "amending" the Constitution are based on general or "mandate" elections.

The Fifth Republic Constitution was also legitimated by its internal character, that is, by virtue of the fact that it included certain traditional republican principles. First, the principle of universal suffrage applies as before to the election of the Assembly. Second, the government, although selected in the first place by the president, continues to be subject to criticism and revocation by the Parliament. Third, there is an independent judiciary. The inclusion of these features had been demanded by the multipartite Consultative Committee, the Council of State, and other agencies and individuals whose advice had been sought at the constitution-drafting stage.[27] Without these provisions, the Fifth Republic Constitution would very likely have been rejected in the popular referendum. Finally, the Constitution continues to be legitimated by its growing (and now overwhelming) acceptance by the French people.

CONSTITUTIONAL INTERPRETATION AND ADAPTATION

Most observers agree that the Fifth Republic today is not the same as it was 35 years ago. Yet there is a considerable difference of opinion about the extent to which the Constitution has been stretched beyond the intentions of the "founding fathers" by means of formal amendment, interpretation, and practice.[28] Thus far, the Constitution has worked well enough to make frequent resort to formal amendment (as is the case in the Federal Republic of Germany) unnecessary. The amendment process is not particularly cumbersome; it involves two alternative methods: After an amendment bill has been passed in each house of Parliament, it is ratified either by a "Congress," that is, a joint session of both houses, by a three-fifths vote, or by popular referendum (see Table 1.3). Not all the constitutional changes to date have moved the Fifth Republic in the classic parliamentary direction, possibly because the French today, as in earlier regimes, have not been able to make up their minds between direct (plebiscitary) and representative democracy. Whereas the amendment of November 1962, which provided for the popular election of the president, was a shift in the plebiscitary direction, the failure of the constitutional amendment of April 1969, which would have "reformed" the Senate out of existence, demonstrated that institutions traditionally associated with republican regimes (or with parliamentary supremacy) cannot be abolished so easily.[29] Moreover, in June 1992, in conformity with the Treaty of European Union (which reflected the parliamentary norms of most of France's neighbors), the constitution *was* formally amended (Art. 88, sec. 4) to require parliamentary approval of all legislative proposals submitted to the European Council of Ministers.

TABLE 1.3 Constitutional amendments: Successes and failed attempts

Subject	Date	Ratification
Membership of former colonies in French Community	4 June 1960	Special method*
Election of president by universal suffrage	26 October 1962	Referendum
Dates of parliamentary sessions	20 December 1963	Passed by Congress
Reform of the Senate	27 April 1969	Rejected in referendum
Reduction of presidential term to five years	20 October 1973	Passed by both chambers but not submitted to ratification process
Right of parliamentarians to appeal to Constitutional Council	21 October 1974	Passed by Congress
Death, incapacity, or withdrawal of candidates during presidential election campaign	14 June 1976	Passed by Congress
Extension of use of referendum to matters regarding civil liberties	July–September 1984	Approved by Assembly, rejected by Senate
Right of citizens to appeal to Constitutional Council	April–June 1989	Approved by Assembly, rejected by Senate
Acceptance of selected rules and norms of European Community**	26 June 1992	Passed by Congress
Reform of judicial authority	19 July 1993	Passed by Congress
Reform of right of asylum	19 November 1993	Passed by Congress

*Use of Article 85 of the Constitution, which provided for ratification by Parliament and a special legislative body composed of members of Parliament and of the legislatures of the newly independent states. Since the creation of that Community was aborted, this article and certain others became irrelevant.
**This prepared the groundwork for the popular referendum on the Treaty of European Union itself, which took place the following September.
NOTE: Sessions of ratifying Congress take place at the château in Versailles.

Regardless of the formal balance of power between the executive and the legislature, constitutional *practice* has tended to reinforce habit patterns that are reminiscent of earlier regimes. The Fifth Republic has had to operate at least partially within the parameters of traditional republican expectations because, apart from General de Gaulle himself, a large number of cabinet members and one president (François Mitterrand) had been prominent politicians in the Fourth Republic, and many more deputies, especially in the early years of the new regime, were holdovers from the Fourth Republic's National Assembly. It was natural for such politicians to operate according to their traditional styles and to help perpetuate old practices. Among these have been the (occasional) practice of parliamentary "investiture" of prime ministers, the custom of proxy voting, the enforcement of party discipline, and the simultaneous service of deputies as regional or local councilors or as mayors.

Nevertheless, certain practices have not conformed with the traditions of parliamentary democracy—indeed, they have been situated in the twilight zone between constitutional and unconstitutional behavior. Thus it is not clear that de Gaulle acted constitutionally when, in October 1962, he dissolved Parliament after it had adopted a censure motion against Premier Pompidou. According to Article 50, the premier, when censured, must submit the resignation of his government (therefore ceasing to be premier). According to Article 8, the president names the premier; and according to Article 11, the president can dissolve the Assembly, but before doing so must consult the speakers of the two chambers *and* the premier. The question is whether an ousted premier is still premier, or whether there is any premier left to consult! Even if one admits that these provisions are vague enough to lend themselves to presidential interpretation for political purposes—in this case, the purpose of taking revenge on, and thereby cowing, the Assembly—could one not say that the spirit of the Constitution was violated? It should be noted that the exercise of the dissolution power is not always motivated by vengefulness. After his election to the presidency in 1981 and again after his reelection in 1988, Mitterrand called for new legislative elections in the hope that the new Assembly would be ideologically better aligned with the Socialist-oriented executive, and therefore easier to work with, than the old Assembly.

De Gaulle and at least two of his successors interpreted presidential power in such a way as to undercut the premier's independent position even more than envisaged by the constitutional wording. They did so by retaining responsibility for foreign and defense affairs; interfering, on a selective basis, in domestic policy matters; and "helping" their premiers in the selection of cabinet ministers. But they got away with that because the majority of deputies had been too submissive. During the two "cohabitation" interludes (1986–1988 and after March 1993), the Assembly was more independent vis-à-vis the president; as a result the premier, whom the Assembly had in effect selected, became a more important decision maker than the president. Most Fifth Republic premiers, in turn, have interpreted *their* powers in such a way as to deprive the Parliament of meaningful legislative initiative—by giving legislators little time to debate policies and enacting measures by decree. But one must remember that in the Fourth Republic, a regime characterized by parliamentary supremacy, the prohibition against "delegated legislation" (i.e., lawmaking by the executive) was disregarded when Parliament in fact granted decree powers to cabinets (see Table 1.4).

Having noted the digressions from the explicit text of the Fifth Republic Constitution, one should not assume that France is unique in this respect. In Britain too, adaptations of the Constitution have become necessary in order for government to function effectively. One of these adaptations is the "complementing" of the principle of parliamentary supremacy by the practice of cabinet government. In France, constitutional provisions have been sidetracked or adapted not only in the Fifth Republic but in preceding republics; however, this process has not necessarily been antidemocratic or "dysfunctional" for the system. In the Third Republic, the constitutional provisions regarding strong presidential powers had to be ignored and certain executive powers had to be permitted to wither in order to facilitate democratic political development. In the Fourth Republic, provisions against the delegation of rule-making power had to be ignored in order

TABLE 1.4 Constitutional principles and adaptations

	Principle	Practice
Third Republic	Presidential dissolution and appointive powers	Parliamentary arrogation of these powers
	President to serve seven years	Premature abdication of several presidents forced by Parliament
Fourth Republic	Prohibition against delegated legislation	Decree powers in fact given to the cabinet
	Investiture of prime minister	"Double investiture" of premier and cabinet
Fifth Republic	Selection of cabinet by premier	Presidential involvement in selection process
	Incompatibility of cabinet office with parliamentary mandate (Art. 23)	Ministers permitted to seek parliamentary mandate, and deputies and senators serving as "temporary" ministers
	Prohibition against undemocratic parties (Art. 4)	Certain extremist parties allowed to exist
	No precise enumeration of civil liberties	Continuation of traditional rights due to their "incorporation" by the Constitutional Council
	Separation of church and state (Art. 2)	Governmental support of parochial schools; public salary of clerics in Alsace; church holidays as legal holidays
	Equality of all before the law (Art. 2)	Legal disabilities of women, only recently abolished
	Vote of censure by Parliament leading to dismissal of cabinet	Vote of censure by Parliament leading to its dissolution by the president
	Prohibition against binding instructions upon members of Parliament (Art. 27)	Enforcement of party discipline in most parliamentary parties
	Government determines policy (Art. 20)	President (normally) tells premier what policies to pursue

to allow decisions to be made by *someone* (usually the premier). In the Fifth Republic, not all failures to adhere strictly to constitutional provisions and not all extraconstitutional practices have merely enhanced presidential power. For example, the interpretation of Article 23 that permits cabinet members to seek formal election to parliamentary seats (which they do not occupy) provides a grassroots legitimation of ministers. The constitutional reference (Art. 2) to France as a secular state has not interfered with legislation that provides for governmental support of parochial schools—nor should it, given the historic and present importance of Catholicism in France. In interpreting the constitutional requirement (Art. 4) that political parties adhere to a democratic order, France could have followed the example of the Federal Republic of Germany by declaring extremist groups such as the Communist Party or the National Front to be illegal. But such a "strict construction" might well create disorder, given the commitment and vehemence of supporters of such groups.

Most of the adaptations found in Western constitutions have been legitimated by their popular acceptance and democratic intent. This is also true of the Fifth Republic Constitution; and even the president's interpretations of it that have tended to favor executive power to the detriment of parliamentary power are democratic because the president himself is (since 1965 at any rate) a product of majority rule.

Neither the "rules of the game" nor notions of legitimacy in France—and, indeed, in several other European countries—have been based exclusively on the text of the Constitution currently in effect. Certain constitutional adaptations have been legitimate because they have been based on laws or declarations that antedated, or existed alongside, a particular constitution. Thus, while the preamble of the Fifth Republic Constitution alludes to a tradition of civil liberties in France, there are (still valid) statutes providing for the punishment of speech that is seditious or *lèse-majesté;* and although the Constitution provides for "equality of all citizens before the law" (Art. 2), there were until recently laws that placed women in a legally inferior position. This is similar to the situation in the Federal Republic of Germany, where statutes providing for punishment of seditious statements and laws giving the police extensive power to make preventive arrests coexisted for many years with provisions in the Basic Law regarding freedom of speech and due process protections. French constitutions have been revised too frequently for the legal norms contained therein to be easily absorbed in the French citizen's political consciousness. In the face of this apparent constitutional impermanence, it has been natural for intellectuals, lawyers, and others to base many of their notions of legality on the old statute laws and their ideas of legitimacy on popular sovereignty. It is in this light that constitutional practice must be viewed.

The Fifth Republic Constitution contains its share of imprecisions and internal contradictions, of which the following may be cited as examples. Article 23 provides for the incompatibility of a parliamentary mandate with incumbency in the national executive branch, but Article 25 permits Parliament to provide legislation that may moderate this incompatibility. Article 16 provides for purely presidential action in cases of emergency, but Article 36 provides for the declaration of martial law by the cabinet and the prorogation of that law by Parliament. Article 21 provides that the premier is in charge of national defense, but Article 15 makes the president commander of the armed forces. Article 20 says that the government "determines the policy of the nation," but Article 5 stipulates that the president is the "guarantor of national independence [and] the integrity of its territory."[30]

During the first decade, most of these contradictions were resolved by a kind of "preferred position" doctrine under which—when the situation was in doubt—presidential power would prevail. This was the case because most French citizens knew that the Constitution was tailor-made for General de Gaulle and accepted the fact that he was the main institutional bulwark of the system. The "institutional" (if not regal) qualities of de Gaulle (based largely on charisma) did not carry over to his successors; consequently, they were bound more closely to the letter of constitutional provisions, and they had to contend more seriously with parliamentarians (especially from political parties other than the president's). Thus the Gaullists after 1974—and the right-wing parties in general after 1981—began to complain about the "ostentation of power" made possible by a "bastard" constitution and called for the strengthening of countervailing powers.[31]

For many years, the president was the main interpreter of the Constitution because judicial review in the American (or even Federal German) sense had not yet sufficiently evolved, that is, before the Constitutional Council developed into a guardian of constitutional propriety (see Chapter 7). Practices and laws that violated the Constitution were considered valid if these violations (such as the procedural violation by de Gaulle in 1962 in connection with a referendum to amend the Constitution) were "vindicated" by popular vote, the ultimate expression of popular sovereignty, and other adaptations were legitimated by the fact that they were anchored in French tradition.

The Fifth Republic Constitution is unusual for a twentieth-century "law of the land" in that, like its U.S., British, and Third Republic counterparts, it is essentially "mechanistic" (i.e., confines itself largely to institutional features and relationships); unlike the Italian, German Federal, Spanish, and French Fourth Republic constitutions, it contains virtually no "programmatic" (i.e., policy-oriented) features and no bill of rights. Whereas the Fourth Republic Constitution spelled out (in its preamble) the right to work, to organize trade unions, to strike, to bargain collectively, and to receive social benefits, free and secular education, and so on, the Fifth Republic Constitution shies away from such clear specifications.[32] However, a plethora of customary rights and freedoms exists alongside the Constitution, and these have been periodically extended by means of legislation, especially since the presidency of Valéry Giscard d'Estaing. Furthermore, the preamble of the Fifth Republic Constitution contains an affirmation of "attachment" to the Declaration of the Rights of Man of 1789 and of the civil rights mentioned in the Fourth Republic Constitution; these rights have been gradually incorporated into the operative body of constitutional law by interpretation of the Constitutional Council.[33]

Every constitution is said to be based on a particularly dominant principle and to be instituted for an overriding political purpose. The major principle of the U.S. Constitution is the separation of powers; of the British Constitution, a gradual development of freedoms and the progressive adjustment of relations among certain dominant institutions (e.g., the queen, Parliament, and cabinet); and of the Fourth Republic Constitution, parliamentary supremacy. The guiding principle of the Fifth Republic Constitution has been the maintenance of traditional republican institutions, but with relations between them adjusted in such a way that effective decision making would be possible. For the first two (Gaullist) chiefs of state, this meant that the executive, especially the president, would be strengthened at the expense of the legislature. While in the opposition, the Socialists, and many centrists, had reservations about the Fifth Republic Constitution because they had always equated republicanism with a powerful legislature, and because the first president had been an overly Olympian and conservative figure. But as the years passed, and especially after the Socialists themselves captured the presidency, they came to share a growing national consensus about the Constitution, which they found quite usable and which could be adapted to a variety of institutional relationships. As will be seen later (Chapter 6), Mitterrand had little difficulty in adopting certain Gaullist interpretations of the presidency; at the same time, he never abandoned the idea of leaving behind him a constitution that would be adjusted in favor of the rights of parliament and the citizen. In 1992, he appointed an ad hoc commission (the *Commission Vedel*) to suggest revisions of the Constitution that would embody his own preferences as well as those of parliamentary leaders. Among the recommendations contained in its final report to the president (early in 1993) were the following: the obligation of newly appointed prime ministers to obtain formal parliamentary investiture; the lengthening of ordinary parliamentary sessions; an increase in the number of legislative standing committees; the abolition of Article 16; and the granting to citizens the right to bring cases before the Constitutional Council (see Chapter 7) and to initiate popular referenda.[34] The adoption of most of these recommendations would go a long way toward returning France to a more traditional parliamentary republic.

NOTES

1. See Raymond Rudorff, *The Myth of France* (New York: Coward, McCann, 1970), pp. 183–187.
2. According to the Constitution of January 1852, Napoleon was to be president for a ten-year period. He was proclaimed emperor in December of that year.
3. Emphasis added. The joint sessions were usually held at the royal palace in Versailles.
4. Of the remaining chiefs of state, one died in office, two were assassinated, one resigned after six months in office because of alleged involvement in scandals, one relinquished his position because of insanity, and four were prematurely forced out by the Chamber of Deputies.
5. "Cartesian" refers to the intellectual tradition inspired by René Descartes through his best-known work, *Discours de la méthode* (1637). According to the popular conception of this method, particulars are deduced from general principles (based on reason) in an orderly, logical, and clear fashion. See Ernst Robert Curtius, *The Civilization of France* (New York: Vintage Books, 1962), pp. 93–96.
6. The *Communards*, a motley force of many thousands ranging from pure revolutionaries to anarchists and "federalists," were motivated in their three-month rebellion variously by lack of food, the desire for a moratorium on the repayment of debts, and the quest for local self-government.
7. Charles Morazé, *The French and the Republic* (Ithaca, NY: Cornell University Press, 1958), pp. 20–31.

8. For a massive study of these questions, see William Shirer, *The Collapse of the Third Republic: An Inquiry into the Fall of France in 1940* (New York: Simon and Schuster, 1969).

9. For the most recent crop of studies, see Michèle Cointet, *Vichy capitale (1940-1944)* (Paris: Perrin, 1993); Asher Cohen, *Persécutions et sauvetages: Juifs et Français sous l'Occupation et sous Vichy* (Paris: Cerf, 1993); and "Présence du passé, lenteur de l'histoire: Vichy, l'Occupation, les juifs," *Revue des annales*, May–June 1993 (Paris: Armand Colin).

10. The groundwork for this measure had been laid during the Popular Front government of 1936.

11. Specifically, it was provided that if the prime minister made a bill a matter of confidence, the text of the bill was automatically considered adopted unless the Assembly actually produced a censure (or "no-confidence") vote; that such a vote could be introduced only if there were a government program before Parliament; and that the president could dissolve the legislature if, after having sat for a minimum of 18 months, it censured a prime minister who had been in office less than two years. Some of these features found their way into the Fifth Republic Constitution.

12. For a succinct and useful account of the end of the Fourth Republic, see Nicholas Wahl, *The Fifth Republic: France's New Political System* (New York: Random House, 1959), pp. 18-24.

13. Regarding the haste and confusion amid which the Constitution was drafted, see Nicholas Wahl, "The French Constitution of 1958: The Initial Draft and Its Origins," *American Political Science Review* 53 (June 1959), 358-382.

14. Jean-Jacques Rousseau, *Le Contrat social* (original French edition published in Amsterdam: Rey, 1762), Bk. 3, sect. 4.

15. Charles Secondat, Baron de Montesquieu, *L'Esprit des lois* (first of numerous French editions published in Paris in 1748), Bk. 11, sect. 6.

16. M. C. J. Vile, *Constitutionalism and the Separation of Powers* (New York: Oxford University Press, 1967), pp. 202-203. For a discussion of eighteenth-century constitutional doctrines, see Jean Bart, ed., *1789-1799: Les Premières Expériences constitutionnelles en France: Documents d'études, droit constitutionnel et institutions politiques* (Paris: Documentation Française, 1989); and Yves Guchet, *Histoire constitutionnelle française, 1789-1958* (Paris: Erasme, 1990), esp. pp. 18-28 and 57-105.

17. Léo Hamon, *De Gaulle dans la République* (Paris: Plon, 1958), p. 70.

18. Hughes Tay, *Le Régime présidentiel et la France* (Paris: Librairie Générale de Droit et de Jurisprudence [hereafter cited as LGDJ], 1967), pp. 69ff.

19. Jacquier-Bruère (pseud.), *Refaire la France* (Paris: Plon, 1945), p. 120.

20. Tay, *Le Régime présidentiel*, pp. 185-194.

21. See Club Moulin, *L'Etat et le citoyen* (Paris: Seuil, 1961).

22. See, for example, Marc Paillet, *La Gauche année zéro* (Paris: Gallimard, 1964), pp. 235ff.

23. Hervé Duval et al., *Référendum et plébiscite* (Paris: Armand Colin, 1970), pp. 15-16.

24. The Fourth Republic Constitution (Art. 2) had merely referred to "political associations," the aim of which was "the preservation of the natural . . . rights of man," specifically, "liberty, property, security, and resistance to oppression."

25. Pierre Mendès-France, "De Gaulle's Betrayal of de Gaulle," *Le Monde Weekly*, 18 November 1970. This view was once also shared by François Mitterrand, in his *Le Coup d'Etat permanent* (Paris: Plon, 1964).

26. Michel-Henri Fabre, *Principes républicains de droit constitutionnel*, 2nd ed. (Paris: LGDJ, 1970), pp. 339f.

27. For a recent discussion, see John A. Rohr, *To Write a Constitution* (Lawrence: University Press of Kansas, forthcoming).

28. See the discussion by Olivier Duhamel, "Les Logiques cachées de la Constitution de la Cinquième République," in O. Duhamel and Jean-Luc Parodi, eds., *La Constitution de la Cinquième République* (Paris: Presses de la Fondation Nationale des Sciences Politiques, 1985), pp. 11-23.

29. On formal amendments as "surgical operations," to correct the weaknesses of the Constitution, see François Luchaire, "La Constitution à l'épreuve du temps," *Revue politique et parlementaire*, September–October 1980, pp. 19-31.

30. For a more detailed treatment of textual ambiguities, see Stanley Hoffmann, "The French Constitution of 1958: The Final Text and Its Prospects," *American Political Science Review* 53 (June 1959), 332-357.

31. See the roundtable discussion, "Un Bilan constitutionnel du septennat," *Revue politique et parlementaire*, March–April 1981, pp. 3-95.

32. For a more general discussion of the differences between mechanistic and programmatic constitutions, see Karl Loewenstein, *Political Power and the Governmental Process,* 2nd ed. (Chicago: University of Chicago Press, 1963), pp. 136-143.

33. On the preamble and other sources of "constitutional values," see John Bell, *French Constitutional Law* (Oxford: Clarendon Press, 1992), esp. pp. 57-77.

34. See Charles Zorgbibe, "Le Rapport Vedel: Un Retour aux sources de la Ve République?" *Revue politique et parlementaire*, January–February 1993, pp. 3-12. See also "Les Institutions de la Ve République en question," *Le Monde, Dossiers et Documents* 207 (February 1993), 1-5.

chapter **2**

The Economic and Social Context

ECONOMIC DEVELOPMENT

The analysis of a political system should involve a discussion of the economic and social realities that the system reflects and helps to change. This is especially the case in a country with a long tradition of *étatisme* and *dirigisme*—state intervention in industrial development and economic transactions. The causal relationships among economy, society, culture, and polity in France have remained a matter of controversy, in part because political and economic developments have not always occurred at the same pace. Since the Revolution of 1789, the French economy has gone through cycles of liberalism and interventionism, protectionism and competition, stagnation and growth. The French industrial revolution began during the era of Louis-Philippe in the 1830s, later than in England and somewhat earlier than in Germany. Its development in France was spurred by both a French variant of "Manchester liberalism" (or a *laissez-faire* approach as popularized by Jean-Baptiste Say) and protectionism. French tariffs in the nineteenth and twentieth centuries were among the highest in Europe. Industrial expansion was impressive: Production doubled between 1852 and 1870, tripled between 1870 and 1914, and slackened only after World War I and the onset of the worldwide economic depression.[1]

France, however, was not as rapidly industrialized as England or Germany. Some scholars have cited the lack of resources—coal in particular—as an impediment to industrialization in France, but probably more important reasons were a basically rural outlook, the French distaste for bigness, a fear of competition, and a Malthusian ideology—the notion that resources are limited and cannot be enlarged and hence that one ought to be conservative and careful in their use and at the same time be entitled to a governmental guarantee of one's share of the economic pie.[2] The French had little taste for domestic investment; they were reluctant to buy industrial shares and even to open savings accounts, and the economy suffered from periodic flights of capital to other European countries. Still another reason for the inadequate pace of industrial growth and the under-developed mass-consumption ethos was the distribution bottleneck: Many items produced in the provinces returned to the provincial markets only after having passed through the hands of middlemen in Paris.[3] The economic dependence of the provinces upon the national capital paralleled the political, administrative, and cultural dependence on Paris. Even today, most decisions affecting the prov-inces are channeled through Paris, just as the railroad and highway networks radiate from the capital.

One of the most important impediments to industrialization and mass pro-duction was the insufficient domestic market, which was related to the demo-graphic stagnation that had been caused in part by the many wars in which France was embroiled.[4] As a consequence of these wars, the country had lost much of its productive manpower. In 1789 France, with 26 million inhabitants, had been the most populous country in Europe apart from Russia; in the late 1960s, when the French population reached 50 million, it had long been sur-passed by the populations of Germany, Britain, and Italy. In order to counteract this stagnation, de Gaulle's postwar appeal to French families to produce *"12 millions de beaux bébés"* in the name of patriotism was not enough; it had to be supplemented by a system of income supports to families with two or more children (*allocations familiales*) and by fairly liberal immigration policies.

Between 1946 and 1975, more than 3 million immigrants entered France, in addition to about a million repatriates from the former colonies in North Africa. These figures were augmented by a large number of "temporary" workers from Spain, Portugal, and the Third World now forming a significant percentage of the work force in French factories. Precisely what effect this population influx has had, and will have, on the French economy is unclear. The presence of foreign workers had been welcomed for a number of reasons: They contributed to the growth of the internal market; as they were for the most part unskilled, they formed a cheap labor force; and, as they were largely not unionized and easily subject to deportation, their ability to press for higher wages was limited. They did not require an unreasonable outlay for housing or social benefits, because (at least at the outset) they tended to be young people without dependents. They brought more money into the social security funds than they took out and cost the government less for education than the natives. Yet because of their low labor costs, the incentive of employers for "postindustrial" innovations (e.g., automation) was reduced. Nowadays there is a widespread belief that the pres-ence of large numbers of immigrants will have a negative impact in the long run. The growth of their communities has created resentment among native workers; in addition, the rootlessness and cultural maladjustments from which many of them suffer have caused social disorganization that has, on occasion, erupted into violence. Finally, the dependents they *do* bring into the country have special prob-lems and impose unusual burdens on local welfare and educational facilities.[5]

By all measures, France is one of the most industrialized nations today. Spurred by the French experiment in economic planning inaugurated in 1946, the country's rate of growth, averaging close to 5 percent annually in the 1950s and 1960s, has been much higher than that of the United States or Britain (see Table 2.1).[6] Some of France's industries, notably mass transportation, aeronautics, electronics, and communications, are among the most modern in the world. Its railway system, renovated in the late 1940s, is one of the best in Europe. In recent years, other manifestations of economic modernization—often called "Americanization"—have been in evidence. The mass ownership of television sets, microcomputers, and other durable goods; the proliferation of supermarkets throughout the country; a high per capita ownership of automobiles; and the tendency among increasing numbers of middle-class families to acquire second homes attest to France's economic dynamism.

In the eyes of some observers, this dynamism is uneven; they argue that French creative resources are inadequately focused on economic production and that where such focus exists, it is not accompanied by sufficient attention to marketing, especially on a global scale.[7] It is unclear whether this problem has stemmed from French individualism or, more specifically, from a tendency to divorce intellectual pursuits and technological innovation from commercial pursuits.

In any case, the growth of the national product since the end of World War II has been impressive and is reflected in statistics showing that by the mid-1970s, the per capita income of the French was among the highest in Western Europe. Generally, the hourly wage rates of industrial workers in France kept up with

TABLE 2.1 Comparative economic statistics

	France	Germany (Fed. Rep.)	Italy	Great Britain	United States
Annual rates of growth of GNP at market prices 1969–1979					
Total	4.0	3.3	3.3	2.2	2.9
Per capita	3.4	3.1	2.6	2.1	2.0
1981–1986					
Total	1.7	1.7	1.9	2.6	2.9
Per capita	1.2	1.9	1.7	2.5	1.9
1986–1991					
Total	2.7	3.5	2.8	1.9	1.8
Per capita	2.2	2.5	2.6	1.6	0.9
Indices of real wages in industry Average gross hourly earnings of manual workers, 1991 (1985 = 100)	110.4*	118.2	—	110.3	94.0
Consumer price index, 1992 (1985 = 100)	123.0	115.1	147.5	146.4	121.5**

*1988
**1991
SOURCE: Based on *Eurostat* (Brussels-Luxembourg: European Union, 1988, 1991, 1992, 1993).

inflation better than in the United States, largely as a result of periodic governmental adjustments of the minimum wage. Thus, while the consumer price
index rose from 100 in 1975 to 164.5 in 1980, hourly wage rates in manufacturing rose from 100 to 188.[8] However, the relative inequality of income distribution persisted. In the mid-1970s, the gap between the highest and the lowest
deciles of earners was more than 8:1 (compared to 3:1 in Britain and 4:1 in
Germany). Under Socialist rule after 1981, the situation did not improve much,
despite the redistributive impulses of the Mauroy government during the first two
years. At the same time, the legal maximum workweek (beyond which workers
are entitled to overtime pay), which in 1938 had been 40 hours, was steadily
increased, so that in the early 1970s, at 44 hours, it was among the longest in
Western Europe. Under the Socialist government, the workweek was gradually
reduced to 35 hours, largely on the basis of collective contracts, but raised again
to nearly 39 hours in 1987.

For many years, France's economic growth was impeded by a geographic
maldistribution of its population (due to a variety of factors such as soil conditions, topography, transport facilities, and distances to markets). The Paris region
and parts of the northwest bordering on Belgium are heavily populated, whereas
the Massif Central and parts of southwestern France are sparsely settled and show
little growth. With only four conurbations of over a million inhabitants (Paris,
Lyons, Marseilles, and Lille [see Tables 2.2 and 2.3]), France is still a country of
small towns and rural communes. The agricultural sector, which in 1945
accounted for a third of the labor force, has been reduced to less than 6 percent (in 1992), but it is still larger than in Britain, Germany, and the United States
(see Table 2.4). The majority of French people are recently urbanized, and their
cultural and emotional roots are in the provinces. The French succeeded for a
long time in keeping the economy dominated by small farms and family firms
producing for a limited market. Since the Méline legislation of 1892, which imposed high tariffs on imported wheat, the French farmer has been accustomed
to governmental protection against foreign competition. Indeed, many of the great

TABLE 2.2 Selected demographic changes, 1946–1990

	1946	1975	1985	1990
Total population (in millions)	40.5	52.6	55.0	56.6
Birthrate (per 1000)	20.9	14.1	14.0	13.8
Infant mortality (per 1000 live births)	84.4	13.8	10.1†	7.5*
Longevity of males	61.9	69.1	71.0**	72.3
Longevity of females	67.4	77.0	79.0**	80.6
Number of adolescents over 14 enrolled in schools (in millions)	.65	4.0	4.2	5.45

*1989
**1982
SOURCES: Based on Dominique Borne, *Histoire de la société française depuis 1945* (Paris: Armand
Colin,1988); Dominique and Michèle Frémy, eds., *Quid*, 1988 and 1992 (Paris: Laffont); Rémy Arnaud, ed.,
La France en chiffres (Paris: Hatier, 1990).

TABLE 2.3 The ten largest conurbations in France

Metropolitan Area	Population (in thousands)
Paris	9,060
Lyons	1,262
Marseilles/Aix-en-Provence	1,087
Lille	950
Bordeaux	685
Toulouse	608
Nantes	492
Nice	475
Toulon	437
Grenoble	400

SOURCE: 1990 Census. Brian Hunter, ed. *The Statesman's Yearbook, 1993–1994,* (New York: St. Martin's, 1993), p. 561.

political parties of the Third and Fourth Republics, aware of their dependence on the votes of the provincial farmer and shopkeeper, embraced a protectionist ideology or policy and thereby helped to perpetuate in France what has been called a "peasant republic."[9]

However, in the past 30 years, there has been a "silent revolution" in agriculture,[10] marked by the abandonment of about 900,000 farms, the consolidation of farmland, the modernization of agricultural production, and the reduction of farm subsidies. At the same time, the government made credit more easily available for the purchase of farm machinery, so that the number of tractors increased nearly twentyfold between 1945 and 1970 (to reach 1.5 million by the mid-1980s). Many farmers who left the land sought employment in industry and added to the growth of new urban agglomerations, especially in the environs of Paris and Lyons. Yet despite growing urbanization, the image of a "terminal peasantry" is

TABLE 2.4 Changes in the structure of the active population, 1968–1992 (selected sectors and years, in thousands*)

	1968	1975	1980	1992
Agriculture/fishing	3,123	2,104	1,841	1,142
Mining and quarrying	251	177	144	76
Manufacturing	5,317	5,780	5,445	4,510
Commerce	2,628	3,215	3,386	3,733
Transport	1,388	1,259	1,334	1,426
Services	4,802	4,812	5,436	7,387
Total	20,729	20,714	21,127	22,332

*Rounded to nearest integer.
SOURCES: International Labor Office, *Yearbook of Labor Statistics* (Geneva: ILO, 1983, 1993); *Annuaire statistique de la France* (Paris: INSEE, 1990).

somewhat overdrawn, and some vestiges of rural domination in politics are still to be found. In the Third and Fourth Republics, the rural element, largely because of the electoral system, dominated the Senate, and that element (together with the electorate of small, provincial towns) dominates the Senate today via right-of-center parties.

The pressure for agricultural efficiency was reduced somewhat when the European Community's Common Agricultural Policy (CAP), put in place in the late 1960s, created a captive market for French farm products. Furthermore, growing unemployment in the cities slowed down the rural exodus.[11] Nonetheless, the postwar modernization of the French economy has inevitably contributed to both a consolidation of industries and to the rise of the tertiary sector. Immediately after World War II, when France faced the challenge of rebuilding a war-torn economy, it tried (under pressure from bourgeois and province-based parties that reflected the nonmarket orientations of the peasant, the artisan, and the small shopkeeper) to protect the small entrepreneur through favorable tax and tariff policies. Later, with the competitive pressures of the Common Market and, still later, the energy crisis, French governments changed their policies abruptly. By means of cheap, long-term credit, tax exemptions for capital gains, outright subsidies, a squeeze on social security benefits, and (in 1979–1981) the gradual abolition of price controls, the government encouraged industrial mergers. This policy had been inaugurated with some hesitation in the early 1960s but advanced with particular dogmatism by President Giscard d'Estaing and his prime minister, Raymond Barre (1976–1981), and was taken up again during the "cohabitation" government of Jacques Chirac (1986–1988).

The result of this policy was that after the early 1960s, more than 400,000 independent tradespeople went out of business, and many jobs were lost, particularly in heavy industry. This development was speeded up in the 1970s and 1980s; between 1980 and 1987 alone, total employment declined from 21.6 million to 21.2 million, and the unemployment rate rose to about 10 percent and reached 12 percent at the end of 1993. Yet there remain several hundred thousand small shopkeepers (including about 40,000 bakers). These continue to fight unsympathetic governments by means of lobbying, the ballot, and, if necessary, spontaneous acts of violence. Thus, in 1970, CID-UNATI,[12] an association of small shopkeepers and artisans, kidnapped policemen and destroyed local tax offices in an attempt to fight the takeover of commerce by larger and more dynamic firms. In the early and mid-1970s, several organizations representing small and medium-sized businesses successfully lobbied for legislation to impede the growth of supermarkets and to water down measures regarding worker participation in management. One of the reasons for the dramatic growth of the Socialist party (and for its victories in 1981) was the fact that it had been joined or supported by many small entrepreneurs who had become disgruntled over the apparent favoritism of Giscard d'Estaing and his government to big business.

In recent years, both the remainder of the agricultural sector and the industrial sector have been challenged—the former by the agreements between the European Community and the United States in the context of the General Agreement on Tariffs and Trade (GATT), under which France is obliged to lower its farm price support levels and reduce agricultural production; and the latter, by the relocation of industries from France to countries with lower labor costs. In 1992, for example, 60,000 enterprises closed down.

SOCIAL CLASSES AND MOBILITY

Historically, the social system of France is much like that of any other Western European country that experienced feudalism and inherited a society divided into classes of nobles, clergy, townspeople (bourgeoisie), and peasants. This division was reflected toward the end of the *ancien régime* in the "estate" representation of the old Parliament. Since that time, the bourgeoisie has gained in political and economic power; much of the landed aristocracy has disappeared or lost its importance because of revolutions, expulsions, and the impact of the guillotine. Independent farmers rose in number because of the parceling of land among all the sons of the landowner. In the nineteenth century, with the rise of the factory system, the industrial working class (the proletariat) made its appearance. Today French society is still divided into the following groups: (1) the upper class, including graduates of the prestigious national universities, the upper echelons of the civil service, the directors of large and successful enterprises, bankers, and what remains of the old aristocracy; (2) the bourgeoisie, including members of the liberal professions (e.g., physicians, lawyers, architects), university and lycée professors, engineers and *cadres* (upper-echelon technical and administrative personnel), and owners of medium-sized shops and family firms; (3) the middle and lower-middle class (*classe moyenne*), including white-collar employees, petty shopkeepers, lower-echelon civil servants, elementary schoolteachers, and, possibly, artisans; and finally (4) the lower classes (*classes populaires*), comprising in the main industrial workers and small farmers. There is a correlation between class and ideology: Thus, membership in the working class usually implies membership in the socialist "ideological family," whereas peasant status has implied sociopolitical conservatism and (in many cases) a continuing commitment to Catholicism.

But such correlations are simplistic and of uncertain reliability. It is important to keep in mind the following: (1) In France a person's social origins may be just as important as actual class membership: A middle-class technician or engineer whose father was a worker would be almost twice as likely to vote for the Left as one whose father had himself belonged to the middle class.[13] (2) Ideological and class cleavages have tended to overlap in complex industrial societies; in France (as in Italy) there are workers who are revolutionary, reformist, Catholic, or apathetic,[14] although in recent years both revolutionary inclinations and Catholic commitments have greatly diminished. The perceived status of a unionized factory worker may be enhanced by the presence of foreign workers; the economic insecurity of a bourgeois may be compensated by his becoming a knight in the Legion of Honor; and the diminishing purchasing power of a lycée professor may be made up in part by the "psychic income" of her academic prestige (which itself has suffered as a result of the democratization of education). (3) There is the growing "postindustrial" sector, whose members (e.g., computer technologists and marketing specialists) are difficult to place in terms of the traditional class system. Indeed, a person's social status according to customary "objective" criteria does not clearly correlate with his self-classification (see Table 2.5). Furthermore, geographical variables may influence or compensate for objective class membership: There is still a status difference between living in Paris and living in the provinces. Thus, entry into the National School of Administration (in French, L'Ecole Nationale d'Administration, or ENA), which for the past 45 years has been training virtually all higher civil servants, has been rare for provincials, especially children of workers and farmers (see Chapter 8). Social mobility has tended to be lateral rather than upward; statistics indicate that the majority of the various elites have fathers who were in elite positions and that higher civil servants have had little difficulty in moving to responsible positions in the private sectors of industry, commerce, and banking.[15]

Between 1959 and 1964, 158,000 French men and women passed from salaried-worker status or from agriculture to positions of self-employment. At the same time, 68 percent of workers' sons remained workers.[16] According to more recent (and more optimistic) studies, between 15,000 and 20,000 new enterprises are created every month, and approximately one-fourth of the new businesspeople are descendants of working-class parents.[17] Still, the majority of adults who have left the farm since the 1970s have entered the low-paid urban labor force.[18] This lack of upward mobility in France, fortified by a continuing inequality of educational opportunity, housing conditions, and tax loopholes for the rich—and accompanied by the existence of a pronounced lower-class lifestyle—sharpened the working class's perception of itself as a deprived segment of society.

TABLE 2.5   Social occupational status and self-classification (in percent)

	Working Class	"The Poor," Little People	Middle & Lower-Middle Class	Bourgeoisie*	Other**
Farmers and farm workers	5	42	33	19	—
Shopkeepers & artisans	12	28	31	1	27
Executives, managers, businesspeople, professionals	2	6	53	25	15
Middle management	8	15	57	9	11
White-collar employees	24	25	42	2	8
Blue-collar employees	45	27	23	1	5

*Includes intellectuals.
**Includes those classifying themselves as "independents" or indicating no precise classification.
SOURCES: Centre d'étude de la vie politique française (CEVIPOF), 1988, adapted from Nonna Mayer, "Identité sociale et politique des petits commerçants (1966–1988)," *Vingtième Siècle*, January–March 1993, p. 76.

To some extent, class cleavages and working-class consciousness have been moderated by the gradual democratization of primary and secondary education (or at least by a public commitment to the principle of such democratization), and the somewhat enhanced possibilities of the recruitment of children of working-class and lower middle-class parents to the lower echelons of the national civil service. Class cleavages have also been reduced by the expansion of the welfare state and the introduction of paid vacations and the statutory medical care system. However, the worker has had to finance social security protection with ever-increasing payroll deductions. Although five weeks of paid vacation are guaranteed by law to virtually all employed categories—the fifth week was added in 1981—a sizable number of industrial and agricultural workers do not take full advantage of them. Family allowances are less effective than they might be as a means of encouraging the growth of the birthrate; many of the French delay marriage and having children because of the persistent difficulty of finding adequate housing. Although individual home ownership has become increasingly common (with 51 percent of families owning their homes in 1986), a large number of families (and the majority of the working class) live in substandard apartments. About three decades ago, the government began to build housing for low- and middle-income families (*habitations à loyer modéré*—HLMs) in the center of Paris and other cities, later supplemented by massive projects along the periphery of towns (*zones d'urbanisation à priorité*—ZUPs). (In 1987, 12.7 million people lived in nearly 3 million HLMs.) However, many HLMs came to be inhabited not by poor workers but by petit-bourgeois French families, and the ZUPs often tended to become instant slums—a situation that did not contribute to an easing of interclass resentments.

After the accession of de Gaulle, co-management boards and profit-sharing schemes were introduced in order to "associate" the working class with industrial entrepreneurs and reduce proletarian resentments. In addition, interclass resentments were channeled into nationalistic (and often anti-American) sentiments, which were widespread and were counted on to unite various socioeconomic sectors. With the partial eclipse of Gaullism, beginning with the election of Giscard d'Estaing in 1974, the resentment of the disprivileged had to be addressed in a more concrete fashion. Despite the decline in economic output induced by the petroleum crisis,[19] Giscard allocated generous amounts of money for increases in unemployment and pension payments and even initiated measures aimed at the democratization of the tax system. However, these measures could not immediately reverse the fiscally conservative policies introduced earlier in the Fifth Republic. Among these policies were the reduction of social security benefits and the introduction of the regresssive value-added tax system (*taxe à valeur ajoutée*—TVA). Spurts of inflation and devaluations of the franc could rarely be compensated for by sufficient wage increases, because the fragmented trade union movement was in a very poor position to bargain collectively, and the officially fixed minimum wage (the SMIG or the SMIC[20]) seldom made up for increases in the cost of living. Finally, the decline of the role of Parliament—in which the working classes, through the Socialist and Communist parties, had reasonably effective representation—and the corresponding enhancement of the position of the higher civil service since 1958 had greatly weakened the working classes' access to decision-making organs.

For many years, the gap between the white-collar worker (*salariat*) and the blue-collar worker (*prolétariat*) in France remained one of the largest in Western Europe. The radical trade unions (including the Communist-dominated CGT), in spite of their verbal commitment to social equality, were hesitant about closing this gap because they hoped to recruit and retain as members the very status-conscious white-collar and *cadre* elements. Moreover, some leaders of political parties most given to egalitarian rhetoric, particularly the Socialist party, were of bourgeois descent and status, and they did not wish to lose their social and economic privileges as a result of a precipitate policy of social leveling.

During the past three decades, the salary and status gaps between blue- and white-collar employees have narrowed. In 1954, the median income of the white-collar employee was 13 percent higher than that of the industrial worker; by 1974, the differential had been reduced to 4 percent, and a further reduction had occurred by 1983.[21] These salary convergences could be interpreted as a sign that France had entered the "postindustrial" phase and as proof of the corollary proposition regarding the *embourgeoisement* of the masses, the weakening of the class struggle, and the "end of ideology."[22] But in fact the number and proportion of industrial workers in the labor force have not decreased dramatically: from 8 million, or 39.7 percent, in 1970 to 7.8 million, or 36.9 percent, in 1978; and to 6.4 million, or 30.4 percent, in 1988.[23] However, many of these, particularly the unskilled, are immigrant or temporary workers, and they often tend to be ignored because they are "by definition, hardly members of French society."[24] Conversely, although there has been an increase in the number of white-collar employees as a consequence of the explosion of the service sector (from 9.5 million, or 46.4 percent, in 1970 to 13.3 million, or 62.9 percent, in 1988), there has been a corresponding socioeconomic decline: During the 21-year period (1954–1975) during which the white-collar segment nearly doubled, its "feminization" increased from 54 percent to 64 percent,[25] and women's salaries have continued to lag behind those of men. Furthermore, white-collar workers of both sexes have routinized jobs and low pay, experience unemployment, and resent the inequities of the tax system. Occasionally, industrial and white-collar workers discover that they have interests in common with intellectuals and students— for example, during the events of 1968, these social groups attempted (or pretended) to support one another in public demonstrations against the Gaullist system. But such camaraderie is at best tenuous, largely because of the history of mutual distrust, the different backgrounds, and the divergent concerns of these groups. More than two decades after the May events, the "mandarins" (the Sorbonne professors), no matter how far to the left, still live in their spacious apartments in the bourgeois neighborhoods of Paris, while the poor continue to live in the suburban slums, the "Red Belt," around Paris.

RELIGION AND CULTURE

Constitutionally, France is a secular country. The Catholic church was disestablished three generations ago; public education, even in the provinces, is consciously and officially nonreligious; and many political parties, in addition to a large percentage of the parliamentary deputies (from the Third Republic to the present) have had a decidedly anticlerical outlook. Until well into the Fourth Republic, it was the view of Radical-Socialists that Catholicism was incompatible with republicanism, and it was the view of many Socialists that religion was incompatible with socioeconomic progress and equality. As if to advertise its commitment to laicism in public life, the Third Republic after the 1880s accorded few chances to practicing Catholics to serve as cabinet ministers. With the outbreak of World War II, Catholicism "reestablished" itself as a positive political force when a number of priests joined the Resistance; after the war, a new Catholic party, the MRP, emerged with the fullest republican credentials. In the immediate postwar years France was, nevertheless, considered a "mission" country by the Vatican, which encouraged priests to mingle with workers and to live with them. But in the Vatican's view, such identification went too far; after priests joined unions, participated in strikes, and even left the priesthood, the Vatican suspended the "worker-priest" movement in 1953. (It was revived on a modest scale a decade later.)

In spite of the lessening of attacks on religion by left-wing political parties, especially during the past decade, the convergence between Catholicism and the working-class outlook remains incomplete. In 1988, only 6 percent of French workers considered themselves practicing Catholics, and 79 percent were more or less detached from the Church. According to a recent poll, in 1991 only 27 percent of the total population considered themselves believers in any religion; of the 79 percent who identified themselves as Catholics, only 10 percent went to weekly mass and only 6 percent went to confession.[26] To be sure, there are variations according to region and gender. About two-thirds of practicing Catholics are women. To the extent that France is urbanized, it is largely "de-Christianized." Religious practice is relatively insignificant in selected regions around Paris and more significant in the rural areas of Brittany, Alsace, and Auvergne.[27] But throughout the provinces there are many small communities from which the priest has departed and where churches are in a state of disrepair.

The parochial (mainly Catholic) schools are maintaining their enrollments, which in 1993 embraced about 20 percent of all French schoolchildren from kindergarten through secondary school. There are several explanations for the survival of this aspect of religious culture. Undoubtedly the Debré laws of 1959, under which teachers in Catholic (as well as other private) schools receive their salaries from public funds when these schools "contract" with the national Ministry of Education to include state-approved subject matter in their curricula, have helped to sustain the Catholic school system financially. Furthermore, in some less developed provinces—Brittany, for example, where Catholic school enrollment is high (nearly 40 percent)—parochial education may be viewed as a way of asserting the region's cultural uniqueness. And in the cities, parents may see parochial schools as a means of preserving many traditional moral values that are threatened by industrialization and other social changes or of preserving discipline and ensuring more personalized instruction (and higher standards than those believed to exist in public schools with large proportions of poor immigrant children). It is a reflection of both the persistence of Catholic values and the "republicanization" of most French Catholics that, in the past 15 or 20 years, the Catholic-secular issue has been muted and that many secular French citizens failed to support the Socialist government's attempt in 1983–1984 to bring the parochial schools under closer government control. The issue was revived in 1993 with the introduction of a bill to augment government support of parochial schools (see Chapter 10).

In many respects, France, once considered "the eldest daughter of the Church," manages to be a thoroughly Catholic country. The town cathedral remains in subtle ways a focal point of French culture. Most public holidays (except for May 1, the international Labor Day, and July 14, Bastille Day) are Catholic holidays, and public institutions are shut down. There is still little commerce on Sundays, and the major newspapers do not appear on that day. Until the mid-1960s, the list of officially approved first names for children born in France was based largely on the calendar of saints. Many Catholic charitable, educational, professional, and social-action groups exist; one of them, the Association of Christian Working Youth (*Jeunesse ouvrière chrétienne*), claimed nearly 100,000 members in 1987. Two-thirds of French children born in 1985 were baptized (compared to 84 percent in 1970), and 58 percent of marriages were performed by priests (compared to 95 percent in 1970). But these statistics may relate to cultural-familial more than theological aspects of Catholicism, for only a minority of Catholics identify with the stand of the Church on certain issues (e.g., contraception, abortion, or homosexuality).[28]

Non-Catholics enjoy full religious, civil, and political liberties. Three centuries ago, and until the Revolution of 1789, Protestants (mainly Huguenots) were subjected to forcible conversion, expulsion, and occasional massacres, punctuated by periods of toleration. Today, many Protestants—they are said to number between 800,000 and 1.2 million[29]—are prominent in commerce, banking, the professions, and (since the end of World War II) in the higher civil service and politics, especially in the upper echelons of the Socialist party.[30]

There are about 700,000 to 800,000 Jews in France today. The Nazi Holocaust had nearly decimated the Jewish community, whose roots in France go back to Roman times, but its remnants were augmented by refugees from Eastern Europe during the immediate postwar years. Jewish religious life was revitalized in the early 1960s with the influx of repatriates from North Africa, who now account for more than half of the total Jewish population. Like their Protestant compatriots, Jews have not only consistently supported republicans (rather than monarchists, who were traditionally identified with Catholicism), but they have also shown a preference for Radical-Socialist and (since the beginning of the

postwar period) Socialist politicians. Jews are fully assimilated and have participated prominently in the country's cultural life. Yet anti-Semitism, sometimes
theologically inspired, is never far below the surface. After the Arab-Israeli War
of 1967, anti-Semitism received a new respectability as a result of pronouncements or actions by de Gaulle, Pompidou, and Giscard that were widely construed
as anti-Jewish. The government's pro-Arab and anti-Israel policies were inspired
by economic considerations rather than anti-Semitism, yet these policies had the
effect of sparking the desecration of cemeteries and the bombing of synagogues
and Jewish-owned stores—all of which in turn led to greater Jewish community
solidarity and, subsequently, massive hostility on the part of that community to
Giscard's leadership.[31] Since the election of Mitterrand, the discomfort of Jews
has been greatly reduced, although Jean-Marie Le Pen, the leader of the National
Front, has made them uneasy with his anti-Jewish innuendos.

It is of course possible to exaggerate the extent to which anti-Semitism exists in France. If, as has been suggested, anti-Semitism is one of the constant,
though latent, factors of French sociopolitical thinking common to the bourgeois
and working classes,[32] it cannot always be clearly separated from negative attitudes toward "outgroups" in general. During the height of the Dreyfus affair, most
anti-Semites were also anti-Protestant, anti-Masonic, and anti-foreigner.[33] Many
French people then viewed—and view today—French culture as thoroughly
bound up with Catholicism (albeit in increasingly secularized form) and with the
idea of an organic evolution of Gallic tribes rooted in the soil of France. Like
most European countries, France tended to base citizenship on *jus sanguinis* as
opposed to *jus soli*—in other words, on the fact of French parentage rather than
birth in France. However, during the French Revolution, citizenship came to be
based, in principle, on ideological and "voluntary" criteria, such as the adherence
to republican principles and a willingness to share the fate of the nation. The
acceptance of these criteria, as well as the need to increase the population of
the country, explains why France encouraged immigration and enacted relatively
liberal naturalization laws.[34] In response to growing unemployment and racism
there have been pressures on the government to limit the number of immigrants
and make naturalization more difficult. Nevertheless, there were in 1990 well over
4 million immigrants, about 1.5 million of them already naturalized citizens, apart
from the North African repatriates and tens of thousands of seasonal workers.

France's ambivalent attitude as both a welcoming host country and a hot-
bed of xenophobia is illustrated today most sharply in the case of the Muslim
immigrants from North Africa. The presence of a large community of Muslims—
estimates of their number in France range from 2.5 million to 4.5 million—has
made many French people uncomfortable, because that presence is often equated
with the unemployment problem and with the rising incidence of delinquency
and crime. The National Front, the *Club de l'Horloge*, and (to a lesser extent)
other right-wing organizations have exploited that discomfort for their own ends,
arguing that Islam, unlike Christianity (or what is increasingly referred to as the
"Judeo-Christian" tradition), is not only a religion but an "oriental" and foreign
way of life, and that the cultural background of these "Arabs" makes it difficult

to assimilate them into French society. French citizens are no more racist than Americans, Britons, or Germans;[35] they consider Islam as respectable as Christianity, increasingly accept the construction of mosques throughout France, and continue to consider France as a welcoming country for immigrants; and they have not lost their faith in the role of the public school in the integration of foreigners.[36] That faith has not been misplaced, for although the number of mosques in France is steadily growing,[37] Muslim immigrants (and especially their children) are gradually becoming Westernized and acculturated to French life.[38]

At the same time, the French are worried that certain elements associated with normative Islam—among them a weak commitment to pluralism, the rejection of separation of state and religion, and discrimination against women—may have a harmful effect on principles associated with French republicanism, among them gender equality and *laïcité*. The public debate on this matter was renewed with particular vigor in the wake of an incident involving two Muslim school-girls who came to their public-school classes with their heads covered by shawls. The incident, which was seen as challenging the ability of the public school to shape the secular national identity of children in France, divided the government and the Socialist party, and provided extra ammunition to the National Front.[39]

The notion of France as the center of Western civilization was once inculcated in even the most backward and socially disadvantaged elements of the provinces.[40] According to one scholar, this notion ceased to be popular some decades ago except among the extreme right wing of the political spectrum;[41] still, the idea of French cultural superiority has intermittently surfaced as a defensive posture. Since the end of World War II, with the rise of American power, the relative weakening of the French economic and international position, the inroads made by the English language, and the emergence of a new internationally minded technocracy that appeared to threaten the position of the traditional, humanistically educated elite, there was a resurgence of cultural chauvinism among educated Parisians, even those with leftist leanings.[42] Many French intellectuals are still concerned about preserving the French language from foreign corruptive influences; a number of associations exist specifically for the "defense of the French language," and the governments of France still spend a great deal of money in order to promote the use of French abroad. The French elite's sensitivity to the position of the French language is reflected in attempts to limit the import of American films and, more recently (in June 1992), in the enactment of a constitutional amendment (Art. 2) stipulating that "the language of the Republic is French."

Cultural chauvinism has been directed not only at foreigners. For many years, children in Basque areas were punished for speaking their native tongue in public schools; the same was true in the case of Breton, a language spoken (in several variants) by several hundred thousand people in Brittany. In the past two or three decades there has been a new assertiveness on the part of Bretons, Corsicans, and (to a lesser extent) Alsatians. This assertiveness has many sources: the independence movements of the Third World; the influence of foreign workers; the transnational regionalism and open borders of the European Union; and the examples of culturally focused "regionalization" policies of Belgium, Italy, and other European countries. France has responded to the unique aspirations of its own ethnolinguistic minorities by providing radio broadcasts in Breton and Alsatian, allowing Breton to be taught in public schools, legalizing Celtic proper names, permitting localities to put up bilingual street signs, transforming Corsica into a separate and partly autonomous region, and promising significant increases in economic development aid to that island. Nonetheless, Corsican, Breton, and Basque separatist movements (or "liberation fronts") have been suppressed and their ringleaders were tried (for subversion) in the State Security Court that existed from 1963 to 1981.

For many generations, the suppression of the cultures of ethnic minorities reflected the thinking of much of the French elite. Most intellectuals and politicians, especially of the Left, were committed to the Jacobin tradition, according to which all provincialisms and particularisms were equated with feudal backwardness and antirepublicanism. To the nationalist, the peripheral ethnolinguistic minorities were "internal exiles" who "compromised national ideology";[43] to the Marxist, they impeded the development of class consciousness, without which there could be no class struggle.[44]

But about two decades ago, a change began to take place. Postwar immigration was so massive that France—with its hundreds of thousands of Portuguese, black Africans, and Southeast Asians, and its large Maghrebi (North African) community—has become a multiracial and multiethnic society. Shortly before Giscard was ousted by the voters, he admitted publicly that France was a "pluralistic society." The Socialists, too, adjusted their principles and advocated the teaching of regional languages and, after gaining control of the government in 1981, promoted policies accordingly.[45]

This new outlook reflected a growing recognition of the reality of provincialism, which has persisted despite the heavy hand of the Napoleonic centralizing tradition. The latter had brought about the unquestioned preeminence of Paris, which still has the largest number of industries and controls the financial, cultural, and political life of the country. Despite some halfhearted efforts to bring "culture" to the provinces, music, theater, and dance do not have an impressive existence outside the capital.[46] The continued dominance of Paris explains why ambitious politicians and businesspeople, even though they might pride themselves on their rural roots, have endeavored to maintain a pied-à-terre or an office in the capital and why many provincial university professors—the "turboprofs"—have tried to obtain supplementary lecture assignments in Paris. In order to breathe some economic life into the provinces, and incidentally to limit the excessive urban sprawl around Paris, the government undertook several measures in the 1960s and 1970s, such as the location of selected nationalized enterprises in provincial cities and subsidies or tax exemptions to private firms willing to build industrial plants in the hinterlands, but the measures have not met with much success.

In recent years, provincials have felt less isolated than before because they have been tied more effectively to the national (i.e., Parisian) scene by the constant modernization of telecommunications and the rail transport system (including the wide distribution of telephones and miniature computer terminals and the construction of a high-speed train service between Paris and several provincial cities). As a result of these developments, the differences in attitudes between provincial small town residents and Parisians have narrowed.

To the extent that provincialism has been maintained or revived, it has been emotional rather than functional: Despite the increasing fiscal powers granted to local and regional authorities (see Chapter 8), typical French citizens are still clearly oriented toward the national government in a *policy* sense; they expect the national government to do more for them than the local government, and their participation in national elections is normally higher than in local ones (see Table 4.8 on electoral abstention, Chapter 4). Still, Paris is farther away from the village than the principal city (*chef-lieu*) of the department, and citizens can relate much better to their national parliamentary deputy if (as is often the case) the latter is also their mayor.

THE EDUCATIONAL SYSTEM

The educational system, like so many other aspects of French life and culture, may be viewed as traditional or innovative, depending upon the observer's criteria. Since the nineteenth century, the school system in France has been largely public, compulsory, uniform, and centralized, with the national Ministry of Education determining the educational policy and curricula at all levels and supervising virtually all examinations for diplomas. The primary schools in particular have served as relatively efficacious agencies of republican, secular, and nationally oriented political socialization and have prepared most pupils for finding a productive place in the economy.

Until about three decades ago, the French school system was highly stratified, with the children of working-class or peasant families rarely going beyond the primary school (and entering the labor market at 15 or, more recently, 16 years of age) and bourgeois children advancing to the lycée in early adolescence, and thence to the university. In fact, the educational content of the lycée, which stressed classicism, rationalism, and formalism rather than technical or "modern" subjects, was little related to the labor market and was mainly designed for the leisure class or those who already belonged to educated or otherwise privileged families.

Although in theory most French lycées are equal, certain Parisian lycées have been more highly regarded than the less pretentious secondary schools in the provinces. In higher education, too, a distinction has been made between the ordinary universities and the specialized *grandes écoles*, such as the Ecole Polytechnique and the Ecole Normale Supérieure; most of the latter were established in the nineteenth century. The *grandes écoles,* which have catered largely to the upper-middle and upper classes, have provided France with its intellectual and political leadership.[47] The status distinctions among the university faculty ranks (*professeur titulaire, maître de conférences, chargé de cours,* and *assistant*) and between these and the student have traditionally been precise and rigid, and have been a microcosm of the hierarchism of society at large.

Nevertheless, there has been an impulse toward the democratization of education, particularly since the beginning of the Fifth Republic. In 1959, the government decided to raise the school-leaving age to 16 (a decision fully implemented only in 1971), and soon there was widespread agreement that secondary schooling was the right of all French children. The traditional screening of pupils for entry into the lycée at the ages of 10 to 11 was replaced by a system (*cycle d'observation*) in which a uniform curriculum was provided for all students up to the age of 14 or 15; this system evolved into a kind of comprehensive middle school, or junior high school (the *collège*, which comprises the lower four years of the lycée). Thereafter (i.e., during the final three years—in the lycée properly speaking), students are guided into one of several "streams" (*filières*): letters, social sciences, physical sciences, mathematics, the life sciences, and (since 1983) agriculture, music and art, physical education, and other tracks in specialized secondary schools. As a consequence of the baby boom in the immediate postwar period, growing social pressures, and easier access, the number of students in secondary schools rose from 1 million in 1950–1951 to 3 million in 1964–1965 and more than 5.5 million in 1990–1991.

The demand for admission in universities created by this growth caused serious problems for the system of higher education, which in 1991 encompassed about 1.2 million students in 76 universities and enrolled about 30 percent of the age group of 20- to 24-year-olds.[48] The overcrowding of lecture halls, the inadequacy of physical facilities and libraries, and above all the persistence of a university curriculum that, notwithstanding its overall excellence, bore an ever-diminishing relationship to the labor market—these were problems that demanded solutions.

In the 1960s, the government began to build additional universities, often with American-style campuses, and introduced more "technical" courses. But these reforms were inadequate and came too late, and the clamor for a thorough overhauling of the French system of higher education figured heavily in the rebellion of May 1968. After this event, Edgar Faure, the minister of education, initiated several significant reforms, including the granting of some autonomy to universities in determining curricula, the creation of new technical institutes, the forming of American-style academic departments (UERs[49]), and a system of "participatory democracy" under which a university's governing personnel would in part be elected by professors, staff, and students. Olivier Guichard, Faure's successor, continued these reforms, particularly in regard to greater decentralization of academic decision making, the shaping of interdisciplinary curricula, and the founding of new university centers in the Paris region to relieve the congestion of the old Sorbonne. The reforms introduced in the mid-1970s by René Haby soon after Giscard's election to the presidency continued the emphasis on making higher education more relevant to the modern economy by giving a larger place in the curriculum to economics, mathematics, business management, and a variety of technical subjects.

The academic establishment welcomed some aspects of educational reform because they were in consonance with its egalitarian principles. These reforms included the virtual universalization of the public nursery school (*école maternelle*); the mixing of the sexes in elementary schools (at first in Paris, and later in the provinces); and the program of literacy and basic education for adults, which was inaugurated in the early 1970s. But the academic elite has been concerned about the decline in overall standards of culture and in levels of literacy resulting from the *massification* of education. There have been numerous complaints that many students taking the examinations for the *baccalauréat* (the lycée diploma) are insufficiently prepared in grammar and writing. Many of these complaints were substantiated by reports issuing from special committees of inquiry set up shortly after the Socialist government was installed in 1981.[50] Despite such complaints, however, the government was committed to a continuing democratization of education: It hoped that the proportion of secondary-school students who received the *baccalauréat* would rise from 60 percent in 1983 to 80 percent in 1993, and it thought that this goal could be achieved by an enlarged budget, better counseling, and a further modernization of the curriculum.

Some professors have objected to the increased attention to modern subjects because these do not conform to an idealized conception of culture; these professors see their own elite status threatened by a cheapening of the commodity they produce. Such an attitude was brought into sharp focus in 1976, in reaction to a government proposal to reform the university curriculum in order to channel a large number of students from humanistic to more practical subjects. This aim was to be accomplished with the participation of the business community. Many professors opposed the reform on the ground that it would destroy the function of the universities "as places where culture is dispensed to those worthy to receive it."[51] Despite the good intentions of politicians, the rate of expansion of university admissions was reduced, and between 1978 and 1980 the Ministry of Education abruptly dismantled selected graduate programs at various universities, reduced the financial support of institutions that had taken their autonomy too seriously, and even disaccredited a university (Vincennes, near Paris) whose curriculum had been too innovative. Under the Socialist governments between 1981 and 1986 as well as succeeding governments, a number of reforms have been advocated that would appear to move France in an "American" direction: the downgrading of the prestige of the professor; the end of automatic admission of holders of lycée diplomas to selected faculties; pressure on universities to seek grants from the private sector; and the suggestion that universities take account of the market in paying higher salaries to professors of business administration, engineering, and other "practical" fields than to professors of the more traditional subjects.[52] In the meantime the number of entrants into universities continued to grow so rapidly—it was well over 1.5 million in 1993—that individual faculties began to limit the number of students admitted to graduate ("third cycle") studies.

Irrespective of the changing commitments to structural reforms in education, the democratization of education at all levels is likely to continue.[53] The commitment to democratization was an article of faith under governments run by

Socialists, because they were wedded to the Napoleonic principle of admission to universities on the basis of objective academic achievement rather than ascribed status; because of the close ties between the National Education Association (in French, Fédération de l'éducation Nationale—FEN) and the Socialist party; and because of the dominance of educators in the higher echelons of the party and in the government. For these reasons, the scholarship aid to university students (*bourses*), especially those from low-income families, was increased and the salaries of teachers were raised. To what extent such democratization will continue under conservative governments is unclear, especially in the face of competing pressures on the public treasury coming from the unemployed, the farmers, and the aged.

THE POSITION OF WOMEN

Nowhere is the ambiguous relationship between modernism and traditionalism illustrated better than in the position of women in France. As a Latin and predominantly Roman Catholic country, France tended to assign the customary family and household roles to women. The Napoleonic code of 1804, under which women were legally incompetent, remained in force until 1938. Since that time, the legal and political disabilities of women have gradually been removed. In 1945, women obtained the right to vote; in 1965, married women were granted the right to open bank accounts without their husbands' express permission and the right to dispose of property in their own name, and subsequently, to be legal heirs; in 1972, children born out of wedlock obtained the same rights as other children; and in 1986, French citizens obtained the right to carry the maiden name of their mothers.

Women have made even greater strides economically. Between the mid-1950s and mid-1960s, the number of women in the professions (in particular teaching) rose by nearly 70 percent. In 1992 women accounted for 56 percent of graduates of secondary schools and nearly 54 percent of university students, over 75 percent of elementary schoolteachers and about 60 percent of secondary schoolteachers, but only 20 percent of university professors.[54] The proportion of women in the medical and related professions has grown considerably (see Table 2.6). The entry of women into the labor market has been facilitated by a generous system of paid maternity leave—it was raised to 16 weeks in 1980—and by the availability (especially in the Paris region) of free nursery schools for children from the age of three up. It should be noted that the proportion of women in France's working population as a whole has changed very little in this century: It was 39 percent in 1906, 38 percent in 1979, and 44 percent in 1991. It is unclear whether this situation should be attributed to the rising income of men and the family's growing prosperity, to the fact that the foreign-worker sector includes relatively few women, or to the continuing importance of traditional sex-role distinctions. Although the pay differential has narrowed somewhat in the past decade, the average salary of women in the private sector was still about 30 percent lower than that of men in 1981; since the passage of a law in 1983

TABLE 2.6   Women in selected professions, 1982–1990 (percentage of total)

Profession	1982	1990
Specialized physicians	22	31.5
General practice physicians	13	27
Dental surgeons	26	31
Psychologists and psychotherapists	71	73.5
Veterinarians	12	27
Pharmacists	49	52
Lawyers	33	40
Certified accountants	11.5	16
Architects	5	15

SOURCE: Based on INSEE, as cited in Marie-Claude Betbeder, "La souplesse des professions libérales," *Le Monde*, 17 February 1993.

forbidding wage discrimination based on sex, this differential has been reduced, but in 1991 it was still 24 percent.[55] Nevertheless, the unemployment rate of women (with more than 15 percent in 1992) is still much higher than that of men (11 percent), as is the proportion of women holding part-time or temporary jobs.[56]

The political role of women is more difficult to assess. Most observers agree that women have traditionally been somewhat more conservative ideologically than men and that their rate of electoral abstention has been somewhat higher. Thus in the parliamentary elections of 1967, 65 percent of the women voted for right-wing candidates, compared to 48 percent of the men; by 1978, this 17-point differential had been reduced to 6 points, and by 1986, when the Right got 55 percent of the vote of both sexes, the differential had virtually disappeared. The one remaining difference had to do with support for extremist parties.[57] In the last several elections, women have voted less heavily than men for candidates of the Communist Party and the National Front. In the first round of the presidential elections of 1988, only 10 percent of women voters (as compared to 17 percent of male voters) supported Jean-Marie Le Pen. In the elections of 1993, the right/left preferences of women approximated those of men, except that women were somewhat more attracted to candidates of environmentalist parties.[58]

Women running for political office have tended to choose leftist rather than conservative sides. For example, of the 10 first-round presidential candidates in 1981, 3 were women, and 2 of these ran on leftist labels;[59] and of the 26 women elected to the Assembly that year (compared to 18 elected in 1978), 19 were Socialists and 3 Communists. In the parliamentary elections of 1988, the situation was more balanced: Of the 32 women elected to the Assembly that year, 16 were Socialists or close to that party; one was a Communist; 14 belonged to the Gaullist-Giscardist alliance, and one was elected on the ticket of the National Front.[60] In the parliamentary elections of 1993, 35 women were victorious.[61] The only three women cabinet members during the Third Republic served (as junior ministers) in the Popular Front government of Léon Blum in 1936. Since 1946, only about two dozen women have held ministerial posts: five during the Giscard presidency and the remainder since the election of Mitterrand.[62] Women were particularly important in the Socialist government headed by Edith Cresson (1991); 8 of her 46 ministers were women: of them, 5 were full members of the cabinet. In the Balladur government set up in March 1993, only 3 of the 30 ministers were women; one of them, however (Simone Veil), held 3 portfolios (social affairs, health, and urban affairs) and was the highest-ranking cabinet officer after the prime minister.

Women have fared no better in other political offices. Although since the end of the 1970s, women have constituted about 53 percent of the electorate, they have provided less than 3 percent of senators,[63] about 20 percent of the municipal councilors, 5 percent of the general councilors, and 4 percent of the mayors in the 1980s. During the municipal elections of 1989, 17 cities with over 20,000 inhabitants chose women as mayors, among them Strasbourg; and the general council elections of 1992 resulted in the election, for the first time, of a woman (and member of an ecologist party) as president of a regional council. Although women have made up more than 50 percent of the total number of civil servants, they have accounted for fewer than 7 percent of the deputy or assistant directors of ministries. In 1984, women accounted for only 5.2 percent of the members of the Council of State, 6.5 percent of the Court of Accounts, and 3.3 percent of the Inspectors of Finance. This situation has improved since the enactment of a law in 1982 that provided for equality of access to public employment. Thus the proportion of women among the entrants to the National School of Administration (ENA) grew from 20 percent in 1980 to nearly a third in 1990. Nevertheless, women do not often reach the highest positions in the civil service. In 1991, less than 10 percent of the incumbents in the *grand corps* (the Council of State, the Court of Accounts, and the Inspectorate of Finances) were women. Moreover, the average salaries of women in all echelons of the civil service were 17 percent lower than those of men.[64] A bill passed in 1982 provided that at least 25 percent of candidates in municipal elections (in communes of more than 3,500 inhabitants) be women, but the bill was voided by the Constitutional Council. Women have represented about 25 to 35 percent of the membership of the various trade unions, but fewer than 10 percent of the leadership positions. However, in 1993 Nicole Notat was the first woman to be elected secretary-general of a major trade union confederation, the CFDT. Another breakthrough occurred in 1992 with the appointment (by the National Assembly) of the first woman to the Constitutional Council.

One indication of the changing societal position of women has to do with birth control. The Gaullist party had disapproved of contraception and abortion because of the leadership's social conservatism and its desire to encourage the growth of population. But in the past three decades, family planning has become more acceptable, and since 1969 contraceptive devices for women could be purchased legally. After the accession of Giscard, the policy of liberalization in regard to women's rights advanced considerably. Abortions were legalized, and (since 1980) their cost covered by the social security funds. Between 1970 and

1980, women achieved equality with men with respect to choice of domicile, authority over children, retention of surname, and initiative in divorce proceedings; and in 1985, women were given equal rights in the administration of family property. As a sign of his commitment to women's rights, Giscard created a Ministry for the Condition of Women, and Mitterrand retained such an office during the first few years of his presidency.[65] Much of the credit for these achievements must go to the women's movement, the independent existence of which is of fairly recent date.[66] Among the most important organizations have been the *Union des femmes françaises*, which was formed in 1945 out of Resistance committees, and which now has about 200,000 members; the *Mouvement de la libération des femmes*, established in 1968 as a federation of several associations of different leftist tendencies; and the *Mouvement pour la liberté de l'avortement et de la contraception.*[67] In 1989 a new women's organization, the *Alliance des femmes pour la démocratisation*, was founded; it included representatives of virtually all political parties and age groups and concerned itself with general political issues, in particular on local levels. It was largely in response to the pressure of women's organizations that a bill was enacted in 1992 that made sexual harassment subject to criminal penalties.

NOTES

1. See Gordon Wright, *France in Modern Times* (Chicago: Rand McNally, 1960), pp. 343–353.
2. On French Malthusianism, see Charles Morazé, *The French and the Republic* (Ithaca, NY: Cornell University Press, 1958), pp. 49–62.
3. Herbert Luethy, *France Against Herself* (New York: Meridian, 1957), pp. 21–24.
4. War was not the only reason for the demographic stagnation. A lowering of the birthrate before World War II and again in the mid-1960s was caused by people delaying marriage in response to the difficulty of finding housing and subsequently by the relative increase in middle-class households and the deliberate decision by many to have smaller families.
5. See "Immigrés: Le Dossier explosif," a series of articles in *L'Express*, 4 February 1983, pp. 46–66, for statistics and public-opinion data.
6. It should be noted, however, that the *initial* postwar levels of industrialization of the United States and Britain were much higher than that of France.
7. See, for example, Michel Crozier, *L'Entreprise à l'écoute: Apprendre le management post-industriel* (Paris: Inter-Editions, 1989).
8. Thus, in 1983, the increase in the minimum wage (SMIC) was 12.3 percent, while the rise in prices was 9.0 percent; in 1984, 6.9 percent and 6.5 percent; in 1985, 6.9 percent and 4.2 percent; and in 1986, 3.3 percent and 3.0 percent. In 1990, the SMIC was 2.5 percent.
9. Gordon Wright, *Rural Revolution in France: The Peasantry in the Twentieth Century* (Stanford: Stanford University Press, 1964), p. 1.
10. Ibid., pp. 143ff.
11. Many farmers are facing financial difficulties, and it is estimated that every year, 2,000 to 3,000 farms close down. See François Colson and Alain Blogowski, "Des Agriculteurs en difficulté," *Projet* 234 (Summer 1993), 55–63.
12. CID-UNATI—*Comité d'information et de défense-Union nationale des artisans et travailleurs indépendants.*

13. Daniel Boy, "Origine sociale et comportement politique," *Revue française de sociologie* 19 (January–March 1978), 73–102. According to a 1988 poll on the relationship between class membership or social status on the one hand and political orientation on the other, 63 percent of the working class considered itself to be on the Left and 20 percent, on the Right; those who described themselves as "poor" were 45 percent on the Left and 38 percent on the Right; and those who classified themselves as middle class were 30 percent on the Left and 49 percent on the Right. Nonna Mayer, "Identité sociale et politique des petits commerçants (1966–1988)," *Vingtième siècle*, January–March 1993, p. 77.

14. Mattei Dogan, "Political Cleavage and Social Stratification in France and Italy," in S. M. Lipset and S. Rokkan, eds., *Party Systems and Voter Alignments* (New York: Free Press, 1967), pp. 175–177.

15. Pierre Birnbaum, *La Classe dirigeante française* (Paris: Presses Universitaires de France [hereafter referred to as PUF], 1978), pp. 68–70. In this study it is noted (p. 104) that in 1974, 15 percent of the "ruling class" was composed of sons of members of the middle and lower classes, and 4 percent of sons of farmers—at a time when sons of members of the lower classes constituted 40 percent of the population and sons of farmers 26 percent. This was a slight improvement over 1954. See also Pierre Birnbaum, ed., *Les Élites socialistes au pouvoir, 1981–1985* (Paris: PUF, 1985).

16. Daniel Bertaux, "Mobilité sociale biographique: Une critique de l'approche transversale," *Revue française de sociologie* 15 (July–September 1974), 329–360. On the "mythology" of the tertiary sector, see André Glucksmann, "Nous ne sommes pas tous prolétaires," *Temps modernes* 29 (January 1974), 330.

17. See Jean Lajkine, "Bourgeoisie, qui es-tu?" *La Pensée* 290 (November–December 1992), 13–22.

18. See Dominique Borne, *Histoire de la société française depuis 1945* (Paris: Armand Colin, 1988), pp. 103ff.

19. This crisis resulted from a quadrupling of oil prices by the Organization of Petroleum Exporting Countries (OPEC) following the Arab-Israeli war of October 1973.

20. SMIG—*salaire minimum industriel garanti*, the ordinary minimum wage; SMIC—*salaire minimum industriel de croissance*, a minimum wage dependent upon productivity growth. The SMIC applies to about 10 percent of the working population.

21. According to statistics of the *Centre d'études des revenus et des coûts* (CERC), the average earnings of male *cadres supérieurs* were 7.5 times higher than those of female industrial workers in 1967, 6.6 times higher in 1973, and 5.1 times higher in 1983. Cited by Michel Noblecourt, "De l'inégalité à la différence légitime," *Le Monde Aujourd'hui*, 16-17 March 1986.

22. On the meaning of "postindustrial society," see Todd La Porte and C. J. Abrams, "Alternative Patterns of Postindustria," in Leon N. Lindberg, ed., *Politics and the Future of Industrial Society* (New York: McKay, 1976), pp. 21–24.

23. *Eurostat Review 1970–1979* (Luxembourg: European Communities, 1981), pp. 129–130; and *Eurostat*, 27th ed. (1990), pp. 116–117.

24. Jacques Lautman, "Où sont les classes d'antan?" in Henri Mendras, ed., *La Sagesse et le désordre* (Paris: Gallimard, 1980), p. 81.

25. Ibid., p. 85. For somewhat conflicting statistics, see Laurent Thevenot, "Les Catégories sociales en 1975," *Economie et statistique* 91 (July/August 1977), 4–5, 12.

26. Poll of November 1991 in *Madame Figaro*, cited in SOFRES, *L'Etat de l'opinion 1993* (Paris: Seuil, 1993), p. 216.

27. Ibid., p. 218.

28. About 60 percent of the population (outside the Paris region) favor the maintenance of Sunday "blue laws," but only 15 percent do so for reasons of religion. Poll of 1991, in SOFRES, *L'Etat de l'opinion 1993* (Paris: Seuil, 1993), p. 218. For an overall statistical analysis of religious attitudes and practices, see Guy Michelat, Julien Potel, Jacques Sutter, and Jacques Maître, *Les Français sont-ils encore catholiques?* (Paris: Le Cerf, 1991).

29. Half of the French Protestants are members of the Reformed Church, most of the remainder belonging to the Lutheran and Evangelical sects. They are led by about 1,200 clergy (100 of whom are women).

30. Former Prime Minister Rocard is a Protestant, as are at least six of the cabinet ministers who served under him. According to a recent source, about 25 percent of regional prefects and more than 20 percent of the members of the diplomatic corps are Protestant. See Michel Richard, Christian Makarian, and Corinne Lhaïk, "Le Pouvoir des Protestants," *Le Point*, 10 October 1988, pp. 30-35.

31. See Alain de Sédouy and André Harris, *Juifs et Français* (Paris: Seuil, 1979). See also William Safran, "France and Her Jews: From 'Culte Israélite' to 'Lobby Juif,'" *Tocqueville Review* 5:1 (Spring–Summer 1983), 101-135; and Maurice Szafran, *Les Juifs dans la politique française* (Paris: Flammarion, 1990).

32. See Pierre Birnbaum, *Un Mythe politique: La "République juive"* (Paris: Fayard, 1988).

33. Anti-Semitism was a component of the "integral nationalism" of ultraconservative thinkers like Charles Maurras, who disliked Jews because they were not Catholics; and Maurice Barrès, who disliked Jews because they were "different." J. S. McClelland, ed., *The French Right* (London: Jonathan Cape, 1970), pp. 25-32. For instances of survival of small-town, petit-bourgeois anti-Semitism, see Edgar Morin, *Rumor in Orléans* (New York: Random House, 1971), esp. pp. 11-79.

34. Until recently, a child born in France of foreign parents acquired citizenship automatically upon reaching majority (i.e., the age of 18) if he or she had lived in France for the preceding five years. Immigrants could be naturalized upon demand after a minimum of five years' residence and proof of acculturation (including fluency in French). In 1993 legislation was enacted providing for tighter controls over immigration and immigrants and removing the automatic grant of citizenship. Henceforth local authorities will be able to exercise discretion in responding to requests for naturalization. See Philippe Bernard, "Nationalité française, nouveau mode d'emploi," *Le Monde*, 1 January 1994. See also Catherine Wihtol de Wenden, *Citoyenneté, nationalité et immigration* (Paris: Arcantère Editions, 1987); and William Rogers Brubaker, "Citizenship and Naturalization: Policies and Politics," in Brubaker, ed., *Immigration and the Politics of Citizenship in Europe and North America* (Lanham, MD: University Press of America, 1989), pp. 99-127.

35. According to a poll conducted in 1992, 57 percent do not think of themselves as racists. Sondage CSA of November 1992. Cited in *Le Monde*, 26 February 1993, p. 12.

36. For a particularly strong argument, see Dominique Schnapper, *La France de l'intégration: Sociologie de la nation en 1990* (Paris: Gallimard, 1991).

37. There are now more than 900 mosques in France, of which about 360 are in the Paris region. For a discussion of Islamic institutions, see "L'Islam en France," *Le Point*, 28 August 1993, pp. 45-58.

38. See Rémy Leveau, Catherine Wihtol de Wenden, and Gilles Kepel, "Les Musulmans dans la société française," *RFSP* 37:6 (December 1987), 765-781. See also Gilles Kepel, *Les Banlieues de l'islam, naissance d'une religion en France* (Paris: Seuil, 1987).

39. See "Faut-il laisser entrer l'islam à l'école?" *Le Point*, 22 October 1989, pp. 52-57. See also David Beriss, "Scarves, Schools, and Segregation: The Foulard Affair,"

French Politics and Society 8:1 (Winter 1990), 1-13. A similar incident occurred in 1993.

40. Laurence Wylie, *Village in the Vaucluse* (New York: Harper & Row, 1986), p. 208.

41. Ernst Robert Curtius, *The Civilization of France* (New York: Vintage Books, 1962), p. 28.

42. Including Jack Lang, the Socialist minister of culture from 1981 to 1986 and 1988 to 1993, who (briefly) railed against American "cultural imperialism."

43. Jacques Chevallier, "L'Etat-nation," *Revue du droit public* 96 (September–October 1980), 1271-1302; and William Safran, "The French Left and Ethnic Pluralism," *Ethnic and Racial Studies* 7:4 (October 1984), 447-461.

44. See Roger Martelli, *Comprendre la nation* (Paris: Editions Sociales, 1979), p. 71. According to Martelli, there is no such thing as a Corsican or Breton nation. In a decision in 1990, the Constitutional Council echoed that view.

45. Partie socialiste, *Projet Socialiste pour la France des années 80* (Paris: Club Socialiste du Livre, 1980), pp. 253-258; and William Safran, "Minorities, Ethnics, and Aliens: Pluralist Policies in the Fifth Republic," in Paul Godt, ed., *Policy-Making in France* (London and New York: Pinter, 1989), pp. 176-190; and same author, "The French State and Minority Cultures: Policy Dimensions and Problems," in J. R. Rudolph and R. J. Thompson, eds., *Ethnoterritorial Politics, Policy, and the Western World* (Boulder & London: Lynne Rienner, 1989), pp. 115-157.

46. In the 1960s, under the direction of Minister of Culture André Malraux, centers for the arts (*maisons de la culture*) began to be established in selected cities, with mixed success.

47. There are now about 300 *grandes écoles*, about half of them schools of engineering and commerce. Many of these are private, and their prestige is far below that of the Ecole Polytechnique, the Ecole Normale Supérieure, or the Ecole Nationale d'Administration.

48. This represented more than a fourfold increase from 1960 (when there were 214,000 students).

49. UER—*unité d'enseignement et de recherche* (instruction and research unit).

50. The Commission Laurent Schwartz reported (at the end of 1981) that a third of the graduates of primary schools had not mastered spelling, and that France had some 400,000 illiterate adults. Another report (Commission Louis Legrand) revealed that a large proportion of upper-grade secondary-school students performed poorly in mathematics and foreign languages. See "Ecole, pourquoi tant d'échecs," *Le Point*, 31 January 1983, pp. 50-53.

51. Alfred Kastler, "La Réforme de l'université," *Le Monde*, 23 April 1976. See also Jacques Charpentreau, "Le Snobisme de la culture," *Revue politique et parlementaire* 78 (March–April 1976), 70-79.

52. Frédéric Gaussen, "Les Enseignants et la loi du marché," *Le Monde,* 14 February 1989.

53. For a more pessimistic view, see Liliane Delwasse, "Les Limites de la démocratisation," *Le Monde de l'education*, December 1987.

54. The proportion of women varies according to field of specialization. In 1991 women accounted for a clear majority of students in literature and law, slightly more than 51 percent in the social sciences, but only 40 percent in the sciences, medicine, and engineering. Catherine Leroy, "Les Sciences délaissées," *Le Monde*, 17 February 1993.

55. Marie-Béatrice Baudet, "L'Égalité à pas comptés," *Le Monde*, 17 February 1993.

56. For a recent discussion, see Mariette Sineau, "D'un perspective à l'autre: La politique socialiste en direction des femmes (10 mai 1981-10 mai 1991)," *French Politics and Society* 9:3-4 (Summer-Fall 1991), 63-81.

57. Le Monde, Dossiers et Documents, *L'Election présidentielle de 1988*, p. 43. According to *Jours de France* (7-12 November 1987), in 1977, 35 percent of wives had voted like their husbands; in 1987, only 23 percent did.
58. Janine Mossuz-Lavau and Mariette Sineau, "Le Revirement des femmes," *Le Monde*, 18 August 1993. For a more detailed discussion of voting trends, see Janine Mossuz-Lavau, "Le Vote des femmes en France (1945–1993)," *RFSP* 43:4 (August 1993), 673–689.
59. Huguette Bouchardeau of the left-socialist PSU and Arlette Laguiller of the extreme-leftist *Lutte ouvrière* (Workers' Struggle).
60. In the 1988 presidential election, there was only one woman among the first-ballot candidates: Mme Laguiller.
61. The partisan division of the women deputies was as follows: RPR, 16; UDF, 13; PS, 3; miscellaneous Left, 1; PCF, 2.
62. In the Mauroy government, 6 of the 43 ministers were women; in the Chirac government of 1986, 4 of the 43; in the (second) Rocard government, 6 of the 49.
63. In 1980, 7 of the 305 senators were women, and in 1986, 9 of the 319 senators.
64. Valérie Devillechabrolle, "L'Administration, un nouveau vivier," *Le Monde*, 17 February 1993. See also Michèle Riot-Sarcey, "Les Femmes et le pouvoir," in Jean-Yves Potel, ed., *L'Etat de la France* (Paris: Editions de la Découverte, 1985), pp. 454–456.
65. Under Mitterrand it was called the Ministry for Women's Rights. Chirac abolished that ministry in 1986, and Rocard (in 1988) did not restore it. However, in 1991, Cresson reestablished the position, naming a junior minister for women's rights.
66. The women's organizations that had existed during the Fourth Republic had been connected with other movements (e.g., communist-oriented Resistance forces and Catholic Action Groups).
67. In the parliamentary elections of 1978, a women's organization (*Choisir*) fielded 43 candidates, but it won only 1.4 percent of the first-round votes.

chapter **3**

Patterns and Perspectives
of Political Culture

APPROACHES TO FRENCH POLITICAL CULTURE

The development of constitutional government and the evolution of political patterns in any country are associated not only with "objective" socioeconomic conditions but also with the values and attitudes of citizens. For many years, it was acknowledged that France had long experience with democratic institutions, that it possessed the requisite socioeconomic infrastructure necessary for a stable democracy,[1] and that, in short, it was a "modern" country;[2] yet there was a feeling, widely shared by American and even French political scientists, that the French "national character" contained flaws that made it difficult for such a democracy to be fully achieved. Until recently, discussions of the problems faced by France tended to emphasize a number of political-culture traits that were to be blamed for recurrent revolutions, legitimacy crises, ideological dissensus, and blockages. Thus, American social scientists pointed to the French habit of ideological thinking, the prevalence of class distrust, the tendency to excoriate the political establishment, the absence of civic-mindedness (*incivisme*), and an underdeveloped ethos of participation, itself related to a lack of subsystem autonomy.[3] Some social scientists spoke of a "delinquent society" that made incessant demands upon the state for benefits but refused to accept the necessary social and political obligations.[4]

These characterizations have almost always proceeded from the vantage point of an ideal-type of political culture. Such a culture, which happens to bear a striking resemblance to that which is believed to exist in the United States, is noted for its pragmatism, prosystem orientation, social trust, ethos of participation, significant subsystem (e.g., social group or local government) autonomy, and high degree of civic responsibility. That approach to French political culture was sometimes accepted by French social scientists as well, in part because they shared the habitual self-criticism of French intellectuals, who looked at reality in terms of their own (Jacobin or Marxist) ideals, and in part because American political science was so dominant that French practitioners of the discipline were tempted to imitate U.S. methods of analysis and U.S. approaches to political culture—and with it, to think of the American system as a model.[5]

CIVIC AND ANTICIVIC ATTITUDES

A book published a few years ago contains a list of the following traits of French culture that are regarded as major causes for the "blockages" that have existed in French society: (1) a taste for comfort; (2) an instinct for private property; (3) a collective laziness; (4) a hexagonal vision of reality; (5) a penchant for abstraction; (6) an admiration of the intellectual and a contempt for the businessperson; (7) an "untouchable" past, that is, a sanctification of traditional views of national history and a resistance to change; (8) an orientation to the small world—the locality, the family, and the individual; (9) a concern with aesthetics—with form and appearance; and (10) an immobility based on fear of contact with outsiders.[6]

There are problems with such a catalog: (1) The items in it are often based on questions that are highly selective and not placed in context. (2) The presumably negative (or dysfunctional) traits may be compensated by positive traits that are not adequately studied because they are alien to the American experience. (3) The characterizations have not always correlated with actual political behavior. (4) The list of traits has not fully reflected the dynamic nature of political culture—the fact that the political attitudes of the French have been in a process of constant change since the end of World War II and especially since the watershed events of 1968.

For example, the lack of civic-mindedness in France was said to be illustrated by widespread tax evasion, draft dodging, contempt for law, and that most notorious of symptoms of alienation: alcoholism. This lack of civic-mindedness was illustrated in 1981 by a public-opinion survey that revealed relatively high levels of indulgence toward those who behave in an uncivic manner: 52 percent are tolerant toward draft dodgers; 58 percent, toward those who have illegal ("moonlighting") jobs; 44 percent, toward tax cheats; 32 percent, toward those who use public transport without paying; but only 9 percent toward those who take drugs and 2 percent toward burglars.[7] Nevertheless, occasional violations of the laws, or the circumvention or "rectification" of laws by means of personal arrangements or even bribery, have not been demonstrably more pronounced in France than in the United States, and less so than in Italy. For several generations of republican experience, the French have accepted the *principle* of government of laws, and tended to be law-abiding in *practice* if they were convinced that the laws were just and fair. Today, the growing acceptance of judicial review, as practiced by the Constitutional Council, suggests that government of laws is replacing government legitimation by popular sovereignty as a norm.

Draft dodging was bound to be a problem in a country engaged in wars for a longer period than any other democratic regime in the twentieth century—from the outbreak of World War II in 1939 to the settlement of the Algerian war in the early 1960s. But draft dodging has probably been no more significant in France than it was in the United States during the Vietnam War. Moreover, the French are also known for their patriotism and for the readiness with which many of them sacrificed their lives during World Wars I and II and during the German Occupation.

Tax evasion—a phenomenon about which the French speak constantly (and not without a certain bluster)—is definitely related to an "evaluative" political culture, and to the extent that such evasion exists, it is at least partly indicative of a "low support level" among the population. But tax fraud or tax negotiations were probably inevitable in a society that was incompletely industrialized, and in which taxes were not deducted automatically from payrolls or (until the introduction of the value-added tax) based on itemized production processes. Meanwhile, tax fraud had certain "eufunctional" aspects: Permitting artisans and small shopkeepers to practice selective fiscal evasion cushioned them against the vicissitudes of too-rapid economic modernization, kept their antisystem proclivities in check, and limited the growth of popular fascism, such as Poujadism (see Chapter 4). Finally, in France, tax advantages for the wealthy are not so obviously sanctioned by law as they are in the United States and are partly balanced by the extensive system of "negative income taxes"—family subsidies, university scholarships, and social security payments.

The alcoholism that one (still) encounters in France might similarly be attributed to widespread alienation. But excessive wine drinking, apart from its association with conviviality and "Latin" patterns of social intercourse, is also related to the fact that viticulture is a very important element of the French agricultural economy.

For many years, the educational elitism described in the previous chapter impeded upward mobility, fortified inequality, and contributed to the alienation of those social sectors whose chances of advancement were blocked, while the "unrealistic" and (perhaps excessively) humanistic content of higher education contributed to frustration, as university graduates found their diplomas not particularly suited to the market. But selectivity in school admissions (which continues despite the educational reforms) has also been a means of maintaining standards and providing continuity in a cultural tradition that, today more than ever, is threatened both by mass culture and by foreign influences.

Many French observers have shared a widespread assumption that a modern, democratic political culture depends heavily on an ethic of individual achievement, that the development of such a culture has been promoted best in Protestant countries,[8] and that both economic and political advancement in France have been kept in check by the prevalence of Catholicism.[9] One must, however, keep in mind that (1) there is an authoritarian as well as a democratic Protestantism and France has been subjected to the influences of both kinds;[10] (2) France began the process of intermittent "de-Christianization" with the Revolution of 1789; (3) Napoleonic France (which was still in the grip of Catholicism) was one of the first countries to introduce nonascriptive recruitment to the civil service; and (4) postwar France (like Italy, another Catholic country) has had a more dynamic economy than Britain (where much innovation is promoted by non–Anglo-Saxons). Moreover, as we have seen (Chapter 1), there has been a progressive "Protestantization" of France, as Protestants have become more prominent than ever in business, banking, and politics. (This development has been occurring at a time when the United States is becoming less "Anglo-Saxon" and more "Latino.")

Some years ago a scholar remarked that "in the United States, which has gone further than any other Western society in institutionalizing the ethic of achievement, acute social tensions occur at the lower levels of the reward hierarchy. These are manifested in the exceptionally high incidence of various social phenomena, including homicide, mental illness, drug addiction, alcoholism, juvenile delinquency, petty larceny, and organized crime."[11] All these phenomena can be found in France in increasing measure as that country becomes more modernized and urbanized. The fact that the dimensions of these problems are not as great as in the United States might be attributed to the existence of forms of social orientations that we tend to regard as premodern or parochial, such as the continued stress on family membership and on local patriotism. Despite the growing number of divorces and the increasing proportion of unmarried couples and single-parent families,[12] traditional family ties are still important in France, and despite a growing accent on youth (especially since the presidency of Giscard d'Estaing), there is still a respect for, and a concern with, the older generation. In 1971, information centers for the aged (*le troisième age*) were set up in each department to inform them of their rights, which include generous pension payments, housing allowances, and rebates on public transport. Irrespective of this concern (which contrasts sharply with the institutionalized bias against the aged in the United States, a bias that exists despite the growth of entitlements), a recent poll indicated that 71 percent of the French think that it is primarily the responsibility of the family to take care of the aged (against 22 percent, who believe that it should be largely the concern of the state).[13]

The persistence of local orientations, which might be regarded as a line of defense against an overcentralized state, has been attested to not only by a highly developed municipal pride but also by the fact that the mayor of a town is more favorably regarded than a deputy or senator. This has been the case particularly since the decentralization measures of the early 1980s, under which communes were given greater power and responsibility. A study of the "cognitive" dimension of French political culture shows that 92 percent of respondents to a poll knew the name of their mayor, compared to 44 percent who could identify their deputy.[14]

The localism and familism of French orientations were to some extent symptoms of a fear of outsiders. For many years, this fear was reflected in an avoidance of close relationships outside the family circle,[15] excessively formalized *politesse*, the inability of the French to make friends easily, their reluctance to invite friends to their homes, an unwillingness to join voluntary associations, and an underdeveloped tradition of philanthropy. According to some surveys, the

French still exhibit a relatively low level of trust (a characteristic they are said to share with Italians and Greeks).[16] But according to other surveys, the vast majority of the French believe that people *can* be trusted.[17] In any case, some of these behavior patterns have been less a matter of political culture than a reflection of physical constraints or public policy; as these have changed, the aforementioned patterns of behavior have changed with them. For instance, more French people invite outsiders to their homes as homes become more spacious. Philanthropy, too, is developing, as French families have more money and as governments have used tax concessions to encourage private giving. According to one estimate, between 1975 and 1987 more than 47 percent of the French gave to charity, but the total amount given by the typical family was very small.[18] Nevertheless, in the past few years French voluntary giving has been reflected in "telethons" to fund medical research, in collections of United Nations International Children's Emergency Fund (UNICEF), and in significant contributions to the people of Bosnia.[19] Conversely, government efforts (especially during the cohabitation period of 1986–1988) to encourage wealthy private individuals and corporations to help support museums, theaters, and libraries have not been very successful, in part because the tax incentives have been too low, and in part because the promotion of culture has been considered the proper province of the government.[20] In recent years, the French have increasingly endorsed the "postmaterialist" measures of central and subnational governments and supported movements promoting such measures. These developments are manifested by the growth of local cultural associations, the growing influence of environmental movements, and the promotion of legislation providing for enhanced civil liberties and gender and racial equality (the latter moderating the growing tendencies to xenophobia).

VERBAL AND PRACTICAL BEHAVIOR

The local and familial orientations of the French have frequently been cited as evidences of both a faulty socialization process and a widespread disaffection for the national political system. That disaffection was said to be shown by the prevalence of an ideological approach to politics, revolutionary rhetoric, electoral abstention, and frequent outbursts of political violence. There is no doubt that a generation ago, French politics was informed by a high degree of ideological thinking, by "absolute-value rationalities," and by "apocalyptic visions."[21] This mindset, which has been conditioned by history and by the stress of the educational curriculum on rationalistic, Cartesian, and systematic approaches to social phenomena, has influenced French people's interest in philosophical nuances among competing political formulas. Such approaches were said to be particularly remarkable among "radicals, Socialist and Catholic intellectuals, and Communists,"[22] who had their own diverse views about the imperfections of the existing regime.

Are these divisions significant in terms of practical politics? The French have experienced numerous revolutions or at least have participated in many attempts to replace inadequate regimes by experiments informed by millennial strivings. But none of the revolutions has succeeded completely, and the French have learned not to expect too much from them; as a well-known saying has it, "The more things change, the more they remain the same" (*"Plus ça change, plus c'est la même chose"*). Therefore, "apocalyptic visions" have often been pursued as if they had a life of their own, a situation that has been reflected in the behavior of both political parties and voters (as we shall see in the next chapter).

The functional autonomy of ideological rhetoric (to the extent that such rhetoric still exists), party orientations, and programmatic preferences is illustrated by the fact that although the majority of the French adhere to an anticlerical party, an even greater majority oppose the end of subsidies to Catholic schools.[23] It is also illustrated by the fact that, although there are leftist "collectivist" and redistributive and rightist "anticollectivist" *biases*, there is no clear correlation between general leftist orientations and approval of nationalization policies, or between conservative orientations and privatization policies,[24] and that there are no great differences between Right and Left with respect to the support of minimum incomes (see Table 3.1).

The disjunction between verbal and real political behavior is illustrated in a number of ways. Many French people who embraced revolutionary rhetoric had a penchant for order in their personal lives; many who exhibited verbal antimilitarism admired the warriors of the past; and many who in the past held anti-regime views had respect for civil servants and hoped that their children might enter a career in the service of the state.[25] (This remains true despite the fact that in recent years the image of civil servants has declined—possibly because in the Fifth Republic the distinction between them and politicians has become increasingly obscured.)

TABLE 3.1 Party preferences and attitudes regarding selected policies (in percentages)

Policy	Population as a Whole	Party Preference				
		PCF	PS	UDF	RPR	Nat. Fr.
Reestablishing tax on great wealth						
for	78	98	93	61	57	51
against	15	2	3	30	34	34
Putting in place a minimum income even if that required tax surcharge to finance it						
for	62	45	71	64	57	40
against	24	37	18	21	29	46
Renationalizing a number of enterprises privatized since 1986	18	70	26	2	3	6
Encouraging wives to stay home by granting them a salary	47	39	45	52	54	55

SOURCE: Based on SOFRES, *L'Etat de l'opinion 1989* (Paris: Seuil, 1989), pp. 128 and 129. (Polls conducted in April 1988.)

Herbert Luethy, an astute observer of France, spoke in 1957 about "the lack of consequences of political controversy" in that country.[26] The continued existence of feelings that political arguments have little impact on the content of policy decisions is often said to be "proved" by a decline in party membership, a growing indifference to traditional political parties (especially among the young), and the increasing incidence of electoral abstention. However, the relative indifference to political parties may be due not so much to evaluative orientation with regard to them as to the belief that the old ideologies are no longer very important and that there has been a convergence on issues. Furthermore, the "dealignment" from the mainstream parties is to some extent compensated by the growth of social movements (such as antiracist ones) and single-issue parties (such as environmental ones), a development that might be seen as evidence of interest in fostering democratic expression by a more autonomous "civil society." Similarly, electoral abstentionism may be less a testimony to disillusionment with the political system as such than a sign of protest against too many elections at short intervals (as in 1988) or as an indicator of the belief that the victory of one party rather than another would neither redound to the clear material benefit of the voters nor cause them irreparable harm (see Chapter 4). The rate of participation in presidential elections has remained stable; the highest rates of abstention have been in elections where the outcome has made the least difference in terms of policy: selected national referenda, certain local elections, and elections to the European Parliament (see Chapter 4, Tables 4.8 and 4.9). Moreover, abstention rates in France have not been nearly so high as in the United States in similar elections.[27] Finally, there are other forms of electoral participation, such as voting for factory and university councils and social security boards.

It has been pointed out that many French voters, especially the young, are relatively ignorant of political parties and politicians.[28] A recent study confirms this phenomenon, but it also shows that the cognitive dimension of French political culture is strongly tied to the instrumental dimension: that the knowledge of political subject matter is related not only to a person's place in the social hierarchy and level of education but also to the concrete policy benefits to be derived from such knowledge. Thus, many more farmers (in fact, the majority) know the name of the minister of agriculture than the names of other ministers.[29] Many young people do not inform themselves as much as do adults about politics, in part because they are not yet actively involved in the economic system and in part because they concentrate their efforts on obtaining the lycée diploma.[30]

Until a few years ago, it was customary to refer to incidents of anomic behavior—such as street demonstrations and mass strikes—as indicators of a negative dimension in French political culture. But anomic behavior should not be equated automatically with revolution or construed as evidence of a persistent alienation of the masses. Spontaneous events may in fact provide useful outlets or social catharses that obviate or sidetrack real system changes or revolutions. Most mass protests—by farmers, workers, and students—tend to be issue-specific and are designed to supplement and energize the institutional processes;

moreover, they are not entirely anomic, to the extent that they are encouraged by leaders of political parties and interest groups.

The most interesting (and voluminously discussed) rebellion, the Events of 1968, could be viewed as a case in point. In May of that year, mass demonstrations organized by students and workers in the Paris area broke out, quickly spread to other segments of the population, and culminated in a series of general strikes in several cities that involved more than a third of the nation's labor force, paralyzing France for several days and threatening to bring down the government. The May Events had several causes: the explosion of the number of students in universities and the government's inadequate response to this; the antiquated physical plant and overcrowded conditions, which could not be resolved with jerry-built new structures; an outdated and rigid curriculum that was as ill adapted to the changing labor market as it was to the scientific needs of an advanced industrial society; and a system of relationships (or rather, lack of relationships) between students and faculty that did not respond to the students' demands for greater say in their courses of study. For the workers, there was a growing resentment, in part fanned by the students, over low pay, a long workweek, poor housing, and a perception of general neglect by the government. Both students and workers were impatient with the authoritarian patterns of government initiated by de Gaulle and, finally, bored with the general himself.

Some radicals may have seen the May Events as a prelude to a social and political revolution. For the majority of the rebels, however, the events were little more than a "happening" and a public festival. The events shook up part of France—and provided some momentum for the loosening of social relations. They also broke the spell of de Gaulle and led to increased demands for "participatory democracy" on the part of students and for significant wage increases on the part of workers.

But one should keep in mind that for several years many of the university reforms that were initiated remained innovations on paper only; that such novel manifestations of social solidarity as the collaboration between workers and students hardly outlasted the events; that the rise in consumer demands is not by itself revolutionary; that the radicalization of certain social sectors (for example, the quasi-Catholic trade union, the *Confédération française démocratique du travail* [CFDT]), also coincided, on the one hand, with an impressive victory of Gaullist candidates in the legislative elections of 1968 and, on the other, with the beginning of the "domestication" of the French Communist party (that is, the party's public disavowal of revolutionary methods for achieving power or social change, and a commitment to bourgeois political values); and that the disengagement of the French from Gaullist charisma itself signified a gradual return to institutional normalcy.[31]

To the extent that the events were a spontaneous juvenile uprising rather than an ideologically motivated "proletarian" one, their duration was, by definition, limited.[32] But as an affair of French youth, the events reflected a tendency of that youth to be more critical of the regime and to situate themselves farther on the left of the political spectrum than their elders (which did not necessarily imply voting for specific leftist parties) as well as to challenge traditional assumptions about the political and social order.[33]

CONCEPTIONS OF THE STATE AND NATIONAL IDENTITY

Indeed, it is possible to trace the onset of a process of reexamination of many political attitudes—in short, of changes in the French political culture—to the events of 1968. One of the changes relates to the definition of society itself. Until the early postwar years, the collective consciousness of the French had revolved around an image of society that was based, if not on small-town and village life, on a nostalgia about such a life and the social system and the institutions that informed it: the Catholic church, the public school, the head of the family, and the small commercial establishments. The questioning of the authority of the university professor and the waning influence of the paterfamilias, organized religion, the schoolteacher, and the central bureaucracy have contributed to a lowering of the image of political leaders—as attested to, for instance, by the lampooning of politicians in the public media (see Chapter 9)—and this has led inevitably to a questioning of the role of the state and the foundations upon which it was built. The gradual demystification of the state has been associated with the rediscovery of "civil society"—that is, the various sectors not associated with political parties, elected politicians, or officialdom—a rediscovery that in turn has been reflected in another development: the spread of the idea that many decisions now made by the national government should be made by local governments or by the private sector.

The growing skepticism about the omnipotent state has been accompanied by a more favorable orientation toward the market; increasingly, French citizens find engineers and directors of business firms more useful to society than higher civil servants or deputies.[34] Other surveys reveal that in 1991 only 49 percent considered politics an honorable activity (compared to 65 percent who did so in 1985) and that 58 percent considered elected and appointed officials to be corrupt (compared to 38 percent in 1985).[35] However, the French do not necessarily accept the retreat of the state as a liberating development;[36] they continue to have greater expectations from the state than do Americans, in part, perhaps, because they remember the lack of social responsibility of the traditional entrepreneurial class, and in part because one out of every five members of the work force is paid directly by the state (although this proportion will decrease when the current privatization processes are completed). The continuing relevance of the state as a symbol (a fact that can hardly be explained in terms of the "state-centered" paradigm currently popular among American political scientists) does not imply that the French citizen functions as an authoritarian personality; he or she continues to think about the possibility of rebellion, because such an act may help to rivet the attention of the agents of the state to his or her problems.[37] However, the citizen's attachment to the state is not clearly related to the popularity of the *individual incumbent* of a state position or even to the policy successes and failures of that state. Thus, while President Mitterrand was losing popularity, the French continued to place the president first among the political *institutions* of the country until very recently (see Chapter 10). And while the French increasingly disavowed the Socialist leadership of the country, they continued to acknowledge the various policy achievements of Socialist governments, such as the expansion of civil liberties, the reduction of the workweek, improvements of the welfare state, and decentralization.[38] To be sure, the electorate "punished" the Socialist party for its failure to solve the unemployment problem. However, the disavowal of the Socialist party in 1993 was not simply a reflection of electoral behavior based on economic rationality; it was also related to the party's internal disunity, to widespread corruption among its politicians, and to a growing disenchantment with the "political class" as a whole.

Paradoxically, the desacralization of the state has been occurring at the same time as the growth of a consensus about the constitutional system and even about public policies, which may suggest that the state is no longer desperately needed as a "conceptual glue" for holding the French nation together. Whereas the nation was once defined in terms of a unifying state, it has come increasingly to be defined in terms of a pluralistic society. That society, however, is so ethnically diverse that it has become a plurality of subcultures, in which ethnic consciousness (to some extent filling the void left by a declining religious orientation) is more important than in the past. Thus, while there is no longer a question about the legitimacy of the political system, there are now constant discussions about the foundations of French society and the nature of French "identity."[39] This development, it is argued, has been associated with the decline of the prestige of the French public school as that institution has become increasingly less effective in fulfilling its role as a disseminator of a clear cultural model and an unambiguous sense of Frenchness.[40]

In the past, membership in the French nation was defined in terms of descent. However, the ethnic origins and the provincial cultures of the Hexagon have been so diverse that France had to be "invented":[41] A French national identity had to be fabricated by means of a common language, a centralized republic, an educational system, and the evocation of a common history and common unifying myths. These have included the French Revolution, the Resistance, the May Events, republican values, the universal appeal of the French language and culture, and the idea of France as a great power.[42] For most French people, symbols such as the flag are probably less necessary than for Americans to remind them of the identity of their nation because the French encounter material evidences of their country's history (e.g., châteaux and museums) almost daily, and because several of the specific values, memories, and myths of the French Revolution are now thoroughly internalized by the majority of French citizens, among them equality before the law and universal suffrage.[43]

However, in recent years these myths have been subjected to critical reexamination. The French Revolution has been partly demythologized as historians have evoked the (unnecessary) massacres of antirevolutionaries in the Vendée;

the uncritical acceptance of the France of the Resistance is being modified by a more sober acknowledgement of the crimes of the Vichy regime and the collaboration of the French;[44] and the May Events are increasingly labeled as a collective fiesta that ended as quickly as it began.[45] Claims regarding the uniqueness of French culture have lost much credibility in the face of a mass culture that seems to be the same in various countries, and republican ideas that the French had done so much to disseminate are now accepted by most nations. Finally, the global political importance of France, already deflated by the overwhelming presence of the United States, is being further deflated by the growing international power of Germany. Moreover, there is a feeling that the political myths and values are only incompletely shared by recent immigrants and their immediate descendants.

It is perhaps for these reasons that the French have taken to defining national identity in practical terms. A poll taken a few years ago revealed that for 63 percent of the respondents, French national identity was symbolized by French cuisine; for 62 percent, by human rights; for 42 percent by the French woman; for 34 percent, by church steeples; for 30 percent, by chauvinism; and for 22 percent, by betting on horse races.[46] These images may not reflect objective reality: Cuisine in France is becoming more international; church steeples have more to do with local color than with religion; and although most of the citizens of France are proud to be French (see Table 3.2)—and about half assert that they are ready to die for their country[47]—they are far less chauvinistic today than in earlier times and less so than the British. Nor do these images of national identity correspond clearly with the complicated French attitudes toward outgroups. On the one hand, most French people no longer believe that the majority are descended from "our ancestors the Gauls, and many of them (in principle) accept the idea that membership in French society is open to all who speak French, pay taxes, and are ready to share the fate of France."[48] On the other hand, there are still those who are ill at ease with a purely functional and voluntaristic definition of nationhood,[49] and (for reasons alluded to in the previous chapter) they are reluctant to accept North African Muslims as fully qualified to be French. A major reason for that reluctance is the fear that the number of non-European immigrants might reach a threshold beyond which French cuisine, the commitment

TABLE 3.2 Pride in being French (percentage of each group)

	Population as a Whole	Selected Age Groups		
		18–24	*35–49*	*65 and over*
Very proud to be French	51	35	49	73
Rather proud	27	30	28	21
Not particularly proud	19	30	20	6
Not proud at all	2	2	2	—
No opinion	1	3	1	—

SOURCE: Based on SOFRES, *L'Etat de l'opinion 1988* (Paris: Seuil, 1988), p. 181.

to republican values (e.g., *laïcité* and pluralism), the French language, and even the physical landscape would be denatured beyond recognition.

There is no doubt that over the years the concern of the French with extending individual liberties—and with establishing a certain distance between themselves and the state—has grown. But such a concern is not unqualified and has not converted the French to the laissez-faire ideologies of Ronald Reagan or Margaret Thatcher. Despite the growing fashion of neoliberalism, and despite a disenchantment with the "political class" and a low level of confidence in the ability of politicians to solve the country's economic problems,[50] most French citizens continue to prize economic security (see Table 3.3) and rely on the state to guarantee it.

The concern with concrete socioeconomic payoffs granted by the government has had important behavioral consequences. First, it has moderated the hero-worshipping tendencies (or monarchistic instincts) of French people and has caused them, after a given number of years, to be dissatisfied with the merely symbolic outputs of presidents and governments. Second, it has moderated their distrust of their fellow citizens and has led them to combine in voluntary associations in order to make demands on the public authorities.

The nature of the French people's expectations from their government, their assessment of their leaders' capabilities, and their political culture as a whole are likely to be affected by the progressive integration of France into a supranational European Union and a transatlantic network of relationships. This process began several years ago; as a result of it, many of the distinctive attitudes of the French have already been transformed. There is now less concern with ideology and more with technology, and there has been a gradual displacement of the traditional historical and national orientation by a utilitarian and global one. Although many French intellectuals are still in the grip of cultural insecurity

TABLE 3.3   Major concerns of the electorate, 1993

Percentage of Voters Citing Each Problem:

Unemployment	70
Education	22
Social inequality	17
Crime and violence	16
Inflation	14
Immigration	14
Environment	13
European unity	11
Rise of extreme Right	8
Foreign affairs	6
Political scandals	6

SOURCE: IFOP poll cited by Alain Riding, "France Goes to the Right, by Default," *New York Times,* 11 April 1993.

and a somewhat narcissistic concern with the French language, an increasing proportion of French men and women are learning other languages.[51] Although some members of the French elite still profess a contempt for material values, many other French citizens are oriented toward production, efficiency, and prosperity and point with pride to the fact that the country has become the world's fourth largest exporter. At the same time, they are looking outward for models of economic management.[52] In short, the political attitudes and behavior of the French have come increasingly to resemble those of people in other Western democracies, a development that has spelled the end of French exceptionalism.[53]

NOTES

1. Conditions such as wealth, literacy, industrialization, urbanization, the number of physicians, etc. See S. M. Lipset, *Political Man: The Social Bases of Politics,* expanded ed. (Baltimore: Johns Hopkins University Press, 1981), pp. 27ff.
2. A "modern" political system is one in which traditional authority has been replaced by "a single national authority," decision-making patterns have become rationalized, political functions have become differentiated, political life in general has become secularized, elite recruitment is by merit rather than ascription, and meaningful institutions of (popular) political participation have developed. Samuel Huntington, "Political Modernization," *World Politics* 18 (April 1966), 378–414.
3. Gabriel Almond and Sidney Verba, *The Civic Culture* (Boston: Little, Brown, 1965), esp. pp. 7, 35–36, and 86–97; and Gabriel Almond and G. Bingham Powell, Jr., *Comparative Politics: A Developmental Approach* (Boston: Little, Brown, 1966), pp. 62, 260–266; 321ff and passim.
4. Jesse R. Pitts, "Les Français et l'autorité," in Jean-Daniel Reynaud and Yves Grafmeyer, eds., *Français, qui êtes-vous?* (Paris: Documentation Française, 1981), pp. 285–299.
5. See, for example, Michel Crozier, *The Stalled Society* (New York: Viking, 1973), pp. 97–98 passim; his *The Bureaucratic Phenomenon* (Chicago: University of Chicago Press, 1967), esp. pp. 220ff.; Raymond Aron, *The Opium of the Intellectuals* (New York: Norton, 1962), pp. 227–229; Jean-Jacques Servan-Schreiber, *Le Défi américain* (Paris: Denoel, 1967); and Jean-François Revel, *Without Marx or Jesus: The American Revolution Has Begun* (Garden City, NY: Doubleday, 1971).
6. Gérard Mermet, *Francoscopie: Les Français: Qui sont-ils? Où vont-ils?* (Paris: Larousse, 1988), pp. 200–202.
7. *Nouvel Observateur*-Europe No. 1/SOFRES poll, May 1987.
8. See H. H. Gerth and C. Wright Mills, eds., *From Max Weber* (New York: Oxford University Press, 1958), esp. pp. 302–357.
9. Alain Peyrefitte, *The Trouble with France* (New York: Knopf, 1981), pp. 99–100, 121–131, 155–159, passim.
10. Cf. Emmanuel Todd, *La Nouvelle France* (Paris: Seuil, 1988), pp. 106–120.
11. Frank Parkin, *Class Inequality and Political Order* (New York: Praeger, 1971), p. 68.
12. The number of divorces grew from 37,447 in 1970 to 104,997 in 1987, and about 2 million couples are unmarried. See Gérard Vincent, "La France en 1991: Une Centrifugeuse?" *Contemporary French Civilization* 15:2 (Summer-Fall 1991), 203–204.
13. *Figaro*-SOFRES poll, January 1988.

14. IFOP poll, 1976, and SOFRES poll, 1983. Cited by Pascal Perrineau in "La Dimension cognitive de la culture politique," *Revue française de science politique* [hereafter cited as *RFSP*] 35:1 (February 1985), 72–89. However, a more recent (1992) poll reveals considerable confusion or lack of knowledge about the role of subnational assemblies and the operation of regional elections. SOFRES, *L'Etat de l'opinion 1993*, pp. 217–218.

15. See Henry W. Ehrmann, *Politics in France*, 2nd. ed. (Boston: Little, Brown, 1971), pp. 151ff; and Crozier, *The Stalled Society*, pp. 65–70, 93–99, 112–119.

16. See Ronald Inglehart, *Culture Shift in Advanced Industrial Societies* (Princeton, NJ: Princeton University Press, 1989). According to a composite of World Values surveys for 1981–1984 (p. 30), only about 25 percent of French respondents felt that "most people can be trusted."

17. According to a composite of Euro-Barometer surveys for 1976–1986, more than 80 percent of the French respondents considered people of their own nationality trustworthy. Ibid., p. 17.

18. Mermet, *Francoscopie*, p. 83. According to this source, only 4.7 percent gave more than 500 francs (i.e., more than $80).

19. This has taken place despite the fact that only 40 percent of gifts are tax deductible and that no more than 5 percent of individual income and 3 percent of business income may be deducted. See Danielle Rouard, "Les Aventuriers de la générosité," *Le Monde*, 4, 5, and 6 August 1993.

20. According to some estimates, the total contributions of enterprises to culture and the arts in 1987 was 400 million francs (or about $65 million). See "Le Grand Air du mécénat," *Le Point*, 30 March 1987, pp. 136–137; and Jean-Yves Kaced, "Le Mécénat culturel d'entreprise," *Regards sur l'actualité* 145 (November 1988), 43–53.

21. Gabriel Almond and James S. Coleman, eds., *The Politics of Developing Areas* (Princeton, NJ: Princeton University Press, 1960), p. 37. See also Charles Morazé, *The French and the Republic* (Ithaca, NY: Cornell University Press, 1958), pp. 20ff, which discusses the "passion for theory" prevalent among the French.

22. Almond and Coleman, *Politics of Developing Areas*, p. 37.

23. In a public-opinion poll (Expansion-SOFRES) in 1983, 77 percent of the respondents would consider the abolition of "the free choice of school where children are sent" a very serious matter, 19 percent as a serious matter, and only 2 percent as not serious. SOFRES, *Opinion publique: Enquêtes et commentaires 1984* (Paris: Gallimard, 1984), p. 154.

24. According to a public-opinion poll in mid-1987, while only 25 percent of Socialist voters (compared to 41 percent of the total sample of respondents) approved of the Gaullists' privatization policies, 34 percent of the new owners of privatized industries were Socialists! SOFRES, *L'Etat de l'opinion 1988* (Paris: Seuil, 1988), pp. 33, 36.

25. See François Nourissier, *The French* (New York: Knopf, 1968), pp. 117–122.

26. Herbert Luethy, *France Against Herself* (New York: Meridian, 1957), p. 39.

27. Concerning the extent of electoral abstentionism in France as compared to that in the United States, see William R. Schonfeld and Marie-France Toinet, "Les Abstentionnistes: Ont-Ils toujours tort?" *RFSP* 25 (August 1975), 645–676.

28. For older studies, see P. E. Converse and G. Dupeux, "Politicization of the Electorate in France and the United States," *Public Opinion Quarterly* 25:1 (1962), 11; Frank A. Pinner, "Parental Overprotection and Political Distrust," *Annals of the American Academy of Political and Social Science* 361 (September 1965), 58–70; and Yves Agnès, "Les jeunes et la politique," *Le Monde*, 17 February 1973.

29. Perrineau, "La Dimension cognitive," pp. 75ff. According to a recent poll, only 48 percent could describe the role of the conseil général, and only 23 percent had current information about regional elections. Poll of February 1992, cited in SOFRES, *L'Etat de l'opinion 1993* (Paris: Seuil, 1993), p. 27.
30. For detailed statistics on voting patterns of the young compared to the electorate as a whole, see Annick Percheron, "Peut-on parler d'un incivisme des jeunes? Le Cas de la France," *International Political Science Review* 8:3 (July 1987), 273-282.
31. Of the numerous works on the 1968 rebellion, the following may be mentioned: Patrick Seale and Maureen McConville, *Red Flag, Black Flag* (New York: Hill & Wang, 1970); Alain Touraine, *The May Movement* (New York: Random House, 1971); Bernard E. Brown, *Protest in Paris: Anatomy of a Revolt* (Morristown, NJ: General Learning Press, 1974). For an interesting (though somewhat premature) discussion of the subject, see Philippe Bénéton and Jean Touchard, "Les interprétations de la crise de mai-juin 1968," *RFSP* 10 (June 1970), 503-544. The 25th anniversary of the revolt in 1993 was the occasion of many additional studies on the subject. According to one of these, the Events introduced for the first time the idea of *fraternity*, however briefly. They were also "the first anticommunist mass movement," for they took the monopoly of revolution away from the Communist Party and, in so doing, laid the groundwork for the end of Marxism in France. See Michel Le Bris, "Trois ou quatre choses que je crois savoir de mai 1968," *Revue des deux mondes*, May 1993, pp. 17-35.
32. On this point, see Edgar Morin, Claude Lefort, and Cornelius Castoriadis, *Mai 68: La Brèche—Suivie de vingts ans après* (Paris: Editions Complexe, 1988), esp. pp. 26, 74, 129, 151, 181. The book represents an effort to see the events from a less romantic and more detached perspective made possible by the lapse of twenty years.
33. According to a SOFRES poll (March 1978) of 13- to 17-year-olds, 32 percent felt close to (extreme to moderate) leftist parties, 17 percent to Giscardist or Gaullists, 32 percent to no party, and 17 percent did not know. According to Harris and SOFRES polls of 1977, less than 30 percent of those age 18 to 24 (and only 17 percent of the population as a whole) wanted radical social changes, while about half of the young wanted the status quo more or less maintained. Cited by Annick Percheron, "Se faire entendre: Morale quotidienne et attitudes politiques des jeunes," in Henri Mendras, ed., *La Sagesse et le désordre* (Paris: Gallimard, 1980), pp. 136-143, 160-163.
34. A survey conducted by SOFRES in September 1990 on a ranking of the societal utility of various professions, on a 0-10 scale, produced the following results: nurses, 9.3; workers, 9.2; general medical practitioners, 9.1; elementary and secondary schoolteachers, 9.0; farmers, 8.8; engineers, 8.6; small businessmen, 8.2; directors of business firms, 8.2; clergy, 6.7; higher civil servants, 6.3; parliamentary deputies, 6.1; prostitutes, 4.1. Selected from results cited in SOFRES, *L'Etat de l'opinion 1992*, p. 32.
35. Surveys conducted between the end of 1991 and early 1992, cited in SOFRES, *L'Etat de l'opinion 1993*, pp. 234-235.
36. Alain Touraine, "Existe-t-il encore une société française?" *Contemporary French Civilization* 15:2 (Summer-Fall 1991), 335-338.
37. See H. S. Jones, *The French State in Question* (Cambridge: Cambridge University Press, 1993), pp. 6-12. See also Peyrefitte, *The Trouble with France*, pp. 260-261 passim.
38. SOFRES, *L'Etat de l'opinion 1992*, pp. 226, 231.
39. See, for example: Espaces 89, *L'Identité française* (Paris: Editions Tiercé, 1985), for a social-democratic and "pluralistic" view; and Club de l'Horloge, *L'Identité de la France* (Paris: Albin Michel, 1985), for a conservative and "monistic" one.

40. Pierre Milza, speaking at a symposium of New York University in 1987, cited by Frederick L. Brown, "Crisis, Decentralization, Cohabitation: Aspects of Change in France," *Tocqueville Review* 9 (1987–88), 371–372.

41. Hervé Le Bras and Emmanuel Todd, *L'Invention de la France* (Paris: Pluriel, 1981). For a sweeping historical approach to the subject, see Fernand Braudel, *L'Identité de la France* (Paris: Arthaud, 1986). See also William Safran, "State, Nation, National Identity, and Citizenship: France as a Test Case," *International Political Science Review* 12:3 (1991), 219–238.

42. See Suzanne Citron, *Le Mythe national: L'Histoire de France en question* (Paris: Editions Ouvrières, 1989).

43. See polls in SOFRES, *L'Opinion publique 1986*, p. 90; and SOFRES, *L'Etat de l'opinion 1988*, pp. 195–196, 198.

44. A majority of young people now know that the French authorities participated in the deportation of Jews during World War II, having learned of this event more often from the media than from their schoolteachers. However, most of the young retain a patriotic view of Marshal Pétain: 31 percent think of him primarily as the victor in the battle of Verdun during World War I; 23 percent, as the person who did his best to protect French lives during World War II; 31 percent, as a collaborator of the Nazis; and only 4 percent, as a fascist dictator. SOFRES, *L'État de l'opinion 1993*, pp. 241–242.

45. See Alan Riding, "The '68 Uprising: Heaven in Its Way," *New York Times*, 28 May 1993; and "Que reste-t-il de 'la pensée 68'?" Interview with Luc Ferry, *Le Point*, 7 May 1993, pp. 60–61.

46. Passages/CSA, October 1987. Cited in Mermet, *Francoscopie*, p. 82. Interviewees were permitted to give several responses.

47. According to a poll (SOFRES, *L'État de l'Opinion 1988*, pp. 181–182), 49 percent were ready to die for France.

48. In a poll on the question "what does it mean to be French?," the answers were as follows: to be born in France, 52 percent; to defend freedom, 51 percent; to defend the country, 42 percent; to have the right to vote, 35 percent; to be attached to a common tradition and a common history, 33 percent; to speak French, 24 percent; to have French parents, 21 percent. Jean Pierre Rioux, "Les Français et leur histoire," *Histoire* 100 (May 1987), 72.

49. In the opinion of some observers, France has entered the "postnational" period, when many of its people feel that "[they] are the children of nobody and of everybody." Steven Englund, "De l'usage du mot 'nation' par les historiens," *Le Monde diplomatique*, March 1988, pp. 28–29. See also Pierre Nora, *Les Lieux de la mémoire*, 2 vols. (Paris: Gallimard, 1984–1986), which discusses at length the changes in the French national consciousness.

50. According to a Harris poll of December 1988, 88 percent are disenchanted with politics; 68 percent believe that governments have failed to solve urgent problems; and 61 percent that politicians have been indecisive. Only 20 percent have confidence in politicians, while 40 percent indicate that they had more confidence in leaders of business. "Les Français et la politique: C'est le divorce," *L'Express*, 16 December 1988, pp. 6–8.

51. According to an official report, nearly 60 percent of the French, and 89 percent of those 15 to 19 years old, have an understanding of one or more foreign languages (compared to only 40 percent of those over 65). The vast majority of these know some English. See *News From France*, 7 February 1992.

52. See Michel Albert, *Capitalisme contre capitalisme* (Paris: Seuil, 1991). The author argues that the "Rhenish" (i.e., German) approach to economic policy might serve as a model for France.
53. See François Furet, Jacques Julliard, and Pierre Rosanvallon, *La République du centre: La Fin de l'exception française* (Paris: Calmann-Lévy, 1988). See also Robert Boyer, "Vers l'érosion du particularisme français?" *French Politics and Society* 10:1 (Winter 1992), 8–24.

chapter **4**

Political Parties and Elections

Toward the end of the Fourth Republic, a well-known commentator on French politics remarked that in France "there are two fundamental principles: that of the Right and that of the Left; three main tendencies, if one adds the center; six political families; ten parties, small and large, each opposed by multiple currents; fourteen parliamentary groups, highly undisciplined; and forty million opinions."[1] From the Third Republic to the present, dozens of political formations have existed, each holding somewhat different views about economic and social policy, the relationship between the executive and the legislature and between the national and local governments, the place of religion in politics, and the role of France in world affairs. Some of these formations have represented distinct social classes; others have attempted to transcend classes and appeal to a broadly based national electorate. Some parties can trace their origins to the Third Republic and an even earlier period; others have been formed recently, either to deal with specific, short-term challenges or to respond to appeals from charismatic leaders. Some have mass memberships and complex national organizations; others are little more than coalitions of local notables, depending on a fragmented electorate. Some have had fully developed ideologies and programs; others are merely clubs, created by intellectuals and politicians for a variety of purposes (subsumed under the heading of "ego trips"), perhaps to express their ideas in small-circulation journals, enhance their visibility, or improve their maneuverability within the existing parliamentary party spectrum.

In the past half-century, a gradual simplification of the party system has taken place. In the mid-1930s, there were 19 recognized parties in the Assembly; in the early 1970s, there were only 6: the Gaullists and Republicans; the (Catholic) Centrists and the (anticlerical) Radical-Socialists; and the Socialists and Communists. In terms of ideology, these pairs could be grouped into Right, Center, and

Left; alternatively, they might be combined into four broad electoral and parliamentary groups or into a Right and a Left alliance system. At present there are only five Assembly groups: the Gaullists; the "Giscardists"; the (Catholic) Centrists; the Socialists; and the Communists (see Table 4.1, pp. 72–73; Table 4.2, p. 74; and Figure 4.1, pp. 76–77).

This simplification of the party system has been the consequence of a number of developments: changes in the electoral system; the modernization of the economy and the restructuring of society (which weakened the traditional class consciousness and reduced religious-anticlerical antagonisms); the blurring or discrediting of the image of a number of parties (because their programs were too vague or irrelevant or their leaders were distrusted); the polarizing impact of de Gaulle; and, finally, the personal efforts and ambitions of politicians who strove to mobilize a "national" electorate and appeal for support beyond traditional parties and classes.[2] To these factors one must add a growing consensus about the legitimacy of the Fifth Republic and, with that consensus, a public impatience with ideological nuances, especially insofar as they related to the very nature of the political system. Yet the six ideological families have persisted in sufficient measure—in terms of organizational reality as well as historical points of reference—to be treated separately.

THE SOCIALISTS

The Socialist party (*Parti socialiste*), which governed France for most of the past decade, has an impressive heritage. It is the oldest existing mass party in the country. Although democratic in orientation, much like the German SPD and the British Labour party, it was for many years far more Marxist than other socialist parties in Western Europe. While appealing to the working class with promises of radical economic change, the party has been led, for the most part, by bourgeois intellectuals. After the establishment of the Fifth Republic, the party was greatly weakened as a national political force, but in the early 1970s it began its recovery, becoming the largest party in terms of popular support and achieving a victory of almost landslide proportions in 1981.

The Socialist party was founded in 1905 in an attempt to unite four dominant varieties of socialism: utopian, syndicalist, revolutionary, and reformist. Officially known as the French Section of the Workers' International (*Section française de l'internationale ouvrière*—SFIO), it was a federation of independent regional units whose parliamentary politicians were subject to fairly strict party discipline. Although in principle committed to the class struggle and the transformation of society, the party entered into a number of coalitions with bourgeois parties, especially when the republic seemed to be in danger. Thus the SFIO joined the government in 1914 in a "sacred union" for the defense of France against the German attackers; in 1936 party leader Léon Blum headed an antifascist "Popular Front" government that included the bourgeois Radical-Socialists; and during World War II, a number of Socialist politicians made common cause with non-Socialists (in the Resistance at home and abroad) in fighting against the Germans.

After Liberation, the SFIO, as the third largest party, participated in a government coalition with the Communists and Christian Democrats. It furnished ministers to various moderate governments until 1951, and headed a cabinet in 1956–1957. Although the SFIO was an arch-defender of the Fourth Republic, many of the party's leaders supported the investiture of de Gaulle and the establishment of the Fifth Republic, fearing that failure to do so might lead to civil war. But the SFIO soon became disillusioned with de Gaulle's conservative domestic policies.

Having been consigned to opposition status and weakened by a massive defection of members, the SFIO experimented with a variety of alliance strategies. In 1963, some SFIO politicians promoted the presidential candidacy of Gaston Defferre, the anti-Communist mayor of Marseilles, in order to encourage a rapprochement with (anti-Gaullist) Center parties, including the Christian Democrats. When this effort collapsed, the party embraced a "united Left" tactic. In 1965, in order to strengthen their position vis-à-vis the Communists, the Socialists formed the Federation of the Democratic and Socialist Left (*Fédération de la gauche démocratique et socialiste*—FGDS), a coalition of the SFIO, the Radical-Socialists, and a few democratic-leftist (or social-democratic) clubs. François Mitterrand, the leader of one of these clubs (the *Convention des institutions républicaines*—CIR), was chosen to be president of this federation and soon thereafter became the joint candidate of the democratic *and* the communist Left in the presidential elections.

The Communist-FGDS electoral alliance continued for the parliamentary elections of 1967 and 1968 but broke down in 1969 as a result of growing ideological conflict between the SFIO and the Communist Party (PCF). The FGDS too had collapsed, and the SFIO had become so weak that in the presidential elections of 1969 its candidate received only 5 percent of the first-ballot votes (compared to over 21 percent for the Communist candidate).

After that election, the SFIO ceased to exist formally. It was succeeded by the *Parti socialiste* (PS), a fusion of the old SFIO, the CIR, and various democratic-leftist clubs. The process of revitalization included the eventual replacement of Guy Mollet, who had been the leader of the SFIO since 1946, by Mitterrand, and an increasingly successful effort to retain—by means of a new, progressive platform[3]— the support of much of the working class and to attract young people, white-collar employees, shopkeepers, farmers, and even Catholics.[4] From a low of fewer than 70,000 in 1968, the party membership rose to more than 150,000 by 1975.

It was from this position of strength that the PS rebuilt its electoral alliance with the Communists. In 1972, the PS and PCF agreed on joint platform, the "Common Program of the Left" (to which leftist elements of the Radical-Socialist party would also subscribe a year later), and to mutual support in future elections. The Common Program called, inter alia, for an increased minimum wage, a reduction of the workweek, the extension of social benefits, the strengthening of union rights, a limiting of government support of parochial schools, and the nationalization of some industries.

The Common Program alliance held up well during the parliamentary elections of 1973 and the presidential elections of 1974, but it began to break down

TABLE 4.1 Parliamentary elections, 1958–1993 (in percentage of votes cast*)

Parliamentary Elections	Left			Center		Right		
	Communists	Socialists	Radicals	MRP	Democratic Center	Moderate Independents	Gaullists	National Front
1958								
First ballot	18.9	15.5	11.5	11.6		19.9	17.6	
Second ballot	20.7	13.7	7.7	7.5		23.6	26.4	
1962								
First ballot	21.7	12.6	7.5	8.9	9.6[a]	4.4[b]	31.9	
Second ballot	21.3	15.2	7.0	5.3	7.8[a]	1.6	40.5	
1967								
First ballot	22.5	18.8[c]		17.9[d]			37.8[e]	
Second ballot	21.4	24.1[c]		10.8[d]			42.6[e]	
1968								
First ballot	20.0	16.5		10.3[f]			43.7[e]	
Second ballot	20.1	21.3		7.8[f]			46.4[e]	
1973								
First ballot	21.5	21.2[g]		13.1[h]		36.4[e]		
Second ballot	20.6	25.1		6.1[h]		46.2[e]		
1978								
First ballot	20.5	24.8[i]				23.9[j]	22.6	
Second ballot	18.6	30.6[i]				24.8[j]	26.1	

72

1981						
First ballot	16.2	37.5[i]	19.2[i]		20.8	
Second ballot	6.9	49.3[i]	18.6[i]		22.4	
1986						
Single ballot**	9.8	31.4[i]	8.3[j]	21.5[k]	11.2	9.7
1988						
First ballot	11.32	37.5[i]	(18.5)[j]	40.4[l]	(19.2)	
Second ballot	3.42	48.7[i]	(21.2)[j]	46.8[l]	(23.1)	
1993						
First ballot	9.2	20.3[m]	(19.1)[j]	39.7[o]	(20.4)	12.4
Second ballot	4.6	31.6[n]	(25.1)[j]	55.0[o]	(27.8)	5.7

NOTE: The separate scores for UDF and RPR are in parentheses.
[a] Anti-Gaullist centrists
[b] Independent Republicans (RI)
[c] FGDS
[d] Democratic Center
[e] UDR and Allies
[f] PDM
[g] UGSD
[h] Reformers
[i] Including Left-Radicals
[j] UDF and other Giscard supporters (including CDS, Radicals, and Republicans)
[k] Gaullist (RPR) and UDF, combined list
[l] *Union du rassemblement et du centre* (URC), the electoral alliance of RPR, UDF, and others
[m] Includes 17.6 PS, 0.9 MRG, 1.8 "presidential majority"
[n] Includes 28.25 PS, 1.15 MRG, 2.17 "presidential majority"
[o] *Union pour la France* (UPF) (electoral alliance of RPR, UDF, and others)
*Rounded off.
**Proportional representation; only one round.

SOURCES: *Bulletin de l'Assemblée nationale*, 10e législature, no.1, 13 April 1993; Le Monde, Dossiers et Documents, *21 mars–28 mars 1993, Elections législatives: la droite sans partage*, pp. 63, 77; and *Pouvoirs* 66 (September 1993), 192–193. There are slight variations among the sources.

TABLE 4.2 Presidential elections, 1958–1988 (in percentage of votes cast*)

Presidential Elections	Left		Center				Right	
	Communists	Socialists	Radicals	MRP	Democratic Center	Moderate Independents	Gaullists	National Front
1965								
First ballot		32.2[a]			15.8[b]		43.7[c]	
Second ballot		45.5[a]					54.5	
1969								
First ballot	21.5[d]	5.1[e]			23.4[f]		43.8[g]	
Second ballot					42.4[f]		57.6[g]	
1974								
First ballot		43.2[a]				32.6[h]	15.1[i]	
Second ballot		49.2[a]				50.8[h]		
1981								
First ballot	15.3[j]	25.8[a]	2.2[k]			28.3[h]	17.9[n]	
Second ballot		51.8[a]				48.2[h]		
1988								
First ballot	6.7[l]	34.1[a]				16.5[m]	19.9[n]	14.4[o]
Second ballot		54.0[a]					45.9[n]	

NOTE: Tixier-Vignancour, a candidate of the extreme Right who received 5.3 percent in the first-ballot presidential election of 1965, has been omitted from the table. All other first-ballot candidates who received less than 5 percent of the total vote have also been omitted.

[a] Mitterand
[b] Lecanuet
[c] de Gaulle
[d] Duclos
[e] Defferre
[f] Poher
[g] Pompidou
[h] Giscard d'Estaing
[i] Chaban-Delmas
[j] Marchais
[k] Michel Crépeau
[l] André Lajoinie. Note that a splinter Communist Party put up a separate candidate.
[m] Barre
[n] Chirac
[o] Le Pen
*Rounded off.

just before the parliamentary elections of 1978. The reasons for this breakdown are complex. There was a bitter quarrel over the meaning of the common platform, specifically the extent of nationalization, the leveling of salaries, and the allocation of cabinet posts in the event of a victory of the Left. While the Communists questioned the good faith and the leftism of the PS, the Socialists doubted that the PCF had "de-Stalinized" itself sufficiently to be trusted with a share of power. A principal cause of the Communists' resentment was the fact that, as public-opinion polls and local election results revealed, the PS had become the major party of the Left and had begun to reduce the PCF to the status of a junior partner. The inability of the Left to seize control of the Assembly during the 1978 elections was widely attributed to the failure of the PCF to support Socialist candidates in the second round in many constituencies. At the same time, the unhappiness of the Communists with the PS and the weakened position of the PCF within the Left alliance increased the voters' perception of the Socialists' moderation and improved the latter's future electoral prospects. One of the major reasons for the impressive victories of the PS in 1981 was the fact that the fear of Communists' having excessive (and destructive) influence on a Socialist-led government—a fear exploited in the past by Gaullists and Giscardists—was increasingly perceived as being without substance.

Some Socialists hoped that their capture of the presidency and the control of the Assembly would give their party the opportunity to embrace "social democracy" along the lines followed by analogous parties in West Germany and Scandinavia. That hope was based on the belief that the PS—with the help of votes from shopkeepers, clerks, farmers, teachers, and other bourgeois and petit-bourgeois elements—had already come to occupy part of the political *center* and that the Communist Party had become too weak to pressure the PS to stray from the path of moderate reform. Other Socialists insisted that the overwhelming victories of the PS would enable the party to promote a program of *socialisme à la française* that would go far beyond the moderate reforms undertaken by social-democratic governments elsewhere in Europe.

After 1981, there were still Socialists, notably among younger party activists and, paradoxically, some of the bourgeois members of the party's top echelons, who were inspired by Marxism and expected the PS to strive for the abolition of capitalism. But it is doubtful whether many of the ordinary members (of whom there were more than 200,000 in 1983) wanted radical changes. At that time, less than 50 percent of the PS electorate consisted of members of the working class; many of the industrial workers who voted Socialist belonged to the middle-income and skilled worker categories, the least skilled and most underpaid workers generally remaining loyal to the Communist Party. Furthermore, a significant proportion of the Socialist voters between 1978 and 1981 were businesspeople, middle- and upper-middle-class managerial personnel (*cadres supérieurs*), and practicing Catholics.[5] The *embourgeoisement* of the PS was reflected also in the professional backgrounds of Socialist deputies elected in 1981. Among 268, only 2 were workers, as compared to 21 physicians, 36 university professors, 84 high school teachers, and 43 higher civil servants[6] (see Chapter 7, Table 7.7, for more recent statistics).

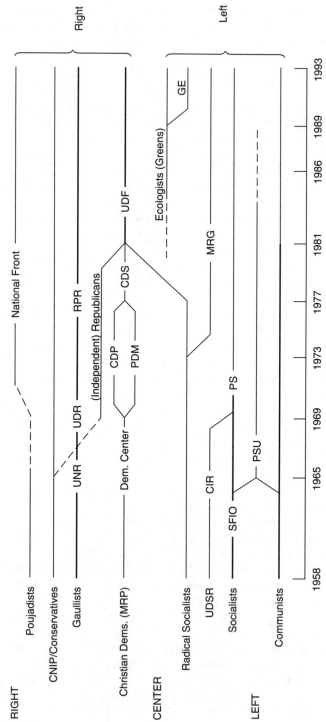

Explanations of Acronyms

CDP   *Centre de la démocratie et du progrès* (Center for Democracy and Progress): pro-Gaullist centrist party established in 1969

CDS   *Centre des démocrates sociaux* (Center of Social Democrats): Catholic centrist party (1976) resulting from the reunification of the CDP and the anti-Gaullist centrists (PDM). In 1988, the CDS constituted itself into a separate parliamentary group, *Union des démocrates et du centre* (UDC).

CIR   *Convention des institutions républicaines* (Convention of Republican Institutions): center-left formation of various political clubs

CNIP   *Centre national des indépendants et paysans* (National Center of Independents and Peasants): an amalgam of various economic conservatives, supporters of business and agricultural elements (increasingly referred to simply as CNI)

FN   *Front national* (National Front): extreme-right party founded in 1972

GE   *Génération écologie*: a left-oriented splinter of the Greens

MRG   *Mouvement des radicaux de gauche* (Left Radicals): split off (1972–1973) from main body of Radical-Socialist party

MRP   *Mouvement républicain populaire* (Popular Republican Movement): major Christian Democratic party of Fourth Republic; ceased to exist in 1966

PDM   *Progrès et démocratie moderne* (Progress and Modern Democracy): anti-Gaullist centrists

PS   *Parti socialiste* (Socialist party): successor (since 1969–1970) to the SFIO

PSU   *Parti socialiste unifié* (Unified Socialist party): established in 1960 by dissidents from SFIO, the Communist Party, and other left-wing groups

RPR   *Rassemblement pour la République* (Rally for the Republic): the "neo-Gaullist party" established in 1976

SFIO   *Section française de l'Internationale ouvrière* (French Section of the Workers' International): name of Socialist party from 1905–1969

UDF   *Union pour la démocratie française* (Union for French Democracy): the Giscardist electoral alliance (1978) of the Republican party, the CDS, the Radical-Socialist party, and smaller groups, each of which retains identity

UDR   *Union pour la défense de la République* (Union for the Defense of the Republic, later renamed Democratic Union for the Republic): Gaullist party, successor (1968) of UNR

UNR   *Union pour la nouvelle République* (Union for the New Republic): Gaullist party, 1958

Electoral Alliances, 1958–1993

Fédération de la Gauche Démocratique et Socialiste (FGDS—Federation of Democratic and Socialist Left): alliance, between 1965 and 1968, of SFIO, CIR, and Radical-Socialists

Réformateurs (Reformers): alliance, 1972–1974, of Radical-Socialists and (anti-Gaullist) Democratic-Centrists

Union de la Gauche Démocrate et Socialiste (UGDS—Union of Democratic and Socialist Left): alliance, 1973, of PS and MRG

Union du Rassemblement et du Centre (URC): alliance of RPR and UDF for the parliamentary elections of 1988

Union pour la France du progrès (UPF): alliance, 1990, of RPR and UDF for the parliamentary elections of 1993

FIGURE 4.1 Fragmentation and consolidation of political parties

NOTE: Heavy lines refer to major presidential/parliamentary formations; broken lines refer to dormant state (e.g., Poujadists), preparty condition (e.g., Ecologists), or disintegration (PSU).

It is unclear to what extent the social composition of the parliamentary contingent of the PS has reflected that of the rank and file of the party. The basic unit of the PS is the department federation, which sends delegates to the national party congress that meets every two years. The congress elects a directorate, which in turns elects an executive committee that meets at least once every two months and is assisted by a secretariat. The federations (some of which, like those of Paris and Marseilles, carry great weight) prepare resolutions for the congresses, promote active rank-and-file involvement, and try to recruit new members. In these tasks the federations are assisted by more than a thousand party sections based in factories.

THE COMMUNISTS

The Communist Party of France (*Parti communiste français*—PCF) was for many years the second largest Communist party in Western Europe (after Italy) and the most disciplined outside the Eastern bloc. It was founded in 1920 at the Congress of Tours held by the SFIO when about three-quarters of the delegates decided to join the Third International, which had been set up by the Russians after the Bolshevik Revolution.

Since its founding, the development of the PCF paralleled to some extent that of the SFIO. The PCF shared many of the SFIO's characteristics, notably its adherence to Marxism, its appeal to the working class, and its espousal of such domestic policies as higher minimum wages, the nationalization of crucial industries, the reform of the tax structure, and the expansion of the welfare state. The PCF had a fairly reliable electoral appeal in the Fourth Republic, obtaining more votes than any other single party. From the beginning of that republic until the installation of a leftist president in 1981, the PCF's share of the total vote ranged from a high of 28.2 percent in November 1946 to a low of 18.6 percent in 1978. It was an important party in the industrial north, in certain rural regions of the Midi and Massif Central, and in the working-class suburbs of Paris. Only about 60 percent of its members, however, and less than 50 percent of its voters have been working class (about 10 percent being intellectuals); only one in four workers has consistently supported the party. In short, the working class is not entirely Communist and the PCF is not entirely working class. Nonetheless, the PCF has been the workers' party par excellence. The party has capitalized on the fact that the French working class has felt a strong sense of alienation, which has not been significantly diminished by improvements in workers' living standards.[7]

For all its revolutionary rhetoric, the PCF made de facto concessions to bourgeois politics. In the early 1930s, the party advocated collaboration with other left-wing parties in order to stem the tide of fascism in Europe, and in 1936, it joined an electoral coalition with the SFIO and the Radical-Socialists and supported (without actually joining) the Socialist-led Popular Front government. As a result of the Nazi-Soviet Pact of 1939 and the PCF's defense of Stalin, many of the party's members became disillusioned. Dissolved by Pétain, the PCF continued in a clandestine fashion and, following the German invasion of the Soviet Union in 1941, began to fight seriously (if belatedly) against fascism, compiling such an impressive record in the Resistance that it emerged from World War II with an enhanced image. The party entered the government for the first time in French political history when it participated in the postwar tripartite coalition.

From 1947 to the end of the Fourth Republic, the PCF was in the opposition. In that role, the party was not only an advocate of "collectivist" domestic legislation but also an apologist for Soviet foreign policies. The PCF opposed German rearmament, the creation of NATO, and the Marshall Plan, and it defended the Soviet invasion of Hungary. Occasionally, the PCF would attempt to use the CGT, the trade union that had ideological affinities to it, as a "transmission belt" for its policies by persuading the union to organize politically motivated general strikes.

In 1958, the PCF opposed both the investiture of de Gaulle as premier and the ratification of the Fifth Republic Constitution. Yet, although the party consistently criticized both the institutions of the new republic and the policies pursued by President de Gaulle, it passed up several chances to promote a revolution against the regime. During the events of May–June 1968, the PCF discouraged a widening of "spontaneous" rebellion and favored a "law-and-order" approach. In the 1965 presidential elections, the PCF, as we have seen, supported the Socialist candidate, but in the presidential elections of 1969, after its own candidate was eliminated in the first round, the PCF sat out the second round, preferring not to exercise a choice between "the cholera and the plague," that is, between Gaullist Pompidou and Catholic Centrist Poher, although the latter was clearly anti-Gaullist. This abstention too may have had a tactical explanation: Odious as the continuation of Gaullist domestic policies would be to the PCF, Pompidou would at least continue to promote a foreign policy favored by the Soviet Union.

Throughout the 1960s and 1970s, the PCF continued to adhere to Marxist-Leninist slogans about revolution, the class struggle, and the dictatorship of the proletariat. The PCF talked about a radical transformation of socioeconomic structures, hoped that the Gaullist regime would discredit itself by its failures, and questioned the utility if not the decency of taking part in bourgeois politics. Yet the PCF participated in all national and local elections, criticized the Soviet Union (though belatedly) for its intervention in Czechoslovakia, embraced bourgeois notions of civil rights (e.g., freedom of speech and press), asserted its belief in competitive elections, and appeared to accept the Fifth Republic Constitution. To some observers, these developments were indicative of a "domestication" of the PCF and of its evolution toward "Eurocommunism"; to others, they were merely a tactic aimed at persuading the noncommunist Left parties to make alliances with it. In any case, by the late 1970s, the image of the PCF had improved considerably. A majority of French citizens no longer believed that the party wanted to make a revolution, and nearly half of the electorate appeared to be favorably inclined to Communist participation in a future government.[8]

The PCF had some reason for optimism about its prospects for obtaining, or sharing, power. It had a core of disciplined activists, a tight organization, a centralized leadership, numerous affiliated organizations (of workers, professionals, students, women, and youth), many journals, a large budget (its expenditures were nearly $25 million in 1980), and a claimed membership of nearly 700,000. Furthermore, it provided more than 700 mayors (including more than 200 in towns of over 9,000).

Yet in the 1978 parliamentary elections, the PCF, although still receiving more than 5.8 million first-ballot votes (and slightly increasing its Assembly representation), was clearly eclipsed by the PS, which had received more than 6.4 million votes. Whereas the image of the PS was improving, that of the PCF was being tarnished by a number of factors. The PCF received the major share of the blame for the defeat of the Left alliance: It was accused of having fomented public disputes with the PS over the interpretation of the Common Program. Before and after the parliamentary elections, there were internal fights regarding the future ideological orientation of the party: One faction called for a de-Stalinization and "Italianization" of the party and for freer internal discussion and less organizational rigidity;[9] another preferred a return to revolutionary Leninism and the abandonment of all "reformist" tendencies.[10] Moreover, Georges Marchais, the party's secretary-general, had an increasingly negative image. His personal integrity was being questioned,[11] and his public appearances were marked by stridently "Stalinist" pronouncements, including a defense of Soviet military actions in Afghanistan.

THE LEFT IN POWER: THE HEADY DAYS OF 1981 AND AFTER

The victories of the Socialists in 1981 were the culmination of two combined strategies: (1) opening their party to a broad spectrum of the electorate and (2) establishing collaborative relationships with other parties of the Left. The "democratic" Left is composed not only of the PS. Two smaller democratic-left formations, the *Parti socialiste unifié* (PSU) and the *Mouvement des radicaux de gauche* (MRG) deserve mention because of their tactical significance or their programmatic influence.

The PSU was by turns a rival and collaborator of the PS. It was not a typical political party—and perhaps not so much a party as a political club. Founded in 1960 by a combination of ex-Socialists, ex-Communists, left-wing Radical-Socialists, and others who opposed the Fifth Republic and resented the SFIO's endorsement of it, the PSU placed itself to the left of the PS (although in *programmatic* terms it was not always clearly "socialist"). During the first few years of its existence, it claimed more than 15,000 members, but in 1981 it had at most 7,000; its popular vote never rose above 4 percent, and it never managed to get more than a handful of deputies into the Assembly. In the mid-1970s, a minority faction of the PSU, including the party's leader, Michel Rocard, accepted the Common Program of the Left and joined the PS.

The PSU is of interest because, as a party composed heavily of intellectuals, it was a source of ideas for the PS. Moreover, the Rocardian faction (which represented about 20 percent of the PS membership) was particularly influential. The Social-ists' evolving positions regarding factory self-management (*autogestion*), economic planning, decentralization, and policies favoring the support of ethnic minority cultures owe a great deal to the PSU.[12] A fairly consistent supporter of Mitterrand's presidential candidacies,[13] the PSU was considered a part of the Left's presiden-tial majority (although it did not always agree with Mitterrand's economic poli-cies), and in 1983 its leader, Huguette Bouchardeau, was given a ministerial post. At the end of 1988, the PSU disbanded.

The MRG consists of those Radical-Socialists who objected to the rapproche-ment between the ("mainline") Radicals and the (Catholic) Democratic Centrists in the early 1970s. Almost from its founding in 1973, the MRG has worked along-side the PS, endorsing the Common Program and supporting the presidential ambitions of Mitterrand. Although fielding its own first-round candidates in par-liamentary elections (and its own presidential candidate in 1981), the MRG has usually cast its lot with the PS in the second round. The MRG differs from the PS mainly in the following respects: It has been less interested in collaboration with the Communists; it has been unenthusiastic about the nationalization of industries; and its attitudes toward income redistribution and social policy have been more reflective of its petit-bourgeois electorate (as contrasted with the working-class electorate of the PS).[14] Despite these differences, the MRG has continued to be closely associated with the PS, especially in the Assembly.

A more problematic element of the Left alliance has been the relationship between the PS and the PCF. Although the Common Program partnership remained officially intact after the 1978 elections, dealings between the two par-ties were embittered by the public trading of charges and countercharges. The PCF accused the PS of being more bourgeois than socialist, of not being com-mitted to genuine reform, and of wanting to use the PCF to gain power and, once having done so, of not giving the Communists their due in policies or positions. The PS, now the dominant partner of the alliance, in turn charged that the PCF still wanted to gain power only in order to destroy democratic institutions.[15]

In 1981, the PCF decided to run its own candidate for president. The party did poorly in the first round and had to support the PS candidate in the second round. In the legislative elections that followed, the PCF did even more poorly: With its Assembly representation halved to 44 (i.e., less than 10 percent of the seats), the party was reduced to relative powerlessness. The PCF put the best face on this unpleasant situation: It chose to interpret Mitterrand's victory as its own and claimed credit for having helped him get elected. Having been granted 4 ministerial posts (out of more than 40) in the Mauroy government, the PCF could be considered to have become part of the ruling coalition; but it could also be said to have been co-opted or imprisoned by it. The ministries given to the Communists were for the most part minor ones; in return for them, the PCF had to accept a number of policy positions laid out by Mitterrand: a respect for public liberties, a democratic (and nonconfiscatory) approach to the nationaliza-tion of industries, a condemnation of Soviet military intervention in Afghanistan, and a commitment to the Western Alliance. Confronted with the choice between programmatic independence and a share of government power, the PCF had become somewhat schizophrenic: While the four cabinet ministers counseled responsibility and solidarity with the government, the leaders of the party executive (the "politburo") sharpened their critiques of that government and imposed ideological discipline. (In late 1981, Marchais purged from the party's organ, *L'Humanité*, about 20 journalists who refused to follow his line.)

In 1982, Marchais was overwhelmingly reelected as secretary-general of the PCF, but his party had been weakened by defections,[16] the formation of dissident groups,[17] and the increasingly independent behavior of the Communist leaders of the *Confédération générale du travail* (CGT), attested by the resignation of Georges Séguy, that union's president, from the party's central committee.[18] Confronted with these difficulties, the Communists were more interested in intra-Left cooperation than the Socialists. In December 1982, the leaders of the PS and PCF agreed to have common first-ballot lists for the municipal elections of March 1983, but in many constituencies, the accord was not observed, and the first ballot ended up as a "wild primary" contest between the two parties.[19]

The Socialists had come to power surrounded by an aura of idealism. Many of the party's supporters had expected it to "govern differently" from the way their predecessors had governed. Because of these expectations, the new government was "condemned to do better."[20] During the first two years of Mitterrand's presidency, many of the policies pursued by the government reflected Socialist ideological tradition: selective nationalizations, increased minimum wages, a reduction of the workweek, the lengthening of paid vacations, and the expansion of public employment. Other projects could not be attributed to socialism specifically (e.g., decentralization and the abolition of capital punishment), and still others were continuations of Giscard's liberal policies—for example, the infusion of capital into globally competitive industries, the promotion of sexual equality, and revisions of the penal code. Finally, the austerity policies inaugurated in March 1983, including a slowdown in salary raises, an increase in social security deductions, and a limit on public-sector jobs, might be attributed to the pressing needs of the day, the evolution of the PS electorate, or the influence of certain "moderate" Socialists in the government.[21]

The government's policy ambiguities also reflected the diversity that had characterized the party since its revitalization in the early 1970s. Its various factions (*courants*) included a social-democratic and vociferously anticommunist group organized around Gaston Defferre; the pro–working class segment oriented around Pierre Mauroy; the supporters of Michel Rocard; and the members of the *Centre d'études, de recherches, et d'éducation socialistes* (CERES), which called itself "revolutionary" and Marxist and was committed to an alliance of all left-wing parties as a matter of principle (despite the fact that about a third of its members came from the Catholic Left).[22] There were those who were relatively indifferent to ideology but tended toward a technocratic approach to problems and who were known for cultivating good relations with the business community, such as Pierre Dreyfus and Jacques Delors, who were appointed, respectively, ministers of industry and economics in the first Mauroy government. Furthermore, there were the *Mitterrandistes* (representing more than 50 percent of the delegates at the party congresses after 1980), who were concerned less with dogma than with electoral strategies, and (since 1981) with the exercise of power. This diversity, which exists to this day, was reflected in the composition of the cabinet and the distribution of legislative committee chairs. For these reasons, the PS paid steadily less attention to the leftist demands of the PCF.

In 1984, the gulf between the two parties widened when Mauroy resigned as premier and a new government was formed under the leadership of Laurent Fabius. The Communist ministers had been invited to stay on; however, the PCF politburo decided to withdraw them because it was unwilling to accept the continuation of the austerity program (begun a year earlier) and the inadequate attention to the unemployment problem. The PCF still considered itself a part of the left-wing Assembly majority; it announced, however, that its support of the government's policies would be selective. (In the investiture vote in the Assembly that followed the appointment of the new government, the Communist deputies abstained.)

The internecine conflicts within the camp of the Left were paralleled by disagreements within the PS itself. For the first several months following the 1981 electoral victories, there was a "honeymoon" atmosphere that fortified a sentiment of unity; the new government seemed prepared to respond to the pent-up expectations and political claims of the varied elements that had brought it to power: trade unionists, schoolteachers, and disgruntled white-collar employees, farmers, and shopkeepers. But in 1982, disaccord surfaced again within the party over a number of issues: the role of Marxism in Socialist ideology and the extent to which the PS was evolving (or should evolve) toward social democracy; economic policy and the role of the unions; the degree to which the continued existence of parochial schools should be supported; and the question whether the PS should cooperate fully with, or maintain its distance from, the government. Whereas Premier Mauroy and party chief Lionel Jospin defended government policies as reasonable and unavoidable, the Rocard wing and the trade unions voiced reservations, and the CERES wing opposed them openly. These disagreements, in addition to the jockeying for positions among party personalities, were evident at the party congress of 1983, with government supporters insisting that public policies faithfully represented traditional socialist values and the feelings of party loyalists, while more critical Socialist deputies demanded a better clearing of signals with the government.[23]

GAULLISM: THE EVOLUTION OF THE RIGHT
FROM TRADITIONAL CONSERVATISM
TO NATIONALIST POPULISM

The Right Before Gaullism

The traditional political Right in France was characterized by its defense of the status quo. It had favored the monarchy against the republicans and had viewed the revolutions of 1789 and 1848 as unfortunate events. It preferred authoritarian to parliamentary government and later developed a taste for heroic figures. Defining society in organic rather than functional terms, it favored a hierarchical and elitist social structure and had contempt for the masses. Originally, the Right was the expression of the "established" pillars of society: the church, the army, the nobility, and the landed gentry. Later, it derived electoral support from big business and those elements of the peasantry that were committed to religious and social conservatism. The traditional Right had tried to bring down the Third Republic, but the Dreyfus affair tarnished the image of the sectors that were identified with that outlook; moreover, the industrial revolution, the growth of the working class, the extension of the franchise, and the rise of socialist parties weakened its position.

After Liberation, the part of the Right that had collaborated with the Germans during World War II had been discredited; most of the remainder had accepted republicanism, and the deputies identified with that remainder labeled themselves "moderates," "independents," or members of "peasant" parties. The main umbrella party was the Party of Independents and Peasants (*Centre national des indépendants et paysans*—CNIP). Founded in 1948, the CNIP was almost evenly divided between representatives of business and industry and representatives of peasants from backward regions, and between pro-Catholic and laic elements. Its Assembly representation gradually increased from 64 in 1945 to 98 in 1951—it was to rise to 129 in the first year of the Fifth Republic—and in 1952 it even contributed a prime minister (Antoine Pinay). But because of its fragmentation, the position of the CNIP (and of the Right as a whole) in the Fourth Republic Assembly was weak. A further source of weakness of the traditional Right was the fact that it had to compete for votes with several centrist parties and, later, with Gaullism.

One right-wing organization that had considerable appeal was the Union for the Defense of Shopkeepers and Artisans (*Union pour la défense des commerçants et des artisans*—UDCA). Founded by Pierre Poujade after World War II as an interest group and combining its hostility to the wealthy with anti-industrialism, antiparliamentarism, and anti-Semitism, the "Poujadists" appeared in the guise of a political party, the *Union et fraternité française*, in the parliamentary elections of 1956, received 12 percent of the popular vote, and got 53 deputies elected. Convinced that de Gaulle would end the hated Fourth Republic and keep Algeria French, most Poujadist deputies favored his return to power, and the majority of their electoral supporters were absorbed into the Gaullist party (with a remnant drifting into the political wilderness). More than a decade later, Poujadism was to reemerge as an important element in the National Front.

The Origins and Evolution of Gaullism

Gaullism is an unusual phenomenon. From its organizational beginnings in 1947 to the end of the Fourth Republic, the Gaullist party claimed not to be a party at all but a national *movement*, an alternative to parties. Whereas other parties were national federations of strong local and regional political machines, often run by notables, the Gaullist party, then called Rally of the French People

(*Rassemblement du peuple français*—RPF), was the expression of the political beliefs and ambitions of one man and a reflection of the mystique surrounding him. The original Gaullists, the leaders of "Free France" in London, were a disparate group. They included devout Catholics, anticlerical intellectuals, and Resistance figures of various political persuasions. After the war, the Gaullist ranks were joined by those who agreed with de Gaulle's criticism of the Fourth Republic and who shared his desire to replace it with a regime that would be better equipped to provide strong leadership and assert France's global role.

Toward the end of the Fourth Republic, support for the Gaullists had declined—the RPF received less than 13 percent of the vote in the legislative elections of 1956—but two years later, with the reentry of General de Gaulle into the political arena, the party's fortunes revived dramatically. Under the new regime, the Gaullist party, relabeled *Union pour la nouvelle République* (UNR), set up numerous local machines, attracted an increasing number of activists, and even acquired a mass electoral base. At the onset of the Fifth Republic, the UNR enjoyed the goodwill of a number of democratic leftists and managed to entice a segment of the working-class electorate. Yet from the early 1960s to 1981 the party increasingly advocated socially conservative and probusiness policies and was heavily supported by entrepreneurs, higher civil servants, professionals, and other well-to-do sectors. However, because of its grassroots aspects and its transformation into a "catchall" party—it got more than 45 percent of the vote in the parliamentary elections of 1968—the Gaullist organization (renamed the *Union pour la défense de la République*—UDR)[24] rejected the label of "right-wing." Moreover, the Gaullist party from the very outset did not behave like a traditional party of the Right: It embraced (or at least gave lip service to) economic planning, looked for technocratic solutions to problems, promoted modernization (e.g., educational reforms and, under Pompidou, high-rises and superhighways), accepted the welfare state, and sought periodic popular endorsements of its policies.

Nonetheless, Gaullism must be considered right-wing because much of the social doctrine (or perhaps mood or style[25]) on which the party has based its populist self-image has related to nationalism and the enhancement of national power. Thus, the Gaullists' support of government subsidies for children stemmed not, as is the case with Catholic-inspired parties, from a belief in large families for their own sake but from an interest in increasing France's population and thus permitting the country to play an enlarged global role.[26] In a similar vein, the Gaullists for many years promoted the defense of national sovereignty by resisting the development of political integration of the European Community, strengthening the country's military capacity, spreading the French language around the world, building up nuclear energy to reduce France's economic dependence, instituting worker-management "participation" schemes in factories to eliminate the class struggle, curbing attempts at administrative decentralization to protect the unity of the French state, and reducing the role of those intermediary institutions (e.g., parties and interest groups) that might interfere in the direct relationship between the government and the people.

Not all Gaullists have adhered to this "classical" Gaullism. Pompidou was a "neoliberal" who stressed industrial modernization and was willing to enhance the economic role of the market and reduce that of the state. Léo Hamon (once the official spokesman of the government) and René Capitant (a professor of law) were self-described left-wing Gaullists who wanted to see the power of a strong government used to expand the welfare state; Olivier Guichard, once chief economic planner, was a technocrat; and the notions of Jacques Chaban-Delmas (mayor of Bordeaux) regarding Gaullist socioeconomic policy (the building of a "new society") had a social-democratic flavor. The factionalism and personalism within the Gaullist movement were illustrated by the fact that in 1981, there were *three* Gaullist presidential candidates![27]

The "personalized" aspect of Gaullism is seen in the case of Chirac, whose political orientation has been marked more heavily by ambition than by ideological clarity. Serving briefly as minister of the interior under Pompidou, he decided, upon the latter's death in 1974, to support Giscard for the presidency, rather than Chaban-Delmas, the official Gaullist nominee. After his election, Giscard rewarded Chirac by appointing him as premier. But Chirac's new position did not prevent him from becoming the secretary-general of the Gaullist party *and*, early in 1976, "coordinator" of Giscard's presidential majority. The "neo-Gaullist" successor party, the Rally for the Republic (*Rassemblement pour la République*—RPR), which was officially founded in late 1976 (a few months after Chirac's resignation as premier), and which Chirac has led ever since, evolved equally as an instrument of Chirac's presidential aspirations and as a repository of Gaullism.[28] In addition to constantly evoking the great general's memory, referring to national independence, and demanding worker "association" in management, the RPR shared with the Giscardists a commitment to fighting the "socialo-communists."

THE POLITICAL "CENTER"

For the sake of symmetry and completeness, one should discuss the fourth political camp currently represented in the two chambers of the French Parliament, that of the "Giscardists," that is, the Union for French Democracy (*Union pour la démocratie française*—UDF). In the past two decades, many writings about the "Giscard phenomenon" have appeared. These have covered the personality and attitudes of Valéry Giscard d'Estaing, the various parties he courted and co-opted in order to promote his presidential ambitions, and the system of government over which he came to preside.[29] In essence, Giscardism represents a confluence of political forces that have rejected both the collectivism of the Left and the nationalism and charismatic populism of the Gaullists, and hence have chosen to describe themselves as "centrists."

Genuine Center parties have represented the petite bourgeoisie and the shopkeeper rather than the industrial working class, big business, or landowners. Their position in the center of the semicircular seating arrangement of the Assembly chamber reflected their ability to turn either right or left, as the occasion demanded, and often to act as balancers in coalition cabinets. The components of the Giscardist electoral alliance system—the Radical-Socialists, the Catholics, and traditional (non-Gaullist) conservatives—are sufficiently disparate to be dealt with separately.

Radicalism

The Radical-Socialist (or simply "Radical") party was officially founded in 1901, but its roots go back to the beginning of the Third Republic, if not earlier. It consistently favored a centralized republic but derived its strength (or weakness) from the fact that it was run by local notables, mayors of towns of various sizes who used their control over a political machine to get themselves elected to the national Parliament. The party's "radicalism" was embodied in its strong anti-Catholic position, its support of a strictly secular national school system, and its advocacy of the separation of church and state. It was "socialist" insofar as it favored a strong bill of rights, universal male suffrage, a progressive tax system, the nationalization of the railroads, and the protection of the small-business proprietor and farmer against the vicissitudes of economic modernization and competition. The party's consistent antimonarchism at the turn of the century made it appear decidedly "leftist." Its center position often made it a crucial partner in government coalitions, so much so that during the Third and Fourth Republics it supplied many prime ministers.

But the party's ideological and programmatic imprecision proved to be its undoing.[30] When a working class emerged as a consequence of industrialization, it turned to the Socialist party, which was preempting the "leftist" label and pushing the Radicals into more moderate and conservative positions. Thus in the mid-1930s, the Radicals supported the left-wing Popular Front government, but in 1940, many Radical deputies voted for the investiture of Marshal Pétain and even served in his fascist puppet regime (while other Radicals joined de Gaulle in his London exile or served in the Resistance). After World War II, the Radicals demonstrated their adaptability by heading, participating in, or supporting government coalitions of both the Right and the Left. To many observers, the party seemed to be run by petty opportunists; yet in Pierre Mendès-France (premier in 1954–1955) it produced the outstanding statesman of the Fourth Republic. When de Gaulle reappeared on the political scene in 1958, much of the Radical-Socialist electorate voted for the general, and many of the party's leaders deserted to the revived Gaullist party, the UNR.

Catholicism

Another "centrist" orientation is that of Christian democracy. The Catholic church was originally monarchist and socially conservative, but toward the end of the Third Republic, a small Catholic party (the *Parti démocrate populaire*) that fully supported republicanism and progressive economic policies was formed. Catholicism became a prominent force in French republican politics after the

Liberation with the founding of the *Mouvement républicain populaire* (MRP). That party, led by individuals who had been prominent in the Resistance, was committed to the idea that clericalism could be successfully combined with republicanism and the welfare state. The party's appeal to the masses, including much of the working class, was such that in the middle of the 1940s, it garnered more than one-fourth of the popular vote in Assembly elections and participated in a tripartite left-oriented government together with the Socialists and Communists and subsequently furnished several prime ministers.

In the early 1950s, the MRP began to weaken, as many of its working-class supporters switched to the Socialists, and as the MRP was forced to compete with the Radicals, and later the Gaullists, for a fragmented petit-bourgeois electorate. By the end of the Fourth Republic, the MRP's Assembly representation had already declined steeply (from 169 in 1946 to 84 in 1956). In 1958, much of the MRP leadership, already more conservative than it had been a decade earlier, joined the Gaullist bandwagon, and the anti-Gaullist rump faced the Fifth Republic with uncertainty.

Centrist Coalition Games

Given the loss of much of their traditional electorate to the Gaullists and the fragmentation of the remainder, both the Radicals and the MRP realized that without allies neither could resist the bipolarizing impact of the electoral system—the second-round runoffs that forced voters to abandon the support of candidates of weak parties and to turn to either a right-wing or a left-wing candidate. Consequently, each of these parties experimented with coalitions involving more powerful partners. In the mid-1960s, the Radical-Socialist party entered an electoral coalition with the Socialists, the FGDS, but that coalition, although it succeeded in electing an increased number of candidates of the noncommunist Left in 1967, broke down by 1969. The reasons were several: (1) Many Radicals felt that the SFIO was using them to shore up its own strength. (2) The FGDS was still too small to overcome de Gaulle's charismatic leadership. (3) An expansion of the noncommunist Left by the inclusion of the MRP—a step then favored by some Radicals—was unacceptable to most Socialists, given their dogmatic commitment to anticlericalism, whereas a broadening of the Left alliance to include the Communists was unacceptable to the Radicals.

After the elections of 1967, the MRP ceased to exist. Those Catholic deputies who remained and had not gone over to the Gaullists had meanwhile reorganized as the Democratic Center. Its leader, Jean Lecanuet, had run for the presidency in 1965 on a program of opposition both to Gaullism and to any kind of alliance with the Communists, but he had received less than 16 percent of the votes. In the elections of 1969, the Democratic Center (organized in the Assembly under the label of *Progrès et démocratie moderne*—PDM) made one last attempt at capturing national office when it fielded Alain Poher, the speaker of the Senate (a position he was to hold until 1993) and a staunch anti-Gaullist, as its presidential candidate. Poher got over 40 percent of the vote, but only because the Socialists supported him in the second round. But when Pompidou was elected, some centrists (who called their group *Centre de la démocratie et du progrès*—CDP) were so starved for political power that they joined the new government, rationalizing their action by pretending that Pompidou would be more receptive to certain centrist policy preferences, notably the promotion of decentralization, greater support for European integration, and a lessened hostility to NATO.

Those centrists who remained in the opposition (still led by Lecanuet) embraced another alternative—an electoral alliance with the Radical-Socialists. This alliance, known as the Reformers' Movement (*Réformateurs*), was put in place in 1971. The movement was not the hoped-for solution to the centrist parties' dilemma, for their electoral base remained too narrow; furthermore, it was fragmented by personal rivalries between the leaders of the two major components and beset by internal contradictions within the Radical party between the "liberal" probusiness faction (led for a time by Jean-Jacques Servan-Schreiber) and the more protectionist faction supported by small shopkeepers.[31] Moreover, those left-wing Radicals who were offended by any collaboration with "clericalists" broke away and formed their own party, the MRG, which, as we have seen, promptly allied itself with the Socialists.

The Election of 1974 and the Emergence of Giscardo-Centrism

President Pompidou's sudden death in April 1974 and the emergence of Valéry Giscard d'Estaing as a presidential candidate seemed to be God-sent opportunity for the Center parties. Positioning himself as an alternative between the Gaullists and the Left, and promising to reverse the artificial bipolarization to which French voters had been subjected, Giscard got both the Radicals and the Democratic Centrists to support him by promising each a part of what they wanted: to the Radicals, an enlargement of civil liberties and a strengthening of the power of local communities; to the Democratic Centrists, an expansion of welfare-state protections and the pursuit of less nationalistic foreign policies. Both groups were promised an extension of the powers of Parliament and a possible change of the electoral system toward proportional representation. At the same time, Giscard appealed to Gaullist voters by promising to safeguard the institutions of the Fifth Republic, a tactic that helped to ensure his election in the second round.

Giscard's background was far from ideal for a politician around whom "centrists" would cluster. A scion of a well-to-do family and a graduate of two very prestigious schools, the Ecole Polytechnique and the Ecole Nationale d'Administration (ENA), he had entered Parliament as a member of the conservative CNIP just before the Fourth Republic collapsed. In 1958 he supported de Gaulle and his new constitution and was soon rewarded with a ministerial appointment,[32] without, however, having joined the Gaullist party. But the CNIP, under whose label he had been reelected to the Assembly in the same year, was too conservative for Giscard's ambitions, for that party had once been lukewarm about republicanism (many of its leaders had supported the Vichy regime) and continued to represent the values of social elitism, family, and religion. Most important, the CNIP had no mass following and no great electoral prospects. In 1962, Giscard, together with a number of deputies, broke away from the CNIP to found his own political organization, the *Républicains indépendants* (RI). This group was pro-Gaullist in that it supported the general on most issues, but it diverged from the Gaullists in favoring an enlarged role for the market (as opposed to the state) in economic affairs; advocating greater political participation by the legislature, the parties, and interest groups; and stressing civil rights. In 1969, Giscard had spoken out against a referendum that would have reformed the Senate; by so doing (since the reform was rejected by the people) he helped to bring about the resignation of de Gaulle. Giscard's public positions were an amalgam of Gaullism, conservatism, economic liberalism, Catholicism, classic parliamentarism, and technocratism—in sum, opportunism—but they were interpreted as sufficiently different from those of orthodox Gaullism to cause the Radicals and Democratic Centrists to be co-opted by Giscard. This co-optation enabled Giscard's supporters, especially those who were on his side in the first round in 1974, to occupy the parliamentary terrain situated between the Gaullists and the Socialists, and thereby to claim the label of "centrist."

However, many observers have suggested that the term was misappropriated and that it rested in large part on wishful thinking—the wish for a depolarization of French political life. In the eyes of the Left, both the Giscardists and the Gaullists were right-wing and therefore indistinguishable from each other in terms of their electoral clientele: shopkeepers, farmers, professionals, middle- and upper-echelon white-collar employees, and pensioners. The Gaullists claimed that whereas *they* were populist, the Giscardists were more genuinely on the Right. This claim was based on (1) the conservative and upper-class origins of Giscard and his "barons";[33] (2) the fact that, unlike the Gaullists in the late 1950s and early 1960s, the Giscardists had never received meaningful working-class support; (3) the laissez-faire liberalism openly embraced by most Giscardists, which made them right-wing by definition; and (4) the fact that the Giscardists' largest and most powerful component, the Independent Republicans (RI), renamed in 1977 the Republican party (*Parti républicain*—PR), could not possibly lay claim to progressivism or centrism but, on the contrary, was solidly conservative.[34]

In January 1978, just two months before the Assembly elections, Giscard inspired the creation of an electoral alliance that included the Radical-Socialists, the Centrists (who had been operating under the label of *Centre des démocrates sociaux* [CDS] since 1976, when the pro-Gaullist and anti-Gaullist factions reunited), the Republicans, and smaller groups.[35] This alliance, the *Union pour la démocratie française* (UDF), was "centrist" in a tactical sense—it hoped to be positioned to attract the more moderate (and anti-Communist) supporters of the Socialist party *and* to push the Gaullist party (the RPR) further to the right while at the same time reducing the presidential chances of Chirac. Some of the Giscardist politicians hoped that the various components of the UDF would soon merge and become a truly centrist political party; others wanted the UDF to remain a loose federation in which the separate identities of the Radicals,

Catholics, and Republicans would be maintained. A compromise between the two positions was soon achieved: Members either could join the UDF directly or they could adhere to the component groups, in which case they would automatically be members of the UDF. It was decided to put up single first-ballot candidates under the UDF label in many constituencies and to support Gaullist candidates only in the second round. In the parliamentary elections of 1978, the UDF did well enough to receive nearly a quarter of the popular votes in the second round, to gain a significant number of Assembly seats (largely at the expense of the Gaullists), and to form a single, if not very disciplined, parliamentary group.

As the presidential elections of 1981 approached, the disunities within the UDF were deemphasized so as not to defeat the purpose for which this organization had been created in the first place: the reelection of Giscard. What provided the requisite unity was the dislike for Giscard's main rival, Mayor Chirac of Paris, the leader of the Gaullists. The politicians of the UDF were heartened by public-opinion polls in 1980 that predicted Giscard's easy reelection. During the campaign, Giscard and Chirac (like Mitterrand and Marchais on the Left) were friendly enemies: Both attacked the candidates on the other side of the political spectrum while questioning the performance and abilities of each other; both ran as first-round presidential candidates, competing for the same right-of-center electorate, and both pledged to support each other on the second ballot if need be. When Giscard emerged as the highest vote-getter in the first round and was forced into a runoff against Mitterrand, the Gaullists officially closed ranks behind Giscard. But Chirac's refusal to issue an unambiguous call to his Gaullist supporters to vote for Giscard probably helped to sabotage the reelection of the incumbent.

There were other reasons for Giscard's defeat. During the first years of his term, the economy grew, the development of high-technology industries was encouraged, and the rate of inflation was kept low; subsequently, however, a recession occurred, unemployment increased, the gap between the well-to-do and the low-income sectors widened, and Giscard's reformist momentum slowed down. Giscard's image had deteriorated amid charges of scandals involving himself, his family, and his ministers. Furthermore, his behavior had become increasingly "imperial" and aloof; and finally, he lost the trust of small but crucial parts of the electorate on whose support he had counted.[36] The Giscardists tried desperately to salvage their position during the legislative elections that followed. In those elections, they formed an alliance with the Gaullists that was labeled, with a certain degree of optimism, the *Union pour la nouvelle majorité*, under which joint first-round candidates were put up in more than 300 constituencies, and the two groups supported each other on the second round. The results of these elections reduced the power of both the Giscardists and the Gaullists.

THE RIGHT AND CENTER IN OPPOSITION

As a result of their loss of power, the Giscardists and Gaullists were beset by a number of problems, apart from having to get used to opposition status. The major loser was the UDF, which, with the ejection of Giscard from the presidency, lost the focal point of its unity, if not its raison d'être. Between 1981 and 1983, many adherents of the UDF were demoralized and confused about what strategy to adopt. Some UDF politicians went over to the Gaullist party; others suggested that the organization strengthen its position by fusing its parts into a genuine party; still others felt that the divergences within the UDF were irreconcilable. With the restraining force of a "progressive" president gone, the Republican party and its ally, the club *Perspectives et réalités*, wanted to use their dominant positions to assert themselves and their probusiness ideas more strongly than before. Conversely, many leaders of the CDS and the Radical-Socialist party talked about making their images more progressive. Whereas the PR and the more conservative elements of the CDS and Radicals favored a policy of close collaboration with the Gaullists and "firm and total opposition" to the government,[37] the more leftist factions of those parties wished to mark themselves off more clearly from the Gaullists and toyed with the idea of leaving the UDF embrace, forming a new center-left coalition, or possibly making overtures to the Socialists.[38]

But these alternatives were straws in the wind: The system of elections, with its bipolarizing tendencies, made the construction of powerful centrist parties difficult; a rapprochement with the new majority was out of the question as long' as the Communist Party was a component of the government coalition. At the same time, the argument made by some Giscardists that the UDF represented the only alternative for those who rejected collectivism on the one hand and charismatic, ultranationalist Gaullism on the other had become somewhat unconvincing since the Socialists' policies turned out to be far from collectivist and the RPR was now much less nationalist or Bonapartist-authoritarian than the old Gaullist party had been. In fact, the new RPR was not so much Gaullist as "Chiraquist"; it had become the political vehicle of the mayor of Paris, who was proving to be ideologically flexible, pragmatic, and fairly successful in attracting middle-of-the-road voters.

The relatively stronger position of the RPR spurred this party to greater efforts at collaboration with the UDF. In 1981, a liaison committee for the two groups was set up in the Assembly, followed in due course by a "reconciliation" meeting between Giscard and Chirac. In the municipal elections of March 1983, there was a degree of second-round collaboration between the two groups, which paved the way for subsequent discussions about a common platform for future elections, but nothing came of this except the signing of a brief Common Charter of Opposition.

Although the UDF was ahead of the RPR in the number of seats in municipal councils (especially in small towns) and was holding its own in the Senate, the Gaullist party, by virtue of its assertive leadership, had become the dominant element within the opposition. Yet the RPR was not without problems. Its leader, Chirac, had proven to be a dynamic politician and had helped bring the party's registered membership to over 700,000 by the mid-1980s, yet he was distrusted by many: Some viewed him as too power hungry, and others doubted his commitment to genuine Gaullism. The party's programs since the early 1980s had been noteworthy for their imprecision, and their Gaullist features were no longer distinct. In fact, it was largely under Chirac's prodding that the RPR abandoned the traditional Gaullist *étatisme* in domestic policy in favor of a "neoliberal" approach (marked by deregulation, tax concessions to business, selective cuts in public spending, and the privatization of industries, banks, and the television networks) and replaced an extreme nationalist outlook in foreign policy by more pro-European and even pro-Atlanticist positions. These changes occurred for several reasons: The mystique of de Gaulle was fading; in order to capture the Giscardist electorate, it was considered necessary to absorb the "liberalism" of the UDF as well as the policy proposals of Raymond Barre, the former premier, whose popularity was reviving; and finally, the opinion of the public at large seemed to be moving away from rigid statism.

THE RISE OF THE NATIONAL FRONT

While the Socialists were benefiting from the steady decline of the Communist Party, the position of the RPR and the UDF, the "republican opposition," began to be threatened by the rise of a new political formation, the National Front (*Front national*). Founded in 1972 by Jean-Marie Le Pen as a conglomerate of fascists, Pétainists, former Poujadists, right-wing Catholics, erstwhile proponents of *Algérie Française*, ultranationalists, anti-Semites, and racists, the party was suddenly thrust onto the political scene during the municipal elections of 1983 when it received 17 percent of the vote in Dreux, a medium-sized industrial town near Paris, and in the elections to the European Parliament in 1984, when it got over 10 percent of the vote. After World War II, Le Pen had served as a paratrooper in Indochina; in 1956 he had been elected to the Assembly on the ticket of the Poujadist movement; later he had fought in Algeria; and in 1965 he had managed the election campaign of Jean-Louis Tixier-Vignancour, who ran for the presidency under the aegis of an extreme-right party.

The National Front appealed to various components of the electorate: the unemployed and those who were afraid of losing their jobs; people who worried about the rising tide of crime in the cities and the decline of old-fashioned values concerning God, country, and family; and those who resented the presence of more than 2 million foreigners on French soil. Given the relatively small number of Jews and the fact of their thorough assimilation, Le Pen's personal anti-Semitism (often expressed with not very subtle innuendo) has had only limited electoral utility. The National Front has concentrated on stirring up hatred against the more numerous North African Muslims (the *Maghrebis*), who are blamed for the above-mentioned problems and accused of taking advantage of France's welfare services and public housing; their presence will, it is argued, ultimately Islamize and "orientalize" French society.[39] For these reasons, the National Front has called for the restoration of capital punishment (abolished in 1981), an end to immigration of non-Europeans, a stricter control of the movements of foreigners, and a change in the citizenship laws to make naturalization difficult. As the appeal of the National Front appeared to increase, many of these policy positions were gradually adopted by the RPR and UDF.

Because of its extreme-right origins, its nationalism and anticommunism, its appeal to racism, and the rabble-rousing behavior of Le Pen, the National Front has often been compared to fascist parties. Yet it has differed from them in several respects. It has officially embraced democratic institutions; it does not wish to replace the Fifth Republic; and, unlike classic fascists, it has asserted that it wants not to strengthen the state but to curb its influence, in particular with regard to economic activity. It insists that it is not on the extreme Right but rather the "liberal" Right; it has frequently expressed its admiration of the United States and of the U.S. Republican party, and its socioeconomic program—with its call for freedom of enterprise, tax concessions to business, the curbing of the trade unions, and a pruning of the welfare state—echoes the policies of Ronald Reagan and Margaret Thatcher.[40] The National Front has appealed not merely to the alienated petite bourgeoisie but to a cross section of the electorate: middle-class suburbanites, farmers, businesspeople, professionals, and industrial workers.

Le Pen has argued that rather than speaking for the "lunatic fringe," he has merely said out loud what others, especially the politicians in the Gaullist and other conservative parties, have thought.[41] Le Pen has attempted to raid the traditional electorate of the RPR and the UDF and, for that reason, embraced a double tactic vis-à-vis these two "respectable" right-wing parties. On the one hand, he has criticized RPR and UDF for being part of the "gang of four," that is, of not being very different from the PS and PCF. On the other hand, he has tried to portray his party as a republican and legitimate alternative. Although Gaullist and Giscardist politicians had made a number of second-round deals with the National Front in the local elections in 1983, the RPR and UDF, which saw no need to add to the respectability of that formation, refused (officially) to make electoral agreements with it for the next parliamentary elections. Despite the threat posed by the National Front to the RPR and UDF, public opinion polls indicated that the Socialists would lose control of the Assembly as a result of the forthcoming elections. In order to contain the damage, the government in 1985 rushed through Parliament a bill that replaced the existing single-member-district method of election with a system of proportional representation. It was anticipated that although under the new system the National Front, the PCF, and perhaps other smaller parties would gain entry into the Assembly, the RPR-UDF majority would be considerably reduced.

THE PARLIAMENTARY ELECTION OF 1986

The results of the elections of 1986 were a mixed blessing for all the political formations. The Socialist party, although it had lost its majority in the Assembly, maintained its position as the most popular party in France. But the party continued to be confused about its identity. Some Socialists felt that the party should continue the process of modernization—cutting away the "dead wood" of ideology—that had been called for at the party congress in Toulouse in 1985; others proposed a more definite turn to a German or Scandinavian type of social democracy; and still others (among them Rocard) yearned for a vaguely defined "ethical" socialism. There were those who (like Pierre Mauroy at the 1987 party congress in Lille) suggested that now that the PS was in the opposition, the time had come for a return to the "sources" of socialism and to its traditional working-class clientele. Others (like the members of the ex-CERES wing) believed that the continued leftist vocation of the PS required that the party mend fences with the PCF. These disagreements were not resolved, nor could they be, since the PS had to speak for a diverse electoral clientele, one in which the blue-collar working class had become a minority. Moreover, under conditions of "cohabitation" with the RPR-UDF, the PS was hardly in a position to translate its orientations into policies.

The RPR and UDF together, with 291 of the 577 seats, had obtained a bare majority. Although it was theoretically sufficient to enable them to produce a government and to pursue a number of policy objectives, they were constrained by several factors: the periodic interference by a president who still retained a number of constitutionally guaranteed reserve powers (see Chapter 6), the conflicts between the RPR and the UDF, and the divisions within the ranks of each of these right-wing formations.

The smaller parties had their problems too. The Communist Party had been "saved" by the new electoral system; but with less than 10 percent of the popular vote and its Assembly representation pared to 35, it could hardly pretend to much influence. Some leaders of the PCF suggested that the party could save its soul and regain the support of the disadvantaged classes by returning to an uncompromising leftist orientation and equipping itself with more-appealing candidates for elective offices. In 1987 the party took the first step in that direction by nominating André Lajoinie (the chairman of the Communist group in the Assembly) rather than Georges Marchais as its candidate in the forthcoming presidential elections. At the same time, however, a number of Communists, led by Pierre Juquin, split from the PCF and formed a rival party of "Reform Communists" (*Rénovateurs*), which in short order chose Juquin as its presidential candidate.[42]

In gaining entry to the Assembly for 35 deputies, the National Front had acquired a degree of legitimacy. But that party was uncertain about how it should subsequently behave. In order to achieve greater respectability, to be considered for some sort of partnership—in terms of policy making or power sharing—by the RPR and UDF, and to entice uncommitted voters in the next presidential elections, the National Front deputies had to eschew the rhetoric of the lunatic fringe and make "responsible" public statements. However, there was a danger that in so doing, the National Front would be perceived as resembling the other right-wing parties too much and risk the loss of its mystique and hence its appeal to what remained of the alienated and antisystem electorate.

THE PRESIDENTIAL AND PARLIAMENTARY
ELECTIONS OF 1988

The appeal of the National Front, with 10 to 15 percent in the popularity polls, was sufficiently high to cause confusion in the ranks of the RPR and UDF. That confusion was compounded when Le Pen, the National Front candidate in the presidential elections of 1988, got 14.5 percent of the vote in the first round, a result that many observers called a "political earthquake." Some Gaullist leaders, among them Charles Pasqua, the minister of interior, attempted to retrieve as many of these votes as possible for their own party in the second round by asserting that the National Front had "the same concerns and the same values" as the RPR; other Gaullists, among them Michel Noir, minister of foreign trade, argued that the RPR should have nothing to do with the National Front, and several UDF politicians openly came out for Mitterrand as the person who could best maintain national unity in the face of the threat posed by Le Pen. In this situation, Chirac temporized; on the one hand, he did not want to alienate those who felt strongly about immigrants, law and order, and other issues stressed by Le Pen. On the other hand, he did not want to risk losing his moderate supporters either to Mitterrand or to Raymond Barre, the candidate of the UDF. Chirac's fence-sitting was apparent during a television debate involving Mitterrand, Barre, and himself. At this debate, Mitterrand accused Chirac of pandering to the National Front electorate; Barre, by appealing for a tolerant and inclusive society, implicitly invited his own first-ballot supporters to transfer their support to Mitterrand.

During the campaign for the Assembly elections following Mitterrand's election to a second presidential term, a modicum of unity between the RPR and UDF was quickly restored, as these parties, under the label of the *Union du rassemblement et du centre* (URC), put up joint candidates in most of the constituencies, with roughly the same number of candidatures for each of the two components.[43] Having restored the old single-member constituency system of elections while in power a few months earlier, these two parties were hoping that the smaller parties, among the National Front, would be weakened and Gaullist-Giscardist control of the Assembly would be maintained.

The Socialists, meanwhile, expected that their candidates would win the Assembly elections on the coattails of Mitterrand's presidential victory. That hope was based in part on the fact that Michel Rocard, who had been appointed prime minister immediately after the presidential elections, projected an image of intelligence and pragmatism and enjoyed wide popularity among Socialists as well as non-Socialists. Indeed, until the very eve of the parliamentary elections, public-opinion polls predicted that the PS would have a comfortable majority in the Assembly. The result, however, fell short of these predictions: The Socialists gained merely a plurality of the Assembly seats. There were a number of reasons for that outcome. Mitterrand had been so confident about a Socialist parliamentary election victory that he had declared that "it was not a good thing for France to be governed by a single party" and had called for an "opening up" (*ouverture*) toward the political center. Therefore, many Socialists thought that their votes would not be needed. Other Socialists felt that their support of Socialist parliamentary candidates would be a wasted effort, since the programmatic differences between the latter and the candidates of the Right were not significant enough. Still others were angry at Rocard for having picked too many centrist ministers and therefore "falsified" the election results, and others again complained that Rocard had appointed too many old-guard Socialists and had thus raised doubts about the Socialist party's interest in an opening toward the center. Finally, there were people who had voted for Mitterrand as a *national leader* but were not necessarily thinking of a Socialist *government.* They joined the many other French citizens who were tired of having to devote yet another Sunday to voting, with the result that the abstention rate (34.25 percent in the first round and 30.05 percent in the second round) was the highest since 1962.

The election outcome, although not a complete victory for the Socialists, represented a significant enough defeat for the Right to leave it in a state of disorientation. The RPR continued to be torn between its right-wingers (i.e., hardliners on law and order such as Pasqua), who did not wish to be outflanked by the National Front and continued to favor a rapprochement with that party, and its moderates, who preferred closer collaboration with the UDF, possibly in the context of an institutionalized (and warmed-over) URC. In addition, there were some politicians in the middle (like former finance minister Edouard Balladur) who dreamed of a large right-of-center confederation comprising the RPR, UDF, and the small, conservative *Centre national des indépendants et paysans* (CNIP). In the meantime, however, the RPR leaders, faced by possible defections of supporters to more moderate parties, announced that the RPR would make no alliances with the National Front in future elections.

The UDF was in a worse position. Almost immediately after the Assembly elections, several leaders of that formation insisted that although it remained an ally of the Gaullists, it was situated in the political center and therefore expected to benefit from Mitterrand's and Rocard's announced efforts at an opening toward the "centrist" mainstream of the electorate. But the UDF leaders disagreed on tactics. Giscard d'Estaing, who had become the official head of the UDF,[44] favored a "constructive opposition"; François Léotard, who led the Republican party, the largest component of the UDF, agreed as long as the principles of his relatively conservative party were maintained; and Barre even went so far as to envisage a future cohabitation with a Rocard government. Meanwhile, when the new Assembly met, the CDS—the most "centrist" of the Center—having increased its representation in that chamber from about 35 to 50, constituted itself into a separate parliamentary party under the label of the *Union du centre* (UDC). One result welcomed by all the major parties was the virtual elimination of the National Front's representation in the Assembly.[45]

Early in 1989, as the French were preparing for the elections to the European Parliament, both the RPR and the UDF were faced by another problem: an incipient rebellion of "young Turks"—Gaullist and Giscardist politicians in their forties—who wished to rejuvenate both formations by wresting the leadership from the "old guard." In order to abort this rebellion, Chirac and Giscard closed ranks and decided that the latter would lead a joint RPR-UDF slate of candidates for the European elections in June 1989.[46] The results were encouraging: With 28.9 percent of the vote (compared to 23.6 percent for the Socialist ticket led by Laurent Fabius), Giscard was considered to have been politically resurrected.[47] The CDS put up its own list, under the label "the Center for Europe," but because of its disappointing performance (8.4 percent of the vote), its political clout was seen as diminished. In mid-1989, a group of "rejuvenators" from both the RPR and the UDF met in Lyons to discuss the possibility of merging the two formations in order to create a more potent center-right party.

THE GREENS

At the end of the 1980s, both the Right and the Left were faced with a new challenge: the rise of the "Greens." Although environmentalist groups had been in existence for several years in France, their political impact was minimal because the electoral system has not favored small parties (see below) and, more important, because problems of ecology were not in the forefront. Attempts were made periodically to sponsor environmentalist candidates on regional and local levels (e.g., in Alsace), but they did not meet with much success. In the presidential elections of 1981, the Ecologists put up a candidate, Brice Lalonde, who received 3.9 percent of the first-round votes. In the parliamentary election of 1986, the new "Green party" (*les Verts*) made a worse showing and (with 1.2 percent of the votes) failed to gain representation in the Assembly. In the presidential elections of 1988 the Greens (under Antoine Waechter, a young Alsatian politician) did surprisingly well, gaining 3.8 percent of the first-ballot votes, but his party (with less than 1 percent of the total national vote in the first round) did poorly in the Assembly elections, and fared similarly (with less than 2 percent of the vote) in the municipal elections of March 1989.[48] There are several explanations for those poor showings. The Greens have appealed to a fairly narrow electorate—the younger and better educated. Until a decade ago, the French public was much more concerned with economic issues than with environmental or other "postmaterialist" ones; before the Chernobyl disaster and the recent oil glut, there was relatively little public worry about the safety of nuclear power stations. Furthermore, many of the platform planks of the Greens were not particularly related to environmental issues and were found also in other (especially left-center) parties,[49] and it was therefore more "rational" to vote for those parties; and finally, the issue of the environment was gradually being taken up by the other parties, notably the PS. In the elections for the European Parliament, the Greens received more than 10 percent of the vote, but these elections had more "expressive" than "instrumental" significance, and the abstention rate was higher than 50 percent.

The position of the Greens as the most credible articulator of environmental concerns was further complicated by the creation by Brice Lalonde of a rival party, *Génération Ecologie* (GE), in 1990. Lalonde had been the candidate of the Greens in the 1981 presidential election, but he came to believe that the environmentalist agenda could be promoted best in alliance with other parties. The relationship between the Greens and GE has been marked by personal rivalry between Waechter and Lalonde, which has weakened both parties. After GE came out slightly ahead in the regional elections of March 1992, the two parties agreed later that year to field a common candidate in every constituency in the next Assembly elections. But the divisions continued to be deep; Waechter envisaged the *Verts* as being neither right nor left, but as an alternative to them both, and shunned any alliances with either. He opposed "productivism" and raised doubts about the limits of technological progress; favored job sharing (a theme to be taken up by Rocard in October 1993); local initiatives and referenda; the restoration of proportional representation; the reduction of the workweek; a lower consumption of energy; and support of Third World countries (including dictatorial regimes).[50] Lalonde, however, had been clearly on the Left. Once a member of the PSU, he was minister for the environment in the governments of Rocard and Cresson, and he has wanted to use GE as base for promoting his own political career, at first as the leader of the environmentalist contingent of the democratic Left and, later, when the disillusionment with the PS became increasingly apparent, as the heir to the electorate of that party. He had some success in his attempt to fashion the GE into a "catchall" party on the model of the PS. Whereas Waechter was considered too dogmatic (much like the German Greens' "fundamentalists"), Lalonde was viewed as too opportunistic.[51]

THE PARLIAMENTARY ELECTIONS OF 1993

The Collapse of the Left

The decade of the 1990s began with clear signals that the Socialist party was in trouble. Many of its former supporters began to be disenchanted with the PS because the government with which it was identified seemed to lose its dynamism and its reformist zeal and proved unable to solve the problems of immigration, student unrest, and above all, unemployment. The credibility of the PS and the government was seriously affected by evidences of incompetence and by a number of scandals involving ministers: questionable business deals, bribes, the distribution of AIDS-contaminated blood to hemophiliacs, and improprieties in party financing (the latter itself a response to the loss of dues-paying party members). An additional factor may have been boredom with Mitterrand, who had been in office as president longer than any predecessor in French history, and who seemed to be losing his touch, particularly in the conduct of foreign affairs.[52] By January 1992, Mitterrand's favorable rating had descended to below 30 percent, and the ratings of Premier Cresson were no better. Mitterrand's attempts to "freshen" the image of his government by a turnover of prime ministers did not help; in the regional and cantonal elections of March 1992 the PS experienced heavy losses (see Table 4.3). Public opinion polls throughout that

TABLE 4.3 Regional, European, and cantonal elections, 1986–1992 (in percentages)

	Regional	European	Regional	Cantonal*
	1986	*1989*	*1992*	*1992*
Abstentions	21.6	50.3	31.3	29.8
Extreme Left	1.3	2.4	1.2	0.8
Communists (PCF)	10.2	7.8	8.0	9.6
Socialists (PS)	29.6	23.6	18.3	18.9
Miscellaneous Left**	1.9	—	2.1	5.0
All Left	43.1	33.8	29.6	34.3
Greens (*Verts*)	2.3	10.7	6.8	7.9
Génération Ecologie	—	—	7.1	2.0
Other environmentalists	—	—	0.8	—
All environmentalists	2.3	10.7	14.7	9.9
RPR/UDF	41.0	37.1	33.0	29.2
Miscellaneous Right	3.7	0.9	4.2	13.8
All republican Right	44.7	38.0	37.2	43.0
National Front	9.7	11.8	· 13.9	12.2
Other extreme Right	—	0.2	0.2	0.2
All extreme Right	9.7	12.0	14.1	12.4
Miscellaneous***	0.2	5.5	4.3	0.3

*1st round.
**Including Left Radicals (MRG).
***Including regional parties and, in the European elections of 1989 and the regional elections of 1992, "Hunting, Fishing, Nature and Traditions" (*Chasse, pêche, nature et traditions*). Figures are for metropolitan France.
SOURCE: Ministry of Interior. Adapted from Nonna Mayer, "Des élections sans vainqueur," *French Politics and Society* 10:2 (Spring 1992) 9.

year and early in 1993 predicted that these losses would be repeated in the forthcoming parliamentary elections.

Nevertheless, the election results came as a shock. They produced the weakest Assembly representation of the PS and its allies since 1968 and plunged the entire Left into disarray. In contrast, conservative parties gained their largest parliamentary majority since 1815. In terms of the popular vote, the PS, with nearly 30 percent of the total, remained the largest *single* party; however, given the existing electoral system (see below), this was of little comfort. Furthermore, many prominent Socialist leaders (including Rocard) and most of the prominent cabinet members lost their bids for election to the Assembly.

The lessons the Socialists drew from this defeat were ambiguous. Several years before the election, the leaders of the party had been aware of the ideological contradictions and programmatic confusions within it. There was the conflict between the two "cultures" within French socialism: (1) Jacobin, centralist, etatist, nationalist, and protectionist; and (2) decentralist, pluralist, regionalist, and European.[53] The former was dominant, but the latter won out on the level of practical politics as the PS successfully harnessed its two conflicting impulses: the urge to reform and the need to govern. But the conflict persisted in the realm of ideas and was aggravated by personal rivalries and antipathies, notably involving representatives of the "old guard," Rocard, and Fabius. At a congress in Rennes in 1990, the party was nearly destroyed by its inability to agree on a program. Subsequent party meetings did not resolve these problems, which were shelved in the interest of holding on to power. The cohesion of the PS was threatened anew early in 1991 with the outbreak of the Gulf War. Many Socialist deputies were inclined against the war but adhered to party discipline in supporting it. The exception was *Socialisme et République*, the faction of Jean-Pierre Chevènement, whose open opposition to France's participation in the war brought about his resignation as minister of defense.

At a congress in Bordeaux in 1992—after the defeat of the Socialists in the regional elections and in anticipation of a legislative election defeat in 1993—Rocard was proclaimed as the party's "natural candidate" for the presidency in the next elections; however, the debate about the future programmatic direction of the PS remained unresolved. In February 1993, Rocard made a speech in which he called for a "big bang," an implosion of the PS and its outdated ideologies so that it could be reconstituted on a different basis. He suggested the creation in its place of a "vast open and modern movement" embracing socialists, reform communists, ecologists, centrists, and other reform-minded citizens.[54] Mitterrand reacted mildly, saying that there was nothing wrong with a party's trying to enlarge itself as long as it did not forget its origins and its basic values and did not abandon socialism itself.[55]

Fabius (who had become secretary-general of the PS in 1991) denounced Rocard's proposal as a move to destroy one of the great traditions of French politics. Chevènement denounced it too; he deplored the absence of clear principles and feared that the new party would be plunged into an ideological "primeval ooze."[56] Rocard's idea was not new; it was the latest of a series of attempts, most of them presided over by Mitterrand—the CIR, FGDS, and even the PS in its founding days—to "reassemble" the democratic Left, and it rivaled Chevènement's own attempts. Chevènement, who had earlier declared his regional federation independent of the PS, quit that party altogether in mid-1993 and formed a new party, *Mouvement des citoyens*, which was to serve as an instrument for the "recomposition" of the whole Left, including "former socialists, ex-communists, left-wing Gaullists, democrats, Christians, and many others without political affiliation."[57] A prototype of such an umbrella group, the *"Refondations"* movement, had in fact been created in 1991. Because that movement contained dissident Communists and disaffected Socialists (including, initially, Chevènement and his allies), it resembled the old PSU in its disorganization; moreover, it competed with Brice Lalonde's own dreams of presiding over a new "green-pink-blue" (i.e., environmentalist, socialist, and European) party.[58]

At the end of 1993, the *Mouvement des citoyens* claimed only 3 deputies and 7,500 members, because Chevènement's leftism was not very convincing to many (except, perhaps, for his continued preference for *dirigisme* and his reservations about decentralization, which appealed to certain old-time socialists). Chevènement's opposition to French participation in the Gulf War had been inspired by ultranationalism, anti-Americanism, and pro-Iraq connections, and not by any specifically "socialist" visions; in fact, after the outbreak of the Gulf War, while still formally a member of the PS, he had proposed to gain supporters by assembling around the "republican idea."[59]

At a conclave in July 1993, which prepared the groundwork for the full party congress scheduled in LeBourget (outside Paris) for later that year, Rocard called for unity. At a meeting of the executive committee in April 1993 (boycotted by Fabius), Rocard, who had been named head of a provisional "directorate" of the party and charged with rebuilding it, called for a statement of "concrete utopias";[60] instead, he got speeches affirming the "values of the Left, [among them] laïcité, humanism, and social justice," but no agreement on specific policies. Ironically, the only Socialist leader who still articulated specific leftist positions—on incomes, immigrants, political asylum, social security, and human rights—was Mitterrand himself; but he could afford this position because he had ceased to function as an active policy maker. However, since the parliamentary elections he had distanced himself as much as possible from the PS—as if to suggest that the disavowal of the party was not a disavowal of his presidency—so that he could continue to act as a transpartisan chief of state.[61] He sent a polite message to the PS but did not specifically congratulate Rocard, who was formally elected secretary-general in mid-1993 at a preliminary meeting of about 100 federation leaders in Lyons. But Fabius could barely contain his hostility, and several younger Socialists—some of them former ministers and others representing the minority faction *Gauche socialiste*—did not show up at all because they objected to the evolving orientations of the majority that had begun to form around the new leadership. That majority produced a resolution, entitled *"Refonder,"* which, while calling for "a break with the Marxist dogma of the nationalized enterprises . . . and [recognizing] the dynamism and efficiency of the market economy,"[62] failed to propose a positive socialist program of action. Rocard was still regarded as the "virtual" (Socialist) candidate for the presidency, but since he lost his own election bid for Parliament in 1993, some questioned this choice and thought of a possible alternative: Jacques Delors, the president of the Commission of the European Union, who appeared to be above the factional fights. At the congress itself these new orientations were reconfirmed; many prominent Socialist politicians were absent (including Edith Cresson and a number of former ministers), ostensibly because the congress failed both to produce a clear program of action on unemployment and other socioeconomic issues and to defend the record of the outgoing government. For despite the weakening of the party's social activism, that record was quite respectable, by and large embodying many of the traditional concerns associated with democratic leftism. But the record was marred by the corruption associated with power, with several ministers having been implicated.[63]

The job of reconstruction of the PS promised to be difficult because the internal divisions of the party persisted—between the "old guard" and the young, the intellectuals and what remained of the working-class activists, and the ideologues and the pragmatists. There was also the problem of lack of support from Mitterrand, although some Socialist politicians thought that in view of the president's own loss of standing nationally, such support was neither necessary nor useful. In fact, some Socialists argued that the party's electoral disaster was largely the consequence of Mitterrand's failing leadership and his indifference, as a lame-duck president, to the fate of the party he had helped to create. As a popular writer put it, "Monsieur Mitterrand is so honest that he intends to give back the Socialist party in the same condition in which he received it."[64]

Efforts at widening the party's support base were impeded by problems in its relationship with other left-wing parties. The Left Radical group (MRG) was still formally allied to the PS, but its relations were disrupted by the failure of the PS leadership to defend Bernard Tapie, one of the leaders of the MRG, against accusations of questionable business practices.[65] It would be even more difficult to recruit the centrist CDS as an ally, for despite the occasional policy disagreements of its leaders (especially the more leftist ones) with the positions of the government, they saw no reason to abandon the UDF, especially since they had been successfully paid off by Balladur with ministerial positions.[66]

There remained the possibility of a future alliance with the Communists. For the time being, however, such a prospect was not favorable, given the mutual hostility between the PCF and Rocard. In 1991, the PCF had joined the Right in voting for censure of Rocard; it had done the same in a vote against Bérégovoy in 1992. The PCF had also shown little leftist solidarity in its voting on Socialist-sponsored legislation. The party remained too "Stalinist" (or "Leninist") for a rapprochement with the PS, even after the collapse of the Soviet Union, as long as Marchais retained the leadership. There had been attempts by certain PCF leaders to reform the party, but these were unsuccessful.[67] One of these leaders, Pierre Juquin, had left the party for the Greens; another, Charles Fiterman (a member of the cabinet in 1981), still carried on the fight to reform the party. The PCF had saved its Assembly seats, but with a membership of fewer than 200,000 (compared to 630,000 fifteen years earlier), it was a shadow of its former self. Its further decline is unavoidable unless it becomes more moderate. Perhaps in recognition of this, Marchais, secretary-general since 1972, announced that he would resign his position in January 1994.[68] He was succeeded by Robert Hue, a relatively young and moderate Communist who was supported by reformers and appeared to be more amenable to intraparty pluralism. However, that development did not guarantee that the PCF would reform itself sufficiently to align with the PS.

Because of these problems, some observers have suggested that the best thing would be for the old party to die so that a new and better one might be born. But this may be neither possible nor necessary, for the PS is still a force to be reckoned with, and it remains the only effective nucleus for any future left-of-center party. It got the largest number of popular votes 1993; its organizational apparatus is still in place, and (despite losses in membership) it still counts at least 120,000 card-carrying adherents, a large proportion of whom are activists. Some of its younger leaders have been among the most popular politicians in the country.[69] Its allies (MRG) and rivals (*Mouvement des citoyens*) lack strength and credibility, and it is more likely than any other party to recapture the votes that had gone to the PCF and the two ecology parties. It is bound to benefit from voter disillusionment with the parties in power, should they fail to solve France's problems. It should be borne in mind that in the first round of the parliamentary election of 1993, the RPR and UDF together got only 44.2 percent of votes (2.8 points more than in 1988 and 4.6 points less than in 1986) and that the overwhelming size of its victory—85 percent of the seats—can be attributed significantly to the nature of the electoral system.[70]

The Victory of the Right

The *Union pour la France* (UPF) was the great victor in the 1993 elections or, rather, the beneficiary of the repudiation of the Socialist government. The UPF had been created in 1990 in response to the double defeat of the Right in 1988. This new alliance was envisaged by some as step to fusion, a step demanded by young "renovators." However, formal fusion was out of the question due to the different traditions of the two major components and above all the continuing rivalry of their leaders. Although the RPR and UDF had cooperated during the campaign for the regional elections of 1992, the losses of the PS had not redounded meaningfully to the benefit of the UPF, for the biggest gainers had been the National Front and the environmentalist parties.

The coherence of the UPF was to some extent impaired by disagreements on the question of European unity. In the summer of 1992, during the public debate preceding the referendum on the Treaty of Maastricht, the vast majority of UDF politicians and their supporters had favored that treaty, whereas the RPR was divided (and Chirac pronounced himself in favor, with qualifications). Ultimately most Gaullists came around in support of the treaty (although they denounced Giscard and other UDF politicians for appearing jointly with Socialists to argue for its support). After the ratification of the treaty by referendum in September 1992, the two components of the UPF concentrated on a joint electoral strategy for the 1993 elections: a common platform, a common position against the Left as well as against the National Front, agreements for mutual support in the second round, and work toward a common presidential candidate. The UPF won by default, despite the competition between the RPR and UDF in the second round.[71]

The fact that the UPF captured 80 percent of the seats in the Assembly and was able to constitute a cohesive government did not mean that the problem of disunity had been resolved. Disagreements on political strategy persisted, specifically regarding the question of the standard bearer in the forthcoming (1995) presidential race. Many Gaullists continued to regard Chirac as the "logical" candidate of the RPR; some Gaullists, like Pasqua, preferred a U.S.-style "primary" to select a common presidential candidate. That was envisaged as a combination of a national selection convention composed of elected officeholders at national and subnational levels and of delegates elected in local primaries by registered party members.[72] The UDF secretary-general, François Bayrou, favored such a primary; Giscard opposed it in case the presidential election were held earlier than 1995;

and Léotard and Barre opposed it altogether. Some UDF politicians continued to support Giscard; others, identified with the UDF as well, preferred to wait and see; still others, inspired by public-opinion polls, were increasingly inclined toward Balladur. Although such a primary is (at least at this writing) still favored by Chirac, not all the Gaullist politicians have accepted it.

Another potential challenger to UPF unity is the CDS component of the UDF. When the new Assembly met, there was uncertainty whether the CDS would organize as a separate parliamentary group. As we have seen, such a group had been constituted after the 1988 elections; moreover, the CDS had asserted its identity by running an independent slate of candidates for the election to the European Parliament in 1989. Now the CDS posed as its condition for remaining in the UDF fold the support of one of their members for Assembly speaker, to which UDF agreed; but when a Gaullist (and an anti-European one) was selected instead, the CDS remained in the fold because Giscard and most of the other leaders of the UDF promised to accept the pro-European orientations of the CDS. Nevertheless, many CDS deputies remained uneasy; they argued that the ministers belonging to their group were ignoring its policy orientations in the interest of government solidarity.[73]

The uneasy relationship between the UDF and the RPR was paralleled by disaccords between the government and Parliament (especially the Senate) and within Parliament itself. There were also tensions between the government and Assembly Speaker Séguin, who differed publicly with Balladur in being both more nationalist (on Europe) and more "social" (on domestic policy, especially on employment). The deputies belonging to the UDF (with individual exceptions, mainly in the ranks of the Republican party) were more welfare-state oriented, more tolerant toward immigrants, and more committed to individual liberties than Gaullist deputies. The UDF also remained more positively oriented to European unity. In constructing his government and choosing his policies, Balladur took these divergences into account; he was open to the development of the European Union, but tough in protecting the interests of the French farmer in GATT negotiations, and his policies on civil rights, immigrants, employment, and constitutional reform represented compromises between conservative and progressive positions as well as between his own preferences and those of Mitterrand.

A major source of conflict was the question of cohabitation, where positions were based less on principle than on tactical considerations. Chirac and (to a lesser extent) Pasqua, the minister of interior, were negative about it; they were hoping that cohabitation would be conflict-ridden, so that Mitterrand would be driven to resign prematurely, thereby provoking an early presidential election, in which Chirac would be better placed than any of his rivals. Most UDF politicians preferred a "soft" cohabitation because of their "centrist" attitudes and because they wanted the government that had given them considerable power to last as long as possible. Furthermore, the longer such a government lasted and governed effectively, the less certain would be Chirac's presidential chances. Giscard had been skeptical about a renewed cohabitation several weeks before the election but afterward softened his position.

A tactically related matter was the conflict between UDF and RPR about who should head the list for the European Parliament elections of June 1994. In mid-1993, Balladur entertained the possibility of leading the RPR-UDF list in these elections, but this idea was opposed by Giscard, who thought of doing so himself (although he had just resigned as deputy from the European Parliament because it conflicted with his other two elective mandates).[74]

Cohabitation with a Socialist president proved to be more bearable and less delicate for Balladur than cohabitation with Chirac, who pretended to support government policy fully but did not want it to be too successful lest Balladur become so popular that he would be preferred as the conservative presidential candidate over Chirac. Conversely, Chirac did not want to see that policy so *unsuccessful* that the French electorate, known for its fickleness, would turn away from the Gaullists.[75] At the end of 1993, Simone Veil and François Léotard, the two top non-Gaullist ministers, came out bluntly in favor of Balladur's presidential candidacy, not only because he would provide the best way out of the endless Chirac-Giscard rivalry but also because he was already the preferred candidate of the public at large as well as of the Gaullist electorate.[76] Only Jacques Toubon, the minister of culture, and Jean-Louis Debré, the deputy secretary-general of the RPR, reaffirmed their personal loyalty to Chirac, whereas Pasqua merely expressed certainty that the candidate would be a Gaullist. Balladur himself continued to insist that his political interests were limited (for the time being) to his governmental tasks and kept Chirac fully informed, while the latter reaffirmed his support for Balladur's conduct.

The Marginalization of the Ecologists and the Extreme Right

One of the consequences of the 1993 elections that was regarded as positive by both the UPF and the PS was the uncertain future faced by their rivals and potential spoilers, respectively the ecologist parties and the National Front. Full support by the ecologists could not have saved the PS, but it could have reduced the extent of its defeat. When the PS, having little to lose, offered to back ecologist candidates unilaterally in the second round if they came out ahead in the first round, both Waechter and Lalonde refused to reciprocate (although the latter had at first been inclined to do so). The ecologists' cockiness could be attributed to their respectable performance (at the expense of the PS) in the European Parliament elections of 1989 and in the regional elections of 1992, which they hoped to repeat. These elections had resulted in the selection of a left-oriented *Vert* (Green) politician as president of the regional council of Nord-Pas-de-Calais, a Socialist stronghold. However, the ecologists ended up with no Assembly seats at all. Some months after Balladur's appointment as premier, Lalonde said that he would not exclude future "cooperation" with a "liberal and social" government, a statement for which the *Verts* denounced him.[77] The "war of the chiefs" was put on hold when Waechter was replaced as secretary-general by Dominique Voynet, who was more open to collaboration with the PS (probably because Waechter's performance had been weaker than that of Lalonde). This change of leadership should incline the *Verts* more to the Left and facilitate the selection of a common ecologist presidential candidate,[78] although Waechter retains enough power to impede the party's attempts to flesh out a clear set of policies.

In terms of its membership, its well-established local machines, and the clarity of its program, the National Front appears to be in a more solid position than the two environmentalist parties. Its performance in recent presidential, local, and European Parliament elections had been so respectable that some Gaullists and Giscardists were ready to make common cause with it. However, most of the UPF politicians were opposed,[79] and in the end the National Front was not needed.[80] That party was not considered a viable alternative to the mainstream right-of-center parties because, as public-opinion polls showed, a large majority of the electorate considered it a threat to democracy.[81]

Nevertheless, the National Front has influenced the dialogue and the policies of the mainstream parties. This was reflected in expressions of intolerance vis-à-vis immigrants on the part of Gaullists and Giscardists—for example, Chirac's statement about the "overdose" of immigrants, with their "noises and odors," and Giscard's article about the "invasion" of the country by foreigners.[82] Even the Socialists were not immune to such rhetoric, as when Rocard suggested that France could not receive the poor of the whole world, and Cresson spoke about chartering airplanes to take some immigrants back to their countries of origin. Furthermore, soon after assuming office, the Balladur government introduced legislation that past and potential supporters of the National Front wholeheartedly approved—to tighten controls over immigrants and to limit rights of asylum.

Such expressions and measures have served to keep many French voters in the "republican" Right. Although the National Front won 14 percent in regional elections in 1992, it ended up with no deputy in Assembly. The electorate was probably also apprehensive about the party's platform of 1991, some of whose 50 "propositions" were plainly unconstitutional. This was particularly true of provisions dealing with the immigrant problem, such as expulsion, separate social security provisions, and detention by the police. Many voters probably also feared that the violence against foreigners in Germany, which has led to murders, might serve as a model for France. Some politicians of the National Front were already thinking of a successor to Le Pen, who would be younger, more dynamic, and less demagogic.[83] Whether the National Front could survive intact without its founder remains to be seen.

THE FUNCTIONAL RELEVANCE
OF POLITICAL PARTIES

The preceding discussion has given the reader some idea of the diversity of French political forces and ideologies. Although such a discussion is meaningful from a historical point of view, the question remains of how ideological distinctions among parties relate to the political process and political behavior. Many scholars have pointed out that in the past, the multiplicity of parties had rendered the maintenance of stable governments difficult, since these governments had been based on tenuous coalitions. Each party's insistence on its uniqueness, an insistence that was a reflection of the importance that French politicians (many of whom have been intellectuals) attached to ideas, impeded the aggregation process. But it did not make the process impossible. In the Fourth Republic, there was a vast area of agreement among most parties about certain essentials, such as the preservation of the republican system, the establishment of minimal welfare-state policies, and the necessity for economic planning.

Among members of Parliament, there has been, from the Third Republic to the present one, the same kind of esprit de corps that is found in other democratic legislatures. Robert de Jouvenel may have exaggerated when he asserted that "there is less difference between two deputies, one of whom is a revolutionary and the other is not, than between two revolutionaries, one of whom is a deputy and the other is not."[84] Nevertheless, it is true that often enough members of political parties have not acted in a manner conforming to the party's ideology when they entered alliances or voted on issues. There has always been a certain degree of opportunism (called "pragmatism" when found in Anglo-American systems) among party leaders, particularly deputies—a phenomenon that has accounted for the widespread notion among the French, from Rousseau's time to the present, that parliamentary parties are mainly power-seeking and selfish, collectively enemies of the people, and guilty of betraying by coalition deals the ideologies to which they are ostensibly committed.

Unnatural Alliances

Such a view can be substantiated by reference to a number of political practices. There have been "unnatural" preelectoral and parliamentary alliances involving political parties representing mutually hostile ideologies. Alliances have been determined by accidents of geography and personality, the institution of the single-member constituency system of elections, and the fear of being left behind by political developments and of having to forgo a share of power. As was pointed out earlier, in 1944 and 1945, the clerical MRP and the anticlerical Socialists and Communists collaborated in a tripartite coalition; in 1971–1972 the anticlerical Radicals and the Catholic Democratic Centrists constructed an electoral alliance and later joined the Giscardist alignment. In 1958, most of the SFIO supported the return of de Gaulle and the ratification of the new constitution, despite the SFIO's frequently articulated reservations about the man and the regime. In 1968 and 1969, the Communists tacitly supported the maintenance of the Gaullist regime despite their criticism of the reactionary nature of Gaullism. In the early 1960s, the Democratic Centrists were in the opposition because of their adamant anti-Gaullism, but they gradually permitted themselves to be co-opted, some of them by Pompidou, into a pro-Gaullist stance in 1969, and the remainder by Giscard, into a new "presidential majority" in 1974. Chirac and other Gaullist leaders have by turns suggested that the National Front is a legitimate party, located within acceptable political parameters, and that it is a danger to democracy. Le Pen himself has on the one hand attacked the RPR and UDF for being in collusion with the Socialists and on the other deplored the refusal of these parties to collaborate with him. In 1984, Raymond Barre asserted that Le Pen was "not a scarecrow" and that he, Barre, could identify with several of Le Pen's themes, such as the problem of immigrants and the threat of domestic violence;[85] but four years later, in a television debate with Chirac, Barre distanced himself from Le Pen. In 1986, Barre considered a "cohabitation" between a right-of-center Assembly majority and a Socialist president unthinkable and called for the resignation of the latter, but in 1988, he was holding open the possibility of collaborating with (and possibly even participating in) a Socialist government.[86] After the Assembly elections in the same year (and again in 1993), the CDS constituted itself as a separate parliamentary party while insisting that it remained a component of the UDF And before and after the presidential elections of 1988, Mitterrand simultaneously played the role of a coordinator of Socialist orientations and strategies and of a transpartisan father figure. The relationships between the Socialists and the Communists from 1965 on, and between the Gaullists and Giscardists from 1962 on, have been, by turns, those of allies, rivals, and antagonists.

Political Wanderings

France has been notorious for the political wanderings of deputies from one parliamentary party to another.[87] Examples of political fence-sitting, pragmatic adaptations, party switches, and even political "bigamy" are numerous. They include Michel Debré and Jacques Chaban-Delmas, who switched from the Radical to the Gaullist party during the Fourth Republic; Mendès-France, who left the Radical party to become a cofounder of a left-socialist party (the *Parti socialiste autonome*, the precursor of the PSU); and Max Lejeune, a Socialist who started his own party, the *Mouvement démocrate-socialiste de France*, and, convinced that the Socialist program had already been achieved, became part of the conservative majority in 1974. Other examples are Jacques Chirac, a Gaullist who in 1974 opposed the official candidate of his party and supported Giscard, only to become his bitter rival from 1976 to the present, a rivalry moderated by intermittent "reconciliations" and appearances of collaboration; Michel Jobert, a Gaullist who was Pompidou's foreign minister in the early 1970s but, when Giscard became president, formed his own party, the *Mouvement des démocrates* (without, however, supporting the opposition), and later, in 1981, supported Mitterrand and was rewarded with a cabinet position; Edgar Faure, who shifted uneasily between Radical party leadership and Gaullism, attempting to *combine* the two in his person. In addition, one may cite the cases of Alain Peyrefitte, who had been a minister of justice under Giscard and who, although himself a Gaullist, was so pro-Giscardist that he tried to help the president in efforts at controlling and co-opting the rest of the Gaullist politicians; Françoise Giroud, a leftist journalist who voted for Mitterrand in 1974 but subsequently became a minister in the government headed by Gaullist Chirac; and Michel Durafour, Jean-Pierre

Soisson, and Lionel Stoléru, all prominent Giscardists who became ministers in the (second) government of Socialist Rocard under the label of *France unie.*[88] More recent examples are Charles Fiterman, who was a prominent member of the *Refondations* movement in 1993 while continuing to be a leading figure in the PCF, and Chevènement, who was a member of the same movement while simultaneously building up his *Mouvement des citoyens* as a rival. Finally, there is the case of Mitterrand himself, who, since the end of World War II, has belonged to and even led four or five political organizations.[89]

The Place of Ideology

In terms of their outlooks, programs, and behavior, the political parties have evolved beyond the ideologies that originally inspired them, either because these ideologies had become irrelevant or because they had ceased to have adequate electoral appeal. Thus, the anticlerical stand is now less meaningful because the rapid urbanization of France has brought about a significant weakening of clericalism. The class-struggle notions of the PCF have become less compelling today, partly as a result of the growing *embourgeoisement* of a segment of the French working class and partly because the most disprivileged segment of that class, the foreign-born workers, have not voted in significant numbers, either because they are not yet politically socialized or because they are not yet naturalized.

The split between parties advocating liberalism and those advocating interventionism is a false dichotomy today; most political parties—from the Giscardists and Gaullists on the Right to the Socialists on the Left—had long ago been converted to some measure of *dirigisme*, and leading politicians of the mainstream parties on both sides of the political divide have (more recently) embraced a variable number of "neoliberal" theses that stress the importance of market forces. The argument that divides the parties is not whether there should be economic planning (or guidance) by the state but what kind of incomes policy, social production, or sectoral participation a particular economic policy should entail. Colonialism or anticolonialism ceased to be relevant issues in the early 1960s, after France had completed its decolonization process.

To be sure, the right-of-center parties continue (to the extent that is electorally feasible) to cater to the more privileged sectors of society; and within the Socialist party, there is still a large faction (once heavily influenced by Mitterrand himself) informed by a redistributive impulse.[90] Despite the conversion of Rocard to a pragmatically centrist orientation, most of the Socialist party factions are still committed to traditional socialist goals: the expansion of the welfare state, a progressive tax system, decent wages, more-democratic access to education, and the promotion of human rights. There is no longer a clear line of division between the PS and the UPF over important foreign-policy questions, such as participation in NATO, the nuclear striking force, and the Arab-Israeli conflict, but (except for European economic integration and the institutional development of the European Union, which all parties save the PCF, the National Front, and a small wing of the Gaullist party favor *in principle*), these are not matters that interest the vast majority of French citizens. One issue on which the Left and the Right have continued to differ is that of the (largely Muslim) immigrants, the former being committed to tolerance and liberal naturalization laws and the latter to more restrictive policies. However, in order to express its hostility to these immigrants, the Right has selectively embraced the *laïciste* positions formerly associated with the Left![91]

Emmanuel Todd, a French sociologist, remarked that "it took centuries to establish [the] ideological structures [of France]" and only five years to liquidate them.[92] This remark may be an overstatement, but it is widely agreed that all the major political parties have been emptied of their traditional ideological content in much the same way as churches have been emptied of worshippers. French voters find it more difficult to adhere to a major political party because they can no longer clearly distinguish its orientation from that of a rival party. In recent national elections, the three mainstream parties—the PS, the RPR, and the UDF—all presented bare-bones platforms and put their emphasis on the leadership qualities of their candidates. The electoral programs presented by the various parties for the parliamentary elections of 1993 were more detailed; however, they also contained more internal contradictions and on many issues tended to resemble one another. The parties themselves have become increasingly nondescript ideologically and have "converged" because of two important developments that have taken place in the past two decades in France (as elsewhere in Western Europe): (1) the decline of the appeal of the Catholic church, which "has drained the Right of its sociological substance"; and (2) the decline of the "smokestack" industries, which has ended "the proletarian dream of the Left."[93] The partisan "wars of religion" (as a well-known commentator on the political scene has called them[94]) have ended in part because of *alternance* (the successful changing of the guard in 1981) and the two "cohabitation" experiences, which have moderated the distinctions between the majority and the opposition; because of a growing consensus about the political system; and, with the recent celebrations of the bicentennial of the French Revolution, the gradual ending of arguments about the heritage of that great event.

Several recent episodes provide illustrations of the growing irrelevance of party labels:

1. The decentralization controversy from 1982 to the present: In most cases, politicians were pitted against one another not so much on the basis of right or left ideology as on the basis of their individual power positions and ambitions.
2. The Gulf War in 1991: French participation was supported by most Socialist politicians (after Mitterrand had decided on that policy for reasons not of principle but of global opportunism) as well as by the leaders of the RPR and UDF and opposed by the PCF, the National Front, and selected ultranationalistically oriented (and anti-American) Socialist and Gaullist politicians.
3. The controversy in 1992 over the question whether France should sign the Treaty of Maastricht that created the European Union: It was favored by Mitterrand and the majority of Socialist politicians, by Giscard and

most of his followers, and by Chirac (in an ambiguous fashion) and half of the RPR politicians, while it was opposed by the PCF, the National Front, and selected nationalists from the Socialist, Gaullist, and Giscardist camps.

In these cases, the "issue" division was so sharply drawn that some commentators have suggested that there are now several orientations that have supplanted the traditional right-left disagreements and that overlap them: (1) Europeanism versus nationalism; (2) decentralization versus centralism; (3) accommodation to the masses versus protection of the elite; (4) a pluralist versus a monistic vision of the state; and (5) the predominance of an interventionist state versus the autonomy of socioeconomic subsystems.[95] To some French political scientists, the various positions expressed during the debate over the referendum on the Maastricht treaty overlapped the traditional party cleavages to such an extent that they posited ten views, images, or "visions" of France instead of the simple left-right distinctions: a positive and optimistic versus a negative and pessimistic outlook; a convergent versus a centrifugal view of society; a tolerant versus a repressive attitude; an urban versus a rural orientation; and a national-laic versus a social-Christian ideology.[96]

The ideological decomposition of parties does not mean that the citizens' identification with parties has come to an end; nor does it suggest that old expectations have totally disappeared. There is still a Left and a Right; however, these are no longer clearly equated, respectively, with the PS and the UPF. In 1993, the voters disavowed the PS not because of the party's leftist traditions but because it failed to resolve urgent problems (see Table 4.4).[97] The lack of clarity of meaning of Right and Left may account for the steady decline of dues-paying members in most of the political parties.[98] It may also explain why party identification is no longer as reliable as it used to be. Today such identification tends to be based not so much on shared beliefs as on narrow instrumental considerations, disappointments in the conduct of rival parties, peer-group imi-

TABLE 4.4   Ideal values and real performance of the Left

	Values the Left Should Embody		Values the Left Embodies Today	
	Percent	*Rank*	*Percent*	*Rank*
The fight against inequality	74	1	30	7
Human rights	63	2	41	2
Job sharing	58	3	31	5
Equality of opportunity	57	4	27	8
The defense of world peace	56	5	32	4
The building of Europe	49	6	45	1

NOTE: The total of the percentages is higher than 100 because of multiple responses.
SOURCE: SOFRES poll, adapted from *Le Monde*, 7 October 1993, p. 8.

tation, feelings of comradeship (as in the case of many who remain members of the PCF), resentments (as in the case of many National Front supporters), and the personal appeal of party politicians.

Voters' Choices, Programs, and Personalities

Political scientists in France continue to argue about the meaning that voters attach to the parties' programs and the influence of the citizens' social condition on their electoral behavior. Low-income and working-class status continue to correlate with voting for a left-wing party; there is an equally impressive correlation between middle-class status, Catholic observance, small-town background, and a conservative orientation (see Table 4.5).

TABLE 4.5 Sociological profile and party identification of the French electorate

	Left	Ecologists	Right	National Front
Total (100%)	42.5	6.0	42.0	9.5
Men	42.0	6.0	43.0	9.0
Women	43.0	6.0	41.5	9.5
Age				
18–24	39.5	11.0	43.5	6.0
25–34	51.0	7.0	34.0	8.0
35–49	42.0	7.0	39.0	12.0
50–64	41.5	3.0	44.5	11.0
65 and over	29.5	2.5	60.0	8.0
Social and professional categories				
Workers	56.5	2.5	31.5	9.5
White collar	47.0	5.0	40.0	7.0
*Cadres moyens**	47.0	6.0	38.0	9.0
Manufacturers, shopkeepers, and artisans	20.0	5.0	61.0	14.0
*Cadres supérieurs***	44.0	10.0	43.5	2.5
Free professions	23.0	16.0	40.0	21.0
Students	37.0	15.0	39.0	9.0
Unemployed	43.0	7.0	39.0	11.0
No profession, retired	33.0	2.0	53.5	11.5
Religion				
Regularly practicing Catholic	15.5	3.0	70.0	11.5
Occasional church-goer	21.0	3.0	61.0	15.0
Nonpracticing Catholic	39.0	2.0	50.0	9.0

*Middle-level management and technical.
**Higher level managerial, supervisory.
SOURCE: Jean-Luc Parodi, "Eclairages sur un scrutin pas comme les autres," Figaro/Etudes Politiques, in Philippe Habert and Colette Ysmal, eds., *Elections Municipales 1989* (Paris: Figaro, 1989), p. 24.

But such correlations are not perfect. Catholics have been voting increasingly for left-wing parties; conversely, there have been workers who have voted for right-wing politicians. In public-opinion surveys of 1980,[99] 35 percent of workers interviewed had confidence in Premier Barre's leadership, as had 52 percent of artisans and 62 percent of small shopkeepers (as compared with 85 percent of industrialists), indicating either that Barre's "neoliberal" economic policies were interpreted as essentially progressive or that many of Barre's supporters had a noninstrumental view of his leadership. Public-opinion polls taken in 1988 revealed that 38 percent of industrial workers voted for a right-wing presidential candidate on the first ballot (about half of them casting their votes for Le Pen); and that, conversely, more than a third of the farmers and about 30 percent of the artisans and shopkeepers voted for Mitterrand.[100] Polls conducted in the past several years reveal that some of the traditional political labels still have positive connotations, but these polls also show that a growing number of respondents no longer consider the notions of "right" and "left" to be useful for an understanding of the positions of political parties.[101]

Furthermore, polls have shown that ideological affinities or self-classifications are not congruent with support of presidential candidates representing political parties usually labeled as right-wing and left-wing—except, perhaps, for supporters

TABLE 4.6 Party identification, ideological self-classification, and presidential candidate preference in 1988—first round (in percentage of total vote cast by each category)

Category	Lajoinie (PCF)	Mitterrand (PS)	Waechter (Greens)	Barre (UDF)	Chirac (RPR)	Le Pen (FN)
Regularly practicing Catholic	0	18	4	31	38	7
No religion	19	41	5	8	9	9
Party preference:						
PCF	71	14	0	2	0	5
PS	5	76	4	3	1	5
Greens	0	17	47	13	9	6
UDF	0	1	1	64	23	10
RPR	0	1	0	13	66	20
National Front	1	2	0	1	3	91
"Political family":						
Extreme left	33	46	3	0	0	2
Left	7	71	7	3	1	5
Center	1	24	5	35	19	15
Right	0	3	1	33	50	13
Extreme right	0	1	0	14	32	53
*"Marais"**	2	31	7	22	17	18

*The political "swamp": the alienated and habitual abstainer.
SOURCE: Adapted from SOFRES, *L'Etat de l'opinion 1989* (Paris: Seuil, 1989), p. 77.

of the PCF and the National Front (see Table 4.6). It has also been noted that the votes for major presidential candidates have often been greater than those received by candidates of their parties in parliamentary and subnational elections, as has been true of de Gaulle in relation to the Gaullist party, Le Pen and the National Front, and Mitterrand and the Socialist party in 1988. The most recent illustration of the lack of clear relationship between the voters' electoral preferences and their views of political leaders on the one hand, and their appreciation of the political system and their policy expectations on the other is a series of public-opinion polls conducted in the fall of 1993 according to which a majority was dissatisfied with the way France was governed and had a pessimistic prognosis with regard to employment, prosperity, and social peace, yet had confidence (ranging from 57 percent to 68 percent) in Balladur's leadership and was likely to vote for him in a presidential contest.[102]

The lack of a clear correlation between ideology, party identification, and policy expectations can be seen from the results of an earlier poll (1978), which revealed that 29 percent of the PS electorate declared itself to be unfavorably inclined toward the Common Program's nationalization plank (and 14 percent of Communist supporters were equally unfavorably inclined).[103] It is true that the extent of support of the Socialists in 1981 roughly corresponded with the extent of popular belief in government intervention in economic and educational matters; but, as noted earlier, it is equally true that French people have come to attach a greater value to economic security than to liberty.[104] At the same time, it is doubtful whether most of the French would accept unlimited nationalization of industry or even a radical leveling of income differentials.[105]

All the major parties or political camps have at times been forced by popular pressure or economic realities to depart from their ideological positions. The Gaullists were obliged to moderate their nationalism and, in the face of perceptions of Soviet threats, their anti-Americanism; the Giscardists embraced the welfare state more enthusiastically than their nucleus, the Republican party, had been willing to do in the past; many Communist politicians realized that a retrieval of the party's lost support might depend on a greater effort at distancing themselves from the Soviet Union; and fiscal pressures forced the Socialists to moderate their redistributive orientations.[106]

Given these compromises, French voters have increasingly made choices on the basis of personality and other nonprogrammatic (or noninstrumental) criteria—a development that has been accentuated by the growing importance of television during election campaigns. For several years, many French people supported Giscard not because they endorsed, or even understood, his "advanced liberalism" (which turned out to be a mixture of government intervention in the economy, a reliance on the market, and welfare-statism),[107] but because of the leadership qualities he was thought to possess. Many French voters on the Left initially preferred Michel Rocard to Mitterrand as the Socialist party's presidential candidate—not so much because they preferred his ideas, but for other reasons: the fact that Rocard was not overly identified with the Fourth Republic, was considered to be a highly intelligent technocrat, and was seen as a "winner."[108] In the late 1970s, many French voters were unenthusiastic about Mitterrand because of the tiredness and staleness he was thought to embody, just as they were impressed by the image of intelligence, reasonableness, and moderation he projected in early 1981. Mitterrand won the presidential election in 1988 not because he was classified as a Socialist but because he was judged to possess "presidential" qualities in greater measure than Chirac.[109] Chirac appears to come off equally unfavorably in comparison with Balladur, who (at the end of 1993) was viewed as more *"présidentiable"* because of his moderate views and his calm and conciliatory behavior.

Similarly, the decline of electoral support for the Communist Party in 1981 and thereafter should not be attributed entirely to the voters' rejection of the party's domestic and foreign policy orientations. Many voters were "turned off" by the buffoonery displayed by that party's leader, Marchais, during television appearances; others refused to vote for the party because they wished to enhance the electoral prospects of Mitterrand, and still others, because the party was seen as having become too strong![110]

THE ELECTORAL SYSTEM: ITS IMPACT
ON PARTIES AND VOTING BEHAVIOR

The electoral successes of a party have often had less to do with the strength of the party's social base or the credibility of its programmatic appeal than with the advantages or disadvantages derived from the electoral system. Under the proportional representation system that prevailed in the early years of the Fourth Republic, in theory, each party had equal chances. The antisystem PCF, the Catholic MRP, and the laic and republican SFIO each had approximately 20 to 25 percent of the parliamentary seats from 1945 to 1951, the number of mandates faithfully reflecting the proportion of the popular vote received by each party. In the parliamentary elections of 1951 and 1956, new electoral laws provided that if any party or combination of parties obtained an absolute majority of the vote in a multimember constituency, that party could take all the seats allocated to the constituency and divide them among various components of the electoral alliance on the basis of prearranged formulas. This measure was intended to favor the prosystem parties near the center—the SFIO, the Radicals, and the MRP—among which electoral alliances were easily possible, and to reduce the representation of those antisystem parties, the PCF and the RPF, that could not easily combine (*s'apparenter*) with "neighboring" parties. Thus, although in the election of 1951 the popular vote of the PCF was nearly twice as large as that of the MRP, the parliamentary representation of the PCF was only slightly larger.[111]

In 1958, France returned to the electoral system that had prevailed throughout most of the Third Republic: the single-member district system of elections with two rounds. Under that system, which is in force today, a candidate is elected on the first ballot if he or she has received an absolute majority of the votes; if no one has received such a majority, there is a runoff election a week later in which a candidate has merely to obtain a plurality of the votes. Since

1976, regulations have provided that any candidate who receives at least 12.5 percent of the total first-round votes in a constituency may stay in the race for the second round; but realism has demanded the withdrawal (*désistement*) of relatively weak candidates in favor of a candidate whose second-round prospects are better and whose party is not too distant ideologically.

Withdrawals are, in principle, based on prior agreements between parties on a national level. Thus, since the early 1970s, agreements between the PS and the PCF provided that whichever of the two parties got the larger first-round vote could expect the other to withdraw in its favor. As we have seen, before the 1993 parliamentary elections, the PS, conscious of its poor electoral outlook and of the loss of many of its traditional electorate to the environmentalist parties, had proposed mutual-withdrawal agreements with those parties but was rebuffed by their national leaders. Often, however, each party has made its own decision on the constituency level, and on many occasions the Socialist candidate, for reasons of personal ambition or of ideological distrust, has preferred either to remain in the race, thus enhancing the electoral chances of a conservative candidate, or to throw his or her support to a Radical or another "centrist" candidate. There have been similar withdrawal agreements between the Gaullist and the Giscardist camps. Because candidates of these two groups have often appealed to a similar electorate and have not differed radically from one another in regard to policy, the first round has served much the same purpose as a "primary" in the United States, in which candidate choices tend to be made on the basis of personality. In fact, the French have come increasingly to refer to the first election rounds as "*primaires*."

The method of electing the president is similar. If none of the several presidential candidates receives an absolute majority of all the votes on the first ballot, there is a second ballot two weeks later in which the two candidates with the largest number of first-ballot votes are the final competitors.[112]

Under the voting system as described above, the preelectoral aggregation process that has traditionally characterized Anglo-American politics has also been at work in France, with the result that the party preferences of French citizens are revealed even less precisely than before by the parliamentary representation of various political parties. The PCF's popular vote was relatively stable from 1951 to 1973, ranging from about 4 million to about 5.5 million, its registered membership remaining stable, too, at about 400,000; its Assembly representation, however, fluctuated from a high of 193 in 1946 to a low of 10 in 1958. Had the proportional representation system of the Fourth Republic been in effect in the November 1958 elections, the PCF would have received 88 seats instead of 10; the SFIO, 72 instead of 40; and the UNR, 82 instead of 189. Had the PR system of 1986 been continued for the Assembly elections of 1988, the PCF would have obtained 43 seats instead of 27; the PS and allies, 233 instead of 276; the FN 32 instead of 1; and the URC (the RPR and UDF combined), 267 instead of 271. Had such a system been in effect in 1993, the RPR and UDF would still have captured control of the Assembly, but the environmentalist parties and the National Front would also have gained seats.

Because there was a general conviction that the electoral system of the Fifth Republic was, until the mid-1970s, heavily weighted in favor of the Gaullists, most of the non-Gaullist parties favored a modification of that system. While in the opposition, the Radicals and Centrists advocated a return to proportional representation, as did the Socialists and Communists. Giscard too had favored such a return but upon becoming president, gave up the idea, especially after the creation of the UDF, a "presidential election machine" that, he hoped, would utilize the second-round bipolarization tendency to his advantage—in other words, keep the Radicals, Centrists, and Republicans in the fold and force the Gaullists to support him as he evoked the specter of a "socialo-communist" government in the event of his defeat.

As leader of the principal opposition party, Mitterrand had been on record as favoring a return to proportional representation, in the belief that under such a system the voters would be able to opt more freely for parties tied neither to the Gaullists nor the Communists, and hence that a democratic changing of the guard (*alternance*) from the Right to the Left would be facilitated. But when the elections of 1981 proved that the Socialists could capture the presidency and the Assembly, Mitterrand's position and that of most Socialists wavered and remained uncertain, especially in the wake of the cantonal elections of March 1982, in which the parties of the Right gained seats at the expense of the Left.

A new electoral law, passed in mid-1982, provided for a partial return to proportional representation for the election of municipal councils in towns of over 3,500 inhabitants[113] (see Table 4.7). The effects of that law, which was first applied in the municipal elections of 1983, were not entirely clear, except for Chirac's massive victory in the Paris elections and the losses incurred by the Socialists in Grenoble and several northern cities (losses that fall under the category of midterm rebuffs of the party in power).[114] The loss of seats to the majority party was not significant enough to be attributed to any specific factor; nonetheless, the law served in a sense as a precedent for a parliamentary act of 1985 that (temporarily) restored the proportional representation system on a national level.

As pointed out earlier, the Socialists revived the system of proportional representation for the elections of 1986 in the hope of reducing the scope of the anticipated victory of the Gaullists and Giscardists. Under the new system, which was based on department party lists—with seats allocated on the basis of the "highest average"[115]—the National Front was able to enter the Assembly and the Communist Party to maintain its presence in it with reasonable representation. As soon as the RPR and UDF gained control of the Assembly, they returned the country to the previous single-member system, but, as it turned out, neither by this change nor by gerrymandering of several constituencies were these parties able to secure victory in the 1988 legislative elections. In any case, it was possible for a "center" party—the CDS—to gain seats even under the restored system.

The French electoral system has been changed more often than the systems of other countries. At the beginning of the Fifth Republic, the abandonment of proportional representation was justified on the grounds that it encouraged the existence of a multiplicity of parties, including powerful extremist ones that threatened the republican regime. But today that threat is no longer credible: the

TABLE 4.7 Systems of election in France at national and subnational levels

Election	Method	Term of Office (Years)	Electoral Constituency
President of Republic	Two rounds; majority	7	Whole country
National Assembly	Two rounds; absolute majority 1st round; plurality 2nd round	5	Single-member constituency
Senate	Indirect; for départements providing 4 or fewer senators: two-round majority system; for départements providing more than 4, proportional representation by party lists[a]	9	Département
European Parliament	Proportional representation by party lists	5	Whole country
Regional councils[b]	Proportional representation by party lists	6	Département
Département council[c] (Conseil général)	Two rounds; absolute majority 1st round; plurality 2nd round	6	Canton
Municipal council[d]	1. For cities of fewer than 3,500 inhabitants: two-round majority "list" system;[e]	6	Commune (except for Paris, Lyons, Marseilles[f])
	2. For cities of more than 3,500: two rounds: 50% to winner; 50% proportional		

[a]"Staggered" elections; one-third of Senate is renewed every three years.
[b]Total number 26 (of which 4 are in overseas regions); size varies from 41 councilors (Limousin) to 197 (Ile-de-France).
[c]Total number 100 (96 metropolitan France, 4 overseas); size varies from 15 to 76. Total number of municipal councilors is 496,700 (1992).
[d]Total number (rounded off) 36,760 (1992); size varies from 9 (communes of under 100 inhabitants) to 163 (Paris).
[e]For cities of fewer than 2,500 there may be individual (i.e., nonlist) candidates.
[f]These cities are subdivided into *arrondissements*, each with its own council, which is elected at the same time as the municipal council. See Chapter 8.
SOURCE: Adapted from *Institutions et vie politique: Les notices* (Paris: Documentation Française, 1991), p. 70.

Communist Party has been marginalized and the National Front (apart from the fact that it has not been able to go beyond the threshold of 15 percent electoral support) has not openly challenged the legitimacy of the system. Because of these developments, there has been a growing demand for a return to proportional representation on the grounds of fairness. For obvious reasons, this demand continues to be made by all the minor parties ranging from Left to Right: the PCF, the CDS, the MRG, and the National Front. In recent years, there has been growing support for this demand within the PS as well.[116]

The effect of the electoral system on voter participation is a matter of controversy. It would be logical to assume that the frequency of elections on various levels, the diversity of electoral modalities, and the constant changes of election laws tend to discourage voter participation. Electoral abstention is relatively high with respect to bodies whose decision-making powers are weak (as in cantonal elections) or in cases where the policy impact is not clearly understood (as in European Parliament elections and in referenda). But abstention has been low in presidential and in all but the most recent parliamentary elections (see Tables 4.8 and 4.9).

The aggregative impact of the electoral system on political parties is much more obvious. However, the electoral system has not been the only factor influencing the performance of political parties. Under existing laws, the number of campaign posters that may be affixed to public buildings (printed at government

TABLE 4.8 Abstentions in elections (percentage of total votes cast)

Year		Presidential	National Assembly	European Parliament	Regional	Cantonal	Municipal
1958	(1)		22.89				
	(2)		31.28				
1962	(1)		31.28				
	(2)		27.92				
1965	(1)	15.25					
	(2)	15.67					
1967	(1)		19.08				
	(2)		31.27				
1968	(1)		20.04				
	(2)		22.17				
1969	(1)	22.41					
	(2)	31.14					
1973	(1)		18.76				
	(2)		18.11				
1974	(1)	15.77					
	(2)	12.66					
1978	(1)		16.68				
	(2)		15.34				
1979				39.29			
1981	(1)	18.91	29.13				
	(2)	14.14					
1982						31.57	
1983							21.63
1984				43.27			
1985							
1986			21.90		22.07		
1988	(1)	18.62	34.26			50.87	
	(2)	15.93	30.05				
1989				51.11			27.18
1992					31.30	29.34	
1993	(1)		30.80				
	(2)		32.44				

(1) First round.
(2) Second round.
SOURCE: *Le Monde* (1958–1993).

TABLE 4.9 National referenda (percentage of total votes cast)

Year	Referendum	Yes	No	Abstentions
1958	Adoption of Constitution	85.14	14.85	19.51
1961	Algerian self-determination	74.99	25.00	26.24
1962	Evian Agreements	90.80	9.19	24.66
	Direct election of president	62.25	37.74	23.02
1969	Reform of regions and Senate	47.58	52.41	19.86
1972	Enlargement of European Community	68.31	31.68	39.75
1988	Autonomy statute for New Caledonia	79.99	20.00	63.10
1992	Adoption of Treaty of Maastricht	51.05	48.95	29.49

SOURCE: Ministry of Interior.

expense) is limited, as is the number of hours (these are cost-free) allocated for party publicity on radio and television. A law enacted in 1988 (which updates legislation passed in 1964) limits the contributions of individuals and corporations for each candidate (to 2,000 and 50,000 francs, respectively). The law allows a maximum expenditure of 500,000 francs per parliamentary-election candidate and limits the expenditure for first-round presidential candidates to 120 million francs and for second-round candidates to 140 million francs.[117] All parliamentary candidates who have received at least 5 percent of the votes are reimbursed for 10 percent of their expenditures; and presidential candidates, for 25 percent. In addition, each presidential candidate may print and distribute one campaign brochure at government expense.[118] There is also a system of government subsidies to parties, under which (according to a law enacted in 1990) allocations to the various parties are based in equal measure on the votes received by them in the preceding national elections and the number of incumbent senators and deputies.[119] Under this formula, the government granted 9.10 francs (about $1.60) for each vote in the legislative elections of 1993. (At the end of that year, the government cut this subsidy by 10 percent.) Despite these contributions, parties are hard pressed to meet the cost of campaigning, which has constantly gone up, owing in part to the growing use of campaign aides. Because of the diminution of the number of registered party members, campaign costs can no longer be easily met with regular party funds (despite the regular contributions from their deputies[120]), a condition that has contributed to party corruption.

POLITICAL FRINGE GROUPS, CLUBS, AND MOVEMENTS

On the periphery of the system of major political parties are numerous political grouplets (*groupuscules*), minor parties, protest movements, and "clubs." Clubs occupy a position midway between parties and interest groups: Like parties, they are purveyors of ideologies and programs, and their leaders may harbor political (and occasionally electoral) ambitions. Like interest groups, they are not primarily interested in capturing political power but in influencing policies.

Clubs are part of an old tradition in France that goes back to the revolutions of 1789, 1848, and 1870. However, clubs were relatively weak in the Fourth Republic, probably because the proportional representation system then in operation made it easy to establish political parties. The club phenomenon reasserted itself during the Fifth Republic, when, in the face of the new electoral law that produced aggregative parties, the (temporary) mass support of de Gaulle, and the weakness of Parliament, parties proved inadequate vehicles for the promotion of specific ideas or programs. Thus, clubs arose for such purposes as criticizing the permissive society resulting from socioeconomic modernization, fighting Gaullism, combatting fascism, promoting laicism, spreading Catholic doctrine, advocating revolution, suggesting a variety of institutional and social reforms, and providing forums of discussion or instruments of political education.[121]

The differences or relationships among clubs, parties, movements, and interest groups are not always precise. Some clubs are structural components of parties or electoral coalitions, as is the case with *Perspectives et réalités* and the *Mouvement démocrate socialiste de France*, both of which are part of the UDF. Some clubs are instrumental in the creation of new parties or electoral coalitions: the *Convention des institutions républicaines* (CIR), which, in the 1960s, helped to create unity within the noncommunist Left and was eventually fused into the new *Parti socialiste*; in the early 1970s the *Fédération des réformateurs*, which attempted to unite the Radicals and Democratic-Centrists; and *Démocratie nouvelle* (founded in 1974), which helped to reunite the majority and opposition Centrists and to create the CDS. Some groups, although formally separate from political parties, are used by them to recruit supporters, such as the *Union des jeunes pour le progrès*, which tried to capture young people for Gaullism; or *Solidarité et liberté*, founded after the 1981 elections by individuals from the RPR and the UDF in order to fight socialism. Other clubs may be the political instruments of individual politicians: among these clubs were *Club 89*, a group of Parisian Gaullists supporting Chirac; the *Comité d'études pour un nouveau contrat social*, established in 1969 by Edgar Faure to create a "majority of ideas," to combine Radical-Socialism with Gaullism, and to keep Faure himself in the limelight; and *Réalisme, efficacité, espérance, liberté* (REEL), a group formed in 1987 to promote the presidential ambitions of Raymond Barre. Similarly, there are organizations that are combinations of clubs, parties, factions within parties, and "movements." Examples of such hybrids are *Refondations* (discussed above); *Alternative Rouge et Verte*, which was founded in 1989 as a fusion of the supporters of the presidential campaign of reform communist Pierre Juquin in 1988, dissident environmentalists, and militant feminists; and *France unie*, formed at the same time by Giscardist Jean-Pierre Soisson when he decided to support the Socialist government of Michel Rocard.[122] Two organizations that combine features of clubs and movements but have transformed themselves into political parties are Chevènement's *Mouvement des citoyens* and the *Mouvement action egalité*, formed in October 1992 as the political expression of poor urban slum dwellers.[123]

Still other clubs, although not formally associated with parties, have contained prominent politicians from various parties and have furnished them with ideas:

for example, the *Club Jean Moulin* (formed in 1958 and now defunct), which included left-wing Catholics, Radicals, and nonpolitical civil servants and published widely respected monographs on institutional reform; the right-wing *Club de l'Horloge*, created in 1974, which appeals to businessmen and higher technocrats (and maintains ties to the National Front);[124] *Echange et projets*, founded in 1973 by Jacques Delors (Mitterrand's first minister of economics) as a link between "productivist" Socialists and the business community; *Espaces 89*, a group of intellectuals who analyze sociopolitical questions from the perspective of the democratic Left; and the *Groupe de recherche et d'étude sur la civilisation européenne* (GRECE), an extreme right-wing, elitist, and racist "study group." The clubs have ranged in membership from several tens of thousands spread over various parts of France (e.g., *Perspectives et réalités*) to only a few dozen members located only in Paris. One of the newer clubs is *Témoignage gaulliste*, which was formed in 1989 by collaborators of de Gaulle who believe that the RPR has departed so far from Gaullism that they can no longer identify with that party.

In addition to the organizations just mentioned, there are numerous small parties. Among these are the CNIP, whose national support has been so diminished that (with barely a handful of deputies) it may become a mere club. In the municipal elections of March 1983 and 1989, there were candidates running under a bewildering variety of leftist, rightist, centrist, regionalist, and unclassifiable labels. Some of these parties have articulated ethnonational claims (e.g., the *Union démocratique bretonne)*; some were politically so extremist as to exist on the fringes of the political spectrum (but others, like the Trotskyist *Lutte ouvrière*, have run candidates for national office); some are single-issue parties, difficult to distinguish from interest groups (e.g., the Ecologists until a few years ago); and others have been promoters of purely local politicians and interests (e.g., the various *Groupes d'action locale*). One of the more interesting (and frivolous) parties was *Chasse, pêche, nature et traditions* (Hunting, fishing, nature, and traditions). Formed in 1989 as an anti-environmentalist party (and concentrated in the southwest), it captured about 4 percent of the vote in the European Parliament elections that year and in the regional elections of 1992 attracted the votes of a number of people who wished to convey their impatience with the mainstream parties. What distinguishes these parties from national ones is that their organization is weak, their membership ephemeral and unreliable, their electoral appeal limited, and their permanent impact on national politics negligible.

The most recent illustration of the tendency to the formation of ad hoc mini-parties was provided during the elections to the European Parliament in June 1994. On that occasion, candidates were put up under the following lists in addition to those of the mainstream parties and smaller existing parties: (1) *Pour l'Europe des travailleurs et la démocratie,* a pro-worker party hostile to a "capitalist" European Union; (2) *L'autre politique,* a leftist anti-Maastricht list headed by Jean-Pierre Chevènement; (3) *Sarajevo,* a list initiated by the philosopher Bernard-Henri Lévy to call attention to the European Community's abandonment of the Bosnian Muslims (and headed by Léon Schwartzenberg, a Left-Radical politician); (4) *Energie radicale,* an independent, leftist, pro-European list intended to promote the political fortunes of Bernard Tapie, a Left-Radical deputy (whose parliamentary immunity had been lifted when he was indicted for the misappropriation of funds); and (5) *L'autre Europe,* a conservative anti-Maastricht list led by Philippe de Villiers, a Gaullist deputy.

SUMMARY AND CONCLUSION

The major theme that emerges from the foregoing analysis is the evolution of the parties' relationships with one another in such a way that the party system as a whole has been transformed from one of centrifugal, or polarized, pluralism to one of centripetal, or moderate, pluralism.[125] There has been a gradual convergence of positive views about the existing constitutional system and a lessened divergence on policies, so that a changeover from a right-wing (or right-of-center) to a leftist (or left-of-center) coalition does not cause a disastrous jolt to the polity. The evolution from a multiparty system toward a four-party system divided into two camps (if one still counts the PCF and does not count the CDS as a separate camp) has been due to changes in the class system, the bipolarizing effect of the single-member constituency method of elections, the reduced relevance of old ideologies, and the factor of presidential coattails.

These changes have been accompanied by changes in the position and character of the individual parties that are components of the system: The Socialist party has become more centrist, more receptive to the orientations of the bourgeois segments of its electorate, less dogmatic, and less fearful of competition from the Communists.[126] The PCF (or what is left of it) has become more moderate or has for tactical reasons pretended to moderation. The Gaullist party, long bereft of its wartime hero, has become more institutionalized, whereas its ideology has become banalized and diffuse; and the UDF, itself the product of a presidential bandwagon effect and a reflection of a lessened antagonism between clerical and anticlerical elements, has become ideologically disoriented.

The emerging bipolarism has been manifested in a number of ways: (1) the increasing tendency, since the late 1970s, of each of the two major camps on the Right and Left to agree on single lists of candidates for the first rounds in many local and parliamentary constituencies, or (in the case of the PS and PCF) at least to better cooperation; (2) the acceptance of common platforms or "understandings"; and (3) more or less cohesive voting in the Assembly. At the same time, one should keep in mind that this bipolarization is neither smooth nor immune to rivalries and other fissiparous influences. Gaullist-Giscardist collaboration on one side, and Communist-Socialist relations on the other, are frequently forced, and politicians of each group continue to resent and distrust one another. Within each group, too, there are conflicts: among conservative, populist, romantic, and pragmatic Gaullists; between business-oriented and social reform–minded Giscardists; among Marxist, social-democratic, and "productivist" Socialists; and between accommodationist and ideologically uncompromising Communists. There are conflicts even between the two major ecologist parties:

the pragmatic and left-of-center *Génération écologie*, which has been close to the PS, and the more idealistic (and somewhat absolutist) Greens.

It is possible to envisage changes in the future that might sharpen these internal differences and arrest, or reverse, the current bipolar arrangement. An economic crisis or the personal failures of their leaders might discredit the recently victorious RPR and UDF, just as rising unemployment and political scandals discredited the Socialist party; the enfranchisement of poor immigrant workers might inject a new, dogmatic radicalism into the PCF and ruin what remains of its relationship with the PS; and a drastic decline in the purchasing power of indigenous workers or a sudden increase in urban violence might give renewed vigor to the National Front. It is also possible that clubs, movements, or other extraparliamentary forces might grow and upset the existing party lineup either by propelling themselves into Parliament or by influencing one or the other of the major parties to change its direction in ways that cannot be envisaged at this time.

NOTES

1. Jacques Fauvet, *La France déchirée* (Paris: Fayard, 1957), p. 22.
2. See Frank L. Wilson, *French Political Parties Under the Fifth Republic* (New York: Praeger, 1982), p. 22.
3. *Changer la vie: Programme de gouvernement du parti socialiste* (Paris: Flammarion, 1971).
4. For a discussion of the founding of the PS, see G. A. Codding Jr. and W. Safran, *Ideology and Politics: The Socialist Party of France* (Boulder, CO: Westview Press, 1979), pp. 211–234. On the evolution of the PS, see D. S. Bell and Byron Criddle, *The French Socialist Party: The Emergence of a Party of Government,* 2nd ed. (Oxford: Clarendon Press, 1988).
5. See Frédéric Bon, *Les Elections en France* (Paris: Seuil, 1978). According to this source (pp. 189 and 193), which bases itself on SOFRES polls, during the elections of 1974, 780,000 industrialists, big businessmen, and *cadres supérieurs* voted for Mitterrand, as did more than 1 million practicing Catholics (compared to the 1.3 million in the first three categories who voted for Giscard).
6. David Hanley, "Les Députés socialistes," *Pouvoirs* 20 (1982), 64.
7. Annie Kriegel, *Les Communistes* (Paris: Seuil, 1968), p. 15.
8. According to a poll conducted in 1976, only 33 percent of respondents believed that the PCF wanted to make a revolution if the time were opportune, while 43 percent were not opposed to PCF participation in government (as compared to 31 percent in 1964). Cited by Raymond Barrillon, "Une Nouvelle Visage," *Le Monde,* 3 February 1976.
9. Led by Jean Elleinstein, a codirector of the PCF's research bureau. See his "La Mutation nécessaire," *Le Monde,* 14 April 1978, and "Aller au fond des choses," *Le Monde,* 15 April 1978.
10. Led by Louis Althusser, a prominent Communist philosopher.
11. In the spring of 1980, *L'Express,* a weekly news magazine, revealed that Marchais had gone to work in Germany as a volunteer during World War II and not as a forced laborer, as he had been claiming.
12. See "Notre Espoir à 20 ans," *Tribune socialiste* 11 (March 1980), 1.

13. Except in the fall of 1980, when most of the party was inclined to support Rocard's short-lived attempt to become the standard bearer of the PS.
14. See *Mouvement des Radicaux de gauche*, présenté par Robert Fabre (Paris: Flash-Actualité-Marabout, 1977), for its standard orientations.
15. Bernard E. Brown, in his *Socialism of a Different Kind: Reshaping the Left in France* (Westport, CT: Greenwood Press, 1982), argues that since the mid-1970s, the PCF has rejected Stalinism, and the PS has refused to embrace social democracy (by opting for extensive nationalization), thus facilitating a PS-PCF convergence. Hindsight suggests that this interesting book may have been premature in its exaggeration of both the "Eurocommunization" of the PCF and the importance of the CERES faction in the PS.
16. In 1982, the PCF's real membership was estimated to be between 300,000 and 400,000, a decline of more than 25 percent in a two-year period. *Le Point*, 1 February 1982, pp. 42f.
17. For example, the group of Parisian Communists led by Paris city councilor Henri Fiszbin, which published its own anti-Marchais journal and had several thousand supporters.
18. But CGT-PCF "unity" was still officially maintained: In December 1981, a large public demonstration was held jointly against aspects of socioeconomic policy.
19. See "Les Primaires sauvages entre PS et PC," *Le Monde*, 26 February 1983.
20. Jean Mitoyen, *C'est dur d'être de gauche* (Paris: Syros, 1985), p. 75. On the euphoria of the new government and subsequent developments, see Julius W. Friend, *Seven Years in France: François Mitterrand and the Unintended Revolution, 1981–1988* (Boulder, CO: Westview Press, 1989).
21. For an interesting discussion of the political and economic pressures weighing on the Socialist government in its first two years, see Albert Lebacqz, *Les Socialists face à la crise* (Paris: Editions France-Empire, 1983).
22. See Michel Charzat, Ghislaine Toutain, and Jean-Pierre Chevènement, *Le CERES: Un Combat pour le socialisme* (Paris: Calmann-Lévy, 1975), for an authoritative statement of CERES ideas. CERES was founded by ENA graduates prominent in the Paris federation of the PS. For a more recent profile of the CERES activist, see David Hanley, *Keeping Left? CERES and the French Socialist Party* (Manchester: University of Manchester Press, 1986).
23. See *Le Monde*, 26 February 1983, pp. 6–8; "Congrès de Bourg-en-Bresse: contributions au débat," *Le Poing et la rose* 101–103 (June 1983); and Anne Chaussebourg, "Les Députés demandent une meilleure coordination et une information reciproque entre le gouvernement, le parti, et le groupe," *Le Monde*, 4 September 1983.
24. In 1971, UDR came to stand for *Union des démocrates pour la République*.
25. See Wilson, *French Political Parties*, pp. 126–134. For a concise analysis of the rise of Gaullism and its condition during the first decade of the Fifth Republic, see Jean Charlot, *The Gaullist Phenomenon* (New York: Praeger, 1971).
26. A clear expression of this "natalist" orientation is found in Michel Debré, *Lettre ouverte aux Français sur la reconquête de la France* (Paris: Albin Michel, 1980), esp. pp. 47–62.
27. In addition to Chirac, the list of Gaullist candidates included Marie-France Garaud, a lawyer who had been Chirac's major advisor during his premiership and had been a cofounder of the RPR but had quit the party in 1979, and Michel Debré, an intimate collaborator of the general.

28. At the same time, Chirac has tried to project the image of a person interested in selflessly rallying the people for their own socioeconomic welfare. See his *La Lueur de l'espérance* (Paris: La Table Ronde, 1978), esp. pp. 13–14. See also Albert Lebacqz, *Les Droites et les gauches sous la Ve République* (Paris: Editions France-Empire, 1984), pp. 147-159, which describes "Chiraquism" as a combination of Gaullist legitimism, pseudoliberalism, "neo-Bonapartism," and "*républicanisme d'autorité*." See also Thierry Desjardins, *Les Chiraquiens* (Paris: Table Ronde, 1986), for a portrait of 16 politicians who began to rally around Chirac—not so much for his Gaullism as for their optimistic assessment of his future.

29. A statement of Giscard's pragmatic and pluralistic thinking is his *Démocratie française* (Paris: Fayard, 1976), transl. as *French Democracy* (Garden City, NY: Doubleday, 1977), and his more recent *Deux Français sur trois* (Paris: Flammarion, 1984). Books written by others include the adulatory biography by Michel Bassi, *Valéry Giscard d'Estaing* (Paris: Grasset, 1968); Daniel Seguin, *Les Nouveaux Giscardiens* (Paris: Calmann-Lévy, 1979), a sympathetic discussion of personalities and of relations between Giscardists and Gaullists; and Olivier Todd, *La Marelle de Giscard* (Paris: Laffont, 1977), which stresses Giscard's alleged talents as political "prestidigitator." Books about the Giscard system include Roger-Gérard Schwartzenberg, *La Droite absolue* (Paris: Flammarion, 1981); and J. R. Frears, *France in the Giscard Presidency* (London: Allen & Unwin, 1981), a knowledgeable effort; and Anne Nourry and Michel Louvois, *Le Combat singulier* (Paris: Denoel, 1980), which concentrates on the convoluted relationship between Giscard and Chirac (and is hostile to both).

30. See Francis de Tarr, *The French Radical Party* (London: Oxford University Press, 1961). The author discusses the factionalism and resulting ideological confusions of the party.

31. For a study of the complicated relations among the Centrists, see William Safran, "Centrism in the Fifth Republic: An Attitude in Search of an Instrument," in William G. Andrews and Stanley Hoffmann, eds., *The Fifth Republic at Twenty* (Albany, NY: SUNY Press, 1981), pp. 123–145.

32. In 1959, Giscard was appointed secretary of state (i.e., junior minister) in the Finance Ministry and three years later, full minister of finance.

33. The group of cofounders and leaders of the RI (later, the Republican party) included Prince Michel Poniatowski, Count Michel d'Ornano, and Prince Jean de Broglie.

34. For René Rémond, author of *La Droite en France*, trans. as *The Right Wing in France from 1915 to de Gaulle,* 2nd ed. (Philadelphia: University of Pennsylvania Press, 1969), Gaullism, in its plebiscitary orientations and populist pretensions, represents the Bonapartist Right; and Giscardism, in its being based on middle-class (especially business) support, represents the Orléanist Right (i.e., evokes the reign of Louis-Philippe between 1830 and 1848, a reign allegedly noted for the self-enrichment propensities of the *grande bourgeoisie*). Another scholar, Colette Ysmal (author of "Nature et réalité de l'affrontement Giscard-Chirac," *Politique aujourd'hui* 3-4 [1978]: 11–23), rejects the notion that Giscardism represents the political Right. She argues that Giscardism is "liberal" in its quest for consensus and its belief in social and economic pluralism. But note that to many French politicians and intellectuals, "liberalism" (viewed in its economic aspect more frequently than its constitutional one) is by definition a right-wing ideology.

35. These included *Perspectives et réalités*, a club of businessmen, politicians, technocrats, and a few intellectuals, which had been an "idea-monger" for the Republican

Party; and the *Mouvement démocrate-socialiste de France* (MDSF), composed of anticommunist former Socialists and other supporters of Giscard.

36. Among them many farmers who were upset because of a steep decline in farm incomes; most of the Jewish electorate, who resented his pro-Arab policies; and environmentalists, who objected to his excessive reliance on nuclear power.

37. *Le Monde*, 31 August 1983.

38. Christine Fauvet-Mycia, "M. François Léotard reproche au CDS d'être tenté par d'autres alliances," *Le Monde*, 28–29 August 1983. See also *Le Monde*, 7 December 1982.

39. See Club de l'Horloge, *L'Identité de la France* (Paris: Albin Michel, 1985); Jean-Yves Le Gallou and Club de l'Horloge, *La Préférence nationale* (Paris: Albin Michel 1985); and Jean-Marie Le Pen, *Les Français d'abord* (Paris: Carrère-Michel Lafon, 1984).

40. See Jean-Pierre Garnier and Louis Janover, *La Deuxième Droite* (Paris: Laffont, 1986). According to this book, the National Front rejects both the capitalist and socialist ideologies, and therefore the traditional right-left cleavage, but advocates an approach to problems that takes into account the realities of the marketplace.

41. See Martin A. Schain, "The National Front in France and the Construction of Political Legitimacy," *West European Politics* 10:2 (April 1987), 229–252; Pierre Bréchon and Subrata Kumar Mitra, "The National Front in France: The Emergence of an Extreme Right Protest Movement," *Comparative Politics* 25:1 (October 1992), 63–82; and William Safran, "The National Front in France: From Lunatic Fringe to Limited Respectability," in Peter H. Merkl and Leonard Weinberg, eds., *Encounters with the Contemporary Radical Right* (Boulder, CO, & Oxford: Westview Press, 1993), pp. 19–49. See also Michael S. Lewis-Beck, "French Electoral Theory: The National Front Test," *Electoral Studies* 12:2 (1993), 112–127. Lewis-Beck emphasizes the "materialist" values of the National Front.

42. The *Rénovateurs*, who were supported by an odd assortment of Trotskyists, anti-Stalinists, and elements of the PSU, put their stress on the environment, women's rights, education, and liberal naturalization laws. At the end of 1988, the Reform Communists transformed themselves into a *groupuscule*, the *Nouvelle gauche*, which was to be a "green and red" movement and was to be joined by the last remnants of the PSU after the latter had dissolved. See *Le Monde*, 20 December 1988.

43. There were agreements in 554 constituencies involving 572 candidates put up by the URC. Of these 283 were from RPR, 278 from UDF, 7 from CNIP, and 4 from various smaller conservative parties. But this implied some duplication: In 18 constituencies, URC endorsed both RPR and UDF candidates, who were to "face off" in the first round for the right to appear in the second round.

44. He replaced Jean Lecanuet, a senator from Rouen, who had led the UDF since its founding in 1978.

45. The National Front did manage to seat a single deputy (Yann Piat) from a Bouches-du-Rhône constituency (Marseilles area), but she was expelled from the party soon thereafter for publicly taking exception to a remark by Le Pen that the gas chambers used by the Nazis to liquidate Jews were a mere "detail of history." In November 1989, the National Front regained a seat in the Assembly when its candidate, Marie-France Stirbois (the widow of the party's second in command), won in a by-election in Dreux.

46. Léotard (a politician in his forties whose relationship with Chirac was strained) did not join the "young Turks" or rejuvenators; he reportedly sided with the "old guard" because he was promised that he would inherit the leadership of the UDF from Giscard if the latter succeeded in becoming the president of the European Parliament.

See "Giscard-Chirac: Le Crépuscule des deux?" *Le Point*, 10 April 1989, pp. 42–43. See also "Droite: Le Plan secret des rénovateurs," *Le Point*, 17 April 1989, pp. 42–49. At the same time, a liaison (*intergroup*) including the RPR, UDF, *and* Centrists (UDC) was formed in the Assembly, largely for the purpose of restraining the rejuvenators.

47. Daniel Carton, "La Résurrection de M. Giscard d'Estaing," *Le Monde*, 20 June 1989.

48. Except for a few Alsatian constituencies, Mulhouse and Colmar, for example; and Breton ones, for example, Quimper and St. Brieuc.

49. The platform of the Ecologists in 1981 included, inter alia, a wider use of the popular referendum, a return to proportional representation, the grant of increased power to mayors, the reduction of the workweek to 35 hours, and a boycott of South Africa.

50. See Parti écologiste, Les Verts: *Valeurs, principes et propositions des Verts*, St. Brieuc, November 1991.

51. Because of Lalonde's socialist orientations and Waechter's "openness" toward selective support of FN politicians on local levels, some cynical French observers distinguished between the "red" Greens and the "brown" Greens (or *"écolos fachos"*).

52. He was widely thought to have mishandled French policy with respect to German reunification and misjudged developments in the Soviet Union; he failed to prevent the breakup of Yugoslavia, to change GATT rules, to influence Middle East negotiations, and to exert significant influence in post-Communist Eastern Europe.

53. Jean-Michel Apathie, "Le PS face à son identité perdue," *Revue politique et parlementaire*, 95 année, no. 964 (March–April 1993), 64–66.

54. For an analysis of the "big bang" speech, see Alain Bergounioux and Gérard Grunberg, "Quel refondation pour le socialisme français?" *Le Monde*, 3 March 1993.

55. For the text of the televised speech, see *Le Monde*, 20 February 1993, pp. 10-11.

56. Patrick Jarreau, "Un Entretien avec M. Chevènement," *Le Monde*, 3 March 1993.

57. *Le Monde*, 27 April 1993, p. 7.

58. See Serge Halimi, "Le Parti socialiste au bout de soufle," *French Politics and Society* 10:4 (Fall 1992), 28.

59. *Le Monde*, 21 February 1991, p. 10. See also Chevènement's own (self-serving) political statement, *Le Temps des citoyens* (Paris: Editions du Rocher, 1993), in which he criticizes France's "capitulation to the European Union and to the U.S.A. and the PS's sellout to capitalism and the abandonment of its leftist vocation."

60. *Le Monde*, 4-5 July 1993, p. 8.

61. In anticipation of the Socialists' defeat, Mitterrand had apparently decided on his noninvolvement even before the elections took place. See Catherine Pégard, "L'Enigme Mitterrand," *Le Point*, 27 March 1993, pp. 21-23.

62. "Les Courants majoritaires du PS préconisent la rupture avec l'orthodoxie économique," *Le Monde*, 23 July 1993.

63. Including ministers Georgina Dufoix (the distribution of contaminated blood) and Roland Dumas (the Habbash affair and improper gifts from the family of a Middle Eastern dictator), Bérégovoy (an interest-free loan), and former Assembly speaker Emmanuelli (the "Urba" affair, involving funds for the PS). See Michel Poniatowski, *La Catastrophe socialiste* (Paris: Bertrand, 1991), and the more neutral Alain Bergounioux and Gérard Grunberg, *Le Long Remords du pouvoir: Le Parti socialiste français* (Paris: Fayard 1993).

64. Guy Bedos, quoted by Jules W. Friend, "Mitterrand's Legatee: The French Socialist Party in 1993," *French Politics and Society* 11:3 (Summer 1993), 1-11.

65. See Patrick Jarreau, "M. Rocard renforce son autorité," *Le Monde*, 6 July 1993. Tapie had been implicated in scandals involving the soccer team (OM-Marseille) he owned.

Relations deteriorated further several months later when Socialist deputies did not fight hard enough to prevent the lifting of Tapie's parliamentary immunity.

66. See Jean-Marie Colombani, "Michel Rocard contre le rocardisme," *Le Monde*, 30 June 1993.

67. For a detailed discussion, see George Ross, "Party Decline and Changing Party Systems: France and the French Communist Party," *Comparative Politics* 25:1 (October 1992), 43-62.

68. See Denis Jeambar, "Dinosaurus Marchais," *Le Point*, 2 October 1993; and *Le Monde*, 30 October 1993, p. 9.

69. Among them Jack Lang, who functioned as minister of culture for a decade, and Bernard Kouchner, minister in charge of humanitarian action.

70. See Pierre Bauby, "Les Législatives 1993 en perspective," *Revue politique et parlementaire* 95:964 (March-April 1993), 59-63.

71. There were mutual withdrawals in only five districts.

72. The basic principle of a *primary* had been adopted in 1990 as part of the founding agreement of the UPF, but the technicalities were not fully worked out.

73. Gilles Paris, "Les Elus du CDS s'inquiètent du silence de leurs ministres," *Le Monde*, 18 November 1993.

74. In the end, Dominique Baudis, the mayor of Toulouse and a UDF politician identified with the CDS, was chosen with the reluctant support of the RPR.

75. See Olivier Biffaud, "La Stratégie chiraquienne de la RPR," *Le Monde*, 6 October 1993.

76. Public-opinion polls for September-November 1993, reported by *Antenne 2*.

77. Later that year, Lalonde aligned himself on the side of Barre and Giscard—and against Balladur and Mitterrand—with respect to their positions on the GATT negotiations. At about the same time, however, he accepted an offer from Balladur to head a "study mission" on the environmental aspects of foreign trade.

78. Presumably this would involve a third ecologist party as well, the *Verts indépendants*.

79. This was especially true of the younger politicians (like Michel Noir, mayor of Lyons) and of the entire CDS.

80. See Nonna Mayer and Henri Rey, "Avancée electorale, isolement politique du Front national," *Revue politique et parlementaire*, 95:964 (March-April 1993), 42-48.

81. For an analysis of the repugnant aspects of Le Pen and his movement and of the anti-Le Pen mobilization, see Nonna Mayer and Pascal Perrineau, "La Puissance et le rejet ou le lepenisme dans l'opinion," SOFRES, *L'Etat de l'opinion 1993*, pp. 63-78.

82. See *Année politique 1991*, pp. 56 and 73. Giscard's article, which stressed kinship (as opposed to naturalization) for entitlement to citizenship, appeared in *Figaro-Magazine*, 21 September 1991.

83. See Jean Noli, "L'Après-Le Pen commence," *Le Point*, 17 April 1993, p. 37.

84. Robert de Jouvenel, *La République des camarades*, 8th ed. (Paris: Grasset, 1914), p. 17.

85. Catherine Pégard, "Faut-il avoir peur de Le Pen?" *Le Point*, 13 February 1984, p. 38.

86. Conversely, Socialist Jacques Delors, a former finance minister (and now president of the Commission of the European Union), said in an interview several months before the 1988 elections that he could see himself as a prime minister under a President Barre, Rocard, or Mitterrand. *Le Monde*, 14 November 1987.

87. This practice is probably facilitated by the semicircular arrangement of the parliamentary chambers, in which a deputy's slight move to the right or left is not nearly so dramatic an exercise as "crossing the aisle" in the British House of Commons.

88. There is also the case of Maurice Duverger, the prominent political scientist who, having been rejected as a candidate for the European Parliament in 1989 by the PS, arranged to have himself put on the slate of the Italian Communist party! The PS had originally wanted to put Duverger on its list, but had changed its mind as a result of letters of protest that recalled his pro-Vichy activities during the Occupation. *Le Point*, 8 May 1989, p. 65.

89. Mitterrand was a leader of the *Union démocratique et socialiste de la Résistance* (UDSR), a pro-Socialist but independent party of former Resistance members; the *Convention des institutions républicaines* (CIR), a collection of democratic-Socialist clubs in the early and middle 1960s; the FGDS (1965–1969), the democratic leftist electoral federation; and finally, the Socialist party—all of these different vehicles for an essentially consistent ideological-tactical position. On Mitterrand's maneuverings from the Fourth Republic on, see Cathérine Nay, *Le Noir et le rouge* (Paris: Grasset, 1984), and her more recent but equally critical *Les Sept Mitterrand ou les méta-morphoses d'un septennat* (Paris: Grasset, 1988).

90. See Alain Rollat, "Les Mitterrandistes, nouveaux partageux," *Le Monde*, 28 July 1989.

91. The Right has argued that the Muslims adhere to a religion that does not accept the principle of separation of religion and state and hence that their massive presence may undermine the principles of French republicanism.

92. Emmanuel Todd, *La Nouvelle France* (Paris: Seuil, 1988), p. 11.

93. Emmanuel Todd, in *Le Point*, 12 June 1989, pp. 44–45.

94. Alain Duhamel, in *Le Complexe d'Astérix* (Paris: Gallimard, 1985), Chapter 1.

95. See Alain Touraine, "Gauche-Droite," *Le Monde*, 8 July 1993; Alain Duhamel, "Les Deux Droites," *Le Point*, 11 September 1993, p. 23; and Olivier Duhamel and Jérôme Jaffré, "Un Paysage politique dévasté," SOFRES, *L'Etat de l'opinion 1993*, pp. 11–17.

96. Oliver Duhamel and Gérard Grunberg, "Référendum: Les Dix France," SOFRES, *L'Etat de l'opinion 1993*, pp. 79–86.

97. In a postelection poll conducted by SOFRES, 54 percent of the respondents in general (and 41 percent of PS sympathizers) thought that the PS had become exhausted; 43 percent (and 33 percent) that it no longer functioned except during election campaigns; 40 percent (and 44 percent) that it is no longer really on the Left; 37 percent (and 26 percent) that it is concerned only with its internal problems; and 31 percent (and 28 percent) that it is no longer interested in changing society. Patrick Jarreau, "La Gauche désincarnée," *Le Monde*, 7 October 1993.

98. Statistics on party memberships are notoriously unreliable because each party tends, for the sake of "boosterism," to provide inflated statistics. But a combination of sources suggest that (with the possible exception of the RPR) the major political parties have lost about half their dues-paying members in the past decade.

99. See Jacques Capdevielle, Elisabeth Dupoirier, Gérard Grunberg, Etienne Schweisguth, and Colette Ysmal, *France de gauche, vote à droite* (Paris: Presses de la Fondation Nationale des Sciences Politiques, 1981), pp. 217–227, and Table 122.

100. IFRES exit poll of 24 April 1988, cited in Philippe Habert and Colette Ysmal, eds., *L'Election présidentielle 1988* (Paris: Le Figaro/Etudes Politiques, 1988), p. 31.

101. According to a *SOFRES* poll, 56 percent of respondents in November 1989 (compared to 33 percent in March 1981) considered the Right-Left labels irrelevant to the positions of parties and politicians. *Le Point*, 27 November 1989, pp. 44–45.

102. IFOP, SOFRES, and BVA polls at the end of September 1993, reported by *Antenne 2*. See also *Figaro Magazine*, 2 October; *Le Monde*, 6 October; and *Paris Match*, 7 October 1993.

103. In another poll (Capdevielle, *France de gauche, vote à droite,* Table 31, p. 257), 8 percent of PCF voters classified themselves as belonging to the Center or Center-Right on an ideological spectrum running from extreme Left to extreme Right; 19 percent of PS-MRG voters classified themselves as belonging in the Center and 4 percent in the Center-Right; 10 percent of the PSU electorate labeled itself as being in the Center, and 3 percent in the Center-Right; and 45 percent of UDF voters considered themselves as belonging to the Center or Center-Left (as contrasted with 37 percent of Gaullist voters who labeled themselves as Centrist or Center-Left!). These outcomes raise some questions regarding the existence of sufficiently objective criteria for ideological self-classification.

104. According to a public-opinion poll conducted in the beginning of 1981 by the *Institut français de démoscopie,* when asked to choose between security and liberty, 26.4 percent of the respondents chose the former and 70.3 percent, the latter. *Le Monde (Dimanche),* 1 March 1981, p. xviii.

105. A poll conducted on 24 April 1988 on the "ideological profile" of the Right and the Left revealed that 78 percent of those identified as being on the Left and 51 percent of those identified as being on the Right had a positive view concerning the right to strike. Other positive views were as follows: the role of trade unions: Left, 69 percent, Right, 41 percent; nationalization: Left, 57 percent, Right, 33 percent; privatizations: Left, 29 percent, Right, 70 percent; employers: Left, 38 percent, Right, 71 percent; private schools: Left, 36 percent, Right, 76 percent. Based on Elisabeth Dupoirier, "Changement et persistance du clivage gauche-droite en 1988," *Le Monde, Dossiers et Documents, L'Election présidentielle* 1988, p. 49.

106. One scholar, Alain Leroux, in *La France des quatre pouvoirs* (Paris: PUF, 1989), has argued that since 1981, all major parties in France have abandoned programmatic orientations in favor of different kinds of pragmatism: political (in the case of the PS); charismatic (the Gaullists); technocratic (Giscardists); and populist (Le Pen).

107. For instance, during Giscard's presidency, deductions of all kinds (*prélèvements obligatoires*) went up from 36.3 percent of GNP in 1974 to 41.6 percent in 1980; investments in nationalized industries went up from 16.9 percent of total industrial investment in 1974 to 27 percent in 1981. Denis Jeambar, "La Pieuvre étatique," *Le Point,* 16-22 February 1981, pp. 36-42.

108. According to Alain Touraine, "Rocardism [could] not be explained in terms of its ideological content" but rather in terms of a variety of favorable (though conflicting) images. Cited in Hervé Hamon and Patrick Rotman, *L'Effet Rocard* (Paris: Stock, 1980), p. 337.

109. According to a SOFRES poll in February/March 1988 concerning the qualities of the three major presidential candidates, Mitterrand (with 40 percent) was judged more competent than Chirac (with 30 percent) while Chirac (with 26 percent) was judged as more aggressive than Mitterrand (with 3 percent). On the eve of the presidential elections a year later, the gap between the two had widened. SOFRES, *L'Etat de l'opinion 1989* (Paris: Seuil, 1989), pp. 102-103. Note, however, that there have been great fluctuations in Mitterrand's popularity as president: from 48 percent in 1981 to 32 percent in 1984, 51 percent in 1986, 56 percent just before the 1988 elections, 60 percent in 1989, between 30 and 40 percent in 1992, about 35 percent just before the 1993 elections, and 47 percent in August 1993, that is, four months after the parliamentary elections.

110. See Jérôme Jaffré, "France de gauche, vote à gauche," *Pouvoirs* 20 (1982), 13.

111. For a treatment of the technicalities of electoral systems from the Third to the Fifth Republics, see Edmond Jouve, ed., *Modes de scrutin et systèmes électoraux*, Documents d'Etudes, Droit constitutionnel et institutions politiques no. 1.05, nouvelle édition (Paris: Documentation Française, 1986).

112. Various details concerning presidential candidacies are established by law, which provides that candidates must be at least 23 years old, must not have been convicted of a felony, and must have been placed in nomination with the signatures of 500 politicians (deputies, senators, general councilors, or mayors). Since 1981, naturalized citizens are eligible for candidacy for the presidency.

113. The law provides for a mixed single-member PR system with two ballots. The party list that receives an absolute majority of the votes on the first ballot gets 50 percent of all seats plus one, the remainder of the seats being divided proportionally among all lists that receive at least 5 percent of the vote. In this way, a majority party or coalition is doubly rewarded, but minor parties obtain *some* representation. See *Le Monde, Dossiers et Documents, Les Elections municipales de mars 1983*, March 1983, pp. 20-23.

114. See John Frears, "1981-1986," in Howard Penniman, ed., *France at the Polls, 1981 and 1986* (Durham, NC: Duke University Press, 1988), pp. 205-207.

115. For a detailed description of the "highest average" system, see Jouve, *Modes de scrutin*, pp. 7-8.

116. See *Année politique 1991*, pp. 78-79. The Vedel Commission on constitutional reform, in its report in February 1993, suggested a possible compromise: electing 10 percent of the Assembly deputies on the basis of proportional representation. Under such a system (roughly modeled on that of the German Federal Republic) each voter would be able to cast two ballots, one for an individual candidate as at present and one for a party list.

117. In December 1993 the Constitutional Council annulled the election to Parliament of Jack Lang, mayor of Blois and minister of culture and education in the outgoing Socialist government, because he had spent 589,000 francs. He was not permitted to run for the Assembly again until March 1994, that is, a year after his abortive election.

118. A candidate for a seat in Parliament must put down a deposit of 1,000 francs for advertising, which is reimbursed if he or she gets a minimum of 5 percent of the vote.

119. There were two qualifications: A party had to put up at least 50 candidates and had to receive at least 5 percent of the national popular vote. The second qualification was nullified by the Constitutional Council in the interest of protecting the smaller parties. See Thierry Bréhier, "Le Financement des partis," *Le Monde*, 10 November 1993. On the evolution of party financing patterns, see André Campana, *L'Argent secret: Le Financement des partis politiques et des campagnes électorales* (Paris: Arthaud, 1976), and Thomas Drysch, "The New French System of Political Finance," in Arthur B. Gunlicks, ed., *Campaign and Party Finance in North America and Western Europe* (Boulder, CO: Westview, 1993), pp. 155-177.

120. Deputies must give up part of their salaries to their parties. Communist deputies transfer their entire salaries to the party, which returns less than 30 percent to them. In contrast, Socialist deputies (in 1988) gave up only 8,000 francs.

121. Frank L. Wilson, "The Club Phenomenon in France," *Comparative Politics* 3 (July 1971): 517-528. For a historical treatment, see Jean-André Faucher, *Les Clubs politiques en France* (Paris: Didier, 1965). See also Janine Mussuz, *Les Clubs et la*

politique (Paris: Colin, 1970). Mussuz distinguishes between clubs that are *sociétés de réflexion* and those engaging in *combat politique*.

122. In 1992, Soisson formed a new mini-party, the *Mouvement réformateur* (not to be confused with a similar group created in the early 1970s).

123. The founder of this movement is Harlem Désir, former leader of *SOS-Racisme*. After being replaced as leader, Désir left the party, joined *Génération écologie*, and subsequently (in 1993) became a member of the Socialist party.

124. The *Club de l'Horloge* also maintains links to the Heritage Foundation, a conservative "think tank" in the United States.

125. For a discussion of these different pluralisms, see Giovanni Sartori, *Parties and Party Systems* (Cambridge, U.K.: Cambridge University Press, 1976), esp. pp. 131–145.

126. On the "postsocialism" of the PS, see Alain Touraine, *L'Après-socialisme* (Paris: Grasset, 1980), and the much more critical book by Alain Peyrefitte, *Quand la rose se fanera* (Paris: Plon, 1983). More recent studies include Jean Poperen, *Socialistes, la chute finale?* (Paris: Plon, 1993), written by a left-oriented insider; and Marc Sadoun, *De la démocratie française: Essai sur le socialisme* (Gallimard, 1993), a political scientist who argues that the PS adapted its rhetoric too readily to that of the PCF although it was unable to produce results expected by the working class.

chapter 5

Interest Groups

$\mathbf{I}$t is only natural that in a country like France, with its social and economic complexities, interest groups should have a significant place. At present, there are thousands of associations, ranging from trade unions and business organizations with large memberships to small, ideologically exclusive groups of students, and from nationally organized professional groups to purely local fellowships.[1] From the Third Republic on, interest groups have played an important part in shaping political attitudes, in policy formulation, and even in the support of republican institutions. Groups have been involved politically not only through their (more or less American-style) "lobbying" activities but also through the linkage of their leadership to the formal decision-making organs, their alliance with political parties, and their direct "colonization" of Parliament and the civil service.

TRADE UNIONS

Among the most important interest groups from the point of view of age, well-established connections to parties, mass membership, and the ability to mobilize support for or against government policies are the trade unions. The oldest trade union "umbrella" organization, the General Confederation of Labor (*Confédération générale du travail*—CGT), was founded in 1895. As a union of anarcho-syndicalist, Marxist, and revolutionary inspiration, it was as much concerned with general political goals (e.g., the restructuring of the whole political system) as with bread-and-butter issues. After World War I, workers inspired by Catholic principles split from the CGT to form their own union, the French Confederation of Christian Workers (*Confédération française des travailleurs chrétiens*—CFTC). In 1947, many workers who disliked the growing dependence of the CGT

135

on the Communist Party and the union's preoccupation with politically inspired general strikes created a new organization, the Workers' Force (*Confédération générale du travail-Force ouvrière*—FO). The CGT was by far the largest union in the 1960s and 1970s, and despite the loss of about half of its membership in the past several years, it remains powerful and its present membership has been estimated to be between 600,000 and 1 million. Although only about one-fourth of its members are Communists, the fact that most of its top leaders have also been prominent in the PCF has often made the CGT appear like an obedient "transmission belt" for the party.[2] The FO has about 500,000 members; during the Fourth Republic, it was a significant union because many of its members (and some of its leaders) were ideologically linked to the Socialist party (SFIO). Unlike the CGT, the FO firmly supported the regime and was convinced that benefits could be gained for workers through collective bargaining and lobbying. The FO has approximated the Anglo-American type of trade union in its acceptance of the (capitalist) political system, its avoidance of dogmatic approaches to labor-management relations, and its staunch anticommunism.

The CFTC was closely allied to the Christian Democratic party (MRP). This alliance, coupled with the CFTC's rejection of the class struggle and the deeply held conviction that "man does not live by bread alone," enabled that union to recruit many traditionalist members of the working class. But the CFTC lacked dynamism and was in danger of losing much of its membership to the CGT, which never tired of pointing out that clericalism could not be credibly combined with the promotion of workers' interests. In response to this claim, the bulk of the CFTC's membership and leadership "deconfessionalized" the union in the 1960s and renamed it the French Democratic Confederation of Labor (*Confédération française démocratique du travail*—CFDT). The bylaws of the CFDT do not mention Christianity but merely refer to man's "spiritual needs." The persistence of a vestigial Catholicism in the CFDT is indicated by a continuing tolerance for the maintenance of government support for a parallel parochial school system.[3] A rump of the old CFTC remains in existence, with about 100,000 members. The CFDT, whose membership is estimated at between 500,000 and 700,000, has become the second-largest trade union federation.[4] In the late 1960s, this union began an ideological evolution that gradually led to its endorsing three principles: the nationalization of the means of production; democratic planning; and factory self-management (*autogestion*).[5] These positions brought most of the CFDT's leadership, and much of its membership, close to the Socialist party. The existence of several ideologically fragmented trade unions has made for a certain amount of competition, which has often forced one or another union to adopt radical rhetoric in order to appeal to potential members, to keep its own members from deserting, or otherwise to trump its rivals.[6]

Ideological conflict has not been the only factor in the fragmentation of the employee sector. In France, as elsewhere in Western Europe, the white-collar segment has organized separately in order to maintain its status distinction. The *Confédération générale des cadres* (CGC) is such a white-collar union, and it counts among its members supervisory or middle-level managerial office personnel and technicians. Not all white-collar employees are in the CGC; many are in fact found within the three major trade union federations. The latter, in order to keep the white-collar elements within their ranks, have insisted that salary differentials between white- and blue-collar workers (which have favored the former) ought to be retained; this is true even of the CGT, which has tried to combine its egalitarian ideology with opposition to a policy of complete leveling of wages. One must be careful, however, not to exaggerate the meaning, or the political implications, of the distinctions between blue- and white-collar employees, as differences in outlook exist within the white-collar sector as well.[7]

The prospect of unity among the various trade unions is uncertain. During Gaullist-Giscardist rule, the ideological divisions among the unions, which had been exacerbated by their relationships to different "patron" parties, had began to weaken, in part because the representation of leftist parties in Parliament had declined, and in part because Parliament, the traditional arena for the promotion of labor interests, had become a less effective decision maker. This situation provided an incentive to the unions to be self-reliant and to combine forces for the promotion of their common interests. All major industrial unions have shared a commitment to higher wages, expanded fringe benefits, higher levels of public welfare spending, more secure protection of the right to organize in the factories, the reform of the tax system, and a general hostility to Gaullism and Giscardism.

However, there has been disagreement on important matters. Although all three industrial unions have favored *some* form of factory democracy, the CFDT had been most insistent about promoting worker self-management, the CGT has been hostile to the idea, and the FO indifferent to it. There have also been differences in approach to general politics, with the CGT and CFDT favoring direct political involvement and the search for parliamentary and other allies, and the FO proclaiming its "independence" from political forces. The commonalities have resulted in (more or less ritualistic) interunion collaboration, especially between the CGT and CFDT, as in joint demonstrations, interunion bargaining committees (e.g., in nationalized industries), common deputations to government officials, common demands, and sometimes common strikes. But the ideological diversities among unions and the personal rivalries among their leaders have been persistent and have been reflected in competing union lists in factory council and social security elections, in the union leaders' periodic trading of insults, and in the failure to promote organizational mergers. The elections to social security boards and labor tribunals, which take place every three years, and (to a lesser extent) the plant committee elections, which occur every two years, provide rough indicators of relative union support among the rank and file.

In several polls conducted since the early 1970s among workers, most of the respondents felt that unions should not mix in politics, but such a view has not been dominant among union leaders (except those of the FO). On the contrary, union leaders have come out clearly in favor of leftist political candidates and have worked actively for their election, although the support of such candidates has been neither unified nor consistent, nor has it necessarily mirrored the preferences of rank-and-file members.[8] In the presidential contest of 1981 (first round), however, the unions were divided: The CGT came out publicly for the Communist candidate, Marchais; the CFDT for Mitterrand; the CFTC for Giscard; and the FO for no one in particular.

A politically activist approach by unions has been unavoidable because "autonomous bargaining" in the Anglo-American sense—leading to collective contracts with employers—has not been particularly effective. The ideological splits in the labor movement have weakened the trade unions' position in bargaining with a relatively unified employer. For factories in which workers' membership is split among several unions, the National Labor Relations Board (*Commission nationale de la négociation collective*—CNNC), which includes union and management representatives, may in theory certify one union as the bargaining agent for all the workers in the plant; in practice, however, the workers are represented at the bargaining table by several unions. There is no union shop in France, and until the early 1980s, union recruiting activities on the factory level were forbidden; if workers wished to join a union, they had to register at a local branch office. Unlike the system in the United States, there is in France no automatic payroll checkoff system; dues have had to be collected (with dismal success) by the local union officials. As a result, less that 15 percent of the workers are unionized, and the union coffers have been relatively empty. Since 1971, collective bargaining at the plant level has been legalized, but the local unions have been so weak that they have tended to rely on national union-management agreements (*accords-cadres*). And because these agreements have often involved the government as a third party, the latter has in effect been a conegotiator whose goodwill is crucial.

In the past, conservative governments often discriminated against the unions because they felt that the political system might be threatened by the unions' historic "revolutionary" ideology; for their part, the unions could not easily replace their belief in the politics of *confrontation* by a politics of *accommodation* (i.e., a businesslike bargaining outlook) so long as they were convinced that bargaining opportunities and fruitful access to government were restricted. Under presidents Pompidou and Giscard, unions resented the government because in its preoccupation with productivity, it did little to moderate the traditional resistance of organized business to collective bargaining (and the tendency of employers to renege on collective contracts).

For these reasons, the election of a Socialist president and a Socialist Assembly majority in 1981 was welcomed by most of the unions. Their optimism was not misplaced: During the Socialists' first year in power, they raised the wages of workers (especially the lowest earners) significantly; expanded social security benefits; increased the taxes on the incomes of wealthy individuals and firms; and introduced legislation (the Auroux Laws) that made it obligatory for management and workers to conduct wage negotiations annually at the plant level and strengthened the unions' representation in factory councils.[9] In addition, a number of union officials were given ministerial posts or were placed on the staffs of individual ministers.

Unfortunately, these legal improvements were counterbalanced by growing unemployment and the loss of jobs, particularly in the "smokestack" industries in which unions had been relatively strong. It has even been argued that the unions have been worse off under Mitterrand's Socialist governments than under previous (Gaullist-Giscardist) governments, the leaders of which were sensitive to charges that their policies were "antisocial."[10] The Socialist government's austerity program, put into effect early in 1983, could not be attributed to any inherently antisocial attitudes on its part, especially in view of the generosity of the social reforms just cited. However, the nationalization policies initiated by the Socialist government promised to have a restrictive effect on the unions' freedom of action, because it is more difficult to denounce (and make tough claims against) the state than against a private employer. Although under the Mauroy government the major unions had their separate axes to grind, the unions articulated only relatively low-key criticisms of government policy, because they did not wish to give too much ammunition to the Gaullist-Giscardist opposition parties. Under the (post-cohabitation) Socialist governments of Rocard, Cresson, and Bérégovoy too, the unions' power was limited by three major factors: the frequent closing of factories, the declining public image of the unions,[11] and pressures on the government to promote productivity and keep the currency stable. Although the majority of union members considered themselves to be on the "Left," had voted for Mitterrand in 1981 and 1988, and had a generally favorable view of Socialist policy (at least as pursued in the early 1980s), they complained about the "politization" of the union leadership, that is, its nearly automatic support of Socialist governments.[12] These were among the reasons why the level of unionization, already low by Western European standards, continued to fall.[13] It was partly in order to improve the image of the unions and renew their energy that the leadership of all the major union federations has been replaced in the past three years.

BUSINESS ASSOCIATIONS

The business community, possessing greater wealth and organizational unity, has usually been in a better position than the trade unions. This is especially true of big business, which since 1946 has been organized in the National Council of French Employers (*Conseil national du patronat français*—CNPF), an umbrella organization of about 900,000 industrial, commercial, and banking firms belonging to some 400 constituent associations, which are, in turn, grouped into 85 federations. During World War II, the business community (then represented by another organization) discredited itself politically by its collaboration with the Vichy regime. The weak Resistance record of industrialists, and their virtual absence from de Gaulle's London entourage, prevented a rapprochement between organized business and postwar governments dominated by left-wing political parties.[14] The poor image of business was in some measure reflected in the nationalization of many industries and in the enactment of numerous laws in favor of workers.

Nevertheless, throughout most of the Fourth Republic the CNPF proved to be an effective interest group. The government's commitment to capitalist planning transformed the business community into a crucial partner in economic policy making; the disunity of organized labor permitted business frequently to ignore collective contracts; and the *pantouflage* relationship of business and the higher civil service gave business a favorable access to the authorities. This relationship made it possible for bureaucrats who had proved their goodwill toward the business community to slip (*pantoufler*) into lucrative positions in that community.

With the establishment of the Fifth Republic, the CNPF acquired much greater power, and the relationship between business and the upper-level civil service intensified. Furthermore, the government had committed itself to a number of goals favored by big business: consolidation, productivity, and exports. This was particularly the case under the premiership of Barre, who was in frequent contact with the CNPF president, François Ceyrac, an older man who personified almost perfectly the conservative, gerontocratic leadership of organized business (and who stepped down in 1981 after a 20-year tenure). In recent years, the CNPF has tried to improve its image and "rejuvenate" its leadership.[15] Under the prodding of the Young Employers (*Jeunes patrons*), a group of dynamic businesspeople vaguely affiliated with the CNPF,[16] the latter has become more sympathetic to free-market competition, collective bargaining, and even a modicum of worker participation in industrial decision—if only in order to weaken the class-struggle approach of some unions and get workers to identify with firms. Nevertheless, differences of opinion on all these matters—and on the "correct" reactions to government policies—continue to exist within the CNPF.[17]

The CNPF is technically open to both big and small business; however, the latter is separately organized in the General Confederation of Small- and Medium-Sized Enterprises (*Confédération générale des petites et moyennes entreprises—* CGPME), an association that, although formally linked to the CNPF, has acted independently in an effort to maintain traditional family business in the face of international competition and the modernization of industry. The CGPME is a federation of some 3,000 constituent associations representing 1.5 million firms, including more than 350,000 commercial establishments, about 100,000 manufacturing firms, and nearly 1 million service enterprises. There are additional associations that have been trying to speak for the interests of the small shopkeeper and artisan. Some of these date back to the Fourth Republic, when France began to commit itself to economic modernization policies. One of the most vocal of these groups was the Union for the Defense of Shopkeepers and Artisans (*Union pour la défense des commerçants et des artisans—*UDCA); founded in 1953, it attracted a membership of more than 350,000, and as a political party (the Poujadists) attained considerable electoral success in 1956 (see Chapter 4). Another organization is the *Confédération intersyndicale de défense-Union nationale des artisans et travailleurs indépendants—*CID-UNATI), whose main strength was in the provinces. Unlike other small-business associations (such as

CGPME, which has tried to lobby in Parliament and to cultivate good relations with conservative or centrist parties), CID-UNATI became quite radicalized and preferred violent forms of political expression—which, in 1970, led to the imprisonment of its founder and leader, Gérard Nicoud. The "martyrdom" of Nicoud may have accounted for the fact that in the early 1970s the membership of that organization grew eightfold, from 23,000 to 189,000. Since then, however, the CID-UNATI has declined and now constitutes hardly more than a political club. Still other organizations are the *Confédération de l'artisanat et des métiers* (CNAM), whose 1,051 affiliated associations encompass about 100,000 individual firms, and the *Union professionnelle artisanale* (UPA), which represents about 350,000 artisans.

If one adds up the membership of all the small-business associations, one arrives at a statistically impressive figure. However, organizational fragmentation has compounded this sector's problems in articulating its interests effectively, given the weakness of the center parties to which it had been ideologically linked, and given the pressures for the consolidation of enterprises, which have contributed to a constantly increasing number of bankruptcies.[18]

In addition to these voluntary, or "associational," business groups there is a network of 153 chambers of commerce and industry, regrouped into 21 regional chambers. The existence of these chambers, which are bodies of public law (*établissements publics*), goes back to the seventeenth century (although their status was redefined by a law of 1898). These chambers, which (through a system of elections) represent local business firms and derive a part of their budget from dues imposed on the firms, are under the authority or supervision (*tutelle*) of the state. Specifically, the minister of industry charges the chambers with a number of public tasks, including the administration of ports and airports (and business concessions in them), warehouses, private business schools, and vocational-training institutes. In order to coordinate the activities of the chambers better and to improve their function as intermediaries between the business community and the state, the government in 1964 established the *Assemblée permanente des Chambres de commerce*, which represents the business organizations by means of periodic elections. A parallel system of chambers exists for artisans and craftsmen (carpenters, plumbers, bakers, et al.), which are topped on a national level by an *Assemblée permanente des Chambres de métiers*. But because of the artisans' organizational fragmentation and their generally precarious economic position, neither their chambers nor the permanent assembly have been very effective in representing their interests vis-à-vis the government.[19]

AGRICULTURE

The weakness of small business is paralleled in the agricultural sector, which has had some difficulty in preserving its position. Whereas until the end of the Fourth Republic agriculture was a dominant economic force and several political parties in Parliament were spokesmen for farmers' interests, today agriculture must rely largely on its own organizational strength. But agriculture, like labor, suffers from fragmentation and internal competition. The largest farmers' organization is the National Federation of Farmers' Unions (*Fédération nationale des syndicats des exploitants agricoles*—FNSEA), an umbrella organization of about 40 specialized farmers' groups. With its 700,000 members (regrouped in more than 30,000 local farmers' associations and 94 department federations), the FNSEA includes only about one-third of the 1.5 million farmers in France, a poor showing compared to the 90 percent of British farmers included in the National Farmers' Union. The FNSEA embraces primarily independent farmers and is generally thought to be conservative in political outlook, although one of its constituent groups, the Young Farmers (*Centre national des jeunes agriculteurs*—CNJA), originally led by the Christian Agricultural Youth (*Jeunesse agricole chrétienne*—JAC),[20] has tried periodically to infuse "progressive" (in addition to Catholic) attitudes into the FNSEA.

The CNJA, with its 80,000 members, is formally "attached" to the FNSEA but maintains organizational autonomy. The FNSEA tries to conciliate the interest of proprietors of small and large farms. In the 1960s, the CNJA charged the FNSEA with being more interested in representing large-scale farmers (especially of cereals) and food processors, and selectively boycotted its activities; but in the 1970s, the CNJA became more influential when one of its leaders, Michel Debatisse, took over the leadership of the FNSEA, became active in the UDF, and eventually (in 1979) became a cabinet minister.

The decline in the number of small landholdings has reduced the numerical weight of the peasantry. Conversely, the adding of land to nearly 300,000 existing farms, and the opening of about 100,000 new large farms, has created new (American-style) modern agricultural producers whose entrepreneurial attitudes are likely to enhance even further the position of the CNJA within the FNSEA and to facilitate closer cooperation with the CNPF.

Fragmentation of agriculture along ideological lines was fairly widespread before the war, when the *Société nationale d'encouragement à l'agriculture* was close to the Radicals, and the *Confédération générale de l'agriculture* related well to the SFIO. Today, there are still agricultural associations that are ideologically oriented. The FNSEA tends to be Catholic and right of center; the *Confédération nationale de la mutualité, de la coopération, et du crédit agricoles* has links to the Center-Left and Socialist parties; and the *Mouvement de coordination de défense des exploitants agricoles familiaux* (MODEF), which represents the very poorest farmers, is sponsored by the Communists. The newest agricultural association—it was formed almost immediately after Mitterrand became president—is the *Confédération nationale syndicale des travailleurs-paysans* (CNSTP), a grouping of several pro-Socialist farmers' movements.

The ideological identification of agricultural associations has been declining, however, and fragmentation is increasingly based on agronomic specialization: single-crop producers, such as wheat growers or winegrowers, and economic groups, such as credit or cooperative-marketing associations.[21] The various agricultural associations are united—if that is the word—under "corporatist" auspices, in the sense that they all elect representatives to the 94 departmental agricultural chambers (with half the members of each chamber elected every three years for six-year terms). These chambers are "bodies of public law" that the government calls upon for expert advice and the performance of selected public administrative tasks, such as marketing, the implementation of farm-price and credit policies, and training programs.[22] At the apex of this organizational pyramid is the *Assemblée permanente des chambres d'agriculture*, which consists of delegates chosen by each of the departmental chambers.

STUDENTS AND TEACHERS

Organizational fragmentation is also found among teachers and students. There are separate Socialist, Communist, Catholic, Gaullist, and liberal student associations. For many years, the largest student organization was the *Union nationale des étudiants de France* (UNEF), which was founded in 1907. Generally leftist, it was weakened in 1960 when the Gaullist government, in response to the UNEF's critique of the government's Algerian policies, cut off the UNEF's public subsidy and refused to have dealings with it.[23] Resentment of this governmental behavior was one of the reasons for the important role played by the UNEF in the rebellions of 1968. Today the UNEF is divided into two rival organizations, *UNEF-Solidarité étudiante*, which is close to the Communist Party, and *UNEF-Indépendante et démocratique*, whose membership is more diverse and includes Trotskyists and socialists of various hues.

The largest and most important teachers' organization for many years was the *Fédération d'éducation nationale* (FEN). Counting about 500,000 members during the 1970s and 1980s, it comprised more than 40 separate subgroups for a variety of educators, the largest of which was the *Syndicat national des instituteurs et professeurs d'enseignement général de collège* (SNI-PEGC), with 300,000 members, mostly elementary and lower-secondary (or "junior high") schoolteachers. Another large affiliated group was the *Syndicat national d'enseignement supérieur* (SNESup), which represented university teachers. The FEN was divided internally also on the basis of several ideological tendencies (e.g., Socialist, Communist, Trotskyist, and self-management–oriented [*autogestionnaire*]), but what held them all together was a common commitment to *laïcité*, that is, a secular public school system. There are some teachers' unions affiliated not with the FEN but with the various industrial unions (e.g., the *Syndicat général d'éducation nationale* [SGEN], a component of the CFDT). Sometimes these teachers' unions compete with one another in elections for the consultative bodies attached to lycées, universities, or the *Conseil supérieur d'éducation nationale*, which is attached to the Ministry of Education; at other times, they collaborate in lobbying for the promotion of *laïcité* or for higher teachers' pay. In the past two years, FEN lost more than half its membership as a result of internal fragmentation over the issue of educational reforms—specifically, the question about the extent to which the increasing official openness toward the rival system of private schools (*écoles libres*) should be tolerated. At the end of 1992 the FEN nearly collapsed and was succeeded by other associations, the most important of which is the *Syndicat national unitaire des instituteurs, professeurs d'école et professeurs de collège* (SNUipp), which includes teachers at all levels from elementary school to university. This new association is egalitarian, "maximalist" in its demands for more teachers, and resolutely opposed to government measures authorizing the expenditure of public funds locally for private schools. Early in 1993, SNUipp joined with others to create a new umbrella organization, the *Fédération syndicale unitaire* (FSU).[24]

Another educational association is the National Union of Parents of Students in Private Schools (*Union nationale des parents d'élèves de l'enseignement libre*—UNAPEL), which speaks for more than 800,000 families. It has joined with teachers' associations and school administrators to lobby for increased government subsidies to parochial schools.[25]

THE ACCESS AND INPUT OF INTEREST GROUPS

The preceding list of the major interest groups, although far from complete, indicates that organizational frameworks exist for the important economic sectors in France. But such existence does not by itself indicate a group's position and power in French political life. In terms of its pluralistic reality, and in conformity with the freedom of association found in all democratic regimes, France (under republics) has been receptive to a vigorous interest-group politics. However, in modern French political history, there has always been a school of thought, inspired in particular by Rousseau and the early Jacobins, that considered any political role for interest groups, secondary associations, and even political parties unnecessary interpositions between the people and the government and therefore destructive of the "general will." In consonance with that doctrine, the Le Chapelier Law in 1791 declared intermediary bodies (*corps intermédiaires*) such as artisans' guilds (or trade unions) illegal, and their reestablishment was not permitted until 1884, when that law was rescinded. A law passed in 1901 allowed the formation of interest groups without prior government authorization. Since that time, interest groups have indeed flourished, and they have made their political influence felt in a variety of ways.

In the Third and Fourth Republics, various economic, professional, or ideological groups were strongly linked to political parties and exerted considerable influence on these parties or were at least close to them. In the Third Republic, the Freemasons considered the Radical party their voice in Parliament; in the Fourth Republic, the MRP was seen as reflecting the views of the Catholic church, and the veterans' organizations supported the RPF because it was thought to represent their interests. A clear party linkage enabled interest groups to colonize the Parliament directly by having their spokespersons elected deputies. Thus, by the end of the Third Republic, the Senate had begun to establish its reputation as the "chamber of agriculture," and in the Fourth Republic, many trade union officials were elected to the National Assembly under Communist or Socialist party labels. Interest group input was facilitated by the specialized legislative standing committees in the Fourth Republic, with the trade unionists securing squatters' rights in the Committee on Labor, and the representatives of the farmers' associations in the Committee on Agriculture. This input was supplemented by the easy access of some interest groups to their "patron" ministry, and by the acceptance of ministerial portfolios by a leader of a client group; for example, the minister of agriculture was usually linked to an agricultural association. In addition, interest group representatives were often recruited (albeit on a temporary basis) to serve on a minister's staff (*cabinet ministériel*). The pervasive presence of interest groups, whether real or imagined, made governmental institutions, from Parliament to the bureaucracy, appear as a complex of fiefdoms. To the extent that this situation blurred the distinction between the public and the private domains, it helped to bring the Fourth Republic into disrepute.

After 1958, the power of interest groups declined considerably. In part this was due to the statist philosophy of de Gaulle, who had as little use for interest groups as for political parties; he viewed both as particularistic and therefore out of harmony with the public interest. Because the concept of *concertation* (translated, for lack of a better word, as "harmonization") was a favorite with de Gaulle and his followers, it has been argued that the general's views regarding groups were proto-fascist.[26] But whereas the Nazis terminated the independent existence of groups by "coordinating" or merging them into the official authority structure, thereby creating the "corporate" (or corporative) state, de Gaulle did not wish to destroy the associational (voluntary) organizational basis of groups; rather, he wished to disarm the trade unions by making them part of a "capital-labor association" and depoliticizing them. Furthermore, we should note that *concertation* has also been a catchword of non-Gaullist planners and post-Gaullist and Socialist politicians, and that it was viewed as a device for technocratic decision making even during the Fourth Republic.

In the Fifth Republic, interest groups could not of course be removed from the political scene, even if political leaders had so wished, but the institutional framework could be arranged so as to minimize or channel their influence. Parliament has not been a consistently reliable access point for interest groups; throughout most of the Fifth Republic, the legislative efforts of organized labor and agriculture have often been hampered by the underrepresentation or fragmentation of their "patron" parties in the Assembly.

The electoral system based on proportional representation that existed in the Fourth Republic had permitted the parties to articulate the views of fairly narrowly defined interests; in contrast, the single-member constituency system of the Fifth Republic has forced the parties to become more aggregative and hence to be less reliable echoes of the demands of particular interest groups. To be sure, the PCF can still be said to represent the workers' point of view—*if* such a representation does not conflict with the party's general strategy at a given period. The Socialist party still reflects the views of such "promotional" groups as the League of Human Rights (*Ligue des droits de l'homme*) and the interests of selected industrial workers; but it must also represent the schoolteachers, civil servants, and other (sometimes rival) interests that compose its electorate.

The ideological affinities between a political party and an interest group may sometimes be more useful to the former than the latter. Moreover, if a group's ideological orientation is too sharply defined, a rival association that does not share that orientation may be formed, with the result that a specific or "objective" interest can no longer be effectively articulated. This has been especially the case with educational groups.

PLURALIST, CORPORATIST, AND OTHER MODELS OF INTEREST GROUP POLITICS

In their variety, their organizational features, their methods of action, and their pursuit of specific policy aims, interest groups in France are in many ways quite comparable to those of the United States. In both countries, workers, industrialists, businesspeople, farmers, and the members of various professions discover their common interests, freely organize, and try to protect and promote these interests by making deals, or bargaining, with one another and by seeking access to, influencing, or lobbying with the political parties, the legislature, the executive, and other official decision-making agencies.

Yet the structure and context of interest group politics in France have diverged in several respects from those in the United States, a country that is said to conform to the *pluralist* model. In the United States, interest groups are organized on a purely voluntary basis; they determine their own organizational structures, define their goals, choose their leaders freely, and have their own sources of funds; and while pursuing these goals, which are usually concerned with concrete but limited policy issues, they maintain their complete autonomy, their distance from the public authorities, and their freedom of action.[27] In France, by contrast, we observe the following: (1) Interest groups and political parties are often linked, sometimes in a formal structural sense and sometimes ideologically. (2) Interest groups may pursue goals that go far beyond single issues and that touch upon the very nature of political institutions, if not the constitutional system as a whole. (3) There is a formal legitimation of the role of interest groups: Unlike the U.S. Constitution, which is silent on the matter of groups, the Fifth Republic Constitution (Art. 4) states that "political parties and groups shall be instrumental in the expression of the suffrage; they shall be formed freely and carry on their activities freely." This legitimation is reflected also in numerous laws granting interest groups official status, providing for their representation in public bodies, and devolving upon them certain tasks of policy implementation. (4) There is a regularized, institutionalized pattern of consultation of interest groups by governmental authorities, so that it is often difficult to determine the source of a set of policies and equally difficult to determine the boundaries between the public (the state) and the private (civil society).

Because of these divergences, some scholars have suggested that France cannot be considered pluralist but must be said to conform to another model—the *corporatist* one—in which the state plays a much more significant role. Originally, the term *corporatism* referred to the position of groups in authoritarian regimes of the fascist type, where group autonomy was severely limited (if not eliminated), lobbying did not take place, collective bargaining did not exist, strikes were forbidden, and all socioeconomic sectors were formally *incorporated* into the state. In recent years, the term has been used increasingly to refer to almost *any* kind of institutionalized relationship between interest groups and the public authorities that departs from the U.S. ideal type, that is, from a situation that is considered the essence of *pluralism*. Thus, in the (U.S.) pluralist system, the "public interest" is a myth: There is only a plurality of interests that sometimes compete and sometimes conflict, complement one another, and converge. Public policy is piecemeal rather than comprehensive and is essentially the outcome of "the legislative struggle"; and the state is little more than a clerk registering the various demands or an umpire who sees to it that the rules are properly observed.[28]

In *corporatist* systems, however, the relationship between interest groups and the public authorities is characterized by some or all of the following: (1) the existence of a limited number of interest groups, which are organized in a hierarchical fashion; (2) special recognition by the state, through licensing or guaranteed access, of the representational monopoly of a group; (3) compulsory membership; (4) a highly formalized and institutionalized access to the public authorities; (5) governmental subvention of interest group activities; and (6) state control over the selection of leaders and the articulation of demands.[29]

It is indeed possible to find empirical evidence of several of these features in France. Thus, the structured nature of interest group access to the formal decision makers is reflected in a variety of institutions. Among them is the Economic and Social Council (ESC), which the government is constitutionally obligated to consult in the preparation of bills involving domestic issues. This agency of "functional representation" includes delegates of trade unions, farmers' organizations, business associations, professional groups, cooperative and mutual societies, and nationalized industries, in addition to unaffiliated experts and civil servants.[30] The ESC (whose members are appointed for five-year terms) is supplemented by numerous advisory bodies that have proliferated around ministries, the "modernization committees" that have helped to shape the French four-year economic plans,[31] and, since the recent decentralization measures, regional economic and social advisory councils. In addition, countless consultative bodies are attached to departmental administrative offices.

French governments have exercised a certain discretion in giving some interest groups favorable representation in advisory councils and in choosing others as privileged interlocutors. In the name of democracy and fairness, the government ought to give all important interests access to decision-making organs; but the fragmentation of and competition among interest groups have strengthened the government's power to determine which association should be considered the "most qualified" defender of a particular socioeconomic sector.

In France, qualification is an important criterion for interest group consultation. French bureaucrats, who have a highly developed sense that they alone represent the public interest, have tended to view the excessive involvement of interest groups in the decision-making process as endangering the "objective" resolution of a problem.[32] Since the civil servants' principal aim is to obtain accurate information, they tend to make a distinction between pressure groups, which they regard as selfish, and professional associations, which, in the civil servants' view, have expertise.[33] This distinction was greatly exaggerated during the Vichy regime when, in a manner characteristic of fascist systems, the government refused to acknowledge "private" groups and dealt only with chambers and other bodies of public law. Today, the existence of privately organized groups is so thoroughly recognized that trade unions, business associations, and other organizations are considered to be de facto participants in government. Nevertheless, all governments have their own hierarchies of organizations with which they prefer to deal. Most governments (or at least the higher civil servants) have preferred to consult professional orders (*ordres professionnels*) where possible rather than pure interest groups (*syndicats*).[34] These "orders" have many tasks: the maintenance of intraprofessional standards and discipline, the control of access to the profession, the supervision of training, and the administration of selective government policies.[35]

Where the criterion of professionalism is inadequate, the question of whether this or that association shall represent a particular interest may be decided by such measures of "representativeness" as an association's inclusiveness, its internal democracy, or even the extent to which a group's outlook is in tune with the public interest. Thus, the Ministry of Social Affairs has bargained on the matter of doctors' fees with the Federation of Medical Associations (*Confédération des syndicats médicaux français*—CSMF) rather than with another medical association, because of the CSMF's "professionalism." (Although the *Ordre des médecins* is even more professional in outlook and membership in it is compulsory for all practicing physicians, it has been less cooperative.[36]) Similarly, the Ministry of Education bargained with the FEN because it was more inclusive and not oriented toward a particular ideology (except laicism).[37] And the Ministry of Education chose to recognize a secularly oriented rather than a confessionally oriented parents' association because it considered the former more "qualified" than the latter. The government's recognition may be influenced by developments within a particular interest. Thus, when the FSU, the newly formed teachers' union, won out over the old FEN in elections to representative councils in educational institutions at the end of 1993, it demanded legitimation as an official interlocutor; such recognition would give the FSU the right to representation on public bodies (e.g., the Superior Council of Civil Servants) and the right to be invited to participate in negotiations on educational policy.[38]

Frequently, when the government has a choice, it selects representatives of the more tractable and less radical trade unions as spokespersons of organized labor. Since the establishment of the Fifth Republic, the number of union delegates in the Economic and Social Council has been approximately equal for the FO and CGT, although for many years the latter had twice as many members as the former. Both labor and agricultural associations have periodically complained about being underrepresented in the ESC, particularly in relation to business and the civil service. In the mid-1980s, the size of the ESC was increased from 200 to 230 and subsequently to 231, and the number of trade union representatives was increased from 50 to 69, while the number of representatives of farmers' associations was reduced from 30 to 25 (see Table 5.1). The growing "governmentalization" of the ESC is indicated by the fact that whereas in 1946, 8 percent of the ESC's members were individuals nominated by the government, the proportion had risen to 30 percent in the Fifth Republic (67 of the 231 in the ESC in 1992).[39] But that governmentalization has not been a bad thing: Because of it, spokespersons of relatively weak interests such as environmentalist and parent-teacher associations have been seated on the ESC.[40] (In any case, the change in the composition of the ESC has not had a decisive effect on its overall public policy impact, which, in the view of many observers, has been very modest.) In the modernization committees dealing with the Economic Plan, trade unions have been chronically underrepresented, in part because the plan has tended (except for the period of 1981 to 1984) to adhere to a business rather

TABLE 5.1 Membership in the Economic and Social Council (changes from 1979 to 1992)

	1979	1984	1992
Wage earners' representatives (trade unions)	50	69	69
(CFDT			17)
(CGT			17)
(FO			17)
(CFTC			6)
(CGC			7)
(FEN			4)
(Agricultural workers' association			1)
Employers' associations	27	27	27
Agricultural associations	30	25	25
Cooperatives and mutual societies	11	19	19
Family, renters', and savers' associations	8	10	17
Public enterprises	6	8	10
Artisans	10	10	10
Free professions	0	3	3
Others	8	7	11*
Other "qualified" individuals appointed by the government	50	48	40
Total	200	226	231

*Includes representatives of associations of departments and overseas territories and of French citizens living abroad.

than a union outlook and to concentrate on growth and productivity rather than wages or social policy.

Even where interest group representation is more equitable, its input can be minimized by the governmental practice of ignoring recommendations that do not fit into a preconceived policy framework. Thus, in the late 1950s, the advice rendered by the *Conseil supérieur de l'éducation* was ignored because it differed from the ideas of the minister of education; in the early 1960s, the government ignored the recommendations made by the multipartite committee of inquiry (the *Commission Toutée*) regarding an "incomes policy" for the public sector. The *Comité supérieur de l'emploi*, in which trade unions could in theory make recommendations regarding manpower training, met only once a year. The National Labor Relations Board, which advised the government on minimum wages and other labor-contract issues, met more often; but during Gaullist-Giscardist rule, the unions claimed that the government representatives on that body usually confronted organized labor with a fait accompli that was not in the interest of the worker. After Mitterrand's election, it was the turn of organized business to complain: While the new president gave audiences to the chief of the CNPF, that organization realized that it could not deflect the government from its nationalization and wage policies (at least in the beginning).[41]

The access and effectiveness of an interest group have depended on a number of factors: the size of its membership, the extent to which it can project an image as an effective agent for an economic or professional sector, the cohesion between the leadership and the rank and file, and the degree to which intrasector fragmentation can be overcome. This fragmentation is particularly apparent in the competing slates of candidates put up by agricultural associations, labor unions, and teachers' associations for elections to agricultural chambers, factory councils, university councils, boards of nationalized industries, social security organs, and labor relations tribunals. On the one hand, this fragmentation may be exploited by a determined government; on the other hand, it is a manifestation of a pluralism *within* interests that the public authorities try to compensate for, if not overcome, by encouraging the kind of "hierarchical organizations" (e.g., in the form of chambers, assemblies of chambers, and *ordres professionnels*) that are said to be symptoms of corporatism! Moreover, hierarchical organization is a reflection of the reality of professionalization and hence is found in large-scale organizations in every advanced society.

Neither hierarchical organization nor equal (or favorable) and formalized access to the public authorities is a sufficient guarantee that an interest group will be taken seriously, for the scope of decision making in a public body in which interest groups are represented may be limited by outside forces or by policy constraints. The administrative councils of most public or mixed enterprises are multipartite in composition, with the workers, the consumers, and the management represented equally. However, the spokespersons of the consumers may vote on the side of the management, and the workers' interests may be slighted by the meddling of the minister of finance, who is concerned with ensuring "budgetary equilibrium" in the nationalized industries.[42]

Similar limitations apply to the *conseils de prud'hommes*, the special functional tribunals, modeled to some extent after the labor courts in Germany, that decide disputes arising in connection with labor legislation.[43] These tribunals (separately organized for industry, commerce, and agriculture) include representatives of trade unions, employers' associations, and other interested organizations that participate in rendering verdicts. It is not clear, however, whether this participation is meaningful for interest groups, except in the most perfunctory sense, for the following reasons: Each group, individually, has only minority representation; the scope of decision is narrowed by codes of labor law; the presiding judge (who is not a spokesperson of any interest group) has considerable prestige and can often sway the lay members; and decisions rendered by the tribunals can be appealed to ordinary courts.

Hence it is not surprising that workers' participation in the elections to the *conseils de prud'hommes* is seldom higher than 60 percent (see Table 5.2).[44] Participation in the elections of trade union representatives to the social security boards (*caisses*), which administer health insurance programs and family subsidies, is somewhat higher, but the elections do not generate great interest. This was particularly true between 1967 and 1982, when the representation ratio favorable to trade unionists was abolished and parity of representation was granted to the employers, in effect giving the latter control over the boards. Under the Mitterrand presidency the trade unions regained their formal majority status on the boards, but such a status is not enough: If trade union input is taken seriously within these boards, as was the case during much of the Fourth Republic, it may be because unions have privileged access to political parties that are well represented in Parliament and can help to alter in the unions' favor the legislation under which the boards operate. These conditions do not always prevail.

TABLE 5.2 Trade unions and elections to labor relations tribunals

	1979	1982	1987	1992
Voters (in thousands)	12,323	13,547	12,256	—
Percent of participation	63.1	58.6	45.9	40.4
Abstentions (in thousands)	4,539	5,608	6,624	—
Percent of abstentions	36.8	41.3	54.0	59.6
Trade unions' shares of employees' votes (in percent):				
CGT	42.4	36.8	36.3	33.3
CFDT	23.1	23.5	23.0	23.8
FO	17.4	17.8	20.4	20.5
CFTC	6.9	8.5	8.3	8.6
CGC	5.2	9.6	7.4	7.0

SOURCE: Based on Jean Magniadas, "Elections prud'homales et syndicalisme de classe," *La Pensée* 263 (May–June 1988) 13.

Yet despite the powers of the government and the limits of pressure groups, the term *corporatism* is misleading. In France, institutionalized relationships between groups and the government are still essentially *pluralist* because (1) the groups themselves have asked for, and helped to develop, the regulations regarding the formalized relationship (and they tend to complain about its "corporatist" nature only if their input does not result in policies they like[45]); (2) there is hardly an economic or professional interest that is articulated by a single organization; (3) the leadership of organized interests, including those that enjoy a relatively privileged access to the authorities, is chosen not by the authorities but by the rank and file; (4) "incorporated" groups may freely boycott the arena of formalized group-government intercourse; (5) privileged links between selected interest groups and official decision makers are found in *all* industrial societies, including the American "pluralist" one; (6) in France, most groups, including highly "incorporated" ones, exhibit *plural* forms of behavior, for example, cooperative ("social-partnership"), co-optative, contentious and claims-asserting (*contestataire*), and uncooperative (*conflictuelle*), depending on the policy issue; and (7) groups continue to engage in such "pluralistic" activities as lobbying, collective bargaining, and strikes. In this sense, "corporatist" patterns should be looked upon not as substitute but as supplementary methods of interest group action.[46]

Moreover, none of the major political parties appears to be interested in a "corporatist" relationship, and recent governments—of the Right and the Left—seem to have tried to move interest group relations with the public authorities in a more "pluralist" direction, sometimes against the wishes of interest groups themselves. Thus the Socialist government in the early 1980s relinquished the power to regulate several aspects of labor-management relations (e.g., the reduction of the workweek) to the unions and employers; furthermore, it deprived the FNSEA of its monopoly status, in the face of that organization's loud protests, by granting equal recognition to three other agricultural associations,[47] and it invited the FNSEA to assert its claims in competition with the other associations. It may be true that the Gaullists had "corporatized" the agricultural sector's relations to the state in the 1960s,[48] but the evolution of the Gaullist party and its ally, the UDF, toward neoliberalism has implied a commitment to an "Anglo-American" kind of pluralism.

The corporatist model, once fashionable, is now increasingly admitted as not really (or no longer) applying to France, yet it is thought to have continued utility as a "heuristic" model.[49] But the concept of corporatism has been stretched to cover so many different political situations[50] that its usefulness has come to be questioned. That is why a new paradigm has recently come into use to differentiate among industrial democracies—specifically, to distinguish France from the United States—that of *statism*.[51] The statist (or "state-centered") model is said to apply to France and other countries where effective decision making is possible because in its confrontations with private interests the state almost always seems to win. Unfortunately, the state, since its "rediscovery" by U.S. scholars several years ago,[52] has not been much more useful as an orienting concept because there has been no agreement on what is meant by it.[53] Ironically, the concept is being applied to France, especially by American scholars, at a time when French politicians, having rediscovered civil society and the market, are increasingly trying to reduce the role of the state and to "degovernmentalize" (*désétatiser*) a range of activities.

An examination of selected issue conflicts in France reveals that the policy process in that country involves a complicated interplay of reciprocal pressures of interest groups and a variety of (sometimes divided) public authorities, in which neither side possesses full autonomy. There are many policy issues on which the government prevailed because it was willing and able to use the powers at its disposal in the face of considerable protest by interest groups. In the early years of the Fifth Republic, de Gaulle succeeded in granting independence to Algeria despite heavy resistance from military officers, nationalist organizations, and a variety of conservative political parties. Under several presidents, agricultural associations failed to obtain sufficient support for family farmers because of governmental emphasis on agricultural competitiveness, a failure that provoked farmers into blocking roads, dumping produce, and threatening violence; the alcohol lobby failed to secure tax exemptions because of the government's concern about alcoholism; the anticlerical associations failed to prevent the passage of the Debré Law in 1959, by which the government could make educational "contracts" with parochial schools because of the Gaullists' interest in retaining the loyalty of the Catholic electorate; and the trade unions failed to secure wage increases commensurate with the rise in the cost of living and, until the early 1970s, to obtain the right to organize in factories. After the 1981 elections, the CNPF was nearly demoralized by its failure to persuade the government to abandon its policies of nationalization, wage increases, and supplementary corporate taxes.

Conversely, there are instances in which the government had to give in to the determined opposition by organized interests. The capital gains tax bills introduced by the government during the Giscard presidency (in 1976–1977) were effectively blocked by big and small business, as was a meaningful extension of factory democracy; the bill introduced by Education Minister Savary in 1983 to integrate the private schools into the national school system was withdrawn in response to opposition by a coalition of Catholic educators, parents' associations, and conservative parties;[54] under the same government (led by Premier Mauroy), the proposals for a reduction of the workweek to 35 hours and the strengthening of the role of workers' councils in factories foundered in the face of opposition by CNPF. Under Chirac's cohabitation government, the bill introduced by Alain Devaquet, the minister for universities, which proposed to make entry into universities more selective, was shelved because of massive student protests. In response to public protests by *SOS-Racisme*, an antiracist organization, the *Ligue des droits de l'homme*, and related groups in 1989 and 1993, the government was forced to modify bills concerning the entry and residence of foreigners. Between 1991 and 1993, the government modified or withdrew a number of educational reform measures in response to protest demonstrations by students' and teachers' organizations. In 1993, the new Gaullist-Giscardist government was forced to abandon part of a medical insurance reform bill that provided for cost sharing for drugs, because the RPR-UDF parliamentary group (which included most of the 55 deputies identified with the medical profession) opposed the provision.[55] In 1994, a government bill to increase the financial support of parochial schools was abandoned in the face of massive demonstrations and the determined opposition of trade unions and left-wing parties.

If current trends toward a more independent role of Parliament continue (see Chapter 7) and the cohesion and discipline of parliamentary parties slacken, one may expect the influence of interest groups on the legislative process to grow. This will be true in particular for groups whose electoral weight is significant. A case in point is the recently created *Bureau de liaison des organisations des retraités* (BLORE), the umbrella organization for eight constituent associations of retired persons. Representing more than 2 million retired, who account for a large proportion of the electorate, it is likely to influence most Assembly election outcomes and eventually to demand formal representation in official organs.[56]

There are times when the government wins against an interest group, but its victory may be at least partially the result of help it has received from other interest groups. Premier Rocard's ability to stand his ground during the Paris transport strikes at the end of 1988 was enhanced by the growing opposition to the behavior of the CGT on the part of the public at large as well as the other trade unions.[57] Conversely, a coalition of private interests may win against one component of the public authority structure because it is supported by another component of that structure. The victory of the unions, immigrant groups, churches, and left-wing organizations in opposing the nationality and citizenship bill introduced by Chirac's government in 1986 was achieved with the encouragement of President Mitterrand. In fact, one of these organizations, *SOS-Racisme*, had been formed in 1984 with the backing of the Socialist government in order to fight racism.[58] Finally, there are policy decisions that are difficult to attribute clearly to the state or the private sector; this would be increasingly true of agricultural policies, which may be made by a combination of forces: private interests, the national government, and the now partly autonomous institutions of the European Union.

In any case, the policy process in France has become more pluralistic and incremental, the result of an interplay of a plurality of public and private preferences. As a consequence of these developments, a mutual adjustment has taken place. On the one hand, Socialist governments, sensing their dependence on business, became more sympathetic to it and more open to its policy suggestions, despite the often harsh ideological rhetoric of Socialist politicians about big business (*le grand patronat*);[59] and even Mitterrand, despite impressive proworker legislation during the first three years of his presidency, reflected the evolution of the Socialist party in response to "postindustrialism" and had no working-class representatives in his entourage.[60] On the other hand, the Gaullists, during the election campaigns of 1988 and 1993, vowed to retain the social achievements of the working-class community. Meanwhile, the trade unions have become more "realistic" in that they no longer expect the government to bring about full employment, and business has become more socially oriented and less hostile to Socialist governments (realizing that these governments have been quite helpful in bringing about the "de-indexation" of salaries).[61] These things have happened because of a recognition of the fact that the power of government is not absolute or even "autonomous." More often than not, policy making (e.g., on issues such as working conditions, wages, and productivity) is a tripartite affair, involving government, labor, and business.[62] The interest groups are the "social partners" (*partenaires sociaux*) of the government, which acts as a coordinator. However, it is increasingly difficult for the government to play that role, for, as a French planning commissioner put it, "it has become practically impossible to assemble in a single place and around a few tables the principal economic and social decision makers. The industrial texture has become diversified; the financial institutions have multiplied . . . in short, our system is much richer but also more complex than it was yesterday, while the [patterns of] behavior have become more and more individualistic."[63] The diversity of the business sector has been accompanied by three related symptoms: *désétatisation, désyndicalisation,* and *déplanification* (denationalization, the decline of unionization, and the reduction of planning).

The role of interest groups is likely to grow in the future, if only because many French people question the excessive role of the state, and the state has itself been attempting to hand over some of its weaponry to the civil society and the market. To be sure, the state still defines the parameters of discussion, but that is also true of the United States and other "pluralist" systems; otherwise, it would not even be possible to speak of states and governments.

NOTES

1. Bernard Stasi, in *Vie associative et démocratie nouvelle* (Paris: PUF, 1979), pp. 47-58, mentions the following as examples of the tens of thousands of associations registered with local prefectures: a group of unpublished authors, organizations of amateur surfers, associations of pedestrians, retirees, apartment renters, former residents of the Suez Canal zone, and consumers', stockholders', and environmental groups. According to Stasi, 25,000 *new* associations were registered in 1977 alone, that is, more than five times the annual average for the period immediately following World War II. Frank L. Wilson, in his *Interest-Group Politics in France* (Cambridge, U.K.: Cambridge University Press, 1987), lists more than 70 nationally organized interest groups whose officials he interviewed (Appendix B, pp. 291-292).

2. See André Barjonet, *La CGT* (Paris: Seuil, 1968), pp. 124-129. According to this source, the CGT is not a complete transmission belt, yet relationships between the leadership of the CGT and that of the PCF have been so close that the CGT has often neglected concrete economic policies in favor of general antisystem policies. For a personal view of these relationships, see Georges Séguy, *Lutter* (Paris: Stock, 1975), esp. Chapter 12. See also René Mouriaux, *La CGT* (Paris: Seuil, 1982), esp. pp. 190-206, for a discussion of the changes in this union's relations to the political parties.

3. According to W. Rand Smith, in *Crisis in the French Labor Movement* (New York: St. Martin's Press, 1987), pp. 64-67, the influence of the Catholic subculture was very

strong among the original membership of the CFDT who had broken from the CFTC but has been much less significant for those who joined subsequently.

4. The membership figures cited in the text are based on a variety of sources, among them the following: René Mouriaux, *Le Syndicalisme face à la crise* (Paris: Editions de la Découverte, 1986); Dominique Borne, *Histoire de la société française* (Paris: Armand Colin, 1988); *Le Monde*, 5 June 1985 and other issues; and Pierre Rosanvallon, *La Question syndicale* (Paris: Calmann-Lévy, 1988). According to the last source, 1988 estimates were as follows: CGT, 600,000; CFDT, 400,000; and FO, 400,000. But all these statistics (like those of party memberships) are unreliable. The figures issued by an organization for its own membership tend to be inflated and those issued for its rivals are usually understated. Thus the CGT still claimed a membership of 2.4 million for 1980, 10 percent of whom were allegedly *cadres*, the FO, 1.1 million (a relatively realistic figure), and the CFTC, 250,000. More recent (1990) figures (provided by the secretary-general of the CFDT) are CFDT, 540,000; CGT, 680,000; FO, 415,000; CFTC, 106,000. See Raymond Soubie, "La Crise des syndicats," in SOFRES, *L'Etat de l'opinion 1993* (Paris: Seuil, 1993), p. 38.

5. See Edmond Maire, *Pour un socialisme démocratique* (Paris: Epi, 1972).

6. There are several additional union confederations (each claiming about 100,000 members), among them the *Confédération des syndicats libres*, which is anti-Marxist and believes in class collaboration; the *Union française du travail*, which favors "pure" collective bargaining; and the *Confédération nationale des salariés de France*, which represents certain white-collar employees as well as truck drivers.

7. A somewhat dated (but still valid) study done several years ago has distinguished on the one hand between the legitimist white-collar workers, who are hostile to unionization and close to the boss, and those who are close to their bosses but favor unionization (preferably separate), for example, most members of the CGC; and, on the other hand, between individualists, who are hostile to unionization but close neither to the boss nor to (blue-collar) wage earners, and the *solidaristes*, that is, those who favor unionization in common with blue-collar workers. The first two are generally on the right politically, and the latter two, on the left. See Gérard Grunberg and René Mouriaux, *L'Univers politique et syndical des cadres* (Paris: Presses de la Fondation Nationale des Sciences Politiques, 1979).

8. Trade union members' diversity in party orientations is illustrated in a poll of the voting intentions in the Assembly election of 1986: Among CGT members, 60 percent favored the PCF, 22 percent the PS, and 8 percent the RPR-UDF; among CFDT members, 12 percent favored the PCF, 63 percent the PS, and 19 percent the RPR-UDF; among FO members, 6 percent favored the PCF, 34 percent the PS, and 54 percent the RPR-UDF. Cited in Mouriaux, *Le Syndicalisme*, p. 65.

9. For a summary of the Auroux Laws, see Smith, *Crisis in the French Labor Movement*, esp. pp. 209–219.

10. Hubert Landier, "Le Syndicalisme français face au changement," *Tocqueville Review*, Spring–Summer 1983, pp. 191–201.

11. A Harris poll of 1987 revealed that while the majority of respondents among the public at large had confidence in the unions, among the workers themselves, the degree of confidence in the unions' ability to represent the aspirations of the working class had declined from 45 percent in 1983 to 25 percent in 1991. Soubie, "La crise des syndicats," p. 48. See also Gérard Mermet, *Francoscopie: Les Français, Qui sont-ils? Où vont-ils?* (Paris: Larousse, 1988), p. 217; and SOFRES, *L'Etat de l'opinion 1989*, p. 220.

12. Dominique Labbé, Maurice Croisat, and Antoine Bévort, *La Désyndicalisation: Le Cas de la CFDT* (Grenoble: CERAT, 1990), pp. 40, 81ff.

13. It is estimated that the three major union confederations lost half of their members between 1978 and 1988, so that by 1990 only 10 percent of wage earners were unionized. See Pierre Rosanvallon, *La Question syndicale* (Calmann-Lévy, 1988), p. 14; and Labbé et al., *La Désyndicalisation*. According to the latter source (p. 7), the departure from the union was a "silent flight": Rather than quitting in a formal sense, members simply stopped paying dues.

14. Henry Ehrmann, *Organized Business in France* (Princeton, NJ: Princeton University Press, 1957), pp. 58–100, 103.

15. Among other things, the CNPF set up new rules providing that the maximum age of the organization's president and vice-president be 70 years, and it encouraged younger entrepreneurs to take a more active part in the organization's executive. Still, in the late 1970s the average age of the typical firm's *président-directeur-général* was 60. See "Les Patrons en France," *Le Monde, Dossiers et Documents* 47 (January 1978), 2.

16. The *Jeunes patrons* have also joined with associations of managing directors, Christian employers (*Centre du patronat chrétien*), and young managers (*Jeunes dirigeants*) to form *Entreprise et progrès*, itself a subgroup of the CNPF.

17. For an interesting journalistic treatment of the diversity of attitudes within the business community, see Alain de Sédouy and André Harris, *Les Patrons* (Paris: Seuil, 1977). For a more recent, and more scholarly, study, see Henri Weber, *Le Parti des patrons: Le CNPF 1946–1986* (Paris: Seuil, 1986), in which the author discusses the "modernization" of attitudes of French business leaders, from Malthusian, protectionist, and paternalistic orientations to a growing readiness for global competition and social responsibility.

18. The average annual number of bankruptcies in the 1980s was about 20,000; in 1990 there were about 40,000, and in 1992–1993 about 60,000.

19. Wilson, *Interest-Group Politics in France*, pp. 105–107.

20. The JAC, which dates back to 1936, is a movement concerned with organizing educational and leisure-time activities and the diffusion of Catholic values among rural youth. In the mid-1980s it formed the agricultural component of the *Mouvement rural de jeunesse chrétienne* and accounted for about 20 percent of the MRJC's membership of 250,000.

21. On the multitude of farmers' groups, see Yves Tavernier et al., *L'Univers politique des paysans dans la France contemporaine* (Paris: Armand Colin, 1972), and, for a more recent description, Jacques Lachaud, *Les Institutions agricoles* (Paris: MA Editions, 1987).

22. For a detailed study of the relationship between agriculture and the public authorities, see John T. S. Keeler, *The Politics of Neocorporatism in France* (New York and Oxford: Oxford University Press, 1987).

23. See A. Belden Fields, *Student Politics in France: A Study of the Union Nationale des Etudiants de France* (New York: Basic Books, 1970).

24. "Le Nouveau Syndicat des instituteurs choisit l'offensive," *Le Monde*, 20–21 June 1993.

25. See Jean-Michel Dumay, "Grandes Manoeuvres dans l'enseignement catholique," *Le Monde*, 14 May 1992.

26. See Alexander Werth, *De Gaulle: A Political Biography* (Baltimore: Penguin, 1967), pp. 197, 203–206.

27. For representative presentations of the (American) pluralist "ideal type," see Robert A. Dahl, *Who Governs* (New Haven, CT: Yale University Press, 1961), *Polyarchy,*

Participation, and Opposition (New Haven, CT: Yale University Press, 1971), and "Pluralism Revisited," *Comparative Politics* 10 (January 1978), 191-204; Gabriel A. Almond, "Research Note: A Comparative Study of Interest Groups and the Political Process," *American Political Science Review* 52:1 (March 1958), and G. A. Almond and G. B. Powell, Jr., *Comparative Politics: A Developmental Approach* (Boston: Little, Brown, 1966), pp. 72-79. See also the summary in Wilson, *Interest-Group Politics in France*, pp. 18-25.

28. See Arthur F. Bentley, *The Process of Government: A Study of Social Pressures* (Evanston, IL: The Principia Press, 1949 reissue), p. 163; Earl Latham, *The Group Basis of Politics* (Ithaca, NY: Cornell University Press, 1952), pp. 1-16; and Bertram M. Gross, *The Legislative Struggle* (New York: McGraw-Hill, 1953).

29. This is a paraphrase of Philippe C. Schmitter, "Modes of Interest Intermediation and Models of Social Change in Western Europe," *Comparative Political Studies* 10:1 (April 1977), 9.

30. Jean Meynaud, *Nouvelles Etudes sur les groupes de pression en France* (Paris: Armand Colin, 1962), p. 272.

31. See Stephen S. Cohen, *Modern Capitalist Planning: The French Model* (Cambridge, MA: Harvard University Press, 1969), pp. 220ff.

32. Ezra Suleiman, *Politics, Power, and Bureaucracy in France* (Princeton, N.J.: Princeton University Press, 1974), pp. 316-351.

33. Henry W. Ehrmann, "French Bureaucracy and Organized Interests," *Administrative Science Quarterly* 5 (1961), 534-555.

34. Bernard Chenot, *Organisation économique de l'état* (Paris: Dalloz, 1965), pp. 257ff.

35. See Jean-Louis Bonnefoy, ed., *Aperçu sur l'administration consultative* (Paris: Documentation Française, 1964).

36. Cf. Jean Meynaud, *Les Groupes de pression* (Paris: PUF, 1962), p. 16. The *Ordre des médecins* suffered from the stigma of having been created during the Vichy regime and hence of being a vestige of fascist corporatism. This fact and the *Ordre*'s attempt to scuttle the implementation of birth control led the government to suggest internal reforms, and the Socialists to encourage the establishment of a rival medical association.

37. James M. Clark, *Teachers and Politics in France* (Syracuse, NY: Syracuse University Press, 1967), pp. 30 passim.

38. The government promised to be "reasonable" but seemed to be in no hurry because of the FSU's negative position regarding public support of parochial schools. Valérie Devillechabrolle, "Les Syndicats réclament une clarification des règles de représentativité dans la fonction publique," *Le Monde*, 22 December 1993.

39. Jack Hayward, *Private Interests and Public Policy: The Experiences of the French Social and Economic Council* (New York: Barnes & Noble, 1966), pp. 23-24. For a more recent study, see Jean Frayssinet, *Le Conseil économique et social*, Notes et Etudes Documentaires, no. 4807 (Paris: Documentation Française, 1986).

40. Wilson, *Interest-Group Politics*, p. 161.

41. *Le Point*, 6 July 1981, p. 41.

42. Alain Bockel, *La Participation des syndicats ouvriers aux fonctions économiques et sociales de l'Etat* (Paris: LGDJ, 1965), pp. 237-238.

43. The workload of the *conseils* has grown steadily. In 1990, they dealt with more than 190,000 cases. See V. Carrasco and A. Jeammaud, "Relations du travail," *Droit ouvrier*, June 1992, pp. 204-207.

44. See Jean Magniadas, "Elections prud'homales et syndicalisme de classe," *La Pensée* 263 (May-June 1988), esp. 18-19.

45. Police officers, hospital nurses, and other public employees have been uncertain whether they preferred an "autonomously bargaining" union (which may give them more freedom) or a "corporatized" one (which would put them into a more advantageous salary category). See Valérie Devillechabrolle, "Les Dérives corporatistes," *Le Monde*, 23 June 1993, p. 32.

46. Among the endless stream of writings on the corporatist or "neocorporatist" paradigm, the following should be mentioned: Gerhard Lehmbruch and Philippe Schmitter, *Patterns of Corporatist Policy-Making*, Sage Modern Politics Series, vol. 7 (Beverly Hills, CA: Sage Publications, 1982); Suzanne Berger, ed., *Organizing Interests in Western Europe: Pluralism, Corporatism, and the Transformation of Politics* (Cambridge, U.K.: Cambridge University Press, 1981); and Reginald J. Harrison, *Pluralism and Corporatism* (London: Allen & Unwin, 1980). For a critique of the use of this paradigm, see William Safran, "Interest Groups in Three Industrial Democracies: France, West Germany, and the United States," in F. Eidlin, ed., *Constitutional Democracy: Essays in Comparative Politics*, Festschrift in honor of Henry W. Ehrmann (Boulder, CO: Westview, 1983), pp. 315–343; and Wilson, *Interest-Group Politics in France*, passim. For a recent attempt to "mediate" between the corporatist and pluralist views, see Yves Mény, "Interest Groups and Politics in the Fifth Republic," in Paul Godt, ed., *Policy-Making in France* (London: Pinter, 1989), pp. 91–101.

47. Keeler, *The Politics of Neocorporatism in France*, p. 5.

48. Ibid., p. 4.

49. Keeler himself (ibid., pp. 3–10), despite the title of his excellent book, seems to be drawing back from the "corporatist" paradigm when he speaks of a "weak corporatism" in France, which is becoming a "structured pluralism."

50. See Dominique Colas, ed., *L'Etat et les corporatismes* (Paris: PUF, 1988). This book, based on a colloquium, contains a bewildering variety of approaches to, and definitions of, corporatism, including an increased role of professional associations in politics, the growing role of politics in social organization, a more orderly pattern of labor-management relations, and a policy-making partnership between the private and public sectors.

51. See M. Donald Hancock, preface to Hancock, David P. Conradt, B. Guy Peters, William Safran, and Raphael Zariski, *Politics in Western Europe* (Chatham, NJ: Chatham House, 1993).

52. See, for example, Eric Nordlinger, *On the Autonomy of the Democratic State* (Cambridge, MA: Harvard University Press, 1981); and Peter B. Evans, Dietrich Rueschemeyer, and Theda Skocpol, *Bringing the State Back In* (Cambridge, U.K.: Cambridge University Press, 1985).

53. The term *state* has been variously used to refer to a strong government, to government as such, to all or most political institutions (hence the "new institutionalism"), to particular institutions (such as the bureaucracy), to the public interest, and to effective decision making.

54. John S. Ambler, "French Education and the Limits of State Autonomy," *Western Political Quarterly* 41:3 (September 1988), 469–488.

55. Jean-Michel Normand, "Simone Veil face au lobby médical," *Le Monde*, 1 July 1993. In this instance, the medical lobby was supported by the trade unions.

56. See Jean-Michel Normand, "Le 'Lobbying' préélectoral des retraités," *Le Monde*, 13 March 1993.

57. There was a widespread feeling that the CGT's tough wage demands (if not the strike itself) had been instigated by the PCF in order to convince the Socialist government to take the PCF more seriously.

58. A mass demonstration in 1985 against the racist propaganda of the National Front was said to have been orchestrated by Jack Lang, the minister of culture. See W. Safran, "The French State and Ethnic Minority Cultures," in J.R. Rudolph and R.J. Thompson, eds., *Ethnoterritorial Politics, Policy, and the Western World* (Boulder, CO: Lynne Rienner, 1989), p. 146.

59. See Michel Bauer, "La Gauche au pouvoir et le grand patronat," in Pierre Birnbaum, ed., *Les Elites socialistes au pouvoir, 1981-1985* (Paris: PUF, 1985), pp. 266-268.

60. Except for Bérégovoy, who had ceased years earlier to identify with his working-class origins. Guy Groux and René Mouriaux, "François Mitterrand et les ouvriers," *French Politics and Society* 9:3-4 (Summer-Fall 1991), 43-62.

61. See François Grosrichard, "Les Patrons snobent le patronat," *Le Monde (Affaires)*, 6 February 1988.

62. See Jean-Daniel Reynaud, *Les Syndicats, les patrons, et l'état* (Paris: Editions ouvrières, 1978).

63. Interview with Pierre-Yves Cossé, in "Le Xe Plan, pour quoi faire," *Regards sur l'actualité* 148 (February 1989), 3-9.

chapter 6

Instruments and Patterns of Decision Making: The Executive

Western democratic regimes usually conform to one of two models. The first is a parliamentary system in which there is an executive composed of two "units": a monarch or a figurehead president and a prime minister (or premier) and his or her cabinet, the latter two selected by, and ultimately responsible to, a parliament. The alternative is a presidential system in which the president, who is popularly elected, functions as both chief of state and head of government and is independent of the legislative branch of government; in such a system, the two branches cooperate with and balance each other.

In terms of both tradition and the political institutions mentioned in its constitution, the Fifth Republic is a hybrid, embodying features of standard continental parliamentary democracies and of various types of presidentialisms. Parliament was retained both for the sake of custom and because a republican system without such an institution was unimaginable. It was invested with sufficient formal powers to appease certain non-Gaullist members of the Constitutional Consultative Committee who, knowing de Gaulle's constitutional preferences, feared that he might set up a dictatorial regime; but it was reduced to a secondary place in the system.

On June 1, 1958, the Assembly invested de Gaulle as prime minister after he had assured the deputies that at the age of 67, he would hardly be likely to launch a career as a dictator. Nevertheless, there was some question in the minds of the deputies whether they could depend upon such assurance. Hence the Parliament, in authorizing de Gaulle to draft a new constitution, passed a law that obliged him to retain the separation of the president's from the premier's office as well as provisions making the premier and the cabinet responsible before Parliament. Yet the Constitution of the Fifth Republic was tailor-made for de Gaulle, with the assumptions that he would be the first president under the new system and that the presidency would be the cornerstone of the political edifice of the Fifth Republic. The president is mentioned first in the Constitution and the legislature second, a reversal of the order of the Fourth Republic Constitution.

THE POSITION OF THE PRESIDENT

Much of the power of the French president is derived from the fact that he or she is virtually independent of other branches of government. The president's term of office is seven years (as it had been in the two previous republics). Whereas in the Fourth Republic a president was limited to two terms, today there is no such limitation. In previous republics, the president was elected by Parliament and was subject to its controls and pressures, and therefore did not possess an independent popular mandate. In the Fifth Republic, the president was until 1962 chosen by an electoral college composed of members of Parliament and municipal councils; thereafter, he has been elected by direct popular vote. The president appoints the prime minister, presides over the cabinet, initiates referenda, and has the authority to dissolve the National Assembly.

A number of labels have been used to describe the special character of the Fifth Republic, among them *principate, elective monarchy*, and *plebiscitary democracy*. The system bears some resemblance to that which prevails today in Austria, Finland, Ireland, and Iceland, in the sense that the president is popularly elected. But in these countries the president is in fact much weaker than their respective constitutions would suggest because his or her role is circumscribed by the president's being subject to ouster by Parliament (as in Iceland) or because the Parliament possesses strong legislative powers (as in Austria, Finland, and Ireland). The French president suffers from none of these limitations. Like the president of the Weimar Republic, he or she is granted special emergency powers in addition to the right of dissolution. Like the U.S. president, he or she "reigns" and "rules." The presidential role is like that of an elective monarch: The president possesses in practice all the powers that the English monarch now possesses only in theory. But the French president can also be compared to an Orléanist monarch (albeit an elective one) because, like Louis-Philippe after the revolution of July 1830, he or she has an important political influence.

The president is the head of state—in fact, "the highest authority of the state"; the guarantor of national independence; the individual chiefly responsible for seeing that the Constitution is observed; the person who (under Art. 5) ensures "the functioning of governmental authorities"; the "arbiter" of political and institutional conflicts; the principal appointing officer and diplomatic negotiator; and the commander-in-chief of the armed forces. He or she is also the "guide of France" and "in charge of the destiny of France and the Republic"; he or she is "the inspirer and orienter of national actions."[1] The president conveys general principles of policy to the people and Parliament through formal and informal messages; he or she has the right of pardon and reprieve; and the presidential signature is necessary in order for acts of Parliament to be valid (although not granted the right to veto legislation in a formal sense, the president may ask Parliament to reconsider a bill he or she does not like). Like a monarch, he or she may choose to be aloof and above political battles—in theory presidents do not demean themselves by overt identification with political parties—and in that he or she represents the continuity of the state.

The presidential "mediation" role was intended to apply primarily to the areas of defense and foreign affairs. The Third Republic Constitution specifically granted the president the initiative in foreign affairs (e.g., in the negotiation of treaties), and early Third Republic presidents had a voice in choosing the foreign minister. Gradually, presidential power to make foreign policy atrophied, especially after World War I, when President Poincaré left Premier Clemenceau free to negotiate the Versailles Treaty. The Fourth Republic Constitution merely stipulated that the president was to be "informed" about international negotiations and that he or she was to sign treaties.

In the Fifth Republic, the president negotiates *and* signs treaties (Art. 52). Because (under Art. 15) the president is commander-in-chief of the armed forces, presidents have always taken defense *policy* as their own domain. For a number of reasons, most of the French accepted de Gaulle's predominance in the two areas of defense and foreign policy. In the first place, the precedent of continuity in foreign affairs had already been set in the Fourth Republic, when in the face of constant reshuffling of cabinets and premiers, there was remarkable stability in the Foreign Ministry: Whereas there were 17 premiers (in 23 governments), there were only 8 foreign ministers. Second, de Gaulle came to power largely because the premiers under the Fourth Republic's institutional arrangements had been unable to solve the Algerian problem. If one of the principal reasons for calling upon de Gaulle was to solve that problem, he had to be given a relatively free hand. Third, implicit in de Gaulle's political philosophy was the reassertion of the international role of France, a position that would necessitate a strong executive.

Although the presidency is associated with other institutions (for which there are specific subheadings in the Constitution), these were for many years underdeveloped and unable to balance presidential power. The Constitution states that the president chooses the premier (or prime minister) and then ratifies or confirms the premier's selection of his or her cabinet colleagues. A rigid interpretation of the Constitution would have it that once the cabinet is constituted, only the Parliament can dismiss it. However, parliamentary dismissal of the cabinet has been difficult and fraught with political risk to the deputies because the Assembly itself is subject to dissolution by the president. Certain bills, constitutional amendments, referenda, and the invocation of emergency powers involve the consultation of the Constitutional Council, but three of its nine members, including its presiding officer, are appointed by the president. One of the few national institutions that would seem to be independent of the president is the Economic and Social Council; that body, however, has only consultative powers.

Many of the powers the premier possessed in the Fourth Republic were allocated to the president in the Fifth Republic. In the former, the president presided over cabinet meetings during ceremonial occasions, but the premier was the real chairperson. In the Fifth Republic, the premier is merely "head of government," whereas the president is (under normal conditions) the actual decision maker. Left to the premier is the role of being a link between the presidency and the Parliament, particularly on matters that have not interested the president very much. Thus, the premier's position has been almost analogous to that of the provincial prefect in France (until 1982), who provided a link between the national government on the one hand and the city council and mayor on the other. Presidents rather than premiers have tended to make all decisions in the "reserved domain" (foreign policy, defense, and constitutional matters), and they have attempted to include in their domain whatever else is of importance to them, such as sensitive social and economic problems. When these latter cease to be headline issues, they devolve upon the ministers.[2] Significant policy decisions made by presidents have included granting Algeria independence in 1962; the blocking of British entry into the Common Market in 1963 and 1967; the initiation of constitutional amendments in 1962 and 1969; the withdrawal of France from the integrated command of NATO in 1966; the embargo on military supplies to certain Mideast countries in 1967; the devaluation of the franc in 1969 and 1971; the reduction of petroleum imports in 1974; the suspension of the construction of nuclear power stations, the abolition of the State Security Court (see Chapter 9), and the building of a number of grandiose public edifices—all in the early 1980s; and the decision to hold a referendum on the Treaty of European Union in 1992.

The list of implied presidential powers and actual decisions is so exhaustive that the notion of the "dual executive" came to be regarded as a myth, at least until 1986. True, the Constitution allows a degree of independence to the premier once he or she has been appointed because according to a strict interpretation, only the National Assembly, and not the president, can get rid of the premier. Moreover, according to the Constitution, the premier has a respectable number of powers and responsibilities. He or she is expected to manage government bills and see them safely through Parliament, but that task is facilitated by the short sessions of Parliament, the government's control over the agenda, and the presidential threat of dissolution. The premier prepares the budget bills, defends government policy in Parliament, and answers parliamentary questions. The premier, as well as the other ministers, supervises the work of the ministries and departments and of the civil servants who staff them, and he or she also issues regulations for the ministries. But these regulations can be vetoed by the president. In addition, the premier's control over the ministries is somewhat limited by the fact that the president may take a direct interest in the work of some ministries or ignore the recommendations of the cabinet.

Some presidential decisions have not required cabinet input or participation at all, such as decisions on the dissolution of the Assembly and the invocation of Article 16 (see below). Although in these two cases consultation with the premier is mandatory, the consultation would probably have little meaning beyond the requirement that the premier be informed of the president's intentions. If the premier should object, the president might react in the same way that President Lincoln was said to have reacted when his seven-member cabinet unanimously voted against a policy he had embraced: "Seven nays, one aye; the ayes have it."

At a press conference in January 1964, de Gaulle said that "it cannot be accepted that a diarchy exist at the top."[3] He was free to listen to or to ignore his premier and in fact to replace him. It has been asserted that this attitude about presidential monopoly, which prevailed from 1958 to 1963, was subsequently modified by the development of a more genuine "copilotage" between president and premier, in the sense that de Gaulle withdrew from clearly articulated leadership in domestic affairs and gave his premier a freer hand in that area.[4] It has also been argued that the role of the premier under de Gaulle's immediate successor increased because Pompidou lacked de Gaulle's charisma, did not face the same domestic and foreign policy problems (e.g., the May Events or Algeria), and, having been victimized by his powerlessness when he was premier, did not in turn become a victimizer as president. But Pompidou fully shared his predecessor's attitude toward the premier. At a press conference in 1972, Pompidou outlined in the following way what he required of his premier: *Weak.*

1. He must have ideas that correspond as closely as possible to those of the President.
2. He must completely accept the institutions of the Fifth Republic, meaning the preeminence of the chief of state in matters of general policy direction and in the most important decisions.
3. "He must be capable of carrying out his own duties—a heavy load . . . since it means not only directing daily policy, but also . . . being responsible for government policy before the Assembly and the Parliament; and, finally, carrying out relations with the Majority."[5]

In the mid-1960s, as finance minister, Giscard d'Estaing had criticized de Gaulle's "lonely exercise of power"; but upon assuming the presidency himself, he endorsed unreservedly the ideas of his predecessors. In a number of interviews and speeches he argued that "the French do not want a president for [receiving] chrysanthemums and for inaugurations . . . [but one who is] responsible for the policy orientations of the country";[6] and he viewed the premier as a "loyal and active" spokesperson for him.[7] It has been suggested that under Giscard, *all* policy matters had become part of the "reserved domain," and that Premier Barre behaved not like a chief of government but like a minister of economic affairs.[8] One of the manifestations of Giscard's unmediated governmental leadership was his practice of issuing to the premier monthly written directives in which details on policy matters, and even the timetable for their discussion, were spelled out.[9]

When Mitterrand assumed the presidency, there was hope that he would be more responsive to Parliament. That hope was based on the fact that as leader of the opposition he had for many years fully identified with the Socialist party's call for a chief of state who would not be authoritarian and would respect the other institutions of government, and whose term of office would be reduced.[10] But during the first five years following his election, he behaved much like his predecessors in insisting that "the premier and the ministers must execute the policies defined by the president, since the president has the duty to put into effect the program for which he had contracted with the nation. The role of the premier is important . . . but when it comes to making decisions at a crucial moment, it is my responsibility to decide."[11]

THE PREMIERS

From the lack of independence of the premier's office that has prevailed under normal circumstances—at least until 1986—one should not infer that premiers of the Fifth Republic have been political nobodies. All premiers thus far have been highly educated and prestigious individuals with wide experience in elective office and/or the civil service. They have been selected because of their qualifications, their political backgrounds, their suitability to the presidential temper, and (even before 1986) their general acceptability to the Assembly.

The original party allegiances of the premiers have been diverse. Michel Debré and Jacques Chaban-Delmas had been Radical-Socialists in the early years of the Fourth Republic; Georges Pompidou and Pierre Messmer had been briefly affiliated with the Socialist party, whereas the backgrounds of Maurice Couve de Murville, Jacques Chirac, and Raymond Barre could be considered more or less "nonpolitical." Pierre Mauroy and Pierre Bérégovoy had been well established members of the old Socialist party (the SFIO) and played prominent roles in the creation and leadership of the new Socialist party (the PS) in 1969–1970. Michel Rocard had been a leader of the PSU and, after his entry into the PS in the early 1970s, controlled an important faction within that party; in late 1980, Rocard briefly vied with Mitterrand for the nomination as the party's candidate for the presidency. Edith Cresson had been active in the Convention of Republican Institutions (CIR), a political formation led by Mitterrand, and a few years after the latter took over the leadership of the PS, she became a member of that party's secretariat. Debré had been a senator, a civil servant, a writer, an important ideologist of Gaullism, and one of the chief architects of the new constitution. Pompidou had been by turns a lycée professor of literature, a member of de Gaulle's "kitchen cabinet" in 1945, a civil servant, and a director of the Rothschild banking house. Couve de Murville had been a respected civil servant and had served as de Gaulle's foreign minister for several years. Chaban-Delmas had been a hero of the Resistance, mayor of Bordeaux (a position he still held as of 1994), and speaker of the Assembly. Messmer had been a civil servant, cabinet minister, and colonial troubleshooter. Chirac had held a number of important civil service positions and, after 1968, a variety of cabinet posts. Barre, a professor of economics, had been minister of foreign trade, and Mauroy had been mayor of Lille, a position he still occupied as of 1994. Laurent Fabius, appointed in 1984—at age 37 the youngest French premier in this century—had been a professional civil

servant who had begun his political career in 1974, when he joined the Socialist party; in quick succession he had become Mitterrand's economic advisor, chief
of staff, and manager of his successful presidential election campaign. Subsequently Fabius had served as Economics Minister Delors's deputy for the budget
and had been credited (or blamed) for much of the government's austerity policy;
later, as minister of industry, he had been responsible for cutting the budgetary
allocations to the public sector and for promoting efficient private industry, even
at the cost of a steep growth of unemployment. Edith Cresson had served as
minister of agriculture and subsequently as minister of foreign trade and minister
in charge of European Community affairs. Pierre Bérégovoy had been secretary-
general of the presidential office when Mitterrand assumed the presidency, subsequently becoming minister of social affairs, finance, and finally (under Cresson)
a "superminister" of economic affairs, finance, and budget. Edouard Balladur, the
current premier (as of 1994), had held a number of high administrative positions
(including membership in the Council of State) and had served as secretary-
general of the presidential office under Pompidou. After an interlude of activity
in the private sector he had been appointed minister of finance in the first
"cohabitation" government headed by Chirac (see Table 6.1).

The six premiers before August 1976 had been loyal Gaullists at one time or
another: They had been prominent in either the Resistance or the Free French
movement (except for Pompidou, who sat out World War II and the Occupation
in Paris, and Chirac, who was too young) or had close personal relations with
de Gaulle; and all but one had experience in the government bureaucracy. Ten
premiers had had parliamentary experience—Debré, Chaban-Delmas, Messmer,
Chirac, Mauroy, Fabius, Rocard, Cresson, Bérégovoy, and Balladur—and three—
Pompidou, Couve de Murville, and Barre—had not, although in 1968 Couve had
run unsuccessfully for a seat in Parliament in a Paris constituency.

All premiers (except during "cohabitation" periods) have stood for a "theme"
considered politically desirable by the president. Debré, the orthodox Gaullist,
helped to launch the new regime he had done so much to shape; Pompidou
represented a technocratic outlook and a business orientation; Couve de Murville,
clearly an interim premier, stood for nonpartisanship; Chaban-Delmas was chosen
to appeal to progressive centrist forces with his quest for a "new society";
Messmer, a conservative Gaullist, was chosen largely for the purpose of retriev-
ing the support of orthodox adherents of Gaullism; and Chirac (in his first term)
was appointed because he combined a background of Gaullism and technocracy
and had the wisdom to prefer Giscard d'Estaing over Chaban-Delmas in the first
round of the presidential elections of 1974. Barre was chosen ostensibly because
of his professional orientation and his seeming lack of political ambition. Mauroy
was selected because of his nearly ideal background: Born into the working class
(and for a time employed as a teacher in a vocational school), he maintained close
ties with the industrial unions of the northeast region; as a moderate, he got along
easily with the leaders of the various party factions. Fabius was chosen partly in
order to help rejuvenate the image of the Mitterrand régime; the president's
popularity had slipped badly in public-opinion polls because of dissatisfaction over

TABLE 6.1   Fifth Republic prime ministers

President	Prime Minister	Month/Year of Appointment	Length of Tenure (in months)	Cumulative Tenure
De Gaulle	Debré	January 1959	39	39
	Pompidou I	April 1962	7	
	II	December 1962	37	
	III	January 1966	15	
	IV	April 1967	15	74
	Couve de Murville	July 1968	11	11
Pompidou	Chaban-Delmas	June 1969	36	36
	Messmer I	July 1972	8	
	II	April 1973	11	
	III	March 1974	3	22
Giscard d'Estaing	Chirac	May 1974	27	27
	Barre I	August 1976	7	
	II	March 1977	12	
	III	April 1978	37	56
Mitterrand	Mauroy I	May 1981	1	
	II	June 1981	21	
	III	March 1983	16	38
	Fabius	July 1984	20	20
	Chirac	March 1986	25	25
	Rocard I	May 1988	1	
	II	June 1988	35	36
	Cresson	May 1991	10	10
	Bérégovoy	April 1992	12	12
	Balladur	March 1993		

NOTE: Months are rounded off.

the unresolved unemployment problem. Fabius was not only brilliant (he was a graduate of the Ecole Normale Supérieure and the Ecole Nationale d'Administration [ENA], the two most prestigious schools of France) but was also identified as a competent pragmatist who was closely associated with the national effort at industrial modernization. Rocard was appointed in part to appease his numerous supporters within the Socialist party and in part because his nonideological approach to problems would facilitate the building of bridges to the political Center—and in so doing, would help to weaken the political Right.[12] Edith Cresson was selected because of her loyalty to the president as well as her identification with a policy of industrial competitiveness, and Bérégovoy was chosen as an interim premier identified with fiscal responsibility.[13]

Despite their qualifications, most premiers have had a subservient relationship to their presidents, especially if such behavior helped to promote their ambitions of someday succeeding to the presidency (as Pompidou had done). However, that subservience has been uneven. A recent study of the French premier includes a "typology of presidential–prime ministerial relations" that distinguishes among premiers who were subordinates, rivals, and opponents of the president.[14] The nature of the relationship has depended on a variety of factors: the "chemistry" of personal interaction, the cohesion within the cabinet, the nature of policy issues, the electoral factor, and the composition of parliament.

COHABITATION I: PRECEDENT-SETTING PATTERN OR POLITICAL PARENTHESIS?

The relationship between president and premier changed dramatically after the parliamentary election of 1986, which produced a Gaullist-Giscardist antipresidential majority in the National Assembly. Some politicians argued that this result should be interpreted as a popular disavowal of Mitterrand's conduct as president and that he should resign.[15] Mitterrand (whose own term of office still had two years left) refused to do so. However, he was obliged to appoint a premier and cabinet to the Assembly's liking rather than his own and had to relinquish most of the decision-making power, at least in domestic matters, to the premier.

The necessity to "cohabit" with a hostile premier and Assembly transformed a hitherto powerful president into a constitutional semimonarch. In effect, Mitterrand now considered his main task "to watch out that the decisions of the government or of the [parliamentary] majority not be detrimental to that which is good, sane, and necessary in [the spirit of] national unity."[16] Much like the British queen (who, in the words of Walter Bagehot, retained "the right to be consulted, to encourage, and to warn"[17]), Mitterrand thought that he retained "in domestic politics [the right], when necessary, to make known his judgment and to warn public opinion against that which . . . was dangerous for national unity and the public interest."[18]

The precise method of power sharing had to be determined in an ad hoc fashion since there was no precedent for it in the Fifth Republic. Cohabitation was an experiment in terms of both government appointments and policy making.[19] Although it was clear from the beginning that the new government would be led by a person who would be supported by the Assembly, it was not certain that that person had to be Chirac. Mitterrand chose Chirac as premier probably because in so doing he averted the possibility of the Assembly's *imposing* him on the president. Mitterrand left the nomination of ministers to Chirac almost entirely, except that he rejected Chirac's original choices for the posts of minister of foreign affairs and defense, the two areas that Mitterrand continued to consider presidential domains. Once the government was constituted, Mitterrand's contact with it collectively was confined to the weekly Wednesday cabinet meetings: These were run by the premier, with Mitterrand confining himself on most occasions to words of admonition and wise counsel.

Driven by ambition, Chirac attempted to "invade" the presidential foreign policy domain or at least to achieve a kind of comanagement of it. Thus, he insisted on accompanying Mitterrand to the economic summit meeting in Tokyo in May 1986; ten months later, he appeared at a French-Spanish summit meeting in Madrid and took the credit for the improvement of relations between the two countries, only to be publicly "corrected" by Mitterrand.

Conversely, although Mitterrand left domestic matters largely in the hands of Chirac, the former was not above interfering in that domain to the extent that he was able to do so and when it suited his political purposes. Thus he did nothing to stop the promotion of Chirac's major policies, among them the denationalization of more than 60 state-owned enterprises, tougher laws to fight terrorism and to control the movement of immigrants, and a return to the single-member constituency system that had been abandoned only a year earlier by the Socialists. But Mitterrand refused to sign government decrees providing for selected policy changes (e.g., changing the boundaries of election districts and privatizing a number of business firms and banks), thereby forcing the government to put these measures through the "normal" (though speeded-up) parliamentary processes.[20] Furthermore, Mitterrand publicly expressed his reservations about projected government policies regarding the treatment of immigrants and changes of the citizenship laws, thereby forcing the government to seek wider consensus for these reforms by means of a specially appointed "committee of experts" (see Chapter 7).

Mitterrand got away with these periodic forays into policy making because the Chirac government was not a monolithic bloc. The government was weakened by its lack of internal unity; it was itself an experiment in "cohabitation" between Gaullist and Giscardist ministers and it had to accommodate to the rivalries between Chirac and François Léotard, the leader of the Republican party (the largest component of the UDF), who was concurrently minister of culture. There were other bones of contention: Thus when Charles Pasqua, the hard-line Gaullist minister of interior, introduced a bill to curb the display of pornographic magazines and their sale to juveniles, Léotard declared his opposition to censorship of the press. Moreover, Léotard's openly avowed interest in becoming a presidential candidate in 1988 was criticized by Chirac as incompatible with Léotard's ministerial responsibilities, a critique that Léotard rejected in a provocative public statement.[21] Between 1986 and 1988, the relations between the RPR and UDF were embittered by feelings that the latter did not get enough consideration from Chirac and that the former was taking the lion's share of top ministerial and other political jobs. In addition, there were arguments *within* the ranks of the Gaullist ministers, as, for example, when Michel Noir, the minister of foreign trade, took exception to Pasqua's (and Chirac's) sympathetic understanding of the National Front's hostility toward resident aliens. This lack of government solidarity made presidential intervention easier and sometimes even provoked it.

In retrospect, it appears that Mitterrand's withdrawal from most of the domestic policy arena enhanced his presidential stature in the eyes of the public (as public-opinion polls show). Conversely, Chirac's increased policy-making responsibilities served as a long rope with which he, so to speak, could hang himself. Chirac's standing was weakened, not merely because he was unable to bring unity to his government but also because while promising firmness, he was not firm enough to maintain his policy directions in the face of public pressures (e.g., in the case of reforms of school administration, social security, the privatization of prisons, the right to enroll in certain university programs, and the reform of the citizenship laws). In any case, whereas in the beginning of Chirac's second premiership, cohabitation proceeded fairly smoothly—in part in response to public opinion, which seemed to be solidly in favor of the experiment—at the end it deteriorated to a strained relationship between president and premier.[22]

COHABITATION II: A "CIVILIZED" WAITING GAME?

With the overwhelming victory of the combined Gaullist-Giscardist forces in the parliamentary elections of March 1993, it became clear that the cohabitation experiment would have to be repeated. Even before the elections, when the outcome was predicted, Mitterrand had prepared himself for renewed power sharing by announcing that he would continue to serve out his presidential term no matter who won the elections and who was prime minister. At a press conference he reminded his audience that the Constitution provided for a division of responsibilities and that "it is not the task of the president of the Republic to govern."[23] The appointment of Edouard Balladur, a moderate Gaullist, to head the new conservative government was a compromise: It accorded with the wishes of both the RPR and the UDF, in the sense that he was their least objectionable choice. Given the rival presidential ambitions of Chirac, the leader of the RPR, and Giscard d'Estaing, the leader of the UDF, neither would be tolerated by the other. Since the RPR had by far the largest number of seats in the new Assembly, Chirac could have insisted on the premiership despite the misgivings of both Giscard and Mitterrand; but he preferred to have someone else take on the job in order to avoid a replay of the first cohabitation episode, that is, to avoid taking direct responsibility for unpopular political decisions that might alienate the voters during the next presidential elections.

The second cohabitation has proved to be a relatively smooth one. Not only have Mitterrand and Balladur respected each other, but each has had an interest in continuing a working relationship as long as possible. For if that relationship broke down, Mitterrand might resign and a speeded-up presidential election would have to take place, in which Chirac (thoroughly detested by Mitterrand) would be the likely winner.[24] For his part, Balladur wished to be prime minister long enough to solve important problems, prove his ability to govern, and come to be regarded as capable of becoming president someday. Balladur did not openly avow any presidential ambitions and Chirac continued to be regarded as the presumptive presidential candidate of the RPR. Nevertheless, Balladur's presidential appetite was probably whetted as his popularity rose (despite growing unemployment) and as public-opinion polls revealed that, among the electorate at large as well as among prospective Gaullist voters, he was a much more popular presidential candidate than Chirac.

To be sure, Mitterrand and Balladur have differed on a number of issues: the unemployment problem, immigration, the right to asylum, constitutional reform, and socioeconomic policies, and the president continues periodically to voice his policy preferences and his concern for social justice. But the two have similar views on foreign policy, defense, and international trade negotiations, a fact that makes it easier for the premier to accept Mitterrand's continued involvement in these matters and permits both the president and the prime minister to test the limits of the presidential "reserved domain."[25] The president and the premier hold frequent consultations, try to avoid public criticism of each other, and often appear together at international meetings. In fact, Balladur sometimes consults with the president *before* he meets with his cabinet.[26] Their collaboration has been facilitated by the harmonious relationship of their respective chief executive officers.[27]

As premier, Balladur has had to perform a multiple balancing act: to avoid needlessly antagonizing the president without incurring the accusation of being his mouthpiece; to ensure a smooth "cohabitation" of the Gaullist and Giscardist members of his government; and to prevent the policy disagreements within his coalition and within the Gaullist leadership group itself (e.g., between the pro- and anti-Europeans and the social progressives and conservatives) from getting out of hand. In addition, he has to make sure that he is not too openly criticized by Chirac from his safe perch outside the national government. For his part, Chirac, too, has had to perform a balancing act: to pretend to support the policies of Balladur lest he be accused of destroying the solidarity of the RPR/UDF coalition and to hope that Balladur's performance will deteriorate and his popularity decline, while he, Chirac, will escape the blame.

THE GOVERNMENT

In size if not power, the typical Fifth Republic government resembles those of earlier French regimes. It has ranged from 24 members under the provisional premiership of de Gaulle in July 1958 to 49 under Premier Rocard in June 1988 (see Table 6.2). The nature and distribution of ministerial portfolios have reflected the problems and pressures of the day. In the Fourth Republic, ministerial posts were established for veterans' affairs, colonies, and even Algerian affairs. Under de Gaulle's presidency, Ministries of Cultural Affairs, Scientific Research, Information, and International Cooperation were created. President Pompidou established a Ministry for Craftsmen and Small Businessmen, and President Giscard d'Estaing added a Ministry for the Quality of Life. Under the Socialist governments of President Mitterrand's first term, a new Ministry for the Economic Plan was formed (both to stress the revival of interest in planning and to satisfy the ambitions of

Michel Rocard); the Ministry of Interior was given the added task of decentralization; and the Ministry of Repatriates was changed to the Ministry of Immigrants. Later, under the premiership of Chirac, the Ministries of Culture and Communication were merged, and a "superministry" of Economic Affairs, Finance, and Privatization was set up. Under the premiership of Balladur, Social Affairs, Health, and Urban Affairs were put under the authority of a single minister of state (Simone Veil). France does not have a "patron" ministry for Bretons, Basques, or Alsatians that would be analogous to the British Ministries for Scottish or Welsh Affairs; there have, however, been instances of prominent Breton and other regional minority politicians being appointed to ministerial positions for reasons of ethnic balance.

Although occasionally a person may be co-opted from the world of business or banking, a cabinet like that of President Eisenhower, which consisted of "nine millionaires and a plumber," would be unthinkable in France. Whereas in the United States an intellectual as a cabinet member is a rarity, the typical French cabinet since the Third Republic has included a high proportion of university and lycée professors and freelance intellectuals. Fifth Republic cabinets have contained a significant number of graduates of the elite schools. For example, 10 of the 15 full ministers (out of a total of 36 ministers of all ranks) in the first Chirac government were graduates of the *grandes écoles*. In the first Mauroy government, 9 ministers were professional civil servants, and of these, 6 were graduates of ENA, but 15 were university professors or public school teachers (including the secretary-general of the major teachers' union). Chirac's second (i.e., cohabitation) government contained 12 ENA graduates ("Enarques") and one graduate of the Ecole Polytechnique. The government constituted by Rocard after the legislative elections of 1988 (one that was to be more representative of "civil society") contained 9 Enarques out of a total of 49 ministers (including the premier himself). Although the Balladur government contained only 8 Enarques (the premier among them), it included no one from outside the "political class": All had been elected to Parliament at least once (4 of them to the Senate).

Cabinet ministers have the specific roles of supervising the civil servants in their particular ministries (which may include several departments or agencies), developing policy in their domain, helping to draft bills and steer them through Parliament, providing expertise to the cabinet, and defending government policy touching on their jurisdiction. The cabinet reflects a complex hierarchy of titles and positions, indicating both the importance of a portfolio and the political position of the minister. At the top are the full ministers, among them the ministers of finance, defense, foreign affairs, justice, interior, and education. Occasionally the title Minister of State may be granted to a full minister in order to indicate his or her special relationship to the president or (as in 1986 and 1993) the premier, as in the cases of André Malraux, de Gaulle's minister of culture; three ministers under Giscard; five in the first Socialist government under President Mitterrand;[28] one each in the Fabius government and in Chirac's "cohabitation" government; four in the second Rocard government, and four in the Balladur government (see Table 6.3). Below the ministers are the "junior ministers"

TABLE 6.2   Party composition of selected Fifth Republic governments

President	de Gaulle				Pompidou		Giscard d'Estaing		
Prime Minister	Debré	Pompidou		Couve de Murville	Chaban-Delmas	Messmer	Chirac	Barre	
	January 1959	April 1962	April 1967	July 1968	June 1969	July 1972	June 1974	August 1976	July 1979
Political Party									
Gaullists	6	9	21	26	29	22	12	9	12
Republicans	—	3	3	4	7	5	8	10	11[g]
Centrists	3[a]	5[a]	—	—	3[c]	3[c]	2	2[e]	4[e]
Radicals	1	1	—	—	—	—	6[d]	5	1[h]
Left Radicals	—	—	—	—	—	—	—	—	—
Socialists	—	—	—	—	—	—	—	—	—
Communists	—	—	—	—	—	—	—	—	—
Miscellaneous	7[b]	—	—	—	—	—	—	—	3[i]
Nonparty	10	11	5	1	—	—	8	10[f]	10[f]
Totals (includes Prime Minister)	27	29	29	31	39	30	36	36	41

[1] 18 full (cabinet) ministers (including 14 Socialists)
[2] 15 cabinet ministers (including 7 Gaullists, 5 various UDF, 3 nonparty)
[3] 19 cabinet ministers (including 14 Socialists)
[4] 22 cabinet ministers (including 14 Socialists, 1 Left Socialist, 4 UDF, 3 nonparty)
[5] 16 cabinet ministers (including 16 Socialists, 1 Centrist [*France Unie*], 1 Ecologist, 2 nonparty)
[6] 21 cabinet ministers
[7] 24 cabinet ministers (including 12 Gaullists, 11 UDF, 1 nonparty)
[a] MRP
[b] Includes 5 Independents
[c] Center for Democracy and Progress (CDP)
[d] Reformers
[e] Center of Social Democrats (CDS)

(*ministres délégués* and *secrétaires d'Etat*), who are usually attached to the office of the premier or a full minister.[29]

The principle of collective cabinet responsibility—that is, the notion that individual cabinet members must publicly agree with the general cabinet position on all issues—has been retained. This principle was often violated in the Fourth Republic because cabinets were coalitions of great ideological diversity and political parties frequently insisted that their representatives in the cabinet stand by the parties' positions on specific issues. Ambitious ministers were sometimes interested in deliberately creating cabinet disunity so that a government would collapse and they would, they hoped, be able to move up when it was reconstituted—for example, from the Ministry of Finance or Labor to the premiership. If, after a reshuffle, ministers did not get any cabinet post, they did not lose everything since they retained their parliamentary seats. In the Fifth Republic, an ousted minister, even though he may have been recruited from Parliament, has no formal right to return to it (see Chapter 7 for a discussion of the "incompatibility" rule).

	Mitterrand							
Mauroy		Fabius	Chirac	Rocard		Cresson	Bérégovoy	Balladur
May 1981	June 1981	July 1984[1]	March 1986[2]	May 1988[3]	June 1988[4]	May 1991[5]	April 1992[6]	March 1993[7]
—	—	—	20	—	—	—	—	14
—	—	—	7[g]	—	1	—	—	6
—	—	—	7[e]	—	1[o]	2[o]	—	5[e]
—	—	—	2	1	1	—	—	1
3	2	3	—	2	3	2[p]	2	—
39	37	36	—	26	25	32	31	—
—	4	—	—	—	—	—	—	—
1[j]	1[j]	1[m]	—	2[n]	3[n]	1[q]	—	3[r]
—	—	3	6	11	15	9	9	1[s]
43	44	43	42	42	49	46	42	30

[f]Collectively designated as "presidential majority"
[g]Known until 1977 as Independent Republicans
[h]"Democratic Left"
[i]Includes one "Social Democrat," one member of CNIP, and the Prime Minister
[j]Movement of Democrats, an ex-Gaullist group supporting Mitterrand in the presidential elections of 1981
[m]*Parti socialiste unifié* (PSU)
[n]Direct (nondifferentiated) members of UDF
[o]*France unie,* a coalition formed in the Assembly of Left Radicals and Centrists to enlarge the presidential majority toward the center and support Michel Rocard
[p]These Left Radicals (MRG) also belonged to *France unie*
[q]Ecologist movement
[r]Includes 2 "direct" adherents of UDF and a member of *Club perspectives et réalités* (a component of UDF)
[s]Simone Veil, a centrist close to Giscard d'Estaing

Although cabinet making no longer *completely* depends on party alignments in Parliament, factionalism within the parties supporting the president (or, during cohabitation, the government) has remained significant, with the result that ideological or programmatic divergences within the cabinet cannot altogether be avoided. Within the Mauroy government, for example, there were disagreements regarding the inclusion of Communists in the government, the nationalization of industries, and the extent to which administrative decentralization should be pursued; within the (second) Chirac government, there were differences of opinion regarding collaboration with the National Front, educational policy, immigrants, and civil liberties. Within the Balladur government, there are differences of opinion regarding the European Union, social security, public investment, law and order issues, and immigration policy, differences that overlap the RPR and UDF.

What power does the cabinet have? In the Fourth Republic, the cabinet was as powerful as the premier; however, the premier's position was insecure because Parliament was so jealous of its prerogatives that it was hesitant to grant meaningful decision-making powers to him or her. It tended to oust premiers who

TABLE 6.3 The French government in April 1993

Prime Minister: **Edouard Balladur (RPR)**

Ministers of State
Social Affairs, Health, Urban Affairs: **Simone Veil**[a]
Interior and Regional Planning: **Charles Pasqua** (RPR)
Justice: **Pierre Méhaignerie** (UDF-CDS)
Defense: **François Léotard** (UDF-PR)

Ministers
Foreign Affairs: **Alain Juppé** (RPR)
Education: **François Bayrou** (UDF-CDS)
Economy: **Edmond Alphandéry** (UDF-CDS)
Posts, Telecommunications, Foreign Trade: **Gérard Longuet** (UDF-PR)
Equipment,[b] Transport, Tourism: **Bernard Bosson** (UDF-CDS)
Industrial Development and Small Business: **Alain Madelin** (UDF-PR)
Labor, Employment, Vocational Training: **Michel Giraud** (RPR)
Culture and French-speaking countries: **Jacques Toubon** (RPR)
Budget, and Government spokesman: **Nicolas Sarkozy** (RPR)
Agriculture and Fisheries: **Jean Puech** (UDF-PR)
Higher Education and research: **François Fillon** (RPR)
Environment: **Michel Barnier** (RPR)
Civil service: **André Rossinot** (UDF-Radical)
Housing: **Hervé de Charette** (UDF-P et R[c])
[International] Cooperation: **Michel Roussin** (RPR)
Overseas Departments and Territories: **Dominique Perben** (RPR)
Youth and Sports: **Michéle Alliot-Marie** (RPR)
Communication: **Alain Carignon** (RPR)
Veterans and War Victims: **Philippe Mestre** (UDF)

Junior Ministers[d]
Relations with National Assembly [Premier]: **Pascal Clément** (UDF-PR)
Relations with Senate and Problems of Repatriates [Premier]: **Roger Romani** (RPR)
Social Affairs, Health, and Urban Affairs [Social Affairs]: **Philippe Douste-Blazy** (UDF-CDS)
Regional Planning and Local Authorities [Interior]: **Daniel Hoeffel** (UDF)
Humanitarian Action and Human Rights [Foreign Affairs]: **Lucette Michaux-Chevry** (RPR)
European Affairs [Foreign Affairs]: **Alain Lamassoure** (UDF-PR)

[a]Nonparty, but close to UDF-CDS
[b]Refers to infrastructure facilities
[c]*Club perspectives et réalités*
[d]*Ministres délégués,* akin to U.S. undersecretaries
[ ] Supervising Minister
SOURCE: *Regards sur l'actualité* 190 (April, 1993), 55.

asserted themselves too much. In the Fifth Republic, premiers and cabinet members have been less powerful because presidents are jealous of *their* prerogatives; hence the constitutional provision (Art. 20) that stipulates that "the government shall determine and direct the policy of the nation" is not a reliable prescription for power sharing with the president, unless (as happened in 1986 and 1993) the premier is fully supported, and the president is opposed, by the Assembly. Because under normal conditions premiers and cabinets depend more on the support of the president than Parliament, the role of the cabinet is frequently that of a sounding board for presidential ideas. This is especially true of foreign affairs, which often fail to be fully discussed in cabinet meetings.

Furthermore, the cabinet and premier share whatever power they have with other bodies, such as the staff of the presidential office, or with personal friends of the president who are part of a "kitchen cabinet." The Presidential Office (the Elysée palace staff) is headed by a secretary-general and includes a growing number (now many more than 500) of legal, financial, military, technical, and political counselors, secretaries, liaisons with other agencies (e.g., the Planning Office, the Economic and Social Council, the Parliament), and a correspondence department.[30] The kitchen cabinet has been institutionalized in the personal staff of the president (*cabinet du président*). The individuals heading this personal staff have sometimes been self-effacing; others have been very much in the limelight.[31] Most of the special counselors have been ambitious, as have the secretaries-general of the Elysée, who have used their office as a stepping-stone to a higher position.[32] Some of the staffers have been recruited from the higher civil service (often via ENA); others from Parliament; still others from the universities or even from interest groups.[33] The president may also consult with individuals who have no official position at all. Giscard often met with leaders of business; Mitterrand has had consultations with officials of trade unions and teachers' associations, business leaders (to the chagrin of some leftist Socialists), and assorted intellectuals. He has, of course, also frequently consulted the secretary-general of the Socialist party and the leader of that party's parliamentary group (though Mitterrand has done this less frequently since his election to a second term).[34]

The frequency of cabinet meetings is in itself no indication of the extent to which the president consults his ministers when he makes a decision. Meetings of the full cabinet of 20 to 25 ministers, which take place every Wednesday morning, are not always conducive to thorough discussions of issues. Therefore, the custom of appointing smaller bodies in which only selected ministers participate has arisen: interministerial committees, usually chaired by the premier, or restricted committees (*comités restreints*), presided over by the president. Some of these committees, such as the Committee on National Defense or the Committee on Foreign Affairs, took on a permanent character, while others will probably remain ad hoc, such as the Committee on Urban Affairs formed by Balladur.

Under Pompidou, a slight upgrading of the cabinet took place, and it met more frequently than it had under his predecessor. This upgrading was probably due to two circumstances: (1) The relative absence of international conflicts involving France turned the president's attention more to domestic problems, in which *arbitrage* functions were less important than economic and other technical expertise (often found in the cabinet); (2) the cabinets contained certain old Gaullists or pro-Gaullists whose stature was too great for Pompidou to ignore them—notably Michel Debré, the first premier under de Gaulle, and Valéry Giscard d'Estaing, minister of finance and leader of a political party (the Independent Republicans) that was of growing importance. But even under Pompidou's presidency, there was no reliable evidence indicating that consultation with the cabinet as a basis of presidential decisions occupied a more prominent place in relation to other consultative mechanisms than it did under de Gaulle.

Under Giscard, the full cabinet ministers met weekly to discuss policy, with the secretaries of state called upon to participate only occasionally. Moreover, Giscard was in almost daily contact with his premier and consulted frequently, and informally, with selected cabinet ministers (notably Michel Poniatowski, a personal friend, who was minister of interior from 1974 to 1977).

Mitterrand continued this pattern, in addition to the practice of convoking on a weekly basis an "inner cabinet" chaired by himself and composed of the secretary-general of the Presidential Office, the premier, and a few ministers. One of Mitterrand's innovations was the creation in 1982 of a *conseil restreint* for economic policy, which included the premier and a small number of ministers, and which met weekly. Although Mitterrand determined the major direction of policy, he allowed his ministers a great deal of discretion on specific issues. Thus, at least until early in 1983, Premier Mauroy had overall responsibility for promoting legislation regarding economic policies and for justifying them to the public. The ministers of interior, justice, and education were given considerable freedom to develop measures concerning administrative decentralization, penal reforms, and the modernization of secondary-school and university curricula, respectively. Mitterrand would, of course, intervene in case of disaccord among the ministers, especially if it could not be resolved by the premier.[35] During the first cohabitation interlude, decision making shifted in the direction of the premier and the cabinet, as Article 20 (which gives the government policy-making power) acquired new significance. This shift applied to some extent even to military and foreign affairs (e.g., matters relating to the European Community and defense spending) to which the president, the premier, and the cabinet developed a more or less collaborative approach.

With Mitterrand's reelection in 1988 and the installation of Rocard's Socialist government, a growing understanding between the president and the premier could be discerned. As Mitterrand's status of a Socialist politician evolved toward that of a nonpartisan statesman, the implementation of his preferences, as outlined in his "Letter to the French" (see note 10), was increasingly left in the hands of Premier Rocard.[36] He was given the credit for the successful handling of delicate problems, among them the crisis in New Caledonia (a French overseas territory), the claims of Corsican civil servants for increased financial support from Paris, and the strikes of transport workers. Furthermore, it was reported that at cabinet meetings, Mitterrand carefully (and even ostentatiously) solicited the advice of Rocard on every question of policy under discussion.[37]

It is a matter of debate whether this was done voluntarily, for the president and the premier did not always agree. Thus, Mitterrand favored a more liberal policy vis-à-vis immigrants and a more benevolent attitude toward the less privileged classes than Rocard; and Mitterrand wanted to keep the flame of leftist unity burning and tried to maintain a bridge to Communists (as if he were still running for the presidency), while Rocard concentrated on developing openings to the centrists, in part in order to cultivate support for his policies in Parliament and improve his ability to govern.[38]

In the eyes of some observers, the relationship between Mitterrand and Rocard was a "paper marriage" marked by a thinly cloaked tension.[39] In any case, the growing civility of that relationship translated into an approval rating of 60 percent for both in the spring of 1989. This result attested to an improved position of the premier, but it was unclear whether that translated into increased power of the cabinet as a whole. In a circular letter addressed to his ministers, Rocard promised to "govern differently" by according greater respect to the Constitution, to Parliament, and to "civil society" outside the political establishment. But he seemed to give little scope to his fellow ministers; on the contrary, he envisaged a "rigorous definition of the role of the premier vis-à-vis his team: [he] would not merely arbitrate [interministerial] disputes but would make decisions." Above all, he would insist on governmental solidarity, as reflected in "a strict discipline with respect to public declarations."[40] In accordance with that principle, he dismissed the minister of health a week after his appointment for having made a number of public policy pronouncements without clearing them with the premier.

In view of the foregoing, it is not always easy to know which decisions arrived at by the cabinet owe their inspiration to the president, the premier, or individual ministers. All presidents have stretched the definition of the "presidential" domain and have made decisions about matters that might well have been left to the discretion of ministers. In the case of de Gaulle, these decisions included the refusal to lower the retirement age of workers; opposition to the reforms of the *baccalauréat* examination; the decision to raise the minimum wage by 3 percent; and frequent intervention in budget making. Under Pompidou, presidential intrusions involved raising the height limits for buildings in the Paris area, vetoing an appointment to the *Académie Française,* and deciding to lower the value-added tax on foodstuffs. In the case of Giscard, an acknowledged expert in economics, presidential decisions involved prices, wages, the floating of the franc, and many other economic matters. He went beyond the practice of his predecessors in scrutinizing the texts of ministerial communiqués and personally editing the language of bills prepared by civil servants (thus bringing the bureaucracy more directly under presidential control).[41] It is unclear whether some of the decisions of the Mauroy government should be attributed primarily to President Mitterrand or the cabinet, among them the decision to seek the abolition of capital punishment, to raise the minimum wage for industrial workers, to replace the holdover administrators of the national radio and television offices, or (under the Cresson government) to move the National School of Administration from Paris to Strasbourg. But the decisions to include Communists in the government and to press ahead with legislation to nationalize certain industries—each decision favored by some and opposed by other ministers—were doubtlessly the president's alone. That was true also with respect to a decision to appoint a program director of a newly built opera house in Paris.

Presidents have shown their independence of the cabinet in other ways as well. De Gaulle undertook periodic *tours de France* in order to "consult" the people,[42] a practice continued by succeeding presidents. Moreover, both de Gaulle and Pompidou used the referendum, which allowed them to bypass the cabinet and obtain legitimation of a purely presidential decision. Although Article 11 of the Constitution specifies that a referendum must be "proposed" by the government before it is submitted to the people, de Gaulle announced to the cabinet in 1962 that *he* would propose to it a referendum on the direct election of the president. Similarly, it was Pompidou, rather than the cabinet, who initiated the referendum (in 1972) on the question of Britain's membership in the Common Market.[43] Under Giscard, consultation with the people did not involve referenda. Instead it took the form of "walking tours" through Paris, frequent meetings with spokespersons of national economic organizations, and highly publicized encounters with ordinary citizens. Mitterrand's attitude toward referenda has been ambiguous. In mid-1984, apparently frustrated by massive public opposition to his proposals concerning the "integration" of parochial schools into the national educational system, Mitterrand announced that he would introduce a constitutional amendment that would provide for the holding of public referenda on questions of civil liberties—in addition to their original use for questions pertaining to "the organization of public powers." There was no follow-through in this instance. However, as mentioned above, Mitterrand resorted to a referendum to ratify the Treaty on European Union in 1992, although he left it up to Parliament to pass an amendment to the Constitution that was made necessary by that treaty.

THE CONSTRUCTION AND RESHUFFLING OF CABINETS

The Constitution requires a ministerial countersignature of a presidential action, a provision that seems to harness individual ministers more precisely to a decision-making role. But ministers have owed their positions to the president in one way or another. Although they are in theory picked by the premier after the latter has himself been selected by the president, many ministers have in fact also been chosen by the president. At a press conference in 1964, de Gaulle referred to "the president who chooses the premier, who has the possibility of changing him, either because he views his task as accomplished, or because he no longer approves of him."[44] De Gaulle's successors have clearly agreed with this interpretation of presidential discretion. Pompidou's position was articulated by his premier, Messmer, when the latter announced on television that after the parliamentary elections of 1973 the president would form a government on the basis of policies he wished to pursue and not on the basis of the ensuing parliamentary lineup.[45] Although Giscard's first premier, Chirac, resigned of his own volition, Giscard admitted that he himself had decided two months earlier to choose a new government.[46]

It is reported that most of the premiers who resigned while still enjoying the support of the Assembly—Debré in 1962, Pompidou in 1968, Chaban in 1972,

Chirac in 1976, Mauroy in 1984—had agreed in advance to resign whenever the president wished it.[47] Whether there is any basis to the rumor that every minister deposits on the president's desk an undated letter of resignation is difficult to confirm. But there is no doubt that all Fifth Republic presidents have had considerable discretion in regard to the selection, retention, and dismissal of cabinet members—except, of course, during periods of cohabitation.

De Gaulle personally selected a number of ministers for the Debré and Pompidou cabinets and was said to have totally constructed the cabinet of Couve de Murville.[48] It has been asserted that Messmer's cabinet colleagues were chosen by a confidant of Pompidou and that the governments of Chirac and Barre were entirely selected by Giscard. In 1981, Mitterrand made the crucial decisions regarding cabinet appointments, although in some cases he did so on the advice of his friends, and in particular that of Premier Mauroy.[49] In 1982 (years before power sharing was envisaged), Mitterrand asserted that he "was not sure" whether he would want to keep the same ministers until 1988.[50] Even in 1986, Mitterrand exercised a certain veto power over ministerial appointments.[51]

The foregoing should not be taken to mean that presidents have been entirely willful in the construction of cabinets. Despite the independence of the presidential role, all the chiefs of state in the Fifth Republic have been concerned with the political composition of the Assembly (even during normal, i.e., noncohabitation, periods), the electorate at large, or both. The first Fifth Republic cabinet, which was installed in January 1959, reflected an attempt to strike a balance between a few old Gaullists, who had to be rewarded for their political loyalties, and leaders of non-Gaullist parties whose support of the Fifth Republic during its initial phase was considered important. However, as if to illustrate de Gaulle's contempt for party politicians, more than a third of the cabinet members were nonparty technicians or civil servants, a ratio that was retained until the end of 1962. The depolitization of the cabinet during those years was also reflected in the *cabinets ministériels* (the ministers' staffs); whereas in the Fourth Republic they had been composed largely of the ministers' party associates or personal friends, there has been a tendency in the Fifth Republic to co-opt civil servants for these offices.[52]

Between the parliamentary elections of 1962 and 1967, the number of civil servants in the cabinet was reduced while the number of Gaullists was increased, roughly in proportion to the growth of the Gaullist majority in the Assembly.[53] After the parliamentary election of 1968, the cabinet assumed an even more Gaullist coloration, clearly corresponding to the overwhelming majority of the UDR in the new Assembly. The repolitization of the cabinet was balanced by the choice of a nonparty technician (Couve de Murville) as premier.

Under Pompidou, the repolitization of the cabinet was virtually complete; more than three-fourths of his ministers were Gaullists, and nonpartisan technocrats were almost totally excluded. Although Pompidou shared de Gaulle's notions about presidential independence and owed his election to a new presidential majority, he was in fact less independent vis-à-vis the Gaullist party establishment. No deputies had been elected on his coattails; although he openly asserted his leadership over the UDR, his Gaullist credentials were being challenged, and he was forced to silence these challenges with political payoffs. Moreover, he had to reward with cabinet positions a certain number of non-Gaullists who had supported him during the presidential election of 1969. After the parliamentary election of 1973 and the collapse of the Gaullist majority in the Assembly, Pompidou's sensitivity to Parliament increased. Although the idea of presidential continuity was conveyed in the retention of a genuine Gaullist as premier, most of the other important holdovers were nonorthodox Gaullists, Independent Republicans, and centrists.

With the election of Giscard, the cabinet was recast in a manner reflecting at once the composition of the Assembly, the new president's penchant for technicians,[54] and his rather centrist presidential majority (see Table 6.2). One-quarter of the cabinet seats were assigned to nonparty people, and Gaullist representation was reduced to one-third of the total. After the parliamentary elections of 1978, the number of Gaullist ministers was reduced in favor of Republicans and the cabinet was progressively "Giscardized."

In the first government headed by Mauroy, the overwhelming majority were Socialists, two-thirds of them recruited from the outgoing Parliament. Mitterrand and Mauroy, in assembling the cabinet, were careful to include the leaders of all the important Socialist party factions, whose full support might be needed for government bills taken up in the Assembly. Nevertheless, the presidential dependence on Parliament should not be exaggerated. Even if the president in constructing a cabinet at some future time should be totally oblivious of party alignments in the Assembly, that body is not likely to take great risks in opposing him because the president is able to distribute favors (including political office and pork-barrel), censure motions are (under normal conditions) difficult to pass, and the president maintains the power of dissolution.

During periods of cohabitation, the construction of cabinets obviously depends much less on the president than on the premier. Nevertheless, the premier operates within certain constraints. In view of the president's visibility and involvement in foreign and military affairs, premiers are not likely to insist on the appointment of foreign and defense ministers to whom the president is clearly hostile. Furthermore, in making his or her ministerial appointments, the premier must satisfy the various factions in the coalition. Chirac's weakness during the first cohabitation period stemmed in part from the feeling on the part of his UDF partners that their camp was underrepresented in the cabinet. Balladur's strength during the second cohabitation period derived in part from the fact that he divided ministerial portfolios neatly between the RPR and the UDF.

Given the fact that presidential discretion applies equally to cabinet appointments and cabinet dismissals, and that there have been only four presidents in the Fifth Republic, three of them representing a continuity of political outlook, there has been much greater cabinet stability in the Fifth than in the Third and Fourth Republics. But this stability has not been absolute. Thus far (1959–1994), there have been only 13 prime ministers (if Chirac is counted only once) and 25 "governments," but there has been a significant turnover of ministers and a corresponding lateral movement of the ministers' higher civil-service staffs.[55] Since 1959 there have been 22 ministers of education and 20 ministers of justice. In contrast, greater stability has prevailed in the Ministries of Foreign Affairs and Defense. There have been more than 45 cabinet reshuffles, but not all of them involved the appointment of new faces. By virtue of their stature or political connections, a number of individuals have been extremely *ministrables* and were moved from one ministry to another (e.g., Michel Debré, who served as premier, finance minister, and defense minister; Edgar Faure, who had been a premier in the Fourth Republic and served in the Social Affairs and Education Ministries in the Fifth; Jacques Chirac, who held the Interior and Agriculture portfolios before becoming premier—and who has been mayor of Paris since 1977; Edith Cresson, who served as minister of agriculture, foreign trade, and European affairs; and Jean-Pierre Chevènement, who was successively minister of industry, education, and defense).

After the first election of Mitterrand there was a thorough turnover of ministers. This was paralleled by a replacement of the staffs of *cabinets ministériels*, often by union officials, journalists, and party hacks—not a surprising move by a party that had been out of power for more than 20 years. But this "reinjection of politics" (as Stanley Hoffmann has called it[56]) was limited: Of the 360 individuals appointed to the aforementioned staffs in the summer of 1981, only 32 were interest group or party officials, whereas 171 were upper- or middle-level civil servants. The element of continuity was not absent even among cabinet members. One cabinet member (Gaston Defferre, interior) had occupied two ministerial posts during the Fourth Republic; another (Claude Cheysson, foreign affairs) had been the *chef de cabinet* of Premier Mendès-France (1954); and still another (Michel Jobert, foreign trade) had been President Pompidou's foreign minister. One minister in the Rocard government (Jean-Pierre Soisson) had been a leader of the Republican party and had held several ministerial posts under Premiers Chirac and Barre.

Whereas in the Fourth Republic, cabinet reshuffles were usually the result of shifting parliamentary-party alignments and disagreements among coalition partners, changes in the Fifth Republic have taken place mostly because of disagreements between ministers and the president. To cite several examples: In 1959, the Socialist and Radical ministers left the cabinet because of disenchantment with de Gaulle's domestic policies; in 1960, the finance minister (Antoine Pinay) quit because he disagreed with Premier Debré and President de Gaulle; in 1962, five ministers, all close to the MRP, resigned in disagreement with de Gaulle's anti-European policies; in 1969, the minister of justice (René Capitant) quit after the resignation of de Gaulle because he was convinced that no successor on the horizon could maintain a genuinely "Gaullist" policy. In 1974, Jean-Jacques Servan-Schreiber was asked to resign from the cabinet shortly after his appointment as minister of administrative reform because of his public disagreement with President Giscard d'Estaing over continued nuclear testing; in 1985 Rocard resigned from the cabinet because he opposed Mitterrand's decision to reinstitute proportional representation for the forthcoming parliamentary elections; and in 1991, Jean-Pierre Chevènement resigned as minister of defense because of his opposition to French participation in the Gulf War.

Sometimes, the president may oust the premier or a cabinet minister because of the need for a scapegoat on whom blame can be fixed for a policy failure. De Gaulle replaced several ministers of education as a consequence of public criticism concerning university reforms, and he replaced Premier Pompidou after the Events of May 1968. In 1975, Giscard sacked the minister of posts because he had mishandled a mail strike (and had insulted postal workers by calling mail sorting "idiots' work"); in the same year, the defense minister was replaced because of unrest in the army over low pay. In 1984, the foreign minister was replaced for having mishandled relations with countries in the Middle East and misled the president; and in 1985, the defense minister was replaced because of the president's embarrassment over the *Greenpeace* affair (in which the French navy sank a foreign vessel in New Zealand waters). In 1992, Bernard Tapie was "suspended" from his function as minister of housing when he faced indictment for a questionable business deal.

There may be occasions when the sacking of ministers over a policy blunder may be more embarrassing to the president than keeping them. A case in point was the Habbash affair in January 1992, in which a notorious Palestinian terrorist was secretly allowed to come to France for medical treatment. When this incident was made public, Mitterrand dismissed, not the responsible ministers of foreign affairs and interior, but their directors-general.[57]

Cabinet changes may also occur if the president decides to give the government a new orientation or image, as when Pompidou appointed Chaban-Delmas as premier in 1969 in order to veer the Gaullists toward the center, and conversely, when he appointed Messmer in 1972 in order to return them to the right, and when Giscard replaced Premier Chirac with Barre in 1976 because the former had demanded too much power and had questioned Giscard's decision to move toward an economic policy of "neoliberalism" (i.e., greater reliance on market forces, a policy that Chirac himself was later to embrace). In 1984, Premier Mauroy was replaced by Fabius in order to signal a shift from a policy of welfare statism to a policy of productivity and austerity. The president may revamp the cabinet in order to make room for politicians whose party has moved from the opposition to the government side, as when the PDM in 1969 supported the Gaullists and its leader, Jacques Duhamel, was rewarded with a cabinet post, and when (in 1981) the Communists gave their unqualified support to Mitterrand in the second round and, after the parliamentary elections, were rewarded with four ministerial posts.

In March 1983, Mitterrand undertook a major restructuring of the cabinet, largely in response to the worsening economic situation. The total number of ministers was only slightly diminished, but the number of full cabinet members was reduced from 35 to 14. This "battle cabinet" was more conservative than the previous one and better suited for carrying out a policy of austerity.[58] Most of Mitterrand's close collaborators retained their positions; but one of his most severe critics (Jean-Pierre Chevènement, leader of the radical CERES faction of the Socialist party) was dismissed, and another, Rocard, was "demoted" from minister of planning to minister of agriculture. Although Mauroy continued as premier, Jacques Delors (a conservative Catholic Socialist and a proponent of tighter fiscal policies) became the "superminister" of economic affairs, finance, and budget and was given the major responsibility for economic policy.

The government's shift to the center was a political *necessity* in view of the fact that in the March 1983 municipal elections, the parties of the Left had lost control of 31 major towns to the Gaullist-Giscardist opposition; it was a political *possibility* because the Communists, having lost more seats than the Socialists, were too weak to resist it. A subsequent restructuring of the cabinet in 1984 signaled even more clearly the shift to the center. Although the Communist ministers had been invited to remain in the government and although several leftist Socialists who had been ousted (including Chevènement) were now returned to the government, the identification of the new premier, Fabius, as a principal architect of the austerity policy that was vehemently opposed by the PCF made it difficult for Communist ministers to remain in the government. Conversely, the departure of the Communists caused a number of centrist politicians within the UDF to express greater interest in supporting the government.

In May 1991, Mitterrand suddenly replaced Rocard with Edith Cresson in order to provide the government with a new dynamism and thus to reverse his own decline of popularity. Mitterrand hoped that Cresson, a loyal ally of the president, would devote greater attention to domestic policies and would restore a sense of unity to the Socialist party, whose left wing had been somewhat alienated by Rocard. After 11 months, Cresson was in turn replaced by Pierre Bérégovoy. This move was occasioned by Cresson's failure to govern effectively, her combative public remarks, and—most important—the poor performance of the Socialist party in the regional and cantonal elections of March 1992.[59] A year later, of course, Bérégovoy had to be replaced by a Gaullist premier in the wake of the Socialists' defeat in the Assembly elections.

The discussion above suggests that the tenure of the premier has been as dependent on the president's goodwill as the tenure of the rest of the cabinet. In the event that the premier should refuse to resign if the president no longer had any use for him or her, the president could "persuade" the Assembly to oust the premier on a vote of no confidence; and even if the president lacked Assembly support, he could accomplish the same purpose by the threat of dissolution. But that is the case only if the president has a parliamentary majority behind him or is reasonably certain that after a fresh election, he will have such a majority.

THE EXECUTIVE AND PARLIAMENT

The fact that half of the premiers have been recruited from Parliament, that many ministers have had parliamentary origins, and that most premiers have found it desirable to go before Parliament to be "invested" (i.e., voted into office by the deputies) may make it seem as though the Fifth Republic has been evolving from pure presidentialism to a more traditional parliamentary democracy. But investiture by Parliament is neither legally required nor essential.[60] Sometimes, in fact, the cabinet is "presented" to the Assembly quite a few days or even weeks after it has already been functioning. The decision to seek investiture is normally made by the president, though it may be influenced by the premier-designate's prior relations with Parliament and the extent to which the president or the premier wishes to show respect for that institution.

For nearly three decades, it was considered almost axiomatic that the parliamentary support of the premier, while it might be desirable, was not a precondition for his or her retention. As Pompidou said, "the President . . . takes the composition of the Assembly into consideration . . . [but] he is not its slave."[61] Whereas in the Fourth Republic a president had to accept the resignation of a premier when the latter lost the confidence of Parliament, a Fifth Republic president could retain the premier despite the latter's loss of Assembly confidence—as de Gaulle did when he retained Pompidou as premier in 1962—as if to demonstrate his indifference to, or even contempt for, the collective preferences of Parliament (for details on censure motions, see Chapter 7).

Conversely, the president could dismiss the premier because the latter enjoyed *too much* confidence in Parliament. Pompidou's dismissal of Chaban-Delmas in 1972 was in part prompted by the latter's receipt of a massive vote of confidence (368 to 96) in the Assembly. The low turnout of the electorate (only 60 percent voted, including 7 percent who cast blank ballots) in the 1972 referendum on Britain's entry into the Common Market had been interpreted as an indicator of President Pompidou's waning popularity. Chaban's dismissal may therefore have been prompted by Pompidou's jealousy of his premier's own strong showing. Chaban's popularity, as measured by public-opinion polls, was consistently higher than that of Pompidou as premier *and* as president (especially during the last three years of Pompidou's presidency).[62] In the words of Pompidou, the retention of Chaban would have created a situation in which "the premier . . . ends up becoming too powerful and reducing the president of the Republic to a symbolic role . . . or else to . . . a kind of director of the cabinet."[63] Political jealousy was not the only reason for the dismissal of Chaban. Negative feelings toward the premier had been developing because of revelations of his failure to pay taxes, and because of his inability to implement his "new society" program, which had promised more telephones, more money to students, more roads, and more housing. As the campaign for the forthcoming parliamentary elections approached, Pompidou needed to restore the image of the Gaullist party, and to do so he had to purge a government in which there had been instances of corruption and scandal. Moreover, he wished to remind the country that in addition to a parliamentary majority there was also a presidential one, and he wished to make the former dependent on the latter. Such a position was not a Gaullist monopoly. In a television debate with Giscard before the presidential election of 1974, and again before the elections of 1981, Mitterrand also affirmed his belief in the dominance of the presidential over the parliamentary majority, and indicated that if elected, he would dissolve the Assembly.

All this was before the legislative election of 1986: Its outcome juxtaposed to the *presidential* majority a competing *parliamentary* majority, the more recent expression of popular sovereignty. To be sure, that majority was neither overwhelming nor particularly disciplined, and Mitterrand might have been tempted to manipulate or undermine it by using the weapons in the presidential arsenal. But it is doubtful whether public opinion would have supported him, for he was at that time not sufficiently popular to set himself against Parliament, which (especially since the mid-1970s) had been asserting its role with increasing confidence.

In 1988 much of the president's power was restored; yet his relationship to Parliament remained ambiguous. In part this was due to the fact that two years of being reduced to a figurehead role had taught him to take Parliament more seriously, and in part to the fact that his premier, Rocard, appeared on occasion to enjoy greater public confidence than the president. Furthermore, the presidential majority that Mitterrand had assembled for his successful bid for reelection in 1988 was gradually replaced by transpartisan (i.e., left-centrist) majorities that Rocard had been building.[64]

One may conclude that the president's relationship to Parliament has remained uncertain. On the one hand, his position is quite comparable to that of a constitutional monarch: He is politically "irresponsible" in that he cannot formally veto bills, does not engage in parliamentary debates, and does not appear in Parliament—with which he is expected to communicate only by means of messages.[65] On the other hand (as the foregoing discussion clearly shows), the president retains several powerful weapons normally associated with the executive in presidential regimes.

ARTICLE 16

One of the most powerful instruments possessed by Fifth Republic presidents is Article 16 of the Constitution. It provides that "when the institutions of the Republic, the independence of the nation and the integrity of its territory . . . are threatened in a grave and immediate manner, and when the regular functioning of the constitutional governmental authorities is interrupted, the president shall take the measures commanded by these circumstances." The constitutions of several democratic countries have contained similar emergency provisions, which have been aimed, not at destroying constitutional government, but at preserving it. Article 16 provides that whenever the president invokes emergency powers, he must inform the nation in a message, and it stipulates that the steps he undertakes "must be inspired by the desire to ensure to the constitutional governmental authorities, in the shortest possible time, the means of fulfilling their assigned functions." The Constitution also provides that the Constitutional Council be consulted with regard to any measures and that Parliament meet during the emergency period. Article 16 has thus far been invoked only once, during the generals' abortive putsch in Algeria. That putsch began on April 23, 1961, and was effectively put down a few days later; yet the state of emergency remained in effect until September 29, that is, for more than five months.

Article 16 leaves open a number of questions. Is it necessary at all, in view of the existence of Article 36, which deals with martial law? That article provides that martial law be decreed by the cabinet but can be extended beyond 12 days only by Parliament. It is therefore not a weapon of the president, and it may have seemed too restrictive to de Gaulle. Article 16, however, may be too open-ended, because it is not clear whether any meaningful checks exist against its abuse or excessively prolonged application. If Parliament is in ordinary session, it cannot be dismissed during the exercise of Article 16; if it is not, it must be called into special session. But what is Parliament entitled to do while sitting? When de Gaulle first announced the invocation of Article 16, he told Parliament that, in its special session, it had legislative and surveillance powers, but at the same time, in a communication to the premier (Debré) he said the opposite, that Parliament could *not* legislate, and that motions of censure would not be allowed. It is difficult in any case for Parliament, in special session or otherwise, to legislate against the wishes of the president, as the government would continue to control the agenda (and the president would, under normal conditions, be able to influence the government).

Furthermore, what are the protections, if any, against an unwarranted interpretation of "danger" to the republic? What measures are allowed, or forbidden, to the president? Can he or she suspend civil liberties? The Weimar Constitution's emergency powers clause (Article 48) authorized the president to suspend only *some* of the rights guaranteed by that constitution, and these were specifically named. But there is no specific bill of rights in the Fifth Republic Constitution; ergo, can the president suspend the rights that exist by statute law or custom? The provision that the measures taken by the president must be inspired by a desire to return to a "normal" state of affairs is not very helpful. What if there is a will to return to normal constitutional government, but no way (as the president sees it) to do so? And what is considered a "regular functioning of . . . institutions"?

De Gaulle's actions during his presidency raised some doubts about the extent to which he was interested in "guaranteeing" the Constitution. He violated Article 11 a number of times when he bypassed Parliament before submitting a bill to a referendum, the most notorious case being the referendum of 1962 that amended the Constitution by providing for the direct election of the president. He violated Article 29 by refusing to accede to the demand of the Assembly for a special session in 1960; Article 38, by unnecessarily asking for special decree powers in 1967; and Article 50, by refusing to dismiss Pompidou as premier in 1962, after the latter had been ousted by a vote of censure in the Assembly. Although de Gaulle adhered to the letter of Articles 23 and 16, he interpreted them so as to violate their spirit or intent. Although emergency powers have traditionally been designed for use during civil disorders, insurrections, or wars, Presidents de Gaulle and Pompidou hinted on a number of occasions that Article 16 might be used for largely political purposes, especially in order to overcome a hostile parliamentary majority.[66]

Most of the Socialists, Communists, and miscellaneous anti-Gaullists, who eventually adjusted to other features of a powerful presidency, have favored the elimination of Article 16, and Mitterrand, as president, has on several occasions formally proposed such action. The opponents of Article 16 are reminded of how a similar provision in the Weimar Constitution was abused by an antirepublican president and contributed to the downfall of democratic government in Germany. They had no illusions about de Gaulle's habit of manipulating the Constitution in order to weaken any institution or policy aimed at minimizing the role of the executive.

For a number of reasons, it appears unlikely that Article 16 will be invoked in the foreseeable future. Wars or invasions are not on the horizon; in the past two decades, terrorism and other domestic disturbances have been handled well enough by normal legislative and executive means; and, in the aftermath of de Gaulle, both Parliament and the Constitutional Council have become more assertive and more interested in both protecting civil liberties and promoting an institutional division of power.[67]

In the final analysis, the decision to invoke Article 16 depends on the degree of public support a president enjoys. With public opinion on his side, he would be less hesitant to dissolve a Parliament that might obstruct his efforts at dealing with emergencies without resorting to Article 16; if public opinion were solidly against the president, the use of Article 16 would not save him. The dissolution power would therefore seem to make Article 16 superfluous. Conversely, it is doubtful whether the elimination of the article would be sufficient to reduce the power of the president, which, after all, depends also on a weak Parliament, weak opposition parties, and lastly, the extent to which a strong executive—whether king, emperor, or charismatic leader—is in consonance with a certain strain in French political tradition.

THE PRESIDENT AND CHARISMA

We have already noted the periodic eruption of charismatic rule in French political history. It is useful to recall that Bonapartism has always appealed to a wide ideological spectrum, and that Napoleon I, Napoleon III, Boulanger, and de Gaulle were supported by both the Right and the Left (though not necessarily at the same time and in the same degree) because these "heroes" were expected to rectify the disorders and evils perpetrated by parliamentary bodies.[68] To be sure, the Right and the Left have been Bonapartist for different reasons: the former because it hoped that a charismatic authority figure would help maintain the existing socioeconomic order and temper a Parliament in which the underprivileged classes were represented; and the latter because it expected such a figure to counterbalance a Parliament that was regarded as the preserve of the privileged classes, and also, perhaps, because the "psychic income" of vicarious glory and national greatness radiating from a hero-executive was a substitute for economic wealth.

According to Michel Crozier, "the conception of authority that continues to prevail in France is universal and absolute, and retains something of the tradition of absolute monarchy with its mixture of rationality and entertainment."[69] Stanley Hoffmann has remarked that most of the French have been socialized to the acceptance of an authority figure who is abstract, impersonal, and removed from the people, yet at the same time embodies personal charisma.[70] Perhaps the reason is that for many years republican constitutions, and the institutional relationships they define, did not enjoy sufficient legitimacy and were not stable enough to serve as reliable foci of identification; or perhaps their relationship to authority is a survival of monarchic nostalgia.

The factors just cited do not quite explain why the French—who have a reputation for rationalism and political skepticism and a preference for institutional orderliness—accepted for more than a decade General de Gaulle's supra-institutional assertions of omnipotence, his claim that he had "embodied national legitimacy for 20 years," and his position (reminiscent of Louis XIV) that "the indivisible authority of the State is confided entirely to the president . . . that there is no [authority]—ministerial, civil, military or judicial—except that which is conferred and maintained by him"; and that it is up to him to share with others that supreme power.[71]

Personalization of power is of course not confined to France. In the United States, the presidential election has become a political popularity contest in this age of television, and the president's collaborators in Congress often owe their election to the presidential coattails; moreover, the way in which the vast powers of the presidency are exercised and expanded depends on the incumbent's unique view of presidential "stewardship." In Britain, the leader of a party is elected or reelected, nowadays in a largely plebiscitary fashion, as prime minister because of his or her views on public policy and the leadership image projected to the British people. However, in both the United States and Britain, "countervailing" powers are found that may be significant: In the United States, Congress can effectively block presidential legislative programs, and even in Britain it is possible for backbenchers to rebel against the leadership. In France, by contrast, countervailing powers are not yet strong enough, even with the recent experiences of cohabitation.

Nevertheless, the personalization of power under de Gaulle should not be compared to that of Hitler, Stalin, or absolute monarchs of an earlier age. In the first place, the presidential office in France is nonhereditary and fallible. Like Hitler and Stalin, de Gaulle wished to be judged by history[72] (as have his successors); but unlike these two, he was also judged by public-opinion polls, a relatively free press, and unfettered plebiscites, whose outcome was not always predictable and which in the end caused him to abandon the presidency peacefully. De Gaulle, like imperious rulers in nondemocratic regimes, virtually monopolized the mass media and used the press conference not so much to enlighten the people as to appeal for national unity, promote excitement, and demand support for his policies. But that support was not a foregone conclusion. He had to submit to elections, the outcome of which would affect his decision-making powers or serve as political weather vanes and, on occasion, inflect his policies. There is the possibility of impeachment, but its use has never been considered necessary.[73]

In France, as in other democracies, the extent to which personal power can be exercised depends on the support of the political parties and, ultimately, the people. Some of the personalization of power is no doubt due to the *vedettisation de la politique* (i.e., the orientation of politics around a celebrity) by the mass media,[74] which capitalize on the average citizen's need for excitement, an emotional focus, and a flesh-and-blood symbol of national aspirations. De Gaulle filled that need more than any corresponding figure in other Western countries because of his towering personality, his martial figure and background, his Resistance leadership, and his image as the prophet of legitimacy—all of which were enhanced even more by comparison with the premiers of the Fourth Republic, most of whom were relatively colorless political birds of passage. None of de Gaulle's qualities, however, proved in the end sufficient to overcome the "anti-executive itch"—a characteristic found especially among the French Left—that helped to secure de Gaulle's departure from the political scene in 1969.[75]

Pompidou had all the constitutional weapons of his predecessor, and in his press conferences he repeatedly emphasized his desire to affirm presidential authority. But he did not inherit the political crises that had brought about de Gaulle's accession to the presidency; although he was the heir of a "president-king,"[76] Pompidou showed, by his frequent outbursts of temper, that he possessed neither the royal hauteur nor the "institutional" qualities of de Gaulle. (It was unlikely that Pompidou could credibly perpetuate de Gaulle's Caesarian habit of referring to himself in the third person.) Instead, Pompidou portrayed himself as an ordinary French citizen. In an appeal to the voters during the presidential election of 1969, he said, "As President of the Republic, I would constantly remind myself that I am only one Frenchman among many, and therefore that I am able to understand them and their problems."[77] Like Alain Poher, his rival for the presidency, who was even more "ordinary," he donned the *petit chapeau* of the typical Frenchman—an illustration of the maxim that in bipolar electoral contests, rivals tend to become mirror images of each other.

In any case, Pompidou's efforts at identification with the populace failed, or perhaps misfired. In his election to the presidency, the abstention rate was 31 percent in the second round, contrasted with abstention rates of less than 16 percent in the case of de Gaulle and less than 13 percent in the case of Giscard.[78] What authority Pompidou had was essentially derived from the fact that he wore de Gaulle's mantle and from his ability to make crucial decisions. Unfortunately, the final two years of his presidency were marked by a politics of drift and indecisiveness, which was exemplified when in April 1972, he relinquished part of the presidential domain by using the referendum on a foreign policy issue—British entry into the Common Market. The public disavowal of his rule (and the temporary eclipse of the presidency) was demonstrated the following year by the UDR's loss of its parliamentary majority.

In the beginning of his term, Giscard's authority rested largely on the image he projected of a modern-minded and competent technocrat, who had less need than his predecessors for full-dress uniforms, parades, and other political prostheses. But there was no question that he believed in a strong presidency. At his first press conference after acceding to the office, he asserted that "as a product of universal suffrage," he was committed to a presidential regime in which the president initiates policies and "propels" them by means of the government he appoints.[79] However, he promised to grant a larger role to the Constitutional Council in safeguarding public liberties and to give a greater role to Parliament and, in particular, the opposition within it. Many of his promises were not kept, among them the reduction of the presidential term of office and meaningful decentralization. Giscard later justified his inaction by saying that as the guardian of the Constitution he was obligated to leave the political institutions to his successor in much the same way as he had inherited them. In fact, he had accumulated much more power than any of his predecessors, but he failed to use it for solving urgent economic problems. That failure contributed to Giscard's increasing preoccupation with the politics of symbolism: trips abroad, spectacular appearances at international conferences, stage-managed press conferences, and carefully packaged addresses to "my dear television viewers." By the end of his tenure, Giscard had become almost imperial in his behavior: contemptuous of Parliament, overly sensitive to the press, yet indifferent to critiques of his egocentric conduct.[80]

Perhaps it is the *role* of the French presidency that imposes a certain kind of behavior or rhetoric on the incumbent, irrespective of his personality or ideology. Mitterrand, who got his political start in the anti-executive climate of the Fourth Republic, came to power in the Fifth Republic on a platform of change and democratization, one that ostensibly rejected Gaullist policies and style. Unlike de Gaulle, who was uncomfortable as a political candidate and as a party politician, Mitterrand did not cease to identify as a party leader and abandon the role of a political candidate until developments of the second cohabitation made his "lame duck" status obvious.[81] But several months after assuming office, Mitterrand began to behave in a manner at least in part reminiscent of his predecessors. Thus, his call for a policy that would "place France at the head of industrial nations" echoed the slogans used earlier by Giscard; in his insistence that "France is not worthy of its history" unless it played a global role, and in his commitment to a national nuclear defense, he echoed de Gaulle's preoccupation with "grandeur."[82] To be sure, his views concerning the balance of institutions have been more democratic; he wanted to replace the authoritarianism under previous chiefs of state by an "authentic republic," which meant that "each institution must be put back in its place: The government governs, the Parliament legislates and participates in the debate without constraints. As for me, while I intend to exercise to the fullest the responsibilities that the sovereign people have entrusted to me, I do not wish to substitute myself for one [institution] or the other."[83]

Nevertheless, Mitterrand, at his first press conference, announced the domestic and foreign policies the government and Parliament were to follow. In his appointments, he used presidential patronage to the fullest. His predecessor had "Giscardized" the executive, the prefectures, the nationalized industries, and the media; Mitterrand systematically "de-Giscardized" them. Even in his style he followed in the footsteps of those who had preceded him. His first press conferences, conducted from the presidential palace, were heavy with pomp and ceremony: Flanked by his cabinet ministers, Mitterrand carefully selected (and grouped together into categories) the questions submitted to him by journalists before answering them, just as de Gaulle and Giscard had done.[84] It has been suggested that the temptation to monarchical behavior on the part of a president is difficult to resist because he is the heir of kings who have embodied historic continuity as well as popular sovereignty;[85] this temptation is increased because of the absence of *political* (as distinct from moral) responsibility on his part: the lack of reliable checks and balances, the practical difficulty of a Parliament pitting itself against the president, and the government's dependence on his confidence (and his whims).[86]

Before these constraints were removed (albeit temporarily) in 1986, and circumstances forced Mitterrand to put into practice his ideas concerning the division of powers, presidents were free to choose their particular brand of monarchy. De Gaulle was a Bonapartist monarch in the sense that he publicly downgraded Parliament and parties and had his rule confirmed periodically by the masses directly by means of referenda. Giscard was an "Orléanist" monarch in the sense that his rule was supported—and much of his policy determined—by the wealthy business sector, the free professionals, and the upper- and middle-echelon technocracy. The beginning of Mitterrand's first term was (somewhat prematurely) labeled a "social monarchy," in the sense that it was a strong presidential rule supported by leftist mass parties and predicated on the expectation that "popular," redistributive policies would be promoted. The first cohabitation experiment, of course, reduced Mitterrand's power, but it gave him practice in acting like a monarch who transcended politics.[87] By playing the role of unifier (*rassembleur*) who fought against selfish (i.e., mostly Gaullist) factions,[88] he acquired a charisma associated with maturity, openness, and avuncular solicitude that enabled him not only to be comfortably reelected but also to assert his power as an "arbiter" of conflicts between the government, the Socialist party, the administration, and the Parliament.[89] However (as Stanley Hoffmann seems to imply), he did not always want to assert that power. His political longevity had been such that (even before the second cohabitation period) he showed an increasing preference for the role of a constitutional monarch—aloof from the technical concerns of daily politics, interested in grand architectural projects, acting as the great impresario of public celebrations (such as the bicentennial of the Revolution), and surrounded by intellectual courtiers who helped to give his "reign" a kind of legitimacy.[90]

SUMMARY

The Fifth Republic has equipped itself with a powerful and stable executive. Yet, as the preceding discussion indicates, the *intraexecutive* relationship is not always clearly established. Although the Constitution makes the president chief of state and entrusts the government to the premier, the distinction between heading a state and leading a government, and between ceremonial duties and decision-making responsibilities, is not as precise as it might be. Presidents are sometimes tempted to intervene forcefully in the decision-making process and at other times to leave the onus for risky policies to someone else, in particular the premier. Most of France's presidents have managed to find their own delicate balance between their "dignified" and "efficient" roles (to use Bagehot's terminology). But there is no guarantee that future presidents will achieve such a balance. Therefore, some have suggested that France straighten out the situation by opting for a U.S. type of president who would be both chief of state and head of government and by abolishing the post of prime minister; others have advocated a return to a more conventional parliamentary model (perhaps a combination of the Fourth Republic, the British, or the German Federal Republic systems) under which the president's role would be more precisely defined as a figure-head one. However, the first option is likely to make the president too strong and resented by an electorate that wants a greater diffusion of power; and the second option might be rejected because it would make the executive too dependent on the parliament and hence introduce the danger of government instability and weakness. A third option might take the form of "aligning" the presidency and the Assembly by giving both the same five-year terms and by eliminating the possibility of premature dissolution. However, thus far there have been no political crises, popular demands, or parliamentary challenges serious enough to necessitate a constitutional redefinition of the position of the executive.

NOTES

1. Radio address by General de Gaulle, 20 September 1962.
2. Michel-Henri Fabre, *Principes républicains de droit constitutionnel,* 2nd ed. (Paris: LGDJ, 1970), p. 371.
3. Charles de Gaulle, *Major Addresses, Statements, and Press Conferences of General de Gaulle, 1958-1964* (New York: French Embassy, 1964), p. 248.
4. Fabre, *Principes républicains*, p. 347. For a more recent interpretation see Roger-Gérard Schwartzenberg, *La Droite absolue* (Paris: Flammarion, 1981). He argues (pp. 37-40) that between 1965 and 1968, most decisions (except for foreign affairs) were made not by de Gaulle but by Premier Pompidou, who even suggested to the president the idea of dissolving Parliament in 1968.
5. Ambassade de France, Service de Presse et d'Information, *Bulletin* 72/65, p. 13. See also *Le Président de la Ve République*, Documents d'études, no. 1.06 (Paris: Documentation Française, November 1977), esp. pp. 25-39.
6. Interview in *La Croix*, 4 May 1974.
7. *New York Times*, 17 June 1976.
8. Schwartzenberg, *La Droite absolue*, p. 37. On Barre's subservience, see Robert Elgie, *The Role of the Prime Minister in France, 1981-1991* (New York: St. Martin's Press, 1993), pp. 142-143.
9. *Le Monde*, 8-9 June and 15 November 1980.

10. In 1973, President Pompidou announced his intention to reduce the presidential term to five years. He even saw to it that an amendment bill to that effect was introduced in Parliament (which passed the bill), but then he failed to convoke Parliament for a joint session, a procedure required for the ratification of the amendment. President Giscard d'Estaing, after *his* election (May 1974), also promised that an amendment would be introduced for the same purpose, but nothing came of that promise. And Mitterrand as a presidential candidate had repeatedly endorsed the notion of a reduction of the presidential term of office to five years, and a two-term limitation—or, alternatively, the retention of the seven-year term, but without the possibility of reelection. He did so most recently in his "Lettre à tous les Français," issued just before the presidential elections of 1988. See *Libération*, 7 April 1988.
11. *Le Monde*, 11 December 1981.
12. On a (favorable) portrait of Rocard by his chief of staff, see Jean-Paul Huchon, *Jours tranquilles à Matignon* (Paris: Grasset, 1993). On his own quest for government by consensus, see M. Rocard, *Le Coeur à l'ouvrage* (Paris: Odile Jacob, 1987).
13. For detailed political biographies, see Arthur Conte, *Les Premiers ministres de la Ve République* (Paris: Le Pré au Clercs, 1986). On the "political styles" of Socialist premiers and their relations between Mitterrand and his premiers, see Thierry Pfister, *A Matignon au temps de l'union de la gauche* (Paris: Hachette, 1985). For a discussion of the economic policies of Barre, Bérégovoy, and Balladur, see Véronique Auger, *Trois Hommes qui comptent* (Paris: Pluriel, 1993).
14. Elgie, *The Role of the Prime Minister in France*, p. 167. According to this typology, Chaban-Delmas, Chirac (under Giscard), and Rocard were rivals of the president; Chirac (under Mitterrand) was an opponent; and the rest played subordinate roles.
15. See Raymond Barre, *Question de confiance* (Paris: Flammarion, 1988), esp. pp. 238, 249–251.
16. *Le Monde*, 20 May 1986.
17. Walter Bagehot, *The English Constitution* (Garden City, NY: Doubleday, n.d.), p. 124.
18. *Le Monde*, 11 December 1986.
19. For an analysis of power sharing in earlier regimes, especially the Third Republic, see Daniel Amson, *La Cohabitation politique en France* (Paris: PUF, 1985).
20. Under the Constitution, the president could not *veto bills* duly enacted by Parliament, and had to sign them within 15 days. But he could refuse to *sign decrees*, thereby nullifying them.
21. There was also a conflict between Léotard, who had been promised that the large wing of the Royal Palace then occupied by the Ministry of Finance would be made available to house additional art treasures of the Louvre, and Edouard Balladur, the Gaullist minister of finance, who refused to vacate the premises and move into a newly built ministerial complex. Chirac chose not to intervene in this matter.
22. For a more positive evaluation, see Marie-Anne Cohendet, *La Cohabitation, leçons d'une expérience* (Paris: PUF, 1993).
23. "Les cérémonies des voeux à l'Elysée," *Le Monde*, 7 January 1993. See also Alain Rollat, "Le Second Tribunat de M. Mitterrand," *Le Monde*, 30 January 1993.
24. See Thomas Ferenczi, "La Tactique du président," *Le Monde*, 12 April 1993.
25. During a television interview (*"Heure de vérité"*) on October 25, 1993, Mitterrand asserted that "there is no reserved domain for the president." Not yet having reached the presidency, Chirac agreed with that view. But in view of the overwhelming control of the Assembly by anti-presidential parties, Chirac and other Gaullists, eager for a confrontation, urged the government to accept no presidential hindrances at all.

26. Such consultation was apparently not perfect. On one foreign policy issue, the expulsion of Iranians suspected of murder (see Chapter 9), Mitterrand was not consulted but informed afterward. *Antenne 2*, 6 January 1994.

27. Hubert Védrine, the secretary-general of the Elysée, and Nicolas Bazire, Balladur's chief of staff. The latter presided over a *cabinet* of 27 *conseillers techniques* and other advisors of various ranks in charge of economic, cultural, budgetary, legal, and parliamentary affairs, relations with the press, and even military affairs (handled by a rear admiral).

28. These included Gaston Defferre, long-time mayor of Marseilles, leader of the Socialist group in the Assembly, and minister in charge of decentralization; Michel Rocard and Jean-Pierre Chevènement, leaders of rival factions in the PS; Charles Fiterman, a Communist; and Michel Jobert, formerly a prominent Gaullist.

29. The "pecking order" established by protocol (and not necessarily based on relative political power) has remained virtually the same as in the Fourth Republic: president of the Republic, premier, president of the Senate, speaker of the Assembly, and finally the rest of the cabinet.

30. The correspondence department, which has grown from 40 under Giscard to more than 80 under Mitterrand, is charged with answering (or forwarding to other units of the executive) an annual average of 200,000-300,000 greetings, complaints, petitions, and invitations from individuals and associations. On the growth of citizen communications to the president, see Yves Agnès, "Cher M. le président," *Le Monde,* 13 September 1981. On the precise breakdown of the Elysée staff and expenditures, see Jean Massot, *La Présidence de la République en France*, Notes et Etudes Documentaires, no. 4801 (Paris: Documentation Française, 1986), esp. pp. 49–66.

31. As in the case of General Lanxade, a member of the Elysée staff, who before and during the Gulf War was consulted by Mitterrand more often than his minister of defense.

32. Thus Michel Jobert, who had been secretary-general of the Elysée under Pompidou, was later (in 1973) promoted to foreign minister, as was Jean-François Poncet, who had held the office under Giscard. Marie-France Garaud, a principal figure on President Pompidou's personal staff, later became an intimate advisor to Premier Chirac and still later (in 1981) a presidential candidate. Among the secretaries-general who subsequently became premiers are Pompidou, Bérégovoy, and Balladur.

33. For example, the chief of Mitterrand's personal cabinet, André Rousselet, was a member of the prefectoral corps who had worked on Mitterrand's staff when the latter was a cabinet minister during the Fourth Republic. See Samy Cohen, *Les Conseillers du Président de Charles de Gaulle à Valéry Giscard d'Estaing* (Paris: Presses Universitaires de France, 1980).

34. Since the election of Rocard as secretary-general of the PS in October 1993, Mitterrand's meetings with that official have been reduced to a minimum owing to the frosty relationship between the two. On presidential consultations, see the excellent summary by Stanley Hoffmann, *Mitterrand's First Year in Power*, Monographs on Europe, no. 5 (Cambridge, MA: Harvard University Center for European Studies, 1982), esp. pp. 5–9. See also *Le Point*, 10 August 1981, p. 32; Maurice Szafran and Sammy Ketz, *Les Familles du Président* (Paris: Grasset, 1982); and Pierre Georges, "Les Hommes du président," in *Le Monde, Bilan du septennat* (Paris, 1988), pp. 41–44.

35. *Le Point*, 10 August 1981, pp. 23–25. On the position of the president in relation to his advisers, see also Maurice Duverger, *La République des citoyens* (Paris: Ramsay, 1982), esp. pp. 145–189.

36. Jean-Louis Andréani, "Un Premier Ministre au long cours," *Le Monde*, 10 May 1989.

37. *Le Point*, 18 July 1988, p. 18.
38. With regard to this last issue, Rocard seemed to be "winning": On the three budget votes in the Assembly in 1989, Rocard obtained more support from centrists than from Communist deputies. Rocard also prevailed in his disagreement with Mitterrand over the leadership of the PS when Mauroy rather than Fabius (whom Mitterrand preferred) was elected first secretary of the party. See Denis Jeambar, "Mitterrand-Rocard: Désaccord en coulisse," *Le Point*, 6 November 1989, pp. 36–37.
39. On this and other points, see Elijah Kaminsky, "The Contemporary French Executive: Stable Governments, Unstable Institutions," paper presented at meeting of American Political Science Association, Atlanta, Georgia, 30 August–3 September 1989, p. 26. See also Jean-Marie Colombani, "Tirs croisés contre M. Rocard," *Le Monde hebdomadaire*, 12-18 October 1989.
40. "Gouverner autrement: La Circulaire Rocard du 25 mai 1988," *Le Monde*, 27 May 1988; and *Regards sur l'actualité* 143 (July–August 1988): 15–18.
41. Bertrand Fessard de Foucault, "Le Grand Conducteur," *Le Monde*, 28–29 July 1974.
42. Between 1959 and 1969 de Gaulle managed to pay a visit to every department in metropolitan France.
43. In addition to the referendum of September 1958, on the Fifth Republic Constitution, there have been seven popular consultations: January 1961, on self-determination for Algeria; April 1962, on the Evian Agreement, granting independence to Algeria; October 1962, on changing the method of electing the president; April 1969, on amending the constitution so as to reform the Senate—a referendum that resulted in a negative vote and culminated in de Gaulle's resignation; the referendum of April 1972; November 1988, on autonomy agreements in New Caledonia; and most recently, September 1992, on the (Maastricht) Treaty on European Union. For rates of abstention see Table 4.9.
44. Massot, *La Présidence de la Ve République en France*, p. 137.
45. *Guardian Weekly*, 13 January 1973.
46. Didier Maus, *Les Grandes Textes de la pratique institutionnelle de la Ve République*, Notes et Etudes Documentaires, no. 4786 (Paris: Documentation Française, 1985), pp. 39–40.
47. Massot, *La Présidence de la Ve République en France*, p. 137.
48. Fabre, *Principes républicains*, p. 367n.
49. According to one source (*Le Point*, 19 June 1981, p. 47), the replacement of Pierre Joxe as minister of industry by Pierre Dreyfus was the idea of Minister of Finance Jacques Delors.
50. Massot, *La Présidence de la Ve République*, p. 137.
51. Thus he vetoed the appointment of UDF leader Jean Lecanuet as foreign minister and of François Léotard as defense minister.
52. A large proportion of them are graduates of the National School of Administration (Enarques). Of the 30 directors of the *cabinets ministériels* in the Balladur government, 21 are Enarques.
53. From 1967 to 1968, the proportion of Gaullists in the cabinet increased despite their loss of majority status.
54. The 43 members of Chirac's cabinet, as reconstituted in January 1976, included 31 with professional civil-service backgrounds. Under de Gaulle, 44.6 percent of the ministers were chosen from outside Parliament; under Pompidou, 43.9 percent; under Giscard, 32.6 percent; and during Mitterrand's first term (1981–1986), 25.8 percent. See Olivier Duhamel, "The Fifth Republic Under François Mitterrand," in George

Ross, Stanley Hoffmann, and Sylvia Malzacher, eds., *The Mitterrand Experiment* (New York: Oxford University Press, 1987), p. 146.

55. On the lateral movement of prime ministers' civil-service staffs under three presidents from and to the Council of State, the Court of Accounts, the prefectoral corps, and private business, see Bertrand Badie and Pierre Birnbaum, "L'Autonomie des institutions politico-administratives: Le Rôle des cabinets des présidents de la République et des premiers ministres sous la Cinquième République," *RFSP* 26 (April 1976), 286–322.

56. Hoffmann, *Mitterrand's First Year in Power*, esp. pp. 5–9. See also *Le Point*, 10 August 1981, p. 32.

57. Presidential protection does not extend to former members of the government. In the same year, Mitterrand refused to intervene when three former ministers (including former premier Fabius) faced indictment for their alleged roles in a scandal involving blood transfusions.

58. Two new personalities were brought in: Roger-Gérard Schwartzenberg, the president of the Left-Radical Movement (MRG), as junior minister of education; and Huguette Bouchardeau, president of the PSU, as junior minister for the environment and quality of life. The minister of foreign trade, Jobert (the lone Gaullist), had resigned earlier.

59. By March 1992, confidence in her leadership had fallen to between 19 percent and 27 percent. She had started her premiership with a confidence level of 49 percent.

60. In Britain, a formal investiture of the cabinet is not necessary; still, there is an implied investiture, because any new cabinet set up after a general election "presents" itself, as it were, together with the government's program—the Queen's Address— which is always voted on. If the address is met with critical amendments that are accepted—an unlikely outcome—this would suggest lack of confidence in the government and would signify parliamentary failure to "invest" it.

61. Press conference of 9 January 1972, Ambassade de France, Service de Presse et d'Information, *Bulletin* 72/12/H.

62. *Sondages* 1–2 (1974), 24–25.

63. *Le Monde*, 23 September 1972.

64. An indication of Rocard's success is the fact that in December 1988, only 2 of the 41 centrists in the Assembly voted for a censure motion against Rocard, and in May 1989, only a third of the Gaullist deputies voted for a censure motion introduced by their colleagues.

65. Presidential messages to Parliament have been used 13 times since 1959: 5 times by de Gaulle, 3 by Pompidou, 4 by Mitterrand, and 1 by Giscard. There have been only two occasions when presidents were permitted to appear personally in Parliament: in 1975, when Giscard appeared at the Senate for the celebration of the centenary of its founding; and in 1982, when Mitterrand came to the Assembly to participate in a ceremony honoring Pierre Mendès-France.

66. Maurice Duverger, "L'Article 16," *Le Monde*, 19 November 1966.

67. Perhaps for these reasons, academic discussion of Article 16 has lessened. In a recent book on the constitution (Olivier Duhamel and Jean-Luc Parodi, eds., *La Constititution de la Cinquième République* [Paris: Presses de la Fondation Nationale des Sciences Politiques, 1985]), the article is not discussed at all; and in a book on the presidency (Massot, *La Présidence de la Ve République en France* [1986]), it is dealt with in two pages.

68. Cf. Jacques Fauvet, *The Cockpit of France* (London: Harvill House, 1960), pp. 80–81. See also Philip Thody, *French Caesarism from Napoleon to Charles de Gaulle* (New

York: St. Martin's, 1989), which (with some exaggeration) traces the historical roots of de Gaulle's authoritarian inclinations.

69. Michel Crozier, *Le Phénomène bureaucratique* (Paris: Seuil, 1963), p. 288.

70. Stanley Hoffmann, "Heroic Leadership: The Case of Modern France," in Lewis Edinger, ed., *Political Leadership in Industrialized Societies* (New York: Wiley, 1967), pp. 108–154.

71. Press conference of 31 January 1964, cited in Lacouture, *Citations du Président de Gaulle*, p. 39.

72. Léo Hamon and Albert Mabileau, eds., *La Personnalisation du pouvoir* (Paris: PUF, 1964), p. 296.

73. Although the president is politically "irresponsible" in that his "ordinary" political actions are not subject to legal challenge, he may be indicted for high treason by the two chambers of Parliament and tried by a special court under Article 67.

74. Hamon and Mabileau, *La Personnalisation du pouvoir*, p. 375.

75. Stanley Hoffmann, *Decline or Renewal? France Since the 1930s* (New York: Viking, 1974), p. 103. To be sure, de Gaulle brought his departure on himself because he had threatened to resign if the 1969 referendum (reforming the Senate) did not pass. But the failure of the referendum was itself a reflection of the people's growing disenchantment with de Gaulle.

76. The expression of Pierre Viansson-Ponté, "Un Dimanche tous les sept ans," *Le Monde*, 1 November 1972.

77. Quoted in Robert Rocca, *Pompi-deux* (Paris: Editions de la Pensée Moderne, 1969), p. 55.

78. An important factor in the abstention rate was the absence of a credible candidate of the Left in the second round.

79. *Le Monde*, 27 July 1974.

80. One critic, Roger-Gérard Schwartzenberg, in *L'Etat-spectacle* (Paris: Flammarion, 1977), p. 64, cites Giscard's remarks (in an interview in October 1974) to the effect that "I attach a great deal of importance to style: Style is the esthetics of action." The same author labeled Giscard's system as a "techno-profitariat" (p. 59).

81. Biographies of Mitterrand are numerous. Among more recent ones, see Catherine Nay, *Le Noir et le rouge* (Paris: Grasset, 1984), and her equally hostile *Les Sept Mitterrand* (Paris: Grasset, 1988); Franz-Olivier Giesbert's critical *Le Président* (Paris: Seuil, 1990); Pierre Favier and Michel Marin-Roland, *La Décennie Mitterrand*, vol. 1: *Les Ruptures, 1981–1984* (Paris: Seuil, 1990); and Wayne Northcutt's (detailed but too chronological) *François Mitterrand: A Political Biography* (New York: Holmes & Meier, 1992). For an interesting comparison of de Gaulle and Mitterrand, see Alain Duhamel, *De Gaulle-Mitterrand: La Marque et la trace* (Paris: Flammarion, 1991).

82. See "Mitterrand: Le Nouveau Ton," *Le Point*, 28 September 1981, pp. 64–69.

83. Press conference of Mitterrand on September 24, 1981. See also "De Gaulle? Non, Mitterrand," *Le Monde*, 26 September 1981.

84. None of de Gaulle's successors could match his style or the sheer number of his press conferences. De Gaulle had 17 conferences during his 10-year presidency; Pompidou, 9 during nearly 5 years; Giscard, 9 during his 7-year term, and Mitterrand, 8 between 1981 and 1992.

85. Jacques Julliard, "La Tentation du Prince-Président," *Pouvoirs* 41 (1987), 27–28.

86. Guillaume Bacot, "Ni se soumettre, ni se démettre," *Revue politique et parlementaire*, January–February 1978, pp. 27–33; and Michel Béranger, "La Responsabilité politique du chef de l'état," *Revue du droit public* 95:5 (September–October 1979),

1265–1314, which compares the president's "arbitrage" to the moral leadership of the British queen.

87. On the monarchic behavior of de Gaulle and his successors, see Charles Zorgbibe, *De Gaulle, Mitterrand, et l'esprit de la constitution* (Paris: Hachette, 1993).

88. See Jean-Yves Lhomeau, "François Mitterrand, sculpteur de sa stature," in *Le Nouveau Contrat de François Mitterrand: L'Élection présidentielle de 1988* (Paris: Le Monde, 1988), pp. 20–21.

89. In 1988, before Mitterrand had officially decided to seek reelection, French citizens (including non-Socialists) appealed to him with the slogan "Uncle, do not leave us!" (*Tonton, ne nous quitte pas*). See Jean-Yves Lhomeau, "1987–1988, La Gloire de 'Tonton,'" *Le Monde*, 22 March 1988.

90. Stanley Hoffmann, "Mitterrand: The Triple Mystery," *French Politics and Society* 6:2 (April 1988), 3–6.

chapter 7

Instruments and Patterns of Decision Making: The Parliament

The conception of republicanism that was traditional in France from the 1870s until 1958 rested on parliamentary supremacy. The Parliament, as the main expression of popular sovereignty, occupied the central role in the French decision-making structure. Parliament was supreme in that it had, at least theoretically, a monopoly on legislative power; it elected the president of the republic; it invested and dismissed prime ministers and cabinets at will; it controlled the budgetary process; it exercised regularly its power of surveillance over the executive by means of questions, interpellations, and votes of censure; and it was the absolute master over such matters as special sessions, internal parliamentary rules, and the dissolution of the Assembly prior to the calling of new elections. Parliamentary legislative monopoly, in principle, did not permit "delegated legislation" (i.e., the granting of power to the executive to enact decrees), nor were parliamentary decisions subject to judicial review.

In many modern societies, the idea (or myth) of the supremacy of parliaments continues to prevail because the legislature is considered to be the agency par excellence of democratic representation and popular sovereignty. But in reality, the power of parliaments has declined in most countries. Among the causes of this decline have been the development of the welfare state, the frequency of plebiscitary elections, the restriction of parliamentary initiative in the interest of efficient decision making, and the increasingly technical content of policies, about which deputies may be ill informed.

The British Parliament has appeared to be an effective legislative body because it is usually dominated by a disciplined party that has an absolute majority in the House of Commons, a chamber "managed" by the prime minister, who is the leader of that party. However, the House of Commons may also be considered a ratifying chamber for decisions initiated by a strong cabinet. Both in Germany and in Italy, the parliament's main role is in effect to confirm decisions made by the leadership of the dominant party (or coalition); and even in the United States, where "all legislative powers [granted by the Constitution] are vested in Congress," the president has virtually preempted the area of foreign affairs, leaving the Senate only an intermittent role in that sphere. Whereas in these countries the formal supremacy of parliament was balanced by the growing importance of the executive, the French Fourth Republic Parliament was not meant to be controlled by any government.

PARLIAMENT IN THE FOURTH REPUBLIC

The dominance of Parliament during the Fourth Republic did not, however, mean that Parliament was a decision maker. The legislature was unable to use its powers because it lacked effective management; none of the parties in Parliament had an absolute majority, and few of them were disciplined. Coalition cabinets were unstable, in part because of the extreme individualism and ambition of the deputies. Many members of Parliament considered themselves capable of being ministers, and deputies were easily persuaded to express lack of confidence in an existing cabinet in the hope that, as a result of the next cabinet "replastering," they would get portfolios.

In order to speed the resignation of a cabinet, the bills initiated by the government were often sabotaged in Parliament. The legislative standing committees (of which there were 19 in the Fourth Republic Assembly) were particularly adept at gutting a government bill. If the committee, which tended to be the preserve of special interests, did not pigeonhole a government bill, its *rapporteur* (the committee member assigned as the principal "steering" person for the bill) would report a "counter-bill" (*contre-projet*) that embarrassed the government and sometimes led to its resignation. In order to stay in power, the government got into the habit of refraining from introducing controversial bills. Budgetary and other crucial measures were frequently dealt with by cabinet decree, based on a broad framework law (*loi cadre*) that Parliament enacted in order to grant the executive full powers and to enable deputies to escape responsibility for unpopular legislation. Yet in the Third and Fourth Republics, it was still meaningful to speak of a parliamentary system; the very existence of a government depended on parliamentary approval, for Parliament could prevent the *permanent* dominance of political leaders by cutting short their terms of office. Despite the fact that in the Fourth Republic many premiers enacted decree laws even after losing the confidence of Parliament (that is, while they were acting as mere chairmen of "caretaker" governments), they did so with the implied permission of Parliament and in the clear knowledge that they would soon be replaced.

Rightly or wrongly, many French citizens came to equate the failures of the Fourth Republic—and not its achievements—with the excessive power of Parliament. They developed a measure of cynicism owing to the deputies' frequent manifestations of opportunism, their endless perorations, and their fruitless ideological quarrels. All of these tendencies made the deputies appear to be the enemies of the electorate and reinforced the substratum of antiparliamentary thinking current in France.[1]

In order to salvage their prestige (and save the republic), deputies during the 1950s had become interested in reforms that would make Parliament more capable of action. For the parliamentary elections of 1951 and 1956, the system of *apparentement* (grouping or joining) was adopted, which provided that any party list gaining an absolute majority of votes in the multimember district would gain not merely a majority of seats but all seats for that district—to encourage various parties to combine and (it was hoped) to reduce the number of parties in Parliament. To the same end, in 1957, the minimum number of deputies required for a parliamentary group was raised from 14 to 28. In 1954, ordinary parliamentary sessions, which sometimes lasted nine or ten months, were limited to a maximum of seven months. In 1956, ordinary members of Parliament ("backbenchers") were barred from obstructing a government budget bill, and in January 1958, a constitutional amendment was proposed that would forbid backbenchers to introduce bills raising expenditures or decreasing revenues. But these attempts at reform came too late. According to a poll conducted in the last days of the Fourth Republic, a vast majority of the French still held negative views about Parliament.[2]

PARLIAMENT IN THE FIFTH REPUBLIC

Despite their preference for plebiscitary rule, the Gaullist drafters of the Constitution knew that Parliament must be preserved because it was the sine qua non of republicanism. But the new Parliament would be rationalized and harnessed for efficient collaboration with the executive. Accordingly, the Fifth Republic Parliament emerged as a mere shadow of its predecessor. The forms are observed: Parliament still has a legislative function, and the government is still responsible to the National Assembly. In terms of its size, structure, and procedures, the Fifth Republic Parliament does not differ radically from parliaments in earlier regimes. The Palais Bourbon, the venue of the Assembly, is a closed and intimate club in which the traditional esprit de corps of politicians, though somewhat weakened since 1958, is still present and often transcends party labels. The deputies spend their working week in much the same way as they might have done during the Fourth Republic. A typical week of a deputy is as follows:

Tuesday	A.M.:	Arrival in Paris by train.
		Reading mail accumulated since Saturday.
	P.M.:	Meeting with parliamentary faction.
		Assembly session. Cocktail.
Wednesday	A.M.:	Working in legislative committees.
	P.M.:	Assembly session. Preparation of reports.
Thursday	A.M.:	Legislative committees.
	P.M.:	Assembly session. Visits to ministries.
		Miscellaneous duties. Meeting with constituents.

Friday	A.M.:	Legislative committees. Visits to ministries.
	P.M.:	Assembly session. Departure for the constituency.
Saturday	A.M.:	At home; visit to city hall; seeing important voters. Meeting with departmental party organization.
	P.M.:	At home.
Sunday	A.M.:	Public gatherings (inaugurations, other ceremonies).
	P.M.:	Attending soccer match. Banquets.
Monday	A.M.:	At home. Contacts with local administration.
	P.M.:	Study of legislative materials. Departure for Paris.[3]

The present Parliament has retained the bicameralism that has been traditional in French politics. The Assembly's 577 members are elected for a five-year term on the basis of universal suffrage;[4] the 321 senators (the number as of 1993) are elected for nine years by an electoral college composed of deputies and local politicians. Each chamber is headed by a speaker, elected by its respective membership. The speaker is assisted by a "steering committee" known as the Presidents' Conference. (The speakers of both chambers are called *présidents*, as are the chairpersons of parliamentary parties.) That body consists of the leaders of the various parliamentary parties and is, in a formal sense, responsible for the allocation of committee seats and the allotment of time for debate on most legislative items. The management of the Assembly and the Senate is the respective *bureau*, which consists of the speaker, 6 deputy speakers, 14 secretaries (who take minutes and count votes), and 3 questors (who are in charge of supplies). In addition, there are nearly 2,000 parliamentary functionaries (about 1,200 in the Assembly) who are concerned with purely administrative or technical-managerial functions.[5]

Formal parliamentary procedure basically follows the pattern established in previous French republics (see Figure 7.1). A distinction is made between government bills (*projets de loi*) and private members' bills (*propositions de loi*), the former accounting for most of the bills passed in the Assembly. When a bill is introduced, it is sent first to the *bureau*; and the speaker, who heads that unit, transmits the bill directly to a legislative committee. After the committee has done its work, the *rapporteur* formally reports the bill to the floor for what is technically the initial "reading." The ensuing debate, which provides an opportunity for the introduction of amendments, is followed by a vote. After its passage in the Assembly, the bill is transmitted to the Senate. If that chamber accepts the original version of the bill, it is sent to the government for signature. If the Senate rejects the bill, the subsequent procedure varies. First, there can be a resort to the shuttle (*navette*), the sending of a bill back and forth between the two chambers until a common version is achieved; second, the government may request the appointment of a conference committee (*commission mixte paritaire*), which is the method most often used; third, the government may ask each chamber for a "second reading" (i.e., a reconsideration and new vote on the original bill); and fourth, if disagreement persists, the government may ask the Assembly to determine the final version of the bill by simple majority vote.[6]

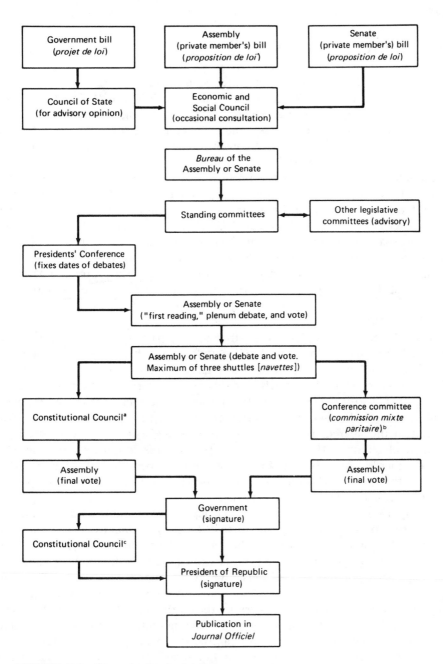

FIGURE 7.1 Steps in the legislative process

[a]In case of disagreement between the government and either chamber on the constitutionality of a bill
[b]In case of disagreement between the two chambers
[c]For organic law
SOURCE: Based on Jean-Charles Maoût and Raymond Muzellac, *Le parlement sous la Ve République* (Paris: Colin, 1971), pp. 68–69.

THE COMMITTEE SYSTEM

The Fifth Republic's legislative committee system is a compromise between the systems found in the U.S. Congress and in the British House of Commons. There are in the Assembly (and in the Senate) only six standing committees, and they are specialized. Their size ranges from 72 members (foreign affairs, defense, financial and economic affairs, and constitutional and administrative matters) to 144 (cultural and social affairs, production and exchange). Deputies are assigned to committees on the basis of the proportional representation of parliamentary parties. The chairperson of a committee, who has little power, is elected by committee members and does not necessarily belong to the largest party. When the new Assembly met after the legislative elections of 1981, the Socialists offered to share the chairs of legislative committees with the opposition parties, but the latter refused. The parties belonging to the majority assumed all the chairs but in so doing followed a kind of *internal* spoils system.[7] After the Assembly elections of 1988, the opposition was offered the chair of the foreign affairs committee, which was assumed by Giscard d'Estaing (who had reentered the Assembly in 1986).

Only deputies who belong to a parliamentary party (*groupe parlementaire*) are allocated membership in the *bureau* and in committees (and only such parties are given office space, ready access to reference materials, and miscellaneous administrative benefits).[8] Formerly, a parliamentary party, in order to be recognized as such, had to have at least 30 deputies, a requirement that forced "loose" deputies to align themselves (*s'apparenter*) with larger groups and thereby contributed to the aggregative process within the legislature. However, after the legislative elections of 1988, the Assembly passed a resolution reducing the minimum number to 20. This was done to accord the benefits of a parliamentary group to the bloc of 27 Communist deputies as a reward for their supporting the election of Laurent Fabius as speaker.

In the beginning of the Fifth Republic, legislative committees met four times a week, from Tuesday to Friday, but since 1969, many committees have met only once a week. Although each bill must be sent to a committee, that body's decision-making power is minimal. Committees are not permitted to produce substitute bills that change or distort the legislative intent of the government. The committees are in any case too large and too unwieldy for the development of genuine expertise. In the early years of the Fifth Republic, the Gaullist party insisted that legislative committees should have no authority to subdivide themselves, probably because that party feared that smaller subcommittees might develop into anti-Gaullist power centers. But such subdivision has in fact taken place; "working groups" (*groupes de travail*) have been formed frequently, and in recent years they have been more or less officially sanctioned. Neither the subcommittees nor the full committees, however, can function meaningfully other than as components of the legislative conveyor belt, for the committee must report back to the chamber within three months or even sooner if the government (which under Art. 48 of the Constitution has the power to assign priority status to a bill) has labeled a bill "urgent." (Between 1959 and 1987, such labels were attached to bills 108 times in the Assembly and 161 times in the Senate.) It has happened that the government has so arranged the agenda and so rushed a bill that it has come up for floor debate before the committee has prepared its report on it or has had time even to discuss it.

At the request of either the government or a parliamentary chamber, a special committee may be named to consider a particular bill. In the past, the government tolerated the Assembly's establishment of special committees in which the subjects under discussion were not highly partisan (e.g., subsidies for repatriates from North Africa, birth control). After 1968, the government became more amenable to the creation of special committees dealing with a broader scope of problems because the absolute majority that the Gaullists enjoyed in the plenum of the Assembly (see Table 7.1) was reflected in the makeup of the special committees. Between 1959 and 1987, 88 demands for special committees were made in the Assembly, of which 57 were approved; all 35 demands for such committees made during the same period in the Senate were approved.

In July 1981, Mitterrand called upon Parliament to do its share to "reequilibrate" the relationship between the executive and the legislature by developing its means of investigation and control.[9] The setting up of parliamentary committees of inquiry into general problems, and of control of government operations (such as the functioning of the public services or nationalized industries), had been authorized by an ordinance of November 1958. But major restrictions on the conduct of such inquiries were imposed. The investigative committees were limited by a set time period and a narrow frame of reference. Such committees could not be created if the problems they were to deal with might give rise to judicial proceedings—a prohibition intended to obviate interference in the work of the Ministry of Justice. Members of commissions of inquiry are selected by vote of the majority, which may decide the rules of conduct of the committee and exclude deputies belonging to minority parties likely to be interested in embarrassing the government. The results of the inquiry must be reported to a permanent (standing) committee, which might reject the report. Finally, the committee meets only in closed session (unlike the standing committees, which since November 1988 may be opened to the public), with the result that government mismanagement can be exposed only by means of leaks (and the parliamentarians' disregard of the pledge of secrecy).

In spite of such restrictions, however, the executive has tended to discourage the appointment of committees of inquiry, and only a small proportion of the deputies' requests for these committees has been met. Between 1971 (the year they were first authorized) and 1986, 18 special investigation committees were set up in the Assembly, and 6 in the Senate, dealing, inter alia, with real estate speculation, environmental pollution, the energy problem, unemployment, the mass media, forest fires, terrorism, and the use of the French language. In addition, the Assembly set up four committees, and the Senate, 13, to look into

TABLE 7.1 Composition of the National Assembly since 1956

Parliamentary Elections	Communists	Socialists & Allies	Radicals & Allies	MRP & Center	Conservatives Moderates, & Independents	Gaullists & Affiliates	Miscellaneous & Unaffiliated	Total Seats
1956	150	99	94	84	97	22	50	596
1958	10	47	40	56	129	206	64	552
1962	41	66	43	55	268[a]		9	482
1967	73		121[b]	41[c]	242[a]		10	487
1968	34		57[b]	34[c]	344[d]		18	487
1973	73	100[e]		34[f]	270[d]		13	490
1978	86	105	10[g]	123[h]	9[i]	153	5	491
1981	44	286[e]			62[i]	88	11	491
1986	35	214[e]			132[j]	158	38[k]	577
1988	27	277[e]			130[j]	129	14[l]	577
1993	23	57[e]			215[j]	257	25[m]	577

[a]Gaullists and independent Republicans
[b]Socialist and Radical alliance
[c]Progress and Modern Democracy
[d]Gaullists, Independent Republicans, and progovernment Centrists
[e]Socialist and Left Radicals
[f]Reformers (Moderate Radicals and Opposition Centrists)
[g]Left Radicals (MRG)
[h]UDF and "presidential majority" (Giscardists)
[i]Independents and Peasants (CNIP)
[j]UDF (Republicans, CDS, and Moderate Radical-Socialists)
[k]Includes 32 National Front and 6 Unaffiliated
[l]Includes 13 miscellaneous Right and 1 National Front deputy
[m]Includes miscellaneous right-wing deputies
SOURCE: (for 1993): *Bulletin de l'Assemblée nationale*, 10e législature, no. 1, 13 April 1993, and *Le Monde* (with variant figures).

government operations (e.g., social security management and the operation of the railroads).

The issue of parliamentary investigative powers had become particularly important in 1973 after revelations about government wiretapping. French parliamentarians were impressed by the Watergate hearings conducted in the U.S. Senate, and they wanted to use them as a model. The wiretapping issue, referred to in France as "Watergate-on-the-Seine," had come before the Senate and the Assembly, and in both chambers the response of the government had been unsatisfactory. Calls by left-wing deputies for an Assembly investigation committee were rejected; the Senate succeeded in appointing such a committee, but the government refused to cooperate with it (and the Senate, in turn, took revenge by cutting appropriations for wiretapping). After the election of Giscard to the presidency, the Senate had a freer hand and formed committees to investigate the television authority, price fixing by nationalized petroleum companies, and the management of the telephone system.

However, the handful of investigative committees set up by the Assembly during Giscard's presidency remained ineffectual. Thus the committee of inquiry into the electronic media, set up in 1979, concluded its work six months later with a report of 15 lines—this after 38 sessions and after questioning 96 witnesses. A special committee set up (on the demand of the Socialists) in 1980 to look into the unsolved murder of a Giscardist politician met for nine months and presented a short report that was ambiguous.[10] A committee of inquiry into the problems of the textile industry, set up in 1980, came up a year later with detailed recommendations, but these did not lead to any legislation because the government did not like them. These results were due not only to the inherent weakness of Parliament but also to the self-denying behavior of the deputies belonging to the Giscardist-Gaullist majority, who did not want to embarrass the president needlessly.

Several months after the 1981 elections, the Assembly formed three committees of inquiry. The government took the work of these committees seriously, largely because the problems they unearthed (among them alleged police brutalities) were identified with the previous government. During both the period of Socialist domination and the first cohabitation period that followed, the Assembly was by and large a cooperative partner of the government and was careful not to upset it with unnecessary investigations; the only major committee of inquiry that the Assembly formed focused on student demonstrations at the end of 1986. In the fall of 1988, rules were changed to allow any parliamentary group to request the appointment of a committee of inquiry. Since then, the Assembly has set up a variety of committees (see Table 7.2), a development that has signified an enlarged role of Parliament. The investigation committees formed since 1991 have been partly or fully open to the public (except for the committee investigating the Mafia). In 1991 the Assembly passed a bill (introduced by Laurent Fabius, the Assembly speaker) to permit the publication of the hearings of committees of investigation.[11] Despite these improvements, skepticism about the results of committee investigations remains.[12]

TABLE 7.2   Ad hoc assembly committees, 1988–1992

Type of Committee	Year	Subject
Investigation	1989	Privatization of industries and banks
	1990	Water pollution and resource management
		Marketing of beef
	1991	Financing of parties and election campaigns*
		The prospects of automobile industry
	1992	Condition of the press and audiovisual media
		Development of the Loire valley
		Fighting the penetration of Mafia
		Fighting transmission of AIDS
Control	1990	Management of social welfare funds
	1991	Functioning of lower-division university cycle
Info/gathering	1989	Integration of immigrants
	1990	Bioethics
	1990	The future of rural society
Evaluation	1990	Housing and urban problems
	1991	Decentralization of national education

*Headed by an opposition deputy.
SOURCE: Based on *Le Monde*, 1988–1993.

THE SENATE

Physically and institutionally, the French Senate has not changed much through various republican regimes. Senators are elected not by the people directly but by an electoral college composed of the Assembly deputies, more than 3,000 departmental councilors, and more than 100,000 delegates of city councils. Thus, more than 95 percent of the electors are representatives of localities.

During the Third Republic, the Senate was a very powerful legislative chamber. It was virtually equal to the Assembly in the sense that the Senate could render an absolute veto over an Assembly decision. The Senate, like the Assembly, could produce a vote of censure, and it competed with the Assembly as a body from which cabinet members were recruited. In the Fourth Republic, the Senate was abolished; in its stead was a "Council of the Republic," which had only a delaying veto. The founders of the Fifth Republic (among them notably Michel Debré) wished to restore the Senate to the position it had occupied in the Third Republic because they expected that chamber, composed as it was of conservative local politicians, to be a guardian of conservative views as against the more left-wing views traditional in the Assembly and thus be an institutional supporter of de Gaulle's presidency. The writers of the Constitution lengthened the senators' term of office from six to nine years, added to the legislative powers of the Senate, and made its speaker the acting president of the republic in case of a vacancy of that office.

Throughout most of the Third and Fourth Republics, the Senate had been an "agricultural chamber." During the first two decades of the Fifth Republic, it continued to be conservative, but it was often hostile to Gaullist-dominated governments because the economic policies advocated by the latter tended to discriminate against the provincial and more "backward" clientele of the Senate (see Table 7.3). Thus, while the Assembly's complexion reflected that of the president more or less precisely in 1958, 1968, 1981, and 1988 and harmonized its behavior with presidential policy preferences, the Senate retained an independent outlook, at least until 1974 when most of its members rallied to the Giscardist "presidential majority." The Senate's independence was expressed not only in repeated requests for the appointment of committees of inquiry but also in appeals to the Constitutional Council to review government bills it did not like. Even during the Giscard years, the Senate functioned as a forum in which disagreement with government policy was expressed more freely, and more often, than in the Assembly, occasionally even obliging a cabinet minister to appear before the Senate to defend government policy.[13]

Many of the Senate's legislative positions have related to matters about which that body, by virtue of its origins, is quite sensitive: for example, policies relating to regions and localities, the protection of farmers, and the privileges of shopkeepers and artisans. In 1972, the Senate amended government bills on regional reform (in order to give greater fiscal powers to regional councils) and attempted to alter a social security bill (in order to raise old-age pension payments to shopkeepers). In 1982, the Senate voted against a government bill on social security because it objected to one of the bill's provisions, the reimbursement of the cost of abortions. Of course, when the government is adamant about a bill or any of its features (as in the case of the 1982 bill), the Assembly can be asked to override Senate objections to it in a definitive "second reading," thus reducing the action of the Senate to a mere suspensive veto.

Nevertheless, because of the Senate's independent attitudes it was widely viewed as an institutionalized opposition and "censor" of the government.[14] During de Gaulle's presidency, this oppositionist attitude—attributable both to the Senate's resentment of its reduced status as an active participant in the legislative process and its hostility to Gaullist ideology—was aggravated by de Gaulle's decision to ignore the Constitution and bypass the Parliament as a whole when, in 1962, he introduced the referendum to institute the system of direct election of the president. As a result, Gaston Monnerville, the Senate speaker, stopped speaking to de Gaulle. Later Alain Poher, the centrist who succeeded to the speakership in 1968 (and held the office until 1993) ran against Pompidou for the presidency in 1969.[15]

Unable to dissolve the Senate, de Gaulle attempted to neutralize it by "reforming" it. The constitutional amendment bill prepared by the government in the fall of 1968 proposed to have only half the members of future Senates elected by the usual method, by regional and local politicians, and the other half in a corporative fashion (i.e., by organized socioeconomic sectors such as trade unions, farmers' associations, and business groups) and to permit the Senate to co-legislate only on clearly enumerated social, economic, and cultural matters. That

TABLE 7.3 Composition of the Senate since 1959 (selected years)

	Total Seats	Gaullist	Independent	Peasants	MRP/ Democratic Center	Democratic Left (mainly Radicals)	Socialist	Communist	Unaffiliated
1959	307	41	92		34	64	51	14	11
1965	274	30	79		38	50	52	14	11
1968	283	29	80		40	50	54	17	13
1973	283	36[a]	60[b]	16	46[c]	38[d]	48	18	21
1980	305[e]	41	52[f]		67[c]	39[g]	69	23	13
1987	319	77	52[f]		70[c]	35[g]	64	15	4
1989	321	91	52[f]		68[c]	23[h]	66	16	5
1992	321	90	47[f]		66[c]	23[h]	70	15	10

[a] UDR
[b] Independent Republicans (RI)
[c] Center Union
[d] Reformers
[e] One seat vacant
[f] Republicans and Independents
[g] Includes Left Radicals (MRG)
[h] Rassemblement démocratique et europénne

SOURCES: *L'Année politique* (1959–1992), *Le Monde*, and *Regards sur l'actualité*. Figures for each party include affiliated senators (*apparentés*).

chamber would be totally excluded from decision making in "general" political affairs, as defined by the government. To sweeten the pill, the government associated the dismemberment of the Senate with a popular reform: the grant of greater autonomy to regions. Most people favored such regional reform but opposed the reform of the Senate. The referendum lost; de Gaulle, in consequence, resigned from the presidency. Opposition to the referendum occurred in part because the reform was an affront to those who had always associated republicanism with the existence of a viable Senate, and in part because of objections to the *procedure* chosen for the reform (i.e., the referendum).

Having been saved as an institution, the Senate's weakness remained; Edgar Faure, the Gaullist speaker of the Assembly in the mid-1970s, described the activities of the Senate contemptuously as *"litanie, liturgie, léthargie."*[16] A symptom of its weakness, especially under the Gaullists, was the relatively small number of sessions: Between 1959 and 1974, the Senate held an average of 66 sessions a year, compared with the Assembly's 91 sessions. It was also evidenced by the fact that of the small number of bills passed by Parliament between 1959 and 1977 that had a parliamentary (as opposed to governmental) origin, fewer than 20 percent had originated in the Senate.

The legislative influence of the Senate has in large measure depended on the role permitted (or assigned to) it by presidents and prime ministers.[17] Under Gaullist-dominated governments, the Senate was distrusted. During Giscard's presidency, that body was viewed more positively because it was more favorably inclined to Giscardism. This change brought about an increase in the Senate's decision-making role: Of the 1,882 private members' bills originating in that body between 1959 and 1987, 41 percent were introduced between 1974 and 1981 (see Table 7.4). Furthermore, the number of government bills introduced in the

TABLE 7.4 Source of bills introduced in Parliament, 1959–1987 (selected years)

	National Assembly		Senate	
Year	Government Bills	Private Members' Bills	Government Bills	Private Members' Bills
1959	81	206	22	31
1961	65	160	41	41
1965	79	80	5	20
1968	90	421	5	30
1972	82	217	27	48
1976	87	158	33	64
1981	51	412	32	136
1985	90	142	20	89
1986	41	357	34	153
1987	58	272	32	108

SOURCE: Based on Didier Maus, *Les grands textes de la pratique institutionnelle de la Ve République*, Notes et Etudes Documentaires, no. 4864 (Paris: Documentation Française, 1988), pp. 151–152.

Senate, which had been 17.5 percent between 1959 and 1978, increased to over 35 percent.[18] Finally, the executive's perception of the cooperative mood of the Senate was such that in 1975, the government of Premier Chirac submitted its general political program before the Senate and asked that body for a vote of approval, and in 1977 Premier Barre, having reshuffled the cabinet, asked the Senate for a vote of confidence![19]

During the period of Socialist dominance, the Senate asserted itself even more, frequently to the point of obstructing the government's reform efforts (and, in fact, was encouraged to do so by Gaullist members of the Assembly). That assertiveness, which contributed to a "conflictual bicameralism,"[20] was attested to by the growing difference of opinion between the two chambers on specific bills; by the fact that the proportion of bills on which conference committees achieved agreement, which had been 71 percent before 1981, fell to 30 percent during the period 1981–1986;[21] and by the number of Assembly overrides of Senate "vetoes," which increased from 61 for the entire period between 1959 and 1981 to 140 for the period 1981–1986.[22]

LIMITS ON PARLIAMENTARY DECISION MAKING

Despite the survival of the Senate, in the wake of his departure President de Gaulle left a Parliament that had been devalued and put under such effective tutelage of the government that many observers wondered whether France could still be considered a parliamentary democracy. Parliament no longer participates in the election of the president nor in the selection of the premier and his cabinet (except indirectly, and on rare occasions); it no longer enjoys a monopoly in lawmaking but must share legislative power with the executive and the people (via the referendum); and it has lost its power of dissolution. Parliamentary officials no longer determine the agenda; instead, a priority agenda is established by the government, which "informs" the Presidents' Conference about matters to be taken up, and a complementary agenda is determined by the speaker of each chamber and approved by it. (The latter agenda, in the Assembly at least, is influenced strongly by the government majority.) The duration of parliamentary sessions has been reduced to five and one-half months a year: two and one-half months in the fall (October–December) and three months in the spring session (April–June). Special sessions may be called by the premier or by a majority of deputies for a specific agenda, but for no more than 12 days. (De Gaulle refused all requests for special sessions. Of the 50 special sessions so far, only 2 were convoked on the request of the deputies.[23]) No backbencher input or obstruction is allowed when budget bills are considered.

Whereas in the Fourth Republic, Parliament's legislative competence was absolute, the Fifth Republic Constitution spells out in detail what falls into the domain of "laws" requiring parliamentary participation. Article 34 specifically mentions civil rights, military conscription, criminal law, taxation, education, social security, the nationalization of industries, property rights, employment, and the jurisdiction of local communities. Presumably, all matters not enumerated can be decided by the president and/or the government. Such decisions are decrees or ordinances rather than laws, yet they have the force of a law enacted by Parliament. Virtually the entire area of foreign and defense policy has been preempted by the executive. There may be debates in the legislative committees of Parliament on aspects of foreign policy, but often these debates are in closed session and do not cause the government to modify its decisions. The Assembly does vote to ratify treaties, most often on European Union matters, where parliamentary ratification is stipulated, but it rarely if ever rejects a treaty.

Even areas that are constitutionally within the competence of Parliament can be "invaded" by the executive. Article 38 of the Constitution provides that the government may ask the legislature to delegate to it the power to make ordinance (albeit for a limited period and purpose). By their nature, such legislative grants are not much different from British "statutory instruments." French governments have resorted to delegated legislation more than 20 times since 1959. In 1960, for example, Parliament authorized the government to make ordinances to deal with alcoholism and prostitution and, in the same year, to control disturbances in connection with the government's policy in Algeria. During the last years of Giscard's presidency, Article 38 was not used, but it was revived under Mitterrand, whose government invoked it (in 1981) for enacting 40 measures, including the reduction of the workweek, the lowering of the retirement age, and the lengthening of the period of paid vacations. Premier Chirac also used that article several times but, as was pointed out in Chapter 6, he was prevented from doing so by Mitterrand on three occasions.

By means of its power to determine the agenda, the government can ensure that its bills have priority over private members' bills. Furthermore, it can stipulate in the case of a particular bill what the extent of debate shall be, what sections of the bill shall be open to amendments, and how much time shall be allocated to specific sections of a bill, often on its integral, unamended text. This procedure, the "blocked vote," as provided for by Article 44 of the Constitution, effectively eliminates parliamentary input on detail (except for those changes, often made by deputies informally, that the government decides to accept). Under de Gaulle and Pompidou, the blocked vote was used frequently; until the late 1960s, more than 100 bills were introduced in this fashion in each chamber. Despite Giscard's professed respect for Parliament, Premier Barre resorted to the blocked vote on many occasions, sometimes in an openly contemptuous manner.[24] This applied to a budget bill in 1979 and to a penal-reform bill in 1980.[25] Under the Socialist governments between 1981 and 1986, the blocked vote was used only three times in the Assembly and seven in the Senate,[26] but Chirac's cohabitation government used the procedure with a vengeance,[27] possibly because of the fact (or belief) that it did not have reliable enough parliamentary majorities to resort to ordinary legislative procedures.

Blocked-vote bills have not always had easy passage in the Senate, which has rejected a sizable number of them. But the Senate's opposition can easily be overcome because the degree of legislative involvement of that chamber depends to a large extent on the government's discretion. Because most of the blocked votes relate to financial matters, the Senate's relative lack of cooperation with the government is of little consequence. On the annual budget bill, the government is virtually complete master. According to Article 47 of the Constitution, the Assembly is limited to 40 days in which to process a finance bill, the Senate to 15 days. If within a 70-day period the two houses of Parliament have not formally approved a budget bill submitted to them by the government, the latter may enact the budget by decree. Because of the invocation of that article, or the threat of its use, comprehensive budget bills have gone through the legislative process in both houses of Parliament very quickly almost every year.

The prohibition against private members' bills on appropriations may be extended to virtually any public matter. If, as one politician remarked, a deputy introduced a bill to abolish the death penalty, this bill could be declared inadmissible, inasmuch as guarding a prisoner under a life sentence would cost more than executing him.[28] Such an interpretation may be extreme, but it may be assumed that the possibility of the government's use of its various trump cards has had a chilling effect on the introduction of bills by private members. In 1957, at the end of the Fourth Republic, 71 of the 198 bills passed by Parliament were private members' bills; in 1959, during the first legislature of the Fifth Republic, only 1 of the 52 bills was a private member's bill; in the second legislature (1962–1967), 55 out of 437; and in the third legislature (1967–1968), 40 out of 168. Only 40 (less than 9 percent) of about 500 bills passed in the seventh legislature (1981–1986) had been introduced by private members, whereas 33 (18 percent) of the 179 laws passed in the eighth (the first "cohabitation") legislature (1986–1988) were of private-member origin.[29] Of the 40 bills enacted by the newly elected Parliament between April and July 1993, none was of private-member origin.[30]

THE CONSTITUTIONAL COUNCIL

The power of Parliament was to be further reduced by the creation of a new institution, the Constitutional Council, which was assigned certain functions that had once been exercised by the legislature. In the Fourth Republic, Parliament could deal with any nonfinance bill or resolution it wished; today the French Constitution distinguishes among several types of laws or "rules." They are the following:

1. Ordinary laws, relating to social, economic, and other matters enumerated in Article 34, which are enacted by Parliament.
2. Organic laws, relating to the organization of public powers and their relationship to each other (Art. 46), which are also passed by Parliament, but only after the Constitutional Council has certified that they are in accord with the Constitution.
3. Constitutional amendments, which the executive proposes, the Parliament advises on, and the people may ratify.

4 Regulations (*règlements complémentaires*), which are made by the president or the premier in order to implement parliamentary law.

5. Decrees (*règlements autonomes*), which are made by the president or the premier without any reference to Parliament whatsoever as long as the Constitutional Council certifies that the matters dealt with by decree have a regulatory character.

Regulations of all kinds may be submitted to the Council of State, which determines their scope and legality and may modify them (see Chapter 8). But it is the Constitutional Council that decides which problems are subsumed under the various laws or rules; in short, it determines what is within the purview of government or Parliament. (Between early 1960 and mid-1989, the council made more than 170 such determinations.) The council must be consulted whenever the government decides to invoke Article 16 and whenever there is a question about the constitutionality of any bill (*before* it is officially enacted) or an international treaty (*before* it is ratified). Finally, the council is responsible for certifying election results.

During the first decade of the Fifth Republic, most of the Constitutional Council's decisions tended to favor the government, even to the point of permitting a government decision to violate constitutional procedures. The most famous case was the constitutional amendment of October 28, 1962, providing for the direct election of the president, in which the government had decided to use the popular referendum, bypassing Parliament. The council, in an advisory opinion, had originally asserted that the procedure chosen by the government was unconstitutional: It violated Article 89, which stipulated that a referendum could be used only *after* each chamber of Parliament had passed the amendment bill by simple majority. (An alternative method of amendment, which obviates a referendum, requires a vote of three-fifths of the members of both houses sitting jointly—see Chapter 1.) After its advisory opinion had been ignored and the referendum had taken place, the Constitutional Council, impressed by the popular verdict in favor of the amendment, declared itself unable to judge on the issue.

For many years, the Constitutional Council was not expected to function as a checks-and-balances device in relation to the executive. Between 1958 and 1975, the council made 484 "decisions," which included 35 certifications of election and referenda results. During the same period, it examined the constitutionality of organic laws only 20 times, of Assembly regulations 22 times, of ordinary laws 11 times, and of international treaties only once.[31] The judicial self-restraint of the council must be attributed in part to the fact that it is given only one month to rule on a piece of legislation. More important, that self-restraint derived from the absence of a tradition of constitutional review (in the U.S. sense) as well as from the council's method of appointment. Of its nine members, who serve nine-year terms, three are chosen by the president, three by the speaker of the Assembly, and three by the speaker of the Senate.[32]

Despite the proexecutive (and, until 1981, the pro-Gaullist or conservative) bias of many of its members, the Constitutional Council gradually widened the scope of its interpretations and came to be viewed as the protector of the rights of citizens against the claims of the state. In 1971, the government had introduced a bill that would infringe on the right to form associations (confirmed by statute in 1901) by permitting prefects to block the formation of groups the aims of which were viewed as subversive. The bill was passed by the Assembly but rejected by the Senate; the Senate speaker (Alain Poher) referred the bill to the Constitutional Council, which declared it unconstitutional. In this landmark case, the council based its decision on the contention that the bill violated one of the rights of French citizens. This right was not explicitly stated in the body of the Constitution of 1958; the preamble of the Constitution, however, referred to the Declaration of the Rights of Man and the Citizen of 1789, which contained a detailed catalogue of civil rights. In giving operative validity to the preamble, the council in effect "inserted" a bill of rights into the Constitution.

The Constitutional Council's preoccupation with civil liberties became more or less institutionalized after 1974. In that year, the Constitution was amended to permit the council to examine a bill's constitutionality (after parliamentary passage but before signature by the president) not only on the request of the president, the premier, or the speakers of the two chambers but also on the petition of 60 deputies or senators.[33] Between 1974 and 1980, the council took up 38 bills at the behest of parliamentarians, in most cases Socialist or Communist deputies. Although the council upheld the government on 24 bills, there was a spate of decisions that had the effect of enlarging or "creating" a catalogue of rights. In 1977, the council voided a government bill that would have allowed the police to search parked cars without securing a warrant, because such a search would contravene a constitutional provision (Art. 66) designed to protect against arbitrary detention. In 1979, and again in 1993, the council rejected as contrary to the right of asylum a government bill that would have restricted clandestine immigration. In 1980, it nullified a bill providing for special surveillance of foreign workers and parts of a bill that would have allowed them to be deported without judicial action, on the grounds that the bills violated the principle of equality before the law (Art. 2). The council also widened the powers of the Assembly by a series of rulings, from the mid-1960s through the 1970s, according to which Parliament's legislative competence was based not only on Article 34 (which listed areas of ordinary legislation) but on other articles as well.[34] Furthermore, the council voided several finance bills for not following proper procedure.

This "quasi-judicial review" falls far short of the U.S. or German practice.[35] Nonetheless, the council's *potential* as a genuine constitutional review mechanism and as a means of checking a reactionary or autocratic executive was valued by the Left in opposition.[36] Conversely, it was condemned by the Gaullists and their allies, who regarded the council as "a supreme oligarchy, totally irresponsible."[37] But after the Socialists came to power, it was the turn of the right-of-center parties (especially in the Senate) to invoke the Constitutional Council against the Left on several occasions. Thus, at the end of 1981 the opposition appealed to the council in an effort to fight the government's nationalization policies. The effort was partly successful in that the council judged the indemnification payments to the private shareholders as too low (and hence as an unconstitutional deprivation of property) and forced the government to modify the legislation, thus delaying the implementation of nationalization. Early in 1982, the opposition used the council again, in order to fight against the decentralization policies, in particular a bill granting partial autonomy to the island of Corsica. In this instance, the council upheld the bill, interposing only minor, and largely procedural, objections. In both cases, however, the government and its obedient Assembly majority complained that the council's activities amounted to an undemocratic "meddling" in the work of duly elected representatives of the sovereign people.[38] In 1990, the council nullified a section of a bill to increase the autonomy of Corsica that referred to "the Corsican people, a component of the French people." Both the Right and the Left, when in power, have tried to "pack" the council with politically reliable people.[39] In any case, it is clear that the council has been equally active under left-wing and right-wing governments, especially in recent years (see Table 7.5).

Between the beginning of its activity and mid-1988, the Constitutional Council took up 149 bills and about 36 regulations. There would probably have been even more but for the fact that the very existence of the council—and the probability of its intervention based on precedent—has produced a certain amount of legislative and executive self-restraint.[40] For example, in the spring of 1993, the new conservative government, in its effort to curb illegal immigration, introduced a bill permitting the police to check the identity papers of suspicious-looking people; its acceptance of an amendment to that bill eliminating its racist features was doubtlessly due to the desire to avoid its submission to the council.[41]

TABLE 7.5 Types of decisions by the Constitutional Council during Mitterrand's first term as president

	Socialist Governments (1981–1986)	Chirac Government (1986–1988)	Total
On the constitutionality of organic laws and parliamentary rules	10	10	20
Ordinary legislative bills	66	26	92
Constitutionality of decrees and regulations	25	7	32
Challenges of election procedures and results	83	37	120
Miscellaneous	2	2	4
Total	186	82	268

NOTE: Many of the electoral challenges refer to the presidential election of May 1981.
SOURCES: Based on reports of Constitutional Council from 1 June 1981 to 15 January 1988, and *Le Monde, Bilan du Septennat* (1988), p. 48 (as adapted).

Occasionally, the government may ask the council to judge on the constitutionality of a bill or treaty in order to depoliticize an issue. For example, in 1992 President Mitterrand referred the Treaty of European Union to the council after the government had signed it; the council's ruling that its provisions conflicted with the Constitution set in motion a process that resulted in a formal Constitutional amendment (Art. 88).[42]

Since the resumption of parliamentary control by the Right, it was again the turn of the Left to look to the council for recourse. However, although there has been an increasing acceptance of judicial review, the corresponding growth of judicial self-restraint has led to a greater selectivity on the part of opposition parliamentarians in sending a bill to the council. For example, only 9 of the 25 bills passed by the new majority in the spring of 1993 were sent to the council for review; of these, only 1 was declared unconstitutional, the others being subjected to partial invalidation or reserved interpretation.[43]

When Parliament has succeeded in opposing or modifying government bills, it has done so less by resorting to the Constitutional Council than by utilizing external, nonjudicial forces. This was the case in the "Anti-Breakers" bill of 1970 and the "Security and Liberty" bill of 1980. These bills, as finally passed—in the one case, providing for punishment of participants in an assemblage that results in disorder or damage to property, and in the other, making the sentencing for violent crimes more uniform—were less harsh than the original versions, as a result of modifications introduced by the Assembly. Behind the modifications of these bills, and of bills on agriculture, veterans' benefits, shopkeepers, and education, were the pressures exerted from outside of Parliament by interest groups.

Even if a law that significantly reflects the ideas of parliamentarians is passed, it may not take effect. The executive may express contempt for parliamentary lawmaking by failing to implement the legislation. For example, Parliament passed a law on birth control in 1967, but the law was not applied until 1975. An act legalizing abortion passed in 1975 (substantially confirming a similar act passed earlier), but although the more recent act stipulated that implementing regulations had to be passed within six months, the minister of health refrained from doing so as long as possible. Several laws have been enacted since the 1960s dealing with immigrants, but the public authorities (including the police) have often disregarded them.[44] (In order to reduce the lapse of time between the passage of laws and their implementation, the government in 1981 appointed an official specifically charged with "pushing" for follow-up regulations as soon as possible.)

QUESTIONS AND CENSURE MOTIONS

In conformity with French republican tradition and of Article 48 of the Constitution, members of Parliament have the right to ask questions of the government. There is a question period once a week (since 1974 on Wednesdays in the Assembly, and on Thursdays in the Senate); a deputy or senator addresses written queries (*questions au gouvernement*) to a minister, and the deputy may supplement them with extemporaneous oral questions. The latter are divided by the Presidents' Conference into questions with or without debate. In the former, the deputy is given 15 or 20 minutes for comment after the minister's response; in the latter, only 5 minutes. Written questions are much more numerous than oral questions. In addition, there are written questions addressed to particular ministers, whose reply is also written (and published, together with the question, in the *Journal officiel*).

During the first two decades of the Fifth Republic, doubts were expressed about the effectiveness of the question period. There were complaints that most questions were not answered within the required time period (one month after submission); that ministers often deliberately delayed answering in order to blunt the immediacy of a particular problem; that they sometimes refused to respond at all; and that they delegated "incompetent" junior ministers to read unsatisfactory replies prepared by the ministry, on which the reader was unable to elaborate orally.[45]

Since the mid-1970s, the situation has improved. The oral exchanges have become somewhat more informal; more important, the number of written questions has increased dramatically, as has the number of written responses. One hour each week has been devoted to "questions on current topics" (*questions d'actualité*)—half of them posed (orally) by majority deputies and half by the opposition—a practice that has resulted in somewhat more relaxed exchanges of views. A procedural reform, instituted by the speaker (Laurent Fabius) in 1989, provides that every Thursday afternoon, a minister or deputy minister is closely interrogated for one hour by deputies of different parliamentary parties, and he or she must respond without preparation. From April 1989 to June 1992, about 1,000 questions requiring an immediate response were posed. The increased utility of the question period is indicated by the steady rise of the number of written and oral questions as well as responses (Table 7.6).

In sum, however, the question period has not proved to be an effective instrument of controlling or embarrassing the government. In the Fourth Republic, inadequate ministerial answers would often lead to an enlargement of the scope of "innocent" factual questions—that is, to a debate on the general policy of the government. The debate might then be followed by an "interpellation," a vote on the question of confidence in the conduct of the government, and might lead to its resignation. Today, supplementary oral questions (of which there are very few compared to the number of written questions)[46] might still be followed by a debate; however, these debates no longer generate great interest or have dramatic political consequences since they cannot culminate directly in a vote of censure (or "no confidence").

Theoretically, distinct procedures are available to Parliament for ousting a government. Under Article 49, the Assembly may wish, on its own initiative, to make a motion of censure (Sec. 2); alternatively, the premier may "provoke" a censure motion by pledging the responsibility of his government to a general policy or program (Sec. 1) or the text of a bill (Sec. 3): That is, the bill is

TABLE 7.6 Written questions and responses in Parliament, 1959–1990 (selected years)

	National Assembly		Senate	
Year	Number of Questions	Number of Responses	Number of Questions	Number of Responses
1959	3,506	2,814	799	588
1964	5,451	5,306	761	584
1969	5,784	5,222	1,000	928
1973	6,756	4,413	1,565	1,507
1977	8,550	7,889	3,068	2,492
1981	13,897	8,932	5,244	3,456
1984	19,139	15,914	6,420	5,243
1986	18,184	11,811	5,111	3,927
1987	19,120	19,109	5,168	4,551
1990	15,249	13,924	5,414	4,684

SOURCES: Based on Didier Maus, *Les grandes textes de la pratique institutionnelle de la Ve République*, Notes et Etudes Documentaires, no. 4864 (Paris: Documentation Française, 1988); and Jean-Louis Quermonne and Dominique Chagnollaud, *Le gouvernement de la France sous la Ve République*, 4th ed. (Paris: Dalloz, 1991), p. 337.

considered adopted unless the Assembly produces a motion of censure within 48 hours after the government has pledged its responsibility. In either case, if the motion passes, the government must resign. But the procedure in the case of an Assembly-initiated censure motion is cumbersome: The motion must be cosigned by at least 10 percent of the members of the Assembly. The vote on the motion can occur only after a cooling-off period of 48 hours, and the motion must be adopted by an absolute majority of *all* members of the Assembly. Any deputy has the right to cosponsor an Assembly-initiated censure motion only once during each parliamentary term.

Since the founding of the Fifth Republic, more than 30 censure motions have been introduced in the Assembly (motivated for the most part by discontent over policy in general or, more specifically, economic policy), but only one of them was successful or, to put it more accurately, *would* have been successful if the president had adhered to the Constitution. De Gaulle's unconstitutional procedure in connection with the change in the method of electing the president had provoked a storm of protest in both houses of Parliament; the Assembly, in October 1962, produced more than the required absolute majority for censure of the government headed by Pompidou. However, instead of dismissing Pompidou, de Gaulle expressed his lack of confidence in the Assembly by dissolving it. After the parliamentary elections that followed, the Gaullists had an absolute majority in the Assembly, and Pompidou was appointed premier of a "new" government.

The "provocation" approach (Art. 49, Sec. 3) has been an effective tool of the executive. Between 1958 and 1991, the government engaged its responsibility 67 times, on each occasion successfully.[47] The fact that the article was used 39 times during the 9th legislature (1988–1993) alone—28 times by Rocard, 8 times by Cresson, and 3 times by Bérégovoy[48]—can be explained easily: During this period the government did not dispose of a disciplined majority that could be relied on to enact without difficulty bills considered important by the premier. Balladur also used the article during the first session of the 10th legislature (spring 1993); for although he had a solid majority, he was confronted with too many amendments introduced by Gaullist and Giscardist deputies, especially to privatization and employment bills. Article 49 (Sec. 3) undoubtedly facilitates the legislative process, but as one scholar has observed, it "denies the Parliament its deliberative function and imposes silence where there should be discussion and decision."[49] In any case, Parliament has thus far failed to oust a single premier (though the Assembly would doubtlessly have had the votes to do so if in 1986 Mitterrand had appointed a Socialist premier). That failure has made it easier for governments to rule by decree or to make policy by simple declaration. The ineffectiveness of the censure procedure must be largely attributed to the fact that the opposition has lacked the necessary votes. Moreover, even opposition deputies can sometimes be dissuaded from voting for censure by possibilities of executive co-optation (i.e., the promise of favorable policy consideration or participation in future governments).[50]

THE INCOMPATIBILITY RULE

The position of government vis-à-vis Parliament has been strengthened by the "incompatibility" clause, Article 23 of the Constitution, which provides that no person may simultaneously hold a parliamentary mandate and a cabinet (or other government) position. The clause was introduced not to provide for separation of powers in the U.S. sense but to reduce the dependence of members of the government on Parliament. Such a dependence prevailed under the Fourth Republic: If a deputy had a reasonably good chance of getting a cabinet post in the event that a government was voted out and a reshuffling took place, then he might be sorely tempted to hasten such a reshuffling by doing everything possible to embarrass the government and cause its resignation. If a government in which he served would in turn fall a few months later, the deputy would still retain his parliamentary seat. Nowadays, the political future of a deputy who becomes part of a newly constituted cabinet is more uncertain. If a cabinet minister offends the legislature, he risks little, in view of the difficulty of passing censure motions; if he loses the president's support and is ousted from the cabinet, he cannot automatically return to the legislative chamber from which he came.

The incompatibility clause has not prevented the government from recruiting many of its members from the Assembly. A deputy who is asked to join the government has a 15-day period in which to make up his or her mind. If the deputy opts for a ministerial position, his or her alternate (*suppléant*) takes over the deputy's parliamentary mandate. The system whereby each candidate for an Assembly seat runs with an alternate, whose name also appears on the election ballot, precludes the necessity of frequent by-elections. A by-election must of course be held if a vacancy is created by the resignation or death of both the deputy and the alternate. Nothing prevents a deputy from having a prior understanding with the alternate that in case the deputy wishes to return to Parliament after a stint in the cabinet, the alternate will resign, thus forcing a by-election and (presumably) facilitating the parliamentary re-entry of the deputy (though the evidence thus far does not provide many instances of such deals). About one-fourth of the approximately 100 by-elections held so far under the Fifth Republic have taken place as a result of the resignation of the *suppléant*.[51]

The spirit if not the letter of Article 23 has been repeatedly violated. Many members of the cabinet have run for seats that they have no intention to occupy. President de Gaulle himself encouraged his ministers to seek parliamentary seats, perhaps in order to enhance the image of a government consisting of members enjoying support in the country at large or at least in important constituencies. But why do electors vote for a candidate for the Assembly if they have reason to believe that he or she will resign the seat right after the elections? The voters are aware of the weakness of Parliament; hence they would rather strengthen their bonds with a person who is closer to power—and who therefore can do much more for his or her constituency than a mere member of Parliament—and they may even hope that the deputy they elected will be "promoted" out of Parliament. The proof that the transfer from Parliament to the cabinet has become quite a normal procedure in the Fifth Republic is seen from the fact that between 1958 and 1967—the period of de Gaulle's unchallenged dominance, during which the reputation of parliamentarians was at an all-time low—73 cabinet ministers were recruited from among the membership of the National Assembly. Between 1959 and 1981, 304 deputies (31 in 1981 alone) and 23 senators gave up their seats in order to accept various government appointments; and of the 44 ministers appointed (or reappointed) after the legislative elections of 1981, 32 had just been elected to the Assembly, and 3 had been members of the Senate.[52] Of the 30 ministers appointed after the legislative elections of 1993, 25 had been formally elected to the Assembly, and 4 to the Senate.[53]

Whereas it has clearly become desirable to the president to use the Parliament as a pool of competent ministers, the political risk to the deputy limits both the deputy and the president. To minimize that risk, the incompatibility rule is circumvented: The government may select several deputies or senators as "parliamentary delegates" (*parlementaires en mission [temporaire]*), who are attached to ministries or who participate in interministerial committees but retain their parliamentary seats (thus becoming, in effect, part-time ministers) provided that their "ministerial" service does not exceed three months. In order to resolve the problem of incompatibility, the first Chirac government supported a constitutional amendment that would have permitted ministers to resume their parliamentary seats automatically six months after relinquishing their cabinet posts. The amendment failed when, in 1974, it fell short of the necessary three-fifths vote in a joint session of Parliament.[54] Since then, more than 80 parliamentarians have served as *parlementaires en mission*.

THE ROLE OF THE DEPUTY

Members of Parliament have themselves been aware of the state of impotence to which the Gaullist regime reduced them. Polls of Assembly deputies conducted in the past 20 years reveal that only a small proportion of legislators believed the role of Parliament to be very important or even satisfactory, although as expected, members of the majority party attached a greater significance to Parliament than opposition party members. In view of this negative institutional self-image, why do deputies choose their political profession, and why has the number of candidates for election to the Assembly steadily increased?[55] One scholar has distinguished among four "typologies of motivation": status (social prestige), program (influencing public policy), mission (giving meaning to one's life), and obligation (the fulfillment of a moral duty to society).[56] (Curiously, power or material payoffs are not listed among the motivations.) The "program" orientation was evident in the case of the Socialist deputies of the seventh Assembly (1981–1986), 193 of whom were elected for the first time. They brought with them a youthful enthusiasm, a feeling of solidarity with a brand-new government, and a recognition that a great number of reforms were overdue and had to be enacted quickly.[57] For that reason, many of them were willing to be docile tools of Mitterrand's presidential majority, cogs in a well-oiled parliamentary machine. There might be a selfish element in the deputies' cooperation with the government: the hope of the ultimate reward of ministerial appointment.

Still, the "mission motivation" of French legislators must play a larger role than it does in the case of U.S. legislators because the payoff is more limited for the former. French deputies do not have the large staffs and salaries of their U.S. congressional counterparts and enjoy fewer fringe benefits. True, only about half of their gross annual salary (in 1990, about $75,000—a sum calculated on the scale for senior civil servants) is taxed. In addition, they receive allowances for secretarial services, housing, and miscellaneous expenses; a reduction in telephone rates; a large number of free airline trips annually to their constituencies; and unlimited railroad travel for themselves and half-fare for their spouses.[58] Yet many deputies are financially hard-pressed, for (in addition to having to give up part of their salary to their party) they must maintain two residences (and sometimes employ two secretaries) and entertain frequently.

Most deputies are not wealthy; in fact, in terms of their social and professional backgrounds, they do not differ greatly from that of the French bourgeoisie as a whole. The contingent of deputies elected to the National Assembly in the past 20 years has included a sizable number of public officials, white-collar employees, many schoolteachers and university professors (especially among the Socialists), and a modest number of lawyers, physicians, pharmacists, and businesspeople. The number of farmers has been insignificant, as has the number of blue-collar workers (except, on occasion, for the Communists) (see Table 7.7).

Deputies are not as indignant about their limited powers and benefits as they might be because most of them enjoy compensatory prestige and emoluments as active local politicians—mayors or regional councilors. Thus, 202 of the 577

TABLE 7.7 Identified professions of members of the National Assembly (metropolitan France)

Profession	1988		1993	
	Number	*Percent*	*Number*	*Percent*
Teachers	153	27.5*	73	13.0
High government officials (*grands corps*)	53	9.6	42	7.6
Health professionals	41	7.5	55	10.0
Lawyers	27	4.9	31	5.6
Professional politicians	26	4.7	28	5.0
Senior managers of private firms	25	4.5	26	4.7
Without declared occupation	25	4.5	27	4.9
Other public servants	21	3.8	21	3.8
Owners/directors of business	16	2.9	33	6.0
Journalists	11	2.0	13	2.4
Farmers	10	1.8	20	3.6
Employees of public enterprises	8	1.4	8	1.4
Workers	6**	1.2	3	0.5
Judges	4	0.7	5	1.0
Accountants	3	0.5	4	0.7
N (metropolitan France)	550	100.0	550	100.0

*Percentages of teachers in previous Assemblies: 1981, 25; 1978, 15.2; 1973, 9.7.
**Number of workers in: 1981, 6; 1978, 11; 1973, 16.
SOURCE: *Le Monde*, 1 April 1993, p. 11. Slightly different statistics in *Pouvoirs* 66 (September 1993), 180.

deputies elected in 1993 were (and continued to be) mayors, 14 were members of regional councils, and 24 were members of general (departmental) councils.[59] This multiple officeholding (*cumul des mandats*), which has been traditional in France and which was not affected by the incompatibility clause, has served the purpose of "connecting" a politician's national and local concerns.[60] It has also provided a modicum of job security to the deputy in case of loss of his parliamentary mandate, and it has compensated the deputy for his reduced status in a weakened Parliament.[61] However, the weakness of Parliament has in part been precipitated by the *cumul* insofar as it has contributed to the deputies' tendencies to absenteeism.

The regulations providing for a reduction in the per diem pay of deputies for excessive absence have not reversed such tendencies, as these regulations are not consistently implemented.[62] At attempt was made a few years ago to counteract the Fourth Republic pattern under which an absent deputy could have his vote cast for him by proxy, by instituting a system of electronic voting. This in turn led to a new practice, that of having colleagues press the buttons for absent deputies. That practice is officially outlawed, but it has continued nonetheless. In 1987, a group of deputies asked the Constitutional Council to nullify an Assembly vote that had involved proxy voting, on the grounds that it violated Article 27, which states that "the right [of a deputy] to vote is personal." The council refused to rule, arguing that the outcome of the vote would have been no different had the absent deputies been present.[63] In 1991 Assembly speaker Laurent Fabius on several occasions withheld per diem pay from deputies who voted by proxy, but he dropped the practice in the face of hostile reactions by many deputies.[64] In 1993, Philippe Séguin, the newly elected speaker, reintroduced the application of the *vote personnel*, but it is uncertain whether he will have much success. Several deputies, including members of his own party, have accused the speaker of "galloping megalomania" and have suggested that his approach discriminates against deputies from the provinces.[65] Except for censure motions or the government's pledging its confidence in a particular bill (where the roll call is used), the various other methods of voting in the Assembly—by raising of hands, rising and sitting, or secret ballot (as for the election of the speaker)—have been equally ineffective in controlling absenteeism.[66]

Another measure intended to reduce absenteeism and to increase the attention span of deputies with respect to their parliamentary business was a bill passed at the end of 1985 to limit to *two* the number of elective offices that could be held at the same time.[67] Since the law became operational only in 1987, it is too early to assess its effect; however, it would seem that the decentralization measures (giving local communities and regions much greater power) and the enhanced ambitions of Parliament would require a disjunction of a deputy's position from that of a mayor (see Chapter 8).[68]

The absenteeism of deputies is a reflection of their sense of frustration. In the past, that condition was due largely to the deputies' own awareness of the streamlined nature of the legislative process; more recently, it has been due to the recognition that Parliament must contend with rival arenas of deliberation and decision.

Among these rivals are the "committees of experts" (*comités de sages*), which, paradoxically, have proliferated particularly in recent years (i.e., the period in which the executive has been expressing a willingness to give Parliament an enlarged role). These committees, which have been compared to the Royal Commissions in Britain or Sweden, are appointed by the cabinet; they are composed of nonparliamentarians, such as academicians, higher civil servants, independent lawyers, and other professionals.[69] The committees conduct lengthy hearings, taking testimony from representatives of interest groups and from individual experts.[70] When the committees are finished with their investigations, they submit a report (often quite detailed) with policy recommendations to the appropriate minister, who then submits it to the whole cabinet. On the positive side, these committees can be viewed as able to gather information from a variety of sources in an unhurried manner and free from partisan pressures. But they can also be seen as attempts to depoliticize a delicate public issue, that is, as a means of buck-passing used by the government (and tolerated by Parliament). Since the inauguration of President Mitterrand, "committees of experts" have been appointed for (among other problems) university reform, ethics in government, AIDS, the cultures of ethnic minorities, the rehabilitation of slums, nationality and naturalization, social security, and the construction of a new national library.[71]

The weakening of Parliament, particularly of the power of individual deputies, was not entirely a Gaullist invention. As we have seen, the immobility of Parliament in the Fourth Republic had provoked measures to streamline the legislative process. These measures were sufficient neither to save the Fourth Republic nor to satisfy the growing number of French citizens who criticized, and wished to reduce, the role of Parliament. Among these critics were not only adherents of the (Gaullist and non-Gaullist) Right, but also liberal Anglophiles who envied the tight management of the House of Commons and certain leftists who, although as a matter of principle or tactics, they wished to have *no* effective decision-making institution, criticized the failure of Parliament to resolve urgent problems. Even a number of politicians most strongly identified with traditional parliamentary government occasionally voiced doubts about a strong, uncontrolled legislature. For example, Mendès-France, the Radical leader of the Fourth Republic, argued that Parliament could not function alone and ought to be aided by a specialized, quasi-corporative chamber (representing not geographical units but economic and professional groups).[72] It could even be said that those who were skeptical about the dominant role of Parliament spoke for the majority of the French. In the past 100 years, French citizens tended frequently to vote for opposition parties that were undemocratic or whose commitment to parliamentary government was questionable, parties that could not (for lack of discipline) effectively transform Parliament into an instrument of government, or a charismatic leadership that was antiparliamentary; or else have participated in periodic "happenings" that were intended to supplement the decision-making work of Parliament.

The negative views of Parliament evinced by politicians in the past have been reflected by the general public in somewhat ambivalent fashion. According to a poll conducted in 1972, 59 percent of French respondents thought Parliament should determine basic policies, while 27 percent thought the president should.[73] According to an earlier poll (1969), 52 percent found Parliament useful, as against only 15 percent who did not.[74] Over the years, the public confidence in Parliament has improved as the public consensus about Fifth Republic institutions in general has gradually developed; in a poll taken in mid-1989, 68 percent said that the National Assembly played a useful role (against 24 percent who disagreed and 8 percent who had no opinion).[75] Among specific political institutions or positions, that of the deputy has engendered relatively low confidence (see Chapter 10, Table 10.1). According to another poll, in which respondents were asked what profession they would choose if they were to do so now, 32 percent would want to be heads of enterprises, 24 percent physicians, 9 percent lawyers, and only 4 percent deputies.[76]

Many French citizens who vote for a deputy doubt not only the latter's "instrumental" efficacy as a legislator but also a deputy's ability to intervene on behalf of his or her constituency with the higher civil service. The reputation for relative powerlessness of deputies may be attributed to the appropriation of legislative functions by the executive as well as to the fact that many political debates have been "delocalized" from the national to supranational and infranational levels, to the Commission of the European Community (for instance, on agricultural legislation) and, since the decentralization laws of 1982, to municipalities and regional councils.[77] But there is a paradox: The negative image citizens have of deputies as a categoric group does not necessarily apply to "their" deputy, whom they may know personally in his or her capacity as mayor.[78]

It has been asserted that "if the relations between the administration and the minister are characterized by a deep mutual distrust, those that exist between the administrator and the deputy bear witness to such an abyss that one may doubt even the existence of any sort of relationship."[79] The gulf between the deputy and the civil servant, which dates to the Third Republic and is based on the existence of two conflicting perspectives, has never been bridged, but it has narrowed appreciably since 1959. In the past, many deputies, in particular those belonging to Gaullist and allied parties, shared de Gaulle's affinity for nonpartisan professionals as representatives of the state, or shared social and educational backgrounds with higher civil servants. In the Parliaments elected in 1981 and thereafter, civil servants have been well represented, especially in Socialist ranks.

The negative view of the importance of the French deputy is not endorsed by all political scientists. Some would argue that backbenchers today have nearly as much opportunity to participate meaningfully in debate as they had in previous republics, particularly on domestic issues; others suggest that Article 34, which enumerates the areas of parliamentary jurisdiction, has not taken any powers away from Parliament that it had possessed previously. They assert that as many important bills are passed by the Assembly today as had been passed during the Third Republic.[80] Although deputies are now accorded less time for debate than previously, they *need* less time because the new system has obviated onerous and fruitless debates on government competence. Because parliamentary investiture of newly constituted governments is no longer required, there is no call for a discussion of their merits. Moreover, owing to the consolidation of parliamentary parties and the diminished importance of ideology, there is less scope for long-winded oratory about matters of principle.

One should not equate the formal weakness of Parliament with lack of participation in all instances. Many government bills, especially since the early 1970s, have been subjected to important changes by deputies. Government bills on farm prices, social security, and educational reforms have been extensively modified during the parliamentary process; the penal-reform bill of 1980 was subjected (in both chambers) to numerous alterations;[81] and the land-transfer and inheritance-tax bill of 1976 was virtually gutted in Parliament. Statistically, the success rate of deputies' amendments (introduced in the plenary session) to government bills between 1970 and 1977 was impressive, ranging from 27 percent for amendments introduced by Gaullists to 5 percent for those introduced by Communists. The rate was equally good between 1986 and 1988, when 24 percent of the more than 9,000 amendments introduced in the Assembly that were of parliamentary origin were adopted.[82] The 9th Assembly (1988–1993) was particularly active. It passed 455 bills (60 of parliamentary origin)[83] and several thousand regulations connected with the European Community and voted on 18 motions of censure. It made significant contributions to legislation concerning immigration, environment, education, minimum wages, and the reform of the penal code (see Table 7.8).[84] Many bills were successfully amended in committee;[85] others were subjected to changes by the government itself in response to *informal* suggestions by deputies (who in turn sometimes responded to the external pressures of interest groups). This increased involvement has not necessarily improved the quality of the laws; it has, however, resulted in the growth of the average size of bills (from 93 lines in 1950 to 220 lines in 1990) and of the bulk of the *Journal officiel* (from 7,070 pages in 1976 to 17,141 pages in 1990).[86]

However, much of the success of deputies in the legislative process depends upon the goodwill of the executive: Many of the private members' bills or amendments that are adopted have been accepted (and occasionally even encouraged) by the government, and besides, many of them have dealt with such politically innocuous topics as the limitation of imports of household pets, the medical coverage of domestics, and so on. Occasionally private members' bills are of greater importance, and the government endorses them because opposing them might be embarrassing.[87] Most often, however, the deputy's role seems increasingly to be that of processing requests from local constituents to the government. The "pork-barrel" concerns of deputies have been to some extent forced on them by the single-member-district system of elections, under which they tend, in Anglo-American fashion, to be victors in local popularity contests. They continue to justify their popularity, and assure their future reelection, by securing the help of the national government in solving local problems. But in order to do this, deputies must cooperate with the government and not alienate it by being parliamentary troublemakers. This explains why some opposition deputies, whose parties have no realistic prospects of assuming control over the Assembly or blocking the majority steamroller, break ranks and vote for selected government bills.[88]

Parliament was impotent in the first decade of the Fifth Republic because until 1969, the chief of state was General de Gaulle, who regarded himself (and was regarded) as an institution eclipsing all others, and who reinforced the special

TABLE 7.8 Amendments to bills in the Assembly (selected years)

	Proposed	Adopted
1978	2,394	936
1981	5,060	1,370
1982	9,804	4,273
1984	1,081	3,609
1986*	6,189	873
1988	2,826	1,178
1990	9,910	2,275

*Nine of these had been introduced and adopted during the pre-cohabitation period.
SOURCE: Adapted from J. L. Quermonne and D. Chagnollaud, *Le Gouvernement de la Ve République*, 4th ed. (Paris: Dalloz, 1991), p. 317.

legitimacy of his position by periodic popular mandates, and also because there was usually a cooperative majority of Gaullists in the Assembly. After the collapse of that majority in 1973 and its replacement by more disparate "presidential majorities" (except for the 1986–1988 interlude), a number of Assembly speakers—of whom two had once served as premiers[89]—have demanded "structural changes" that would enhance the role of legislators, and a succession of premiers, particularly at the beginning of their terms of office, have avowed their intention to support such demands. Perhaps they did so for the sake of public relations or to ensure that their government programs would receive a resoundingly affirmative vote. But lest the premiers create illusions among deputies—and irritate the president of the Republic—they have accompanied their promises to Parliament with the reminder that the executive remained the chief decision maker.

The inauguration of Giscard d'Estaing in 1974 raised new hope that Parliament would be called upon to participate in legislative activity more meaningfully than under the first two presidents. The blatant violations of the Constitution in regard to Parliament that had occurred under de Gaulle[90] were not repeated under Giscard. On the contrary, the restricted options available in an economy beset by difficulties had rendered many policy initiatives politically risky and tempted Giscard to share the onus with Parliament. Indeed, between mid-1974 and the end of 1975, the formal input of the legislature on important government bills—divorce, abortion, budget, education, and conditions of employment in the public sector—was significant. However, this burst of activity did not transform the deputies into genuine co-decision makers, particularly on financial matters. Moreover, it was short-lived, for by the end of 1978 the government increasingly ignored Parliament. Although nearly half the hours of discussion in both chambers were devoted to an examination of the budget, one deputy (a Communist), complained that "the budget [still] leaves the Assembly in practically the same condition in which it entered"; and even the Assembly speaker (Edgar Faure) admitted that Parliament did little more than perform an "autopsy" on the budget.[91]

When in opposition, the Socialist party had repeatedly complained about the contempt shown for Parliament by Gaullist and conservative presidents and premiers; the party's platforms had called for an enlarged role for that institution, and Mitterrand had advocated such a role both before and after his election to the presidency. One measure of that enlarged role has been the growth of the operating budget for both chambers.[92] However, the newly elected and Socialist-dominated Assembly that met in July 1981 was held to a very tight schedule by a government determined to see a speedy enactment of legislation it considered urgent. The government allocated only three days for debate on a bill concerning administrative decentralization, a delicate topic on which Parliament (and especially the Senate) had dragged its feet some years earlier. The government may have resorted to various "railroading" tactics because of its inexperience or because decentralization was a "hot" topic; in any case, several Socialist deputies, although approving the substance of the bill, voted against it because of their resentment of the procedures used.

For many years, much of the submissive behavior of the majority deputies could be attributed to their belonging to a disciplined party that had been elected on the presidential coattails; in addition, there was the psychological impact of the bipolar situation: If a deputy did not support his party, he gave aid and comfort to the other side. But gradually this bipolar situation has been changing because of the existence of factions within each party, the transpartisan interest-group connections of individual deputies, and the support groups (*amicales*) containing both majority and opposition deputies favoring specific causes. In 1988, bipolarity was modified by the fact that many deputies did not owe their election to the Assembly to the presidential coattails; lacking an absolute Socialist majority, Premier Rocard had to construct ad hoc majorities for different policy issues by depending by turns on the supplementary votes of centrists, Communists, and occasionally even Gaullists.[93] In 1993, although the Right achieved an overwhelming victory in the parliamentary elections, its Assembly majority remained fragile, given the conflicts between and within the RPR and the UDF.

This fragility should give deputies more freedom to express themselves, especially since during recent decades the number of hours devoted annually to plenary sessions in the Assembly has nearly doubled.[94] However, the government retains tight control of the calendar; and in a situation in which deputies are given five or six working days for examining a score of government bills (and sometimes only three days during special sessions) and opposition deputies are allowed two minutes each for a discussion of farmers' benefits, the problems of artisans, or overall economic policy, the Parliament cannot make the most informed contributions.

The election of former premier Laurent Fabius as speaker of the Assembly in 1988 was a promising sign for that chamber. Under his leadership (aided by an ambitious chief of staff),[95] the Assembly's national and international prestige and its general atmosphere improved, and it became the destination of visits by prominent personalities. In addition to this *"politique de réception,"*[96] Fabius suggested other innovations, among them (in addition to the abortive attempt to eliminate proxy voting) the right of the speaker to call a meeting of a standing committee during periods when the Assembly is not in session.

The newly appointed Gaullist speaker, Philippe Séguin, reiterated the demand for interim sessions of standing committees. He also continued the "politics of reception" by (unsuccessfully) inviting British Prime Minister John Major to the National Assembly, subsequently (and successfully) inviting King Juan Carlos of Spain to address the plenum of that chamber,[97] and, as if to snub the Foreign Office, notifying President Mitterrand of the visit before the foreign minister. (Not to be outdone, René Monory, the speaker of the Senate, had earlier invited German Chancellor Helmut Kohl to *his* chamber.) In addition, Séguin took up the demand, first made by Fabius, to lengthen ordinary parliamentary sessions from five and a half to nine months. He also called for the automatic meeting of a special standing committee of the Assembly during periods when the full Parliament is not in session. Such a committee, composed of members of various parties, would be able to call on ministers to answer questions on current topics.

(Fabius had proposed such a standing committee, but one to be convoked only at the request of the President.)

Among other concrete measures announced by Séguin were the following: (1) the right of chairpersons of standing committees to demand the appearance of ministers to defend specific provisions of government bills; (2) the requirement that the text of bills to be debated in plenary session be the amended version that had been adopted by the *standing committees* rather than (as is the case today) the original text submitted by the government;[98] and (3) the rebroadcasting of parliamentary debates on television (to begin on an experimental basis on the cable network of the Paris region). There is no doubt that the efficiency of Parliament has improved in the past several years and is likely to improve even further, both in consequence of Séguin's prodding and in response to the Treaty of European Union, which stipulates the specific involvement of the Parliament in future elaborations of European legislation.

Premier Balladur pronounced himself in favor of efforts to strengthen the decision-making role of Parliament, but he envisaged them as part of a package of constitutional reforms (some of them suggested by the president and a "blue ribbon" committee on the subject).[99] In the meantime, he repeated his assurance to the deputies that he wanted a continuing "dialogue" with them and looked eagerly forward to backbencher bills on social policy matters, but it remains to be seen whether this will result in making Parliament an equal partner of the executive in the legislative process.

NOTES

1. On the French tradition of antiparliamentarism, see Philippe Lavaux, "Récurrences et paradoxes: une histoire contrapuntique," *Pouvoirs* 64 (February 1993), 5–22.
2. Pierre Fougeyrollas, *La Conscience politique dans la France contemporaine* (Paris: Denoël, 1963), Chapter 3.
3. Adapted from Jean-Claude Lamy and Marc Kunstlé, *Au petit bonheur la chambre* (Paris: Julliard, 1972), pp. 36–38. Because of the improvement of rail service (especially the spread of high-speed trains), some deputies now depart for Paris early Tuesday morning.
4. As Table 7.1 shows, the number of Assembly members has varied over the years, depending on the nature of the electoral system and the splitting up of constituencies.
5. They include secretaries, stenographers, word-processor operators, drivers, supply agents, guards, and others, to whom the rules for the ordinary civil service do not apply. They are politically neutral, though many of them are unionized (for the most part in the CFDT). See Jacques Klein, "Une Carrière administrative peu connue: Le fonctionnaire parlementaire," *Revue administrative* 33:194 (March–April 1980), 131–138; and, for more recent data, *Le Monde*, 14 July 1989.
6. For example, of the 58 bills adopted in 1991, 31 had been submitted to the conference committee; but in the case of 16 of these, the committee failed to resolve the difference. *Année politique, 1991,* p. 177.

7. Thus, those Socialist deputies belonging to the Mitterrand faction got the chair of the finance and defense committees; an adherent of the Mauroy faction became chief steering officer (*rapporteur*) for the budget; the chair of the committee for cultural and social affairs was given to a supporter of Rocard, and that of the committee on laws to a member of (the now defunct) CERES. The Left Radicals, allies of the Socialists, got the chair of the foreign affairs committee, and the Communists, that of production. Furthermore, the division of chairs aimed at a regional and generational balance. *Le Monde*, 5, 6, 8, and 9 July 1981.

8. However, deputies who belong to a *groupe parlementaire* pay a certain price: Not only are they subject to party discipline (although this is less strict in some parties, e.g., the UDF, than in others, e.g., the PCF), but they must also give up part of their salaries to their g*roupe parlementaire* or to the party as a whole. The sum varied, in 1988, from 1,500 francs for the UDF deputy to 20,000 francs for the PCF deputy.

9. Thierry Bréhier, "Parlement: Deux Chances pour rien," in Le Monde, *Bilan du septennat: L'Alternance dans l'alternance* (Paris:, 1988), pp. 49-52.

10. The politician, Jean de Broglie, had been murdered in 1977. It was alleged that Michel Poniatowski, a former interior minister and, like the victim, a friend of Giscard, had covered up the matter.

11. The bill was cosponsored by the leaders of all the parliamentary parties except the PCF. *Le Monde*, 16 January 1993.

12. In the fall of 1992 the (right-wing) opposition deputies, convinced that the government would be whitewashed, refused to participate in a special committee to investigate the government's responsibility in the use of AIDS-infected blood for transfusions. See *Pouvoirs* 65 (April 1993), 203.

13. See Pierre Avril, "Les Contre-Pouvoirs constitutionnels," *Projet*, December 1980, pp. 1189-1198.

14. See Jean-Pierre Marichy, *La Deuxième Chambre dans la vie politique française* (Paris: LGDJ, 1970); Jean Mastias, *Le Sénat de la Ve République: Réforme et renouveau* (Paris: Economica, 1980), for a discussion of that body's legislative and control functions; and for a more recent analysis, Didier Maus, "Le Sénat, l'Assemblée nationale et le Gouvernement," *Pouvoirs* 44 (1988).

15. In 1988 Poher was reelected (at the age of 80) for another term to the speakership, an office to which both Charles Pasqua and Jean Lecanuet aspired but which was finally, in 1993, inherited by René Monory, a prominent centrist (and UDF politician).

16. *Le Monde*, 11 July 1989. The continued reputation of the Senate as a relatively relaxed body explains why Michel Charasse decided in 1992 to quit as minister of the budget (a role that, in his opinion, required too much work) and renew his political career in that chamber.

17. See Arnaud Tardan, "Le Rôle législatif du Sénat," *Pouvoirs* 44 (1988), 104-110.

18. More graphically, in 1969 only 1 government bill was introduced in the Senate, and in 1975 (the high point), 59 bills.

19. Of course the Senate approved; but it is not clear what if any effect a disapproval would have had on the legitimacy and continuation of the government.

20. The expression of Olivier Duhamel, "The Fifth Republic Under François Mitterrand," in George Ross et al., eds., *The Mitterrand Experiment* (New York: Oxford University Press, 1987), p. 152.

21. Ibid.

22. Didier Maus, *Les Grandes Textes de la pratique institutionnelle de la Ve République*, Notes et Etudes Documentaires, no. 4864 (Paris: Documentation Française, 1988),

p. 162. Note that 20 of the bills thus overridden were subsequently voided by the Constitutional Council.

23. Forty-three special sessions were called by the premier; one was convoked automatically in connection with the use of emergency powers (Art. 16), and three met upon the election of a new Assembly after dissolution of the old. One special session was convoked at the behest of the president in June 1992 when he decided that the amendment of the Constitution (made necessary by the [Maastricht] Treaty on European Union) should be by joint session of Parliament rather than by referendum. The most recent special sessions convoked (in June and July 1992) by the deputies during the ninth legislature dealt with the Habbash affair (see Chapter 6) and minimum wages.

24. Between 1959 and 1987, the "blocked vote" was used 197 times in the Assembly and 249 times in the Senate (90 percent of the time successfully). A more precise breakdown of the use of the "blocked vote" under various presidents is as follows: de Gaulle: 114 in the Assembly, 110 in the Senate; Pompidou, 11 and 32; and Giscard, 32 and 19. Based on Le Monde, Dossiers et Documents, *L'Election présidentielle 26 avril–10 mai 1981*, p. 16; Pierre Birnbaum et al., *Réinventer le parlement* (Paris: Flammarion, 1977), p. 126; Maus, *La Pratique institutionnelle* (1988), p. 160; and *Regards sur l'actualité*, May 1988, p. 5—all of which give conflicting figures.

25. At about the same time, the Assembly actually *rejected* a blocked-vote government bill that would have provided increased subsidies to families with numerous children, when the Gaullists broke majority discipline and voted together with the Socialists against the bill. Although the Gaullists claimed to favor the substance of the bill, they did not like the blocked-vote procedure invoked for it. The Communists, although objecting to the procedure, voted for the measure because of its socially progressive content. See *Le Monde*, 28 June 1980.

26. The government did not quite adhere to the Common Program of the Left of 1972, in which the signatory parties had committed themselves to limit the use of the blocked vote to essential texts and only at a second reading.

27. The Chirac government of 1986–1988 used the blocked vote 36 times in the Assembly and 32 times in the Senate.

28. René Pleven, cited in Michel-Henri Fabre, *Principes républicains de droit constitutionnel* (Paris: LGDJ, 1970), p. 408. Between 1959 and 1987, 321 private members' bills introduced in the Assembly, and 10 in the Senate, were considered inadmissible by the government under Article 40 of the Constitution.

29. Figures (occasionally conflicting) based on Jean-Charles Maoût and Raymond Muzellac, *Le Parlement sous la Ve République* (Paris: Armand Colin, 1971), p. 74; Le Monde, *L'Election présidentielle 26 avril–10 mai 1981*, p. 16; "Bilan législatif 1982," *Regards sur l'actualité* 89 (March 1983), 38f; and "La Pratique parlementaire sous la cohabitation," *Regards sur l'actualité* 141 (May 1988), 10–11.

30. Frédéric Bobin, "La Fin de la nouvelle législature," *Le Monde*, 17 July 1993.

31. Louis Favoreu and Loïc Philip, "La Jurisprudence du conseil constitutionnel," *Revue du droit public et de la science politique* 91 (January–February 1975), 165–200.

32. In addition to the nine appointed members, former presidents of the (Fourth and Fifth) Republic are ex-officio members of the Constitutional Council. However, only Vincent Auriol (a Fourth Republic president) participated in Council sessions until 1960 (and once in 1962), the other ex-presidents (Coty, de Gaulle, and Giscard d'Estaing) choosing not to do so.

33. As part of the amendment bill, the government had proposed that the council be permitted to examine cases on its own initiative (*auto-saisine*) if its members felt

that bills (or laws) violated public liberties. But that part of the amendment was withdrawn when the Assembly opposed it on the grounds that it would result in a "government of judges" and undermine even further the powers of Parliament. François Luchaire, *Le Conseil constitutionnel* (Paris: Economica, 1980), p. 30. On *auto-saisine*, see also *Le Monde*, 6 September 1986, pp. 10–11. For an exhaustive analysis of judicial policy making, see Alec Stone, *The Birth of Judicial Politics in France: The Constitutional Council in Comparative Perspective* (New York: Oxford University Press, 1992).

34. Including various articles (72–74, and 76) that related to the administration of overseas departments. For the full text of 46 decisions from 1958 to 1991, see Louis Favoreu and Loïc Philip, *Les Grandes Décisions du conseil constitutionnel,* 6th ed. (Paris: Sirey, 1991).

35. Unlike the U.S. Supreme Court or the German Constitutional Court, the French Constitutional Council (1) does not judge "cases and controversies" arising under a law already in the statute books; and (2) can be "seized" only by official agents of the state (i.e., the legislative or executive branch) rather than by private individuals (as in the German "constitutional complaint") or by its own volition (as in the American "writ of certiorari"). In 1989 Mitterrand came out in favor of a constitutional amendment that would permit ordinary citizens to appeal to the Constitutional Council. See Michel Kajman, "L'Avenir d'une vieille idée," *Le Monde*, 14 September 1989.

36. In its 1972 program, *Changer la vie*, the Socialist party had proposed the transformation of the Constitutional Council into a "supreme court," to be composed differently from the way it is today: Three members would be *elected* by the Assembly, three elected by the Senate, two chosen by the *Conseil supérieur de la magistrature* (a special body empowered to appoint judges to other courts), and only one appointed by the president.

37. René Lacharrière, "Opinion dissidente," *Pouvoirs* 13 (1980), 133–150.

38. Cf. Loïc Philip, who points out (in "La Loi et les principes," *Le Monde*, 17 December 1981) that *no* French government that has happened to control the legislative process has been enthusiastic about the idea of constitutional supremacy.

39. Early in 1986, anticipating a Socialist defeat in the forthcoming Assembly elections, Mitterrand appointed Robert Badinter, his minister of justice, to the presidency of the Constitutional Council. However, Badinter's decisions have not always favored the Socialist position. See *Le Point*, 25 July 1988, p. 15.

40. For a discussion of judicial self-restraint and the "autolimitation" effect, especially under the Socialist government of 1981–1986, see John T. S. Keeler and Alec Stone, "Judicial Political Confrontation in Mitterrand's France," in Ross et al., *The Mitterrand Experiment*, pp. 161–181.

41. See Philippe Bernard and Erich Inciyan, "Délit de faciès," *Le Monde*, 22 June 1993. Nevertheless, the council declared the amended bill unconstitutional, holding it "incompatible with respect to individual liberty." *Le Monde*, 7 August 1993.

42. On the council's involvement in the debate, see Alec Stone, "Ratifying Maastricht," *French Politics and Society* 11:1 (Winter 1993), 71–88.

43. Guy Carcassonne, "La Loi des sages," *Le Point*, 21 August 1993, p. 19. The partial invalidation referred to sections of a government bill to curb illegal immigration, sections that provided for administrative detention and forbade "marriages of convenience" with French citizens. *Le Monde*, 15–16 August 1993.

44. For example, of 275 laws voted during the fourth legislature (1968–1972), 74 were not equipped with implementing regulations.

45. Cf. Philip Williams, *The French Parliament* (New York: Praeger, 1968), pp. 19, 46–51; *Le Monde,* 9–10 February 1975; and Michel Ameller, *Les Questions instruments du contrôle parlementaire* (Paris: LGDJ, 1964), pp. 80–81.

46. Thus, in 1981, only 113 oral questions that were not followed by a debate were posed in the Assembly, leading to 86 responses; in 1986, 172 questions, with 149 responses; and in 1987, 172 questions, with 150 responses. In 1981, only 2 oral questions that were followed by a debate were posed, but there were no government responses to the questions; and in 1987, there were no such oral questions.

47. Data are from Jean-Louis Quermonne and Dominique Chagnollaud, *Le Gouvernement de la France,* 4th ed. (Paris: Dalloz, 1991), pp. 707–709. On some bills, the government engaged its responsibility more than once, that is, during several readings. On more than a dozen occasions, the "engagements" were not even followed by censure motions.

48. Data are from *Pouvoirs* 65 (April 1993).

49. Joël Boudant, "La Crise identitaire du Parlement français," *Revue du droit public,* September–October 1992, pp. 1322–1402.

50. In 1972, the "moderate" Radicals, led by Jean-Jacques Servan-Schreiber, did not support a censure motion because they anticipated continued Gaullist control of the Assembly after the 1973 Assembly elections, and they wished to keep the door open to the UDR in the hope of being asked to join a postelection coalition. Between 1984 and 1986, and again in 1988, the Communists refrained from supporting the Gaullists and their allies in censure motions against Socialist governments despite growing disagreements with these governments over economic policy.

51. The following former ministers, for example, reentered the Assembly upon the resignation of their *suppléants*: Edgar Faure in 1969, Pierre Messmer in 1974, and Jacques Chirac in 1976.

52. During the first legislature (1958–1962), 28 deputies (or 4.8 percent of the 579 members of the Assembly) became ministers; 61 (or 12.5 percent of 487) during the fourth legislature (1968–1973); and 69 (or 14 percent of 490) during the fifth legislature (1973–1978). The Mauroy government appointed in June 1981 included 27 (or 5.5 percent of 491) who had been members of the sixth legislature (1978–1981). Cf. *Revue du droit public* 95:6 (November–December 1979), 1559–1590, and 96:4 (July–August 1980), 1151; and *Le Monde, Dossiers et Documents, Les Elections législatives de juin 1981* (Paris), pp. 20–23 et passim.

53. *Le Monde, Dossiers et Documents, Elections législatives: La Droite sans partage* (Paris: 1993), p. 158.

54. On this occasion most of the deputies who had entered the Assembly as *suppléants* understandably voted with the opposition, and signed a statement refusing to resign and thus bring about a by-election. Georges Morin, "L'Impossible Réforme du statut des suppléants parlementaires," *Revue du droit public* 95:6 (November–December 1979), 1559–1590.

55. In 1993, there were 5,167 candidates for the 555 legislative constituencies in metropolitan France, that is, an average of 9.3 candidates for each constituency. This compares to 8.3 in 1986 and 5 in 1988. In Paris alone there were 13 candidates for each constituency in 1993.

56. Oliver H. Woshinsky, *The French Deputy* (Lexington, MA: Lexington Books, 1973), esp. Chapter 1. The author's findings: 38 percent, mission-motivated; 28 percent, program; 20 percent, status; 14 percent, obligation. The interview responses about the *effect* of deputies on public policy are inconclusive.

57. Jean-Yves Lhomeau, "Le Métier de député," *Le Monde*, 5 August 1981.

58. For further details, see *Le Point*, 26 September 1988, p. 19.

59. *Pouvoirs* 66 (September 1993), 180. This is a considerably smaller *cumul* than for the deputies elected in 1981, of whom 246 were mayors and 249 members of general councils.

60. On the background and effects of *cumul*, see J. Becquart Leclerq, "Multiple Office-holding in Local and National Elective Positions," *Tocqueville Review* 9 (1987-1988), 221-241; and Stéphane Dion, "Le Cumul des mandats en France," *French Politics and Society* 13:3 (1992), 99-126.

61. Support for this argument may be the fact that in the Fourth Republic (when Parliament was relatively powerful) only 36 percent of the deputies had one or more local mandates, whereas in the Fifth Republic the proportion has averaged between 65 percent and 95 percent. See Guy Carcassonne, "Cumul des mandats: L'Anachronisme," *Le Point*, 6 February 1993, p. 36.

62. According to a complicated formula (based on an ordinance issued in December 1958), a deputy loses a third of his allowance for being absent during more than a third of the sessions, and half of his allowance for being absent half of the time.

63. *Le Monde*, 12-13 April 1987.

64. In effect, Fabius compromised by insisting that the personal vote be used only for bills considered important by all the parliamentary parties.

65. See Pascale Robert-David, "Philippe Séguin persiste et signe," *Le Monde*, 6 October 1993. See also "Fronde contre Philippe Séguin," *Le Monde*, 30 September 1993.

66. See "Le Débat sur l'absentéisme parlementaire," *Regards sur l'actualité* 141 (May 1988), 6-7.

67. The anti-*cumul* law provides that politicians may hold no more than two of the following positions simultaneously: deputy or senator; member of the European Parliament; regional councilor; general (departmental) councilor; member of a Paris municipal council; mayor of a town of more than 20,000 inhabitants; deputy mayor of a city of more than 100,000.

68. Because of the 1985 law, Giscard, having been reelected to the National Assembly in 1993, decided to quit as member of the European Parliament, while retaining his positions as president of the regional council of Auvergne and president of the UDF.

69. A committee on defense, named by Balladur shortly after he became prime minister, had 9 high-ranking military officers among its 27 members.

70. The committees are often chaired by prominent individuals. Among those that have been called on several occasions to fulfill this task are Marceau Long, vice-president of the Council of State; Georges Vedel, former member of the Constitutional Council; and René Rémond, historian and president of the *Fondation nationale des sciences politiques*.

71. See Pierre Servent, "La République des commissions," *L'Express*, 3 July 1987, pp. 10-13; Les Commissions parlementaires jalouses de la multiplication des comités de 'sages,'" *Le Monde*, 1 August 1987; and "Les Hommes-Providence de la République," *Le Point*, 11 September 1993, p. 9.

72. Pierre Mendès-France, *La République moderne* (Paris: Gallimard, 1962), pp. 73-108.

73. SOFRES, May 1972, cited in Edouard Bonnefous, "Crise des institutions: Restaurer le contrôle parlementaire," *Revue politique et parlementaire* 74 (October 1972), 16.

74. SOFRES, November 1969.

75. SOFRES poll, cited in *Le Monde*, 15 July 1989.

76. Poll conducted for *Le Figaro* in October 1986. Cited in SOFRES, *L'Etat de l'opinion 1988* (Paris: Seuil, 1988), pp. 222-223.

77. See Pierre Mazeaud, "Le Parlement et ses adversaires," *Pouvoirs* 64 (February 1993), 109-122.
78. See Joël Boudant, "La Crise identitaire du Parlement français," *Revue du droit public*, September-October 1992, pp. 1349-1351.
79. Ezra Suleiman, "L'Administrateur et le député en France," *RFSP* 23 (August 1973), 731.
80. See François Goguel, "Parliament under the Fifth French Republic: Difficulties of Adapting to a New Role," in Gerhard Loewenberg, ed., *Modern Parliaments: Change or Decline?* (Chicago: Aldine-Atherton, 1971), pp. 81-109. For another optimistic view, see Didier Maus, "Parliament in the Fifth Republic: 1958-1988," in Paul Godt, ed., *Policy-Making in France from de Gaulle to Mitterrand* (London: Pinter Publishers, 1989), pp. 12-27.
81. Jean Foyer, "Le Projet du loi 'sécurité et liberté' devant l'Assemblée Nationale," *La Nouvelle Revue des deux mondes*, November 1980, pp. 276-286.
82. Cf. J. R. Frears, "Parliament in the Fifth Republic," in William G. Andrews and Stanley Hoffmann, eds., *The Fifth Republic at Twenty* (Albany: State University of New York Press, 1981), pp. 60-62; and Christian Bigaud, "La pratique parlementaire sous la cohabitation," *Regards sur l'actualité* 141 (May 1988), 10-11. In 1987 alone, 404 amendments were introduced in the Assembly by the government, 990 by the standing committees, and 3,637 by backbenchers, for a total of 5,031. Of these, 1,394 were adopted.
83. Broken down by years as follows: 1988, 48; 1989, 102; 1990, 115; 1991, 94; 1992, 96.
84. See "Bilan d'une legislature," a series of ten articles in *Le Monde*, from 12 to 23 January 1993.
85. In 1990, for example, about two-thirds of the amendments that were adopted had originated in the standing committees.
86. Guy Braibant, "Qui fait la loi?" *Pouvoirs* 64 (1993), 43-47.
87. One such bill, successfully introduced in 1990 by Communist deputies, provided for punishing with a year in prison and a heavy fine those who publicly question the historicity of Nazi crimes.
88. For example, in 1981, 16 Gaullist and 21 UDF deputies voted with the Socialist majority in favor of the bill to abolish capital punishment, despite the fact that public opinion continued to be in favor of its retention.
89. The list of speakers is a short one: Jacques Chaban-Delmas, Gaullist (1958-1969, 1978-1981, and 1986-1988); Achille Peretti, Gaullist (1969-1973); Edgar Faure, pro-Gaullist (1973-1978); Louis Mermaz, Socialist (1981-1986); Laurent Fabius, Socialist (1988-1991); Henri Emmanuelli, Socialist (1991-1993); and Philippe Séguin, Gaullist (1993-).
90. For example, in 1960, the government's refusal to call a special session demanded by Parliament in accordance with Article 29, and in 1962, the government's refusal (in violation of Art. 49) to permit a vote on foreign policy.
91. Patrick Francès, "Les Leçons et promesses de l'année parlementaire," *Le Monde*, 24 December 1975.
92. The budgetary allocation to the National Assembly for 1988 was 1.9 billion francs and to the Senate, about 1.1 billion francs, in each case representing an increase of about 10 percent over the previous year. *Le Point*, 26 September 1988, p. 19. For 1989, the budget for both chambers was increased again by 5.5 percent. *Le Monde*, 14 July 1989.
93. The greater independence of deputies explains why the Assembly involved itself in lengthy debate on matters of foreign policy (especially on the Gulf War and the

Maastricht Treaty) and why it (jointly with the Senate) initiated impeachment procedures aganst three cabinet ministers involved in the affair of the AIDS-contaminated blood.

94. Bernard Tricot and Raphael Hadas-Lebel, *Les Institutions politiques françaises* (Paris: Presses de la Fondation Nationale des Sciences Politiques & Dalloz, 1985), pp. 389–395. See also Guy Carcassonne, "Réhabiliter le parlement," *Pouvoirs* 49 (1989), 37–45.

95. Jean-Claude Colliard, a political scientist who used to be a member of Mitterrand's presidential staff.

96. The expression used by Thierry Bréhier, "Radioscopie de l'Assemblée," *Le Monde*, 14 July 1989.

97. This was the first time since the Second Empire that the head of a foreign state was given this privilege.

98. See Pascale Robert-Diard, "Philippe Séguin persiste à vouloir réformer le travail parlementaire," *Le Monde*, 6 October 1993. See also "Fronde contre Philippe Séguin," *Le Monde*, 30 September 1993; and *Le Monde*, 6 October 1993.

99. The Commission Vedel, which was appointed in 1992 and submitted its recommendations to the president in February 1993.

chapter 8

The Administrative System

BACKGROUND, STRUCTURE, AND RECRUITMENT

In contrast to Parliament and in compensation for the legislature's weakness, the French civil service has retained the role it played in earlier regimes. In fact, the bureaucratic tradition in France, as in Italy and Germany, antedates the republican system. In the fifteenth century, the French monarchs appointed officials who served as tax collectors or commissioners (*intendants*, the precursors of the modern prefects) in the provinces. The sixteenth century witnessed the creation of technical corps, such as the Forest Administration and the Bridges Authority. The function of the bureaucracy was "modern" in that it was an instrument of "forceful national integration."[1] But the basis of its recruitment was distinctly traditional (i.e., ascriptive). Because they had to buy or inherit their positions, most high administrative recruits came from the nobility. As a result of the Revolution of 1789, hereditary office was abolished, and during Napoleon's reign, the criteria of professionalism and merit were introduced, under the dictum of "careers open to talent"; during the July Monarchy, the principles of political independence and permanent tenure of bureaucrats became more generally accepted. Still, bureaucrats were expected to be supporters of the regime and proponents of its ideology. Each change of political system was accompanied by a "purge" of the civil service, for which there existed no overall national organization and no coherent recruitment criteria. Hence, each minister had full discretion in matters of appointment, promotion, and dismissal of civil servants. In the 1830s the Bourbon bureaucracy, composed mainly of landed aristocrats, was replaced by an Orléanist one, consisting largely of the upper bourgeoisie; and in 1848, middle-class prefects were chosen to help fight revolutionary activities in the provinces.

In the Third Republic, the social base of recruitment was expanded some-what. The growth of public education provided greater opportunities for the petite bourgeoisie to find places, particularly in the middle echelons of the civil service. Many prestige positions did remain the preserve of the upper and upper-middle classes, especially in the foreign service and finance; and even middle-echelon bureaucrats tended to reflect the traditional values of statism and conservatism.[2] But the bureaucracy gradually accepted the two dominant values of laicism and republicanism. With the assertion of supremacy by Parliament, the civil service ceased in theory to be a major decision maker. In practice, how-ever, it was as powerful as ever. Because Parliament was disparate in its compo-sition and relatively disorganized, and because the ministers responsible to it held too brief a term to familiarize themselves with their departmental domains, higher civil servants were often left to their own devices. The less France was governed, the more it was "administered."[3] Parliament implicitly recognized its own weak-nesses and its unwillingness to make detailed administrative decisions by adopt-ing the custom of passing framework laws (*lois cadres*) under which ministers were given vast powers to issue decrees and regulations. These powers in fact devolved upon the civil servants.

Many French citizens did not view this lack of political supervision as an evil. In contrast to the American notion of a federal bureaucrat as a "hired hand," an individual employed to implement public policy, the French have considered the civil servant to be one who pursues a respected vocation and who is a member of a superior class, who may be following a family tradition, and whose job, especially at the higher levels, includes policy making. French higher civil servants have represented an awesome entity known as the State—at one time equated with the monarch and later with the republic.

Prior to World War II, relatively little uniformity and cohesion existed in the civil service. The division of grades was imprecise and differed somewhat from one ministry to another because each ministry was in charge of its own organi-zation and recruitment. The Council of State, the pinnacle of the bureaucracy, provided only general supervision. In 1945, the civil service acquired the form it has today: It was unified; a Civil Service Commission (*Direction de la fonction publique*) was created and put under the supervision of the prime minister or (in later years, as under the Rocard government) that of a separate minister; hierarchical grades were set up; training and recruitment methods were standard-ized; and fiscal responsibility for the bureaucracy was delegated to the Ministry of Finance.

Today, about 2.6 million people are employed by the state—about 12 per-cent of the total labor force—compared to 135,000 in 1845. The current figure (as of 1992) includes some 900,000 teachers from elementary to university levels, 500,000 employees of the postal and telecommunications services, 200,000 employees of the Finance Ministry (among them tax collectors), and the full-time local agents of the national government (e.g., prefects and their deputies (sub-prefects).[4] If one adds the officials or "public service agents" of departments (100,000) and communes (about 600,000), and the employees of public hospitals

(650,000), the railroads (250,000), gas and electricity (140,000), and other public corporations, one arrives at a figure of about 5 million.[5]

There are four basic categories of civil servants, which are roughly similar to those that prevail in the British Civil Service:

Category	Class
A	Administrative (*fonctionnaire de conception et de direction*)
B	Executive (*fonctionnaire d'application*)
C	Clerical (*fonctionnaire d'exécution spécialisée*)
D	Custodial (*fonctionnaire d'exécution simple*)

Within each category there are corps (e.g., *grand corps* or prefectoral corps), indicating the type of work or agency of the civil servant, and echelons, determining the nature of the position, the rank, and the salary. The most complicated differentiation obtains in the upper ranks of the administrative civil service, the approximately 10,000 higher bureaucrats (*hauts fonctionnaires*) who are technically above category A (*hors échelle*). This class is itself divided into several categories and includes, in ascending order of importance and status: (1) *fonctionnaires principaux* (e.g., attachés to central administrative offices, the revenue service, and prefectures); (2) *fonctionnaires supérieurs* (e.g., engineers and most of the civil administrators); (3) *hauts fonctionnaires* (e.g., inspectors of finance, officials of the Court of Accounts, members of the diplomatic and prefectoral corps); and (4) *grands fonctionnaires* (e.g., secretaries-general of ministries, ambasssadors, the director of the budget, the chief of the Planning Commission, and the top members of the Council of State).

Recruitment to the French civil service is tied to the educational system. Thus for category D, very little formal schooling is required; for C, the requirement is the completion of elementary school; for B, a *baccalauréat* (secondary-school diploma); and for category A, a university education. Prior to 1945, training for the civil service was generally provided by the Ecole libre de science politique (a private institution founded in 1871) and by the law faculties of universities. These institutions prepared the bulk of the recruits either for immediate entry into the higher bureaucracy or for "postgraduate" studies in the Ecole Polytechnique or other *grandes écoles*. Most of these schools are attached to and run by individual ministries. Thus the Ministry of Finance has maintained the Ecole Nationale des Impôts for training tax officials, and the Ecole des Mines has been maintained by the Ministry of Industry for the training of geologists. After World War II, a number of additional *grandes écoles* were founded in order to prepare civil servants for the specialized technocratic functions that were gaining in importance in a growing welfare state.

By far the most interesting postwar innovation in the education of the bureaucracy is the National School of Administration (Ecole Nationale d'Administration—ENA), established in 1946. The original purpose of this "superinstitution" was to deemphasize the legal curriculum that had been traditional for the vast majority of civil servants in favor of more modern subjects such as sociology, economics, statistics, and public administration. (However, a large proportion of the entrants to ENA have been graduates of law faculties.) The curriculum provides for a unique combination of the practical and theoretical. The three-year program begins with a year of work in an administrative office, often in the provinces. The second year is devoted to academic study. The third year consists of further on-the-job training in the particular ministry that the student hopes to enter.

ENA is unique in many other ways. Unlike ordinary university faculties supervised by the minister of national education or minister of universities, ENA is under the authority of the premier; it is politically neutral, in contrast to the ideological tendencies still found in various law faculties; it conducts mostly seminars rather than the formal lectures (*cours magistraux*) to large audiences typical of the ordinary institution of higher education. Furthermore, it has virtually no permanent faculty; professors are lent to ENA from universities, from the civil service, and occasionally from business. Finally, ENA graduates choose their own careers, that is, determine which part of the civil service they wish to enter. A large number of ENA graduates—there are now many more than 3,000—have gone into the upper echelons of the Council of State, the Inspectorate of Finances, the diplomatic services, and the prefectoral corps. Many ENA graduates, or *Enarques* ("Enarchs"), have joined the staffs of prestige ministries; some have become prominent politicians; others have gone into the planning technocracy; and still others, into business.[6]

During the Third and Fourth Republics, most graduates of the *grandes écoles* had been from the upper or upper-middle classes and hailed from Paris. ENA was intended to provide for less ascriptive and more democratic recruitment, not only by means of competitive entrance examinations, but also by a system of financial subsidies (in effect, salaries) paid to the students. The attempt to broaden recruitment did not succeed as anticipated. At the end of the 1970s, no more than 2 percent of were from the working or peasant class. A large proportion of the approximately 100 applicants admitted annually have been Parisians, or at least graduates of a Parisian lycée and a Parisian university, and have tended to be children of civil servants or other professionals.[7] Under the Socialist governments of 1981–1986, special efforts were made to seek out ENA graduates who had come from the petite bourgeoisie and had been active in Socialist party politics and give them important appointments.[8] Furthermore, in an attempt to make the higher civil service more egalitarian, the government in 1983 introduced legislation providing for an alternative path of entry into ENA: Competitive examinations would be open to members of general (departmental) councils, mayors and deputy mayors of medium-sized and larger towns, and officials of mutual societies and social security agencies.[9] These measures were rescinded by the Chirac government in 1987 but were restored in the spring of 1989 by the Rocard government.[10] Such measures have been only partly successful, and even under the Socialists, ENA "dynasties" were found: A significant proportion of entrants to that prestigious institution had fathers who were themselves members of the political establishment.[11] In 1991, in an effort to dilute the Parisian bias of ENA and to further the decentralization of governmental functions, Premier Cresson decided to move that institution to Strasbourg.[12] Such a "delocalization" was highly unpopular with the Parisian elite; nevertheless, when Balladur became prime minister, he reconfirmed the decision, which had already been partly implemented.

THE POLITICAL COMPLEXION OF CIVIL SERVANTS

The social selectivity of *Enarques* has led to the impression that they share not only a high degree of intelligence and technical competence but also outlook and manners and that they feel a certain contempt for other members of the political apparatus, if not for society at large. In turn, the non-ENA elite, and outside observers in general, hold ambiguous impressions of ENA: as a place for ambitious but not necessarily cultured young people where education is practical in orientation but not particularly technical or "professional" and where students learn above all to cultivate useful social relations and to become part of a tightly knit elite network.[13] It may be true that many higher civil servants have an overblown self-image that has expressed itself in a disdain for Parliament, because that body contains a large number of nonexperts. Even though the educational and cultural backgrounds of parliamentarians and *Enarques* are often similar, the professional orientation of the latter leads them to exaggerate the false distinctions commonly made in modern democratic systems between politics and administration. In a democracy, the elected representatives are expected to make the political decisions, and the civil servants to implement them. The former are by necessity partisan, whereas the latter are (ideally) politically neutral; the former are instruments of change, whereas the latter are supposed to provide stability and continuity, while always remaining responsible to the politicians and therefore responsive to demands for change.

However, although the French civil service has often thought of itself as an "objective" counterweight to the parliamentary party system, it has never been completely dissociated from the ideological arguments that often inform politicians. Higher civil servants in France, unlike their colleagues in Britain, are not expected to be completely nonpartisan. They may join the political parties of their choice, express their ideological preferences, and even run for seats in Parliament (in which case they receive a leave of absence without loss of seniority). Occasionally there may be restrictions regarding the civil servants' partisan commitments, as in 1945, when there was a purge of collaborationist bureaucrats, but the purge occurred because those bureaucrats had adhered to the ideology of a regime regarded as illegitimate. During the middle years of the Fourth Republic, some ministers attempted to block the appointment or promotion of Communist civil servants; however, in 1954 the Council of State ruled such discrimination illegal. Nonetheless, certain political parties have almost always enjoyed a preferred status in the civil service.

In the Third and Fourth Republics the staffs of national ministries tended to reflect the ideological diversity of parliaments and coalition cabinets, and there were always many bureaucrats who identified themselves as "leftist," irrespective of the statist outlook implicit in their roles. In the Fifth Republic, the diminished position of Parliament has tended to fortify both the conservative and the technicist orientation of civil servants. They have attained a higher status and greater autonomy in relation to Parliament than they possessed in previous republics, but their political dependence on the executive has increased because the premiers (and sometimes the presidents directly) have asserted their own authority more effectively, as most of them have had civil-service backgrounds. Under de Gaulle's presidency, many civil-service positions were "politicized"; he often preferred his Resistance companions to young ENA graduates whose political reliability was an unknown factor.[14]

There has been a continuation of the Fourth Republic practice of appointing parliamentarians of the favored party, after they have failed in their attempts at reelection (or in anticipation of electoral defeat), to positions in the public sector;[15] however, many of these appointees had a background in the civil service. A good number of higher civil servants, including about half the directors of the central administration, have owed their positions to political collaboration with a minister, and their appointments and promotions have not been justified merely by merit or seniority.[16] Partisan criteria have been particularly important in the staffing of certain "delicate" agencies such as the Foreign Ministry and the television networks, because great importance has been attached to the civil servant's reliability in voicing the official viewpoints. Until 1974, with a strong Gaullist executive and a weakened (and in any case Gaullist) Assembly, many higher civil servants (including prefects) were blatantly Gaullist and participated in UDR activities.[17]

Between 1974 and 1981, the upper echelons of the civil service were increasingly staffed with Giscard's supporters and friends (a significant proportion of whom happened also to be *Enarques*);[18] indeed, the governmental bureaucracy was said to have been so effectively "Giscardized" that Socialist leaders after 1981 rationalized some of their own policy-making failures in terms of alleged roadblocks erected against them by ideologically hostile bureaucratic holdovers. But the Socialists, too, changed the coloration of the civil service: Many appointments to the Elysée staff, the *cabinets ministériels*, the management of railroads and other public enterprises, and the television agencies were made on the basis of a balanced representation of different Socialist party factions, electoral and personal fidelity to Mitterrand, and even family ties.[19] According to one study, the growth of patronage in the civil service was reflected in the replacement of 350 *directeurs d'administration* by more reliable people during the first five years of the Mitterrand presidency (compared to nearly 300 during the Giscard presidency).[20]

A significant ideological diversity and as a result a certain ideological "blending," if not neutrality, have existed for a long time in the non–policy-making middle and lower echelons of the civil service, which are characterized by fragmented unionization. (The more than 1 million unionized civil servants have belonged to a variety of unions—with public-transport workers generally opting for the pro-Communist CGT and the teachers for the pro-Socialist FEN.[21])

While the civil servant's ideological orientations may influence his or her general political conceptions, they do not necessarily determine his or her bureaucratic behavior. "Once in a high post, the administrative civil servants have all accepted the [political] hierarchy."[22] In the highly institutionalized system of France, the roles of civil servants have been so well defined that they have tended to use technical rather than partisan arguments and to identify with their *ressorts* rather than with partisan outlooks. The behavior of members of the Socialist-oriented bureaucratic elite has not been much different from that of their more conservative predecessors. As they have pursued their careers, they have gradually shifted to the right.[23] Moreover, the conflict between the ideology of the ENA and that of the Socialist party has been reduced as that party has itself become partly "Enarchized."[24] That explains why in the 1980s an increasing number of Socialist officials "discovered the virtues of [market] liberalism," just as certain modern-minded directors of private enterprises wanted a larger dose of "the rationalizing action of the state."[25]

At the same time, conservative attitudes have been fortified by extrabureaucratic influences, particularly from the law schools and *grandes écoles* and their faculties, with which higher civil servants are bound to have continuing contact.[26] Although "in France the aroma of political reaction which aspirants for the higher administrative career acquired during their preparation for entrance [into prestige schools] as late as the 1930s has gone out of style," and although ENA has fostered the idea of opposition to government that acts in behalf of special interests,[27] the civil service is constantly influenced by interest groups and indeed even seeks their input. But that influence is unequal because the civil service does not represent the kind of broad cross-section of the population that is organized into competing socioeconomic associations, and therefore does not always reflect the most progressive or democratic ideologies (and sometimes not even the interest of the state[28]). Higher civil servants tend to be rather close to the business sector because both groups are bound to the existing order—the former for professional reasons and the latter because the system has favored the economic advantages of the owning classes. The shared background and, since the beginning of the post–World War II era, a shared commitment to rationalized economic decision making (including planning—see Chapter 10) have strengthened the institutional ties between big business and the higher civil service, and both sectors have in fact used the planning machinery to head off the "unrealistic" demands of the trade unions. The emphasis on productivity has been as characteristic of the *Enarques* of the *grand corps* as of the bureaucrats in the technical services (e.g., electricity, railroads, and nationalized manufacturing industries).

Many of the specialized civil servants who staff these technical services are trained in the Ecole Polytechnique, which was set up in 1795 as a combined civilian-military school and was to be open to the talented of all social classes as long as they were "attached to republican principles."[29] The Polytechnicians, like the *Enarques*, have a respect for efficiency and for entrepreneurial and technological (rather than legal or partisan) approaches to problems, and many hope to get jobs in the private business sector. "One is often told in French business circles that a Polytechnician who is among the top 10 or 20 graduates of his year can, after he has first spent some years in government service in order to solidify his qualifications, choose the private firm into which he wishes to be 'parachuted'!"[30] In addition, the rapport between the technical civil servants and private entrepreneurs is strengthened by the fact that occasionally there are close ties between privately owned and nationalized industries—and sometimes virtual mergers of production and marketing, as, for example, between the public Renault and private Peugeot automobile-manufacturing firms.

To what extent, then, is the French civil service an instrument of democracy? Administrative careers are not quite so open to the masses as are political careers. The sons of bakers (like Daladier) or of café owners (like Laval) could become prime ministers in the Third and Fourth Republics[31] and in the Fifth as well, as illustrated in the case of Bérégovoy, but such people are not likely to enter the higher civil service because it would be relatively difficult for them to climb the educational ladder (and achieve admission to the *grandes écoles*) required for an administrative career. When Parliament was supreme, this upper-class bias of the civil service was moderated by the lower-class ideological orientation of many parliamentarians and cabinet ministers, who theoretically furnished the "political" input into the bureaucracy and also provided an antidote to the conservative and antipopulist extra-administrative influence of law professors and business leaders.

Now the only effective counterforce to bureaucratic conservatism is the president, who appoints the politicians who supervise the civil service. Presidents are products of popular majorities, but not all presidents have interpreted the "public interest" in the same fashion. De Gaulle equated the public interest with the promotion of France's greatness and global influence; and Giscard (as one scholar has argued) so confounded the public interest with the interests of big industries that the autonomy of the state was put in question.[32] It has been contended that the notion of the public interest is largely a myth used by administrators and by governments to perpetuate the existing nonegalitarian social order.[33] But that contention does not quite apply to President Mitterrand and his Socialist government officials who, especially in their first years in office, sponsored many egalitarian policies. In addition, over the past 40 years, the internal reshuffling of civil-service positions has shown a certain democratic trend, in that the staffs of ministries concerned specifically with upward mobility and egalitarian resource allocation—for example, the Ministries of Education, Public Health, Social Affairs, and Labor—have increased dramatically, compared with those of the Foreign Affairs and Defense Ministries.[34]

CONTROLS OVER THE CIVIL SERVICE

The French civil service is not unlimited in its power. In the first place, civil servants can administer only on the basis of laws. During the heyday of parliamentary supremacy, particularly under the Third and Fourth Republics, the laws on which administrative regulations were based had emanated from Parliament, and therefore one could say that Parliament exercised control over bureaucratic behavior. This is less true today, as most parliamentary activities are inspired, directed, and controlled by the government (itself often a product of presidential discretion) and under the present Constitution the executive is given sweeping decree powers.

The second limitation on bureaucratic absolutism traditionally resulted from the "checks and balances" provided by the ideological diversity of civil servants. This diversity was the result of the multiplicity of parties in Parliament and therefore of coalition governments, which ensured that bureaucrats affiliated with a variety of parties be rewarded for loyal service, placed in responsible positions, and promoted. Diversity can still be found, but it has been reduced as a consequence of the simplification of the party system and the narrowing of the ideological gap between the Right and the Left.

The third limitation on bureaucratic absolutism is provided by the input of expertise from social and economic sectors via the ever-expanding consultative machinery. This machinery is of three distinct types. The most widespread consultative bodies are the advisory councils attached to ministries and composed of representatives of interest groups, technicians, and prominent personalities, the latter chosen by the government. The second type is made up of the multipartite boards attached to national and local social security organisms, and composed of spokespersons of trade unions, employers, and other economic or professional sectors. The third type of consultative machinery is found in the regional economic development commissions. There are today more than 15,000 councils and committees with which the bureaucracy deals, and they are of widely divergent characters.[35] These include the Superior Council on Education, the Central Commission for Marketing, the National Committee for the Control of Real Estate, and regional employment and retraining committees. However, it is a matter of controversy whether these consultative bodies provide adequate checks on the administration because many of them are either ad hoc in nature or have restricted competence (see Chapter 5).

Bureaucratic regulations are based on framework laws (*lois cadres*), and the input of interest groups on these laws (except indirectly through the Economic and Social Council) may not be decisive. Interest-group influence is limited by several factors: the ego of civil servants, which does not easily lend itself to the notion that nonprofessional outsiders can make significant contributions to administrative decisions; the unequal representation of social sectors; and the principle of central government responsibility and supervision (*tutelle*), which permits civil servants to restrict the parameters of consultative input. Moreover, a committee's recommendations may be ignored by the civil servants (even in cases where consultation is obligatory), may merely provide the façade of public participation, or may be cited to promote unpopular regulations, thus permitting the civil servants to escape the blame for these.

A fourth check on bureaucratic absolutism is provided by the administrative court system, in which a citizen may question the legality of bureaucratic regulations or behavior. The pinnacle of this system is the Council of State (*Conseil d'Etat*). This body is not "independent" in the Anglo-American sense, as it is officially a component of the civil service. The Council of State was established in 1799 by Napoleon as a mechanism for resolving disputes *within* the civil service, to advise the government on legal matters, and to protect the government from challenges on the part of citizens by hearing (and heading off) grievances. One important reason for the creation of the Council of State was to prevent interference by ordinary courts in administrative acts (i.e., to shut off juridical and political surveillance of the civil service).[36]

The independence of the Council of State was strengthened when, in 1875, its members obtained security of tenure and when subsequently appointments to it were based not on political considerations but on competence and competitive examinations. These changes led to the transformation of the nature of the Council of State. During the early part of the Third Republic, the council was one of the main pillars of authority, whereas Parliament was the arena of partisan controversy and opposition to the executive. Gradually the council developed a degree of detachment from the executive and concerned itself with protecting citizens against administrative arbitrariness.[37] But because the council is formally still part of the executive elite (in the social as well as juridical sense), there is considerable lateral movement between it and a variety of political positions. Some councilors run for Parliament (obtaining a leave of absence when elected); others are detailed to service as ambassadors, ministers of state, cabinet secretaries, or members of ad hoc "blue ribbon" commissions (*comités de sages*); and still others may serve as officials in public corporations.

The Council of State still resolves intrabureaucratic disputes and advises the government on the language of draft bills. It examines not the constitutionality of laws (this role belongs to the Constitutional Council) but the legality of regulations and the behavior of the executive in implementing them. The Council of State, meeting in general assembly, is presided over by the prime minister (or, in his absence, the minister of justice—see Figure 8.1), but that official is only the nominal head of the council and does not interfere in its activities. The actual chairperson, the vice-president, is chosen from among the councilors. Nearly half of the councilors are members of the juridical or redress (*contentieux*) section, which operates separately from the other four sections that deal with administrative and advisory matters. (There are more than 200 higher civil servants in the Council of State, of whom only about one-third are councilors of state, the remainder being the subordinate *maîtres de requêtes* and auditors.) Despite the size of the redress section of the Council of State and despite the fact that only five councilors are required to sit in judgment on a case, it may take several years for a case to be decided by the council because the "judicial explosion" has been such that the docket is often full, and auditors and *maîtres de requêtes* may need a great deal of time to complete an investigation.[38] The judicial explosion is in turn a consequence of the rapid growth of laws, regulations, and decrees.[39] The Parliament has enacted many of these laws in haste and has demanded equal haste of the Council of State in examining their proper formulation.

In the early 1950s, the burden of the Council of State was lightened when the original jurisdiction of the two dozen inferior courts (*tribunaux administratifs*) was

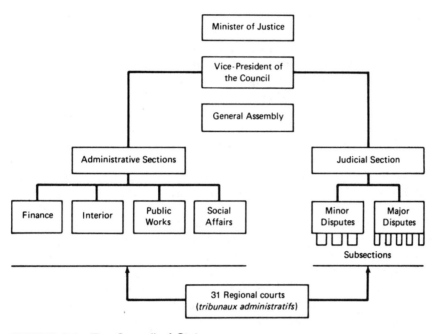

FIGURE 8.1 The Council of State

SOURCE: Based on Ambassade de France, Service de Presse et d'Information, *France,* May 1975, updated.

enlarged and the Council of State was transformed into a largely appellate court. At the end of 1987, in another attempt to deal with the "asphyxiation" of the council, Parliament passed a law creating five interregional administrative appeals courts (located in Paris and other large cities).[40]

Although councilors have come mainly from the upper-middle class, there has not been in France the kind of class justice one frequently finds in the administrative courts of Germanic countries; and although the Council of State is said to have a highly developed "sense of state" and a sympathetic understanding of public authority, and to be reticent about interfering in acts of government,[41] that body has been at least as likely to find in favor of the citizen as of the government (especially since the end of World War II). The council has enriched the concept of civil liberties by "deducing" them from existing laws. Thus, its decisions have contributed to promoting sexual equality before the law, limiting the administrative internment of foreigners, and affirming civil servants' right to strike, freedom of the press, the principle of public trials, and the equality of access of candidates to state examinations regardless of their political orientations.[42]

Nevertheless, the council is not completely effective as an instrument for safeguarding the individual against governmental excesses or arbitrariness. Many a seemingly harsh or undemocratic decision or regulation is based on laws whose constitutionality can hardly be challenged and whose lack of wisdom can be questioned only by Parliament. Also, the government has a hand in nominating councilors, whose tenure is a specified number of years;[43] and finally, the council's decisions may be ignored by the executive.

It was perhaps for these reasons that the French instituted an "ombudsman," or mediator (*médiateur*) system.[44] In accordance with a law of January 1973, the government appointed the first mediator (Antoine Pinay, a former Fourth Republic premier) to a six-year, nonrenewable term.[45] Unlike the Swedish ombudsman, the French mediator receives complaints not directly from the citizen but through the "filter" of a deputy or senator. The mediator's competence extends to all areas of administration: ordinary, social security, nationalized industries, and justice. The mediator can request from administrative agencies any information he or she considers pertinent and can initiate proceedings against malfeasant civil servants. The mediator submits an annual report to the president and Parliament that contains a summary of cases dealt with as well as recommendations for desirable legislative and administrative reforms (of which more than 500 had been introduced by 1991). If possible, the mediator tries to find amicable solutions to problems; but he or she may, if necessary, issue injunctions and initiate litigation. The number of complaints received by the mediator has grown steadily—from 1,600 in 1974 to 23,000 in 1990. The budget nearly tripled between 1978 and 1986, and the staff has increased correspondingly, so that the mediator's office had nearly 50 employees by 1987.[46]

The office of mediator, which was modeled largely on that of the British parliamentary commissioner, represents an institutional grafting that is not entirely appropriate to the French context. Theoretically, the administrative court system already provides the French citizen with a redress mechanism against illegal bureaucratic actions, and checks against maladministration (the proper province of the mediator) are provided (albeit with mixed success) by the government itself in the form of commissions of inspection and inquiry. Thus far, the mediator has not been spectacularly successful because neither civil servants nor their ministers have been very cooperative in revealing information.[47]

In order to remedy this situation, Parliament in 1978 passed legislation enabling citizens to find out whether or what compromising personal data about them is contained in official computerized files and guaranteeing them access to documents. In order to implement these rights, two special bodies were created: the *Commission nationale de l'informatique et des libertés* (CNIL) and the *Commission d'accès aux documents administratifs* (CADA).[48] In 1979, another act obliged bureaucrats to justify their decisions to the citizens.[49] But it is doubtful whether these reforms have rendered the civil service responsive enough to the citizenry.

The less than perfect redress machinery is a minor matter compared to what many perceive to be the structural deficiencies and lack of modernity of the French civil service. Some of the problems of that civil service are endemic to government bureaucracies everywhere, such as the rivalry among different agencies; the conflict between the Finance Ministry, which allocates money, and the ministries that are on the fiscal receiving end; the tendency toward duplication of services; the political interference in administrative work; and the question of the efficiency of bureaucrats.

There is relatively little corruption among higher administrative bureaucrats, not only because of their professional self-esteem but also because they are well paid and therefore are not tempted to supplement their incomes by taking bribes. Traditionally, certain civil servants—particularly those recruited to the administrative staff of a minister (the *cabinet ministériel*)—retained their connections with, and derived additional income from, their private business or professional activities, but some years ago (owing to various scandals) the regulations concerning such connections were tightened.[50]

The prestige of the lower-echelon civil servants is not high enough to compensate for their relatively low pay, and consequently their unions engage in tough bargaining and occasionally call strikes.[51] But even among higher civil servants there is sometimes a problem of salary inequities. A "pecking order" exists not only among administrative grades but also within a particular grade. Thus, an ENA graduate who works for the Ministry of Finance receives more pay than one who works for the Ministry of Culture. Despite the postwar organizational reforms that created greater unity within the civil service, it is difficult to move a higher civil servant from one ministry to another against his will, a situation that has resulted in the overstaffing of some ministries and the understaffing of others. The proliferation of administrative staff is in part a response to the pressure to create enough positions to employ bureaucrats in the service grades to which their educational attainments entitle them, without a clear regard to efficient operations.

SUBNATIONAL ADMINISTRATION

During the last three generations of the *ancien régime*, local government was severely circumscribed by the Bourbon monarchy's policy of centralizing control over localities and provinces in the hands of the Crown and its emissaries. After the Revolution of 1789, the old provinces were abolished and replaced by smaller units, and a decade later, Napoleon established a pattern of centralization of administrative functions that prevailed well into the middle of the twentieth century and is still, mutatis mutandis, in effect today. Under this system, the communes, cantons, districts (*arrondissements*), and counties or departments (*départements*) are not independent decision-making centers possessing "original jurisdiction" as clearly spelled out in the constitutions of federal regimes; rather they are subnational units existing for national administrative convenience. Each of the units presumably has a specific rationale and administrative function. In the commune, the citizen is dealt with most directly; the canton contains a police squad of the national gendarmerie and in addition functions as the constituency for general (i.e., departmental) council elections; the *arrondissement* serves as the basic (single-member) constituency for National Assembly elections; and the department is the immediate subdivision of the national government and the locus operandi of its chief agent, the prefect.

Although some units—the commune, with its council and mayor, and the department, with its assembly (the *conseil général*)—contain elected bodies, locally generated decision-making power has been relatively limited. The prefects, who administered the 96 (metropolitan) departments, were neither elected by the local constituency nor directly responsible to it. Rather, they were national civil servants appointed by the minister of the interior and responsible to him. The prefect was assisted by a subprefect and a cabinet composed of specialists for public works, agriculture, water supply, public health, housing, finances, and so on. Until 1960, the prefect's task of supervising *all* local services was rendered difficult because the specialists not only had to take orders from him but also had to clear their activities with the relevant national ministries. After 1960, the prefect was empowered to deal with these ministries himself, a change that facilitated his coordinating efforts.

As the chief liaison between the national government and local administrative units, the prefect was expected to maintain good relations with mayors and members of regional and local councils and to process local complaints and demands. Prefects could fulfill their roles as liaisons only as long as they enjoyed the confidence of the minister of the interior, who could shift them from one department to another or even dismiss them. After the end of the purges of the immediate post–World War II years, the suspension of prefects became a rare occurrence. However, during the year following the inauguration of Giscard in May 1974, 27 prefects were suspended by the interior minister for "inadequate" performance of their functions,[52] in 1981 and 1982, the new Socialist government replaced 103 of the 124 prefects in metropolitan and overseas departments, and the "cohabitation" government of 1986–1987 replaced 69.

THE COMMUNE

The commune is the basic administrative unit. Originating in the old, prerevolutionary parish, the commune was established in 1789. Each commune has a municipal council elected for a six-year term (the elections for a partial renewal of the council taking place every three years). The number of councilors varies with the size of the commune: For localities of fewer that 100 souls there are 9 councilors; for towns of 5,000 to fewer than 10,000, there are 29; for cities of between 150,000 and 200,000, 59; and for Lyons there are, since 1983, 73; Marseilles, 101; and Paris, 163.[53] The council selects one of its members as mayor and supervises his governmental activities. In 1992 there were about 500,000 communal councilors.

Just as the prefect was the chief executive of the department, the mayor has been the chief executive of the commune in addition to being the major elected spokesperson of the people. The mayor and municipal council have had a number of responsibilities, including the control of traffic; fire protection; trash disposal; the maintenance of nurseries, elementary school buildings, and sports facilities; and the provision of welfare services for the poor, the aged, and others in need. Not all of the responsibilities of the mayor could be associated with local self-government: He or she has been charged with implementing national laws; the registration of births, marriages, and deaths; the maintenance of electoral lists;

and the issuing of building permits. The mayor keeps order, but the police service is financed and controlled by the national government. He or she drafts the budget, but many of the expenditures of the commune have been made mandatory by the national government. Just as the laws pertaining to the election of municipal councilors and the selection of the mayor are made by the national government (which bears the cost of printing ballots and posters in the elections of most communes), so the national government was for many years empowered to veto acts of the mayor and even to dismiss him or her from the post, although this step has been resorted to rarely.[54]

Controversy has continued about the extent to which the mayor is a genuine decision maker, a symbol of local electoral legitimacy, or a figure of folklore. One scholar has emphasized the strong leadership of mayors: their control over the political machine, their initiative in local improvement projects, and their role in obtaining for their communities the necessary financial assistance from the national government. That scholar insisted that "local governments [were] in fact free to make numerous choices," that they "determine[d] policy," and that "the particular choices made by local government [had] consequences for the commune." But he also admitted that local governments "[were] relatively inactive and [did] not play a vital role in meeting local needs."[55] After the family, the commune has been perhaps the most important socialization agent in France, but it has certainly not been an important decision-making unit. Rather, it has been an administrative unit created and maintained for the purpose of carrying out policies decided by the national government. Its legal powers have been determined by that government, and to the extent that mayors had significant power, they derived it not merely from their position as mayor or chief local notable, but—especially if their commune was large—from the fact that they could use their position in order to exert influence on a political party on the national level and get themselves elected to Parliament.

According to another scholar, the fact that mayors have often also been deputies has not reduced their dependence on the prefect. In interviews conducted in 1973, it was revealed that 47.9 percent of the mayors received special favors through the prefectural system, as against 11.1 percent through ministerial offices.[56] The position of the mayor in his or her relationship to the prefecture—specifically, his or her ability to function as "a 'policy broker' between the national government and the town, and between the bureaucracy and the politicians"[57]—might be strengthened if the mayor had an additional public office, such as the chairmanship of a mixed (public-private) construction agency or housing or social aid office. Furthermore, the prefecture could sometimes be bypassed, particularly in large towns whose mayors had direct dealings with the Finance Ministry via the Delegation for Space Planning and Regional Action (*Délégation à l'aménagement du territoire et à l'action régionale*—DATAR), which helped to secure funds for regional and local economic projects.

Still another scholar stresses (and exaggerates) the hereditary ("dynastic") elements in the mayor's (and the commune's) politics,[58] whereas a fourth scholar suggests that strong mayors often derive part of their power (and their ability to confront the national government) from the support of trade unions, teachers' associations, and other well-organized interest groups.[59] (The mayor may be pressured into action by local voluntary associations; conversely, he may encourage the formation of such associations, sometimes in order to relieve himself of tasks for which he has insufficient funds or manpower.) Finally, it should be noted that the mayor of a large town would have less need for the intercession of the prefecture if he or she were appointed to the cabinet. Among the numerous examples of mayors simultaneously holding national cabinet office are former premiers Chaban-Delmas, Mauroy, and Chirac, who are still mayors respectively of Bordeaux, Lille, and Paris, and the late Gaston Defferre, who was minister of the interior and mayor of Marseilles.

To a large extent, the administrative powerlessness of local governmental units was caused by their relative poverty. Budgetary options were limited by the lack of financial resources of the locality and by its underdeveloped revenue-generating powers. Some of the locally collected taxes, voted on by the municipal council, were quite petty, such as dog-license charges, hunting and fishing fees, and surtaxes on the income tax. Other, more important, taxes (e.g., assessments on property, on rents, and on shops, which were collected by the local government) were based on the national government's calculation of the taxable worth of each community, a calculation that local economic developments rendered unrealistic in many communes. These revenues covered little more than half the expenses incurred in the administration of required services, the rest coming from the national government in the form of grants-in-aid. Much of this national subsidy came from the value-added tax that was collected locally, transferred to the national government, and then reallocated by the central government to local communities (a sum rising from $700 million in 1958 to $1.5 billion in 1964 to $2 billion in 1970). In 1975, about 85 percent of the personal income taxes collected by the national government was in fact paid out to localities, but the localities' share of the total governmental expenditures remained quite small (below 20 percent in 1970, or proportionally less than in West Germany and especially the United States).[60] In recent years there has been a growth of both local revenue collection and national government allocations, but not enough to enable local governments to provide the services increasingly demanded of them.

The ineffectiveness of municipalities was due also to the character of their locally recruited administrative personnel, which has been described as "top-heavy, bureaucratic, and archaic," and as "reproducing and often multiplying the faults of the national bureaucracies." In many of the smaller towns, the municipal employee was "aged, not well educated, [and] lethargic," and had little job mobility.[61] According to one estimate, 62 percent of the mayors in 1980 were more than 50 years old; and 55 percent were farmers or pensioners.[62]

Finally, the lack of viability of local communities stemmed from the excessive multiplicity and archaic nature of local units. There are still more than 36,400 communes in France, compared to 1,350 in Britain, 8,000 in Italy, and 16,000 in Germany.[63] The large number in France was perfectly realistic about 150 years ago, when much of the country was rural and the extent of local services was limited. Gradually, many communes were rendered inadequate as administrative units because of their depopulation, loss of an economic base, and consequent inability to maintain basic services efficiently. In 1975, a little over 10 percent of the communes were "urban" settlements of more than 2,000 inhabitants, while 22,700 communes (i.e., nearly two-thirds of the total) had fewer than 500 inhabitants—and as recently as 1992, about 4,000 communes had fewer than 100 inhabitants. Many residents of rural communes had moved to the cities, a move that spurred the growth of metropolitan areas that spilled over into several traditional administrative subdivisions. Grenoble, for example, increased in population from 80,000 in 1950 to 150,000 in 1990 and its metropolitan area to more than 400,000. Some "bedroom" suburbs of Paris grew even faster; Sarcelles, for example, increased from 8,400 in 1954 to 56,000 in 1990.

Raymond Marcellin, who was minister of the interior until 1973, seemed to be interested in giving greater authority to the communes. In 1970 he declared at a meeting of the National Association of Mayors: "The city hall (*la mairie*) is the most perfect symbol of an administration accessible to those who are being administered and the most responsive to human concerns. The commune is also the most natural arena for civic training."[64] That civic training, unfortunately, was likely to result in anticentralistic and antistate attitudes as long as local administrative units possessed only phantom powers.

ADMINISTRATIVE REFORM AND DECENTRALIZATION

The preceding discussion refers in part to an ongoing situation and in part to the past, because the relationship between the national and local governments is in a state of flux. That relationship has been a subject of debate for two centuries; from the early nineteenth century on, numerous proposals were advanced by intellectuals and politicians to modify the extreme centralization of government.

After World War II the debate quickened; French governments seemed to have become more seriously concerned with the reform of subnational administration for a variety of reasons: (1) population movements and inequalities;[65] (2) the need for new forms of functional administration for which old units were insufficient; (3) the problems of duplication and inefficiency; (4) the recognition of the fact that regional provincial attitudes had survived strongly in some areas (e.g., Alsace, Brittany, and Provence) and that these attitudes (and the localism of political parties) had become inconsistent with existing patterns of overcentralization; and (5) the popular desire to participate in a more meaningful type of grassroots politics. Similar developments can be found in other Western European countries with unitary political structures, and it is quite probable that the attempts by France's neighbors—Italy and the Low Countries—to devise novel administrative formulas have inspired French politicians and technocrats.[66]

Decentralization does not, however, mean the establishment of federalism, for that would constitute too drastic a departure from French administrative tradition. In addition, different sectors are opposed to meaningful decentralization of any kind: the "Jacobin" Left and the Communists, who have feared that it would encourage reactionary particularism and social (Catholic) conservatism; orthodox Gaullists, who have argued that it would undermine the unity of the nation and the authority of the state and lead to separatism; the prefectoral corps, which has feared a loss of power; and even certain local politicians, who have themselves been part of the national elite and therefore apprehensive about the creation of rival subnational centers of power.[67] In view of this, the record of decentralization, was, until recently, largely one of campaign rhetoric and half-measures.

Decentralization implies, among other things, the creation of better and more realistic instruments for the regional or local execution of centrally conceived policies. A controversial instance of this approach to decentralization was the ill-fated proposal, couched in the form of a constitutional amendment, by de Gaulle in April 1969 to establish (or reestablish) the *region* as a formal territorial unit of the French state. In the popular referendum, the amendment was rejected (an event causing de Gaulle's resignation) for several reasons, among them not only the uncertainty about the actual powers attributed to the regions but also, and perhaps primarily, the growing unpopularity of de Gaulle, with whom the referendum was intimately associated.

One way in which local government has been modernized has been the passing of laws permitting the merger of communes that have become too small and inefficient to perform mandatory services by themselves. (By 1977, 838 fusions, involving 2,045 communes, had taken place.) As an alternative to mergers, a law passed in 1971 permitted the formation of commune associations for the joint administration of selected public services, and laws passed subsequently extended the communes' powers in financial matters. In 1988 there were more than 14,000 such associations serving more than 19,000 communes.[68]

Another approach to administrative reform was the creation of economic regions. These were first established during the Fourth Republic to provide the means for local, and therefore more relevant, input of economic information necessary for economic planning and to have more realistic units to which to apply regional plans (*plans nationaux d'aménagement du territoire*), containing a catalogue of needs and resources for the purpose of deconcentrating industry and population. In 1964, the government gave greater recognition to those regions by naming one of the department prefects of each region a "superprefect" (see Figure 8.2). The superprefect did not replace the department prefect; rather, he or she was a coordinator: He or she "stimulate[d] and [held] conferences."[69] The superprefect was assisted in this task by Regional Economic Development Commissions (*Commissions de développement économique régional*—CODERs), bodies in which local politicians, deputies and senators, interest group spokespersons, and technicians participated not in the making of policy but in advising the superprefect about regional needs and prospects.

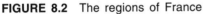

FIGURE 8.2 The regions of France

SOURCE: Based on Ambassade de France, Service de Presse et d'Information, *France,* October 1973, p. 5. In 1975, Corsica (Corse) was constituted as a separate region and divided into two *départements*.

The hope that the CODERs would provide an arena of regional economic policy inputs was not fulfilled; they were abolished at the end of 1974, and their tasks were vested in the regional councils. These councils, established by Parliament in 1972, were given the power to obtain revenues from drivers' license fees and taxes on real estate transfers, to be used to finance regional investments. But the 1972 reforms fell short of instituting meaningful provincial self-government;[70] they were seen as providing for only a symbolic transfer of financial resources to subnational units and as constituting merely "a caricature of decentralization."[71] Giscard had been one of the critics, and he was elected under a widely held assumption that he would make decentralization a major policy priority.[72] But owing to a variety of constraints, including pressure from his Gaullist allies, he failed to live up to these expectations. As president, Giscard said: "The role of the region is not to administer, but to provide an [additional] coordinating echelon. France is not rich enough to have four echelons of administration—local, departmental, regional, and national. It is too divided to wish to introduce new political games."[73]

THE REFORMS OF 1981–1983

The most significant innovations since the French Revolution were undertaken after the Socialist electoral victories of 1981. For the Socialists, decentralization, as an essential step toward bringing government closer to the people, was a major policy objective—*"la grande affaire du septennat"*—and was seen as being associated with industrial "self-management" and the recognition of ethnoregional peculiarities.[74]

A law passed in the spring of 1982—the culmination of a year-long parliamentary debate—set the tone in affirming that "the communes, departments, and regions shall administer themselves freely by means of elected bodies."[75] The office of prefect was abolished, and replaced by that of the "commissioner of the Republic" (*commissaire de la République*). The effective executive powers of the department were relocated in the hands of the president of the general council (elected by direct popular vote, with cantons serving as single-member constituencies).[76] Furthermore, members of regional councils were to be elected by universal suffrage beginning in 1986. Both the city councils and the general councils were to be given increased power to collect revenues (including corporate taxes). The decisions of all three types of councils were to be self-enforcing; in abolishing the a priori veto of these decisions by the commissioner (who would henceforth be merely a "delegate" of the central government), the new legislation was intended to reduce the scope of national *tutelle* (supervision).[77] In 1987, the title of *commissioner* was changed back to *prefect.*

At this writing—a decade after the enactment of the decentralization laws—there are still differences of opinion about the scope of actual decentralization, its success, and its impact on the political system as a whole.[78] There has been an undeniable growth of local budgets, based on both locally collected revenues and increased allocations received from the national government. The powers of local governments have been enlarged in a variety of areas, including the construction and maintenance of school buildings, urban transport, and the control of commercial transactions. Moreover, there have been diverse local and regional initiatives in economic development (see Table 8.1).

To some extent, the increased activities of subnational authorities have been the enforced consequence of buck-passing by the national government, especially

TABLE 8.1 Subnational authorities and jurisdictions (selected tasks)

	Commune	Department	Region
Social action	Application, intake; supplementary benefits; public health office	Services to child-maternity care; shelters for handicapped and aged; social services; preventive care	
Education	Primary	Junior high (*collèges*)	High school (*lycées*); special education; continued (vocational) education
Economic and local development	Indirect assistance; direct supplementary assistance; intercommunal space planning	Direct assistance; direct supplementary assistance; rural development	Research centers; economic development; direct and indirect assistance; space and other planning; regional parks
Transport	Urban	Nonurban; school transport	Regional liaisons
Culture	Archives; municipal museums, libraries, conservatories	Departmental archives, museums, central lending libraries	Regional archives and museums
Environment	Drinking water; drainage; waste disposal	Planning and maintenance of hiking/riding trails	Environmental protection
Road maintenance	Communal; resorts	Departmental; fishing and commercial harbors	

SOURCES: Based on *L'Administration territoriale II: Les collectivités locales*, Documents d'études, no. 2.03 (Paris: Documentation Française, October 1984); *Les cahiers français* 220 (March–April 1985); and *Institutions et vie politiques, Les notices* (Paris: Documentation Française, 1991), pp. 55–60.

since the austerity policies begun in 1983. The increased responsibilities of local authorities have led to a greater professionalization and an improvement of the quality of regionally and locally elected officials. Many of them continue to come from the ranks of physicians, dentists, pharmacists, and educators; but there are now more professional civil servants, fewer farmers, and fewer notables.[79]

Although there is still a large proportion of farmers among the mayors, their professional backgrounds have become more diverse (see Table 8.2). One effect

TABLE 8.2   The occupational profile of mayors

Occupation	Number	In Percent of Elected Mayors	Occupational Breakdown of Electorate
Farmers and farm workers	13,413	36.7	4.6
Inactive or retired	7,039	19.3	46.2
Middle management/middle-level professionals	4,621	12.7	10.9
Senior executives/managers	2,795	7.7	4.2
Artisans, craftsmen	2,615	7.2	5.1
Professions	1,990	5.3	0.8
Owners or managers of business firms	1,700	4.7	0.2
White-collar employees	1,240	3.4	13.2
Workers	1,095	3.0	14.8
Total	36,508	100.0	100.0

SOURCE: Yves Mény, "Le maire nouveau est-il arrivé?" *Elections municipales 1989*, Le Figaro/Etudes Politiques, 1989, p. 9. The mayors were elected in 1983 for six-year terms.

of decentralization has been the rise of a new kind of mayor, especially in the big cities—more dynamic, more managerial, and more charismatic.[80] The charisma of these mayors is often based on excessive ambition, which is reflected in grandiose building projects (e.g., subways and convention centers) that lead to greater indebtedness. In order to cover the costs of such projects, mayors may seek loans from the national government, private sources, and even the European Union (with whose officials mayors sometimes negotiate directly).[81] Furthermore, they may apply pressure on the national government to increase the staffs of their prefectures. It is obvious that a mayor is helped in this effort if he is also a deputy (preferably belonging to the political party that governs).

Most communities, however, are not very successful in such efforts. Because of their relative poverty, their resources are strained by increased pressures on social services; and because of their relatively low political weight, they are less able to appeal to the national government. The fiscal strain has been particularly severe in smaller communities, of which there are still too many.[82] Some of them cannot even pay the salaries of their regular personnel and turn in desperation to their prefecture.[83] They also band together to engage in common lobbying efforts by means of organizations such as the *Association des petites villes de France*. In order to alleviate the fiscal problem of small communes, a law was enacted in 1992 to encourage intercommunal collaboration in the collection of taxes and (after a certain number of years) a common tax structure for clusters of communes. There is a specialized national agency, the *Direction générale des collectivités locales*, which facilitates this process.[84]

Since 1982, there has been a steady growth of the subnational civil service, which in 1992 employed more than 1.2 million people (i.e., more than 50 percent of the total public service, and 6.5 percent of the national workforce). This civil service is divided roughly as follows (in round numbers): region, 5,000;

département, 150,000; commune, 800,000; intercommunal consortiums, 70,000; other, more than 75,000. There is insufficient professional competence, especially within the ranks of the local civil service, in part because of relatively low salaries. This explains the increasing resort to outside "consultants," in particular by the larger cities that can afford to hire them.[85]

Despite the growing fiscal responsibilities of subnational authorities, local spending (as compared to national government spending) has remained lower in France than in other Western democracies.[86] Such spending continues to be conditioned by national resource allocations, which remain significant (see Table 8.3). Because the size and reliability of these allocations is uneven, citizens relate more easily to their mayors and think of the central government as more distant than they did before decentralization.[87] However, because citizens also believe that the state should concern itself more with the economic life of local communities, their relationship to the mayor—and the mayor's democratic legitimacy—is affected by his relationship to the national authorities.

National political parties play a role in this relationship in the sense that they serve as the instrument of recruitment to both local and national elective positions. Local elections are orchestrated by the major national parties (which operate along the traditional right-left axis), but the parties are not the important local actors once the election is over, and that is perhaps why voters do not replicate their national party behavior when they vote locally. To be sure, the national parties' involvement varies from commune to commune; but as the responsibilities of local governments and the authority of mayors increase, relations (and coalitions) between parties on a subnational level are increasingly determined by local considerations.[88] According to a poll conducted in 1989, 86 percent of the mayors think that they are judged in municipal elections on the basis of their municipal management, and only 7 percent believe they are judged according to their political label.[89]

The mayors' growing prestige has been a consequence not only of their enhanced power but also of the limit on multiple-office holding (discussed in Chapter 7), which tends to force politicians to choose between national and subnational office. Thus in 1986, Alain Carignon, the mayor of Grenoble and

TABLE 8.3 Sources of revenue of subnational units (in percent of total)

Source of Revenue	Commune			Department	Region
	1982	1986	1991	1991	
Locally collected	29.6	37.4	39.9	50.9	54.2
Contribution from national government	40.3	35.1	32.2	36.8	29.8
Borrowing	13.7	11.4	15.5	8.8	10.9
Other	16.4	16.1	12.4	3.5	5.1
Total	100.0	100.0	100.0	100.0	100.0

SOURCES: Adapted from *Cahiers français* 239 (January–February 1989), 70; and *Institutions et vie politique 1991* (Paris: Documentation Française, 1991), p. 60.

president of a general council (Isère), gave up his National Assembly seat in order to devote greater attention to the interests of his city.[90]

The continuing uncertainties about the role of mayor are surpassed only by those concerning the general and regional councils. There is confusion especially about the role of the presidents of these bodies: Are they the spokespersons of their subnational geographical constituents or do they control these constituents? Do these councils bring citizens closer to government, or are they unnecessary fiefdoms, as is charged by traditional Jacobin centralizers?[91]

An equally controversial matter is the relationship between decentralization and local democracy. The fact that there is one local councilor for every 100 inhabitants (as compared to every 1,000 in Britain) and that the rate of participation (i.e., 75 percent between the end of World War II and the end of the 1980s) is high does not mean that citizens participate in local administration more meaningfully than before. The mayor makes the decisions, which are of course more important than they were prior to decentralization, and often merely informs the councilors.

FUNCTIONAL DECENTRALIZATION

One of the areas to be affected by the recent reforms is the current system of functional decentralization. Since the end of World War II, the various agencies for the administration of health insurance, family subsidies, and retirement benefits have been based on "activity" as opposed to geographic subdivisions. These agencies, or funds (*caisses*), which are essentially mutual-aid societies that have acquired legal personalities because they have been co-opted for certain administrative tasks and put under the supervision of a national ministry, operate on various subnational levels that do not exactly match the usual administrative units. Thus, whereas there are 22 ordinary regions in metropolitan France (and 4 regions overseas), there are only 16 regional social security offices (*caisses régionales de sécurité sociale*); and whereas there are 96 departments in metropolitan France, there are 114 family-allowance offices and 121 primary social security offices.

Another kind of "functional decentralization" has been the creation of 25 school districts, or *académies*, in which the rector of a particular university is responsible for the administration of the district's entire educational system, including secondary and elementary schools. The university reform laws of Edgar Faure, passed in 1968, and of Olivier Guichard, passed in 1970, have empowered these school districts and the district councils of education to make many decisions without direct prior approval by the national Ministry of Education, decisions about changes in curricula, restructuring of academic departments, and disbursement of certain day-to-day expenditures. In practice, however, this kind of decentralization has been implemented with hesitation. The overlapping of territorial and functional administrative subdivisions is symptomatic of the problems of the French administrative system. This overlapping may provide flexibility, but the jurisdictional rivalries and confusions it introduces must be a nightmare for the specialist in administrative law.

THE ADMINISTRATION OF PARIS

The government of Paris has always been exceptional, and the national government has taken a special interest in it because the capital is the pride and property of the French nation. By special statute promulgated by Napoleon in 1800, the city of Paris was divided into 12 administrative districts (*arrondissements*). During the Second Empire, 8 more districts were added, to form the 20 subdivisions existing to this day. For many years, each *arrondissement* had its own mayor (but no separate council). The mayor's area of competence was quite restricted, hardly encompassing more than the keeping of personal registers and electoral rosters and the performance of marriages. There was an elected municipal council for all 20 *arrondissements,* which had the power to change street names, to recommend budgets, and to issue traffic regulations. The real government of Paris was concentrated in the hands of *two* prefects: the prefect of the Seine and the prefect of police, who were both under the authority of the Ministry of the Interior and whose jurisdictions sometimes overlapped.

Such a centralized administration proved inadequate in view of the urban sprawl around the capital. In order to take into account suburban growth and population shifts, some departments surrounding Paris were subdivided in the early 1960s; in addition, a Paris regional government was set up, with its own (appointed) council that was concerned with certain types of public services and urban planning. In 1975 Parliament passed a bill providing, for the first time since 1870, for a mayor for Paris as a whole (to be elected by an at-large municipal council for a six-year term) and for an enlargement of the capital's municipal-service bureaus. (The two prefects, however, remained in place.)

From a fiscal perspective, the relationship between Paris and the national government has been much more productive than the relationship between large U.S. cities (including the capital) and the federal government. Most of the funding for museums, libraries, universities, theaters, and public transport in Paris has come from the national government. Nevertheless, the relationship has not been immune to partisan politics. The fact that since 1977 the mayor of Paris has been Gaullist leader Chirac has not made the mayor's dealings with the national government easier (except, of course, between 1986 and 1988, when Chirac concurrently held the prime ministership). Relations with Giscard were strained because of Chirac's tendency to use his office to promote his well-known presidential ambitions; relations with Mitterrand and his Socialist prime ministers were difficult because Socialists have constituted a minority in the Paris city council.

In mid-1982 the government introduced legislation ostensibly intended to bring Paris government closer to the people (and incidentally also to reduce the power of Chirac). The government proposed to transform the twenty *arrondissements* into independent municipalities, each equipped with its own legislative council, mayor, and budget—with the mayor of Paris demoted to the role of a mere presiding officer with ceremonial functions. The modified reforms for Paris that Parliament passed and that went into effect in 1984 provided that the mayors of the *arrondissements* be consulted by the mayor of Paris on such matters as the demolition and construction of buildings, the maintenance of streets, and the determination of the municipal investment budget. In addition to retaining their traditional functions (e.g., the registration of births and deaths), the *arrondissements* were to be equipped with their own civil servants—an average of 40 for each—and put in charge of allocating subsidized housing, administering child-care centers and old-age homes, and establishing industrial zones, and were empowered to make their own "mini-budgets." Parallel provisions were enacted for Marseilles and Lyons, cities that are also divided into *arrondissements*. The practical impact of these reforms is not clear, as the budget allocated to each of the *arrondissements* has been quite small.[92]

CORSICA

An important aim of decentralization policy has been to breathe new life into the regions. The first beneficiary of this policy was Corsica; its island status, its relative economic underdevelopment, its special cultural-linguistic heritage, and its sociopolitical traditionalism (manifested, inter alia, in power struggles among rival clans)—all these made for a particularism (expressing itself in autonomist movements of various kinds as well as violence) that Paris could not ignore.

In 1982 Parliament passed special autonomy laws for Corsica. These provided for a regional council, to be known as the "Corsican Assembly," elected for a six-year term under a direct proportional-representation system. The assembly would have wide powers of decision making in agricultural, transport, housing, and educational matters; would be able to formulate economic-development policies; and would collect part of its own revenue (from taxes on vehicles and tobacco, for example), to be supplemented by financial allocations from Paris.[93] Corsican civil servants have periodically complained about the inadequacy of such allocations, and in the spring of 1989 threatened to strike in order to obtain salary supplements. In 1990 the government introduced a bill to expand Corsican autonomy; it was passed after the Constitutional Council forced the government to eliminate as unconstitutional the original reference to "the Corsican people, component of the French people." It was not clear whether the Corsican statute would serve as a prototype for autonomy arrangements for the other French provinces.

BUREAUCRACY, TECHNOCRACY, AND ECONOMIC ADMINISTRATION

It has long been recognized that the reform of administration goes beyond geographical decentralization. Many governments since the end of World War II have shared an intellectual commitment to address themselves to the following "constant themes": the reduction of the number of ministries; better training and more democratic recruitment of civil servants; better coordination of administrative work; the deconcentration of administrative responsibilities; and the reduction of tensions between administrator and administered.[94] One should also note the existence in France of multiple obstacles to reform: the lack of financial resources, the rivalries among administrative offices, and the virtually automatic (seniority-based) advancement of civil servants, which renders them resistant to change. The most recent commitment to reform was made by Michel Rocard, who, in a circular issued shortly after his appointment as premier, called for a greater respect by civil servants for the needs of "civil society," promised to explore possibilities of reorganizing bureaucratic agencies, and in the interest of cost-effectiveness recommended the rescission of "obsolete and unduly constraining" regulations.[95] The Balladur government too has committed itself to further decentralization, but so far has not introduced specific legislation to that end.

One approach to dealing with these problems has been to resort to specialized agencies or "technostructures." The people involved in economic administration (that part of the administrative system concerned with nationalized industries and public corporations) fall outside the ordinary civil-service categories. The economic-industrial sector of the administrative apparatus has been important in France for several generations; its increased significance since the end of World War II is a reflection not only of French *dirigisme* but also of the importance of left-wing political parties during the Fourth Republic and in the Fifth Republic between 1981 and 1993, which committed France to a policy of nationalization of industries and a plethora of welfare-state schemes, the administration of which required the creation of novel, technocratic agencies. Recruitment of personnel to these agencies is according to technical and nonpolitical criteria, at least in theory,[96] which gives the nationalized industries considerably greater flexibility in hiring than is found in the ministries.

In the administration of the economic-industrial sector there are, however, a number of problems. First, there is a lack of uniformity even greater than that which now prevails in the regular bureaucracy. A multitude of legal forms and institutional typologies exist, ranging from the (commercial or industrial) *établissement public* to the *régie autonome* (e.g., the Paris transport authority). Although many of these agencies are supposed to be "autonomous" and to follow purely business or technical rather than political methods in their management, each of the enterprises is in fact under the control of a particular minister. Nevertheless, there is relatively little democratic supervision of these public corporations. Whereas in the Fourth Republic there were special parliamentary "watchdog" committees in charge of specific public corporations, today there is no effective parliamentary control over them, despite the growth of the number and importance of committees of investigation (see Chapter 7). Moreover, the redress mechanism that one finds in the ordinary civil service is lacking; the Council of State has virtually no jurisdiction in cases involving the nationalized industries.

The government's policy on strikes, already confusing with respect to civil servants, appears to be even more unclear for the economic sectors of the public service. It is true that in the Fifth Republic various laws or ordinances have been passed forbidding strikes: In 1963, *grèves tournantes* ("staggered" strikes of short duration by successive segments of the work force in a particular plant or office) were forbidden to all sectors of the nationalized economy; and in 1964, strikes by airline controllers were outlawed; but these measures have not been strictly enforced. In 1988, during a prolonged strike of Paris subway workers, Premier Rocard hinted that no-strike clauses regarding public-service workers might be enforced and strengthened, but he had no time or inclination to follow up. In 1993, there was a strike of employees of Air France, the national air carrier, in response to massive layoffs, but the government responded by replacing the director of the airline.

A certain kind of formal "democratic" input is provided by the multipartite advisory councils attached to the various nationalized industries and composed of representatives of consumers, officials, business managers, and trade unions, but these councils have limited power, owing to their disparate composition, their lack of expertise and information, and their purely consultative nature. The modernization of the administrative structure that has occurred has often been the consequence of pressure from the business sector and has been in the interest of economic expansion; more recently, such modernization has been speeded up in connection with selective deregulation and privatization.

Finally, there is the technocracy of the French Planning Commission, which is in many ways quite different from the traditional civil service. Like many higher civil servants, most of the planning technocrats are graduates of ENA and are subject to supervision by a guardian ministry, in this case the Prime Minister's office (in a formal sense) as well as the Ministry of Economic Affairs and Finance (in practice). But the relatively small number of economic planning officials (about 150 to 200 in all) are economists and statisticians; they are likely to be younger than higher civil servants elsewhere, and they have worked under an aura of "scientific mystique." Whereas ministerial civil servants have tended to be *étatiste* and *dirigiste*, many of the planners have been nonideological and willing to accept both interventionist and liberal principles if these help to promote the objectives of growth and efficiency. But like the traditional civil servants, French planning officials have distrusted Parliament and hoped for the decline of interference from that quarter. The administration of economic policy therefore tends to remain "a partnership between the managers of big business and the managers of the state"[97] rather than a partnership between government and a diversity of social and economic sectors. When the Socialists came to power in 1981, the trade unions were promised a somewhat enlarged role in economic planning, but in subsequent years the fulfillment of that promise was impeded both by the reduction of the plan's relevance in the face of pressures of the market and by the steady decline of the power (and membership) of unions.

NOTES

1. John A. Armstrong, "Old Regime Administrative Elites: Prelude to Modernization in France, Prussia, and Russia," *International Review of Administrative Sciences* (hereafter cited as *IRAS*) 38:1 (1972), 21–40. See also Marceau Long, "The Civil

Service in France," in Louis Fougère, ed., *Civil Service Systems* (Brussels: International Institute of Administrative Sciences, 1967), pp. 67–68.

2. David Thomson, *Democracy in France: The Third and Fourth Republics,* 2nd ed. (London: Oxford University Press, 1958), pp. 58–61.

3. Herbert Luethy, *France Against Herself* (New York: Meridian, 1957), p. 40.

4. These figures are approximate; they are based on the following sources: *La Fonction publique en 1981* (Paris: Documentation Française, 1982); Minelle Verdié, ed., *L'Etat de la France* (Paris: Editions de la Découverte, 1987), pp. 63-88; "Vive l'Etat," *Le Monde,* 14 April 1987; and various issues of *News from France* and *Le Monde,* 1988–1993.

5. During the first few years of Mitterrand's first presidential term, about 80,000 government employees were added—in part to the educational system, and in part to the sector of nationalized industries, although under the Chirac government the number of public employees was reduced as a consequence of the denationalization policies.

6. Examples of ENA graduates who embraced careers outside the government include the presidents of Saint-Gobain, an industrial conglomerate; Peugeot; ELF-Aquitaine, a formerly nationalized petroleum corporation; and Crédit Agricole. See Jean-François Kesler, *L'ENA, la société, l'état* (Paris: Berger-Levrault, 1985), p. 468.

7. On the social and geographical origins of entrants to ENA, see the statistical tables in Ezra Suleiman, *Politics, Power, and Bureaucracy in France* (Princeton, NJ: Princeton University Press, 1974), pp. 54–63; and Pierre Birnbaum, *La Classe dirigeante française* (Paris: PUF, 1978), pp. 55–63. See also Samy Cohen, *Les Conseillers du président* (Paris: PUF, 1980), esp. pp. 51 and 187 (table). In a highly critical book (Jacques Mandrin, *L'Enarchie,* 2nd ed. [Paris: La Table Ronde, 1980]) it is argued that the "Enarchy," originally envisaged as a nonpartisan, neutral, and professionally competent elite holding aloft the mystique of the state, was corrupted by Giscard, who transformed it into a combination of managers close to big business and consisting of his personal friends.

8. See Pierre Birnbaum, *Les Elites socialistes au pouvoir* (Paris: PUF, 1985). For a critique of this pattern, see Michel Poniatowski, *La Catastrophe socialiste* (Paris: Rocher, 1991), pp. 14–15.

9. *Le Monde,* 28 April and 12 November 1983. Applicants for the alternative path (*troisième voie*) had to be at least 41 years old. For earlier attempts to make entrance to ENA more democratic and to modernize its curriculum, see Pierre Racine, "L'Ecole National d'Administration et son évolution," *Revue administrative* 26 (March–April 1973), 131–41.

10. See "La Création d'un troisième concours d'entrée à l'ENA," *Le Monde,* 16-17 April 1989.

11. Thierry Pfister, *La République des fonctionnaires* (Paris: Albin Michel, 1988), p. 46; and Michel Schifres, *L'Enaklatura* (Paris: Lattès, 1987), pp. 20ff.

12. The decision, which followed a recommendation by an interministerial committee, also affected other administrative services, which were to be transferred to 73 cities. It was envisaged that by the end of the decade, 30,000 public employees would be transferred.

13. See Schifres, *L'Enaklatura,* pp. 15–23 et passim.

14. Julien Cheverny, "Le Mode autoritaire de l'anarchie," *L'Esprit,* special issue, January 1970, pp. 61-62.

15. For example, Mitterrand appointed Robert Badinter, the minister of justice, to the presidency of the Constitutional Council just before the anticipated defeat of the Socialist party in the parliamentary election of 1986; and for a similar reason he appointed Pierre Joxe, the minister of defense, to the national audit office (*Cour des*

comptes) early in 1993. Mitterrand's patronage appointments have included numerous ambassadorships. See Michel Colomès, "Les Verroux de Mitterrand," *Le Point*, 27 February 1993, pp. 36–39.

16. Bernard Gournay, "Un Groupe dirigeant de la société française," *RFSP* 25 (April 1964), 215–231.

17. Cf. Philip Williams and Martin Harrison, *Politics and Society in de Gaulle's Republic* (New York: Doubleday Anchor, 1973), p. 242. Officially, partisan involvement on the part of higher civil servants is condemned. In October 1975, a circular issued by the premier's office reaffirmed the illegality of such involvement.

18. Cohen, *Conseillers du président*, p. 188 et passim.

19. Maurice Szafran and Sammy Ketz, *Les Familles du président* (Paris: Grasset, 1982). See especially Chapter 1, "La République des fidélités," pp. 7–32. One source (*Le Point*, 3 August 1981, p. 27) notes that of the 27 rectors of academies (the chief administators of the school districts), 14 were replaced in 1981, mostly by reliable Socialists. One public agency, the Paris subway authority (RATP), was put under a Communist director—no doubt because the new minister of transport was a Communist. On the French "spoils system" under Giscard, Chirac, and the Socialists, see also Christiane de Brie, "La Très Réélle Politisation des hauts fonctionnaires," *Le Monde diplomatique*, April 1987.

20. Marie-France Toinet, "La Morale bureaucratique: Perspectives transatlantiques et franco-américaines," *International Political Science Review* 9:3 (1988), 193–203.

21. For statistics, see Jeanne Siwek-Poudesseau, "Le Syndicalisme des fonctionnaires, 1900–1981," *Vingtième Siècle*, January–March 1993, p. 122.

22. André Passeron, "La Bastille administrative" (Part 1), *Le Monde*, 12 March 1975.

23. Pfister, *République des fonctionnaires*, p. 22.

24. According to Pfister (ibid., p. 23), 19 percent of the members of the PS executive bureau in 1977 were *Enarques*.

25. Birnbaum, *Les Elites socialistes au pouvoir*, pp. 202–203.

26. Alfred Diamant, "Tradition and Innovation in French Administration," *Comparative Political Studies* 1 (July 1968), 255–256. See also Catherine Lalumière, "Les Fonctionnaires et le service public," *Le Monde*, 6 March 1976.

27. F. M. Marx, "The Higher Civil Service as an Action Group in Western Political Development," in J. La Palombara, ed., *Bureaucracy and Political Development* (Princeton, NJ: Princeton University Press, 1963), p. 79.

28. See Ezra Suleiman, *Politics, Power, and Bureaucracy* (Princeton, NJ: Princeton University Press, 1974), Chapters 4 and 12.

29. See Michalina Vaughan, "The Grandes Ecoles," in Rupert Wilkinson, ed., *Governing Elites* (New York: Oxford University Press, 1969), p. 86. The Ecole Polytechnique had originally been set up a year earlier as a school of public works (Ecole centrale des travaux publics).

30. David Granick, *The European Executive* (Garden City, NY: Doubleday Anchor, 1964), p. 74.

31. Thomson, *Democracy in France*, p. 58.

32. Pierre Birnbaum, *Les Sommets de l'état: Essai sur l'élite du pouvoir en France* (Paris: Seuil, 1977), pp. 151ff.

33. Jacques Chevallier, "L'Intérêt général dans l'administration française," *IRAS* 41:4 (1975), 325–350.

34. Gabriel Mignot and Philippe d'Orsay, *La Machine administrative* (Paris: Seuil, 1968), p. 8. See also Jean Montheu, "Un château-fort médiéval: Le ministère de l'économie

et des finances," *L'Esprit*, n.s., special issue, January 1970, p. 147. According to this source, the staff of the tax office (Ministry of Finance) grew from 48,900 in 1963 to nearly 60,000 in 1970. It continued to grow in the 1970s and 1980s, but there are still not enough tax inspectors to resolve the persisting problem of tax evasion.

35. See Georges Langrod, *La Consultation dans l'administration contemporaine* (Paris: Cujas, 1972). This massive work on "consultative administration" lists more than 300 *comités, commissions,* and *conseils* on the national level alone.

36. Charles E. Freedeman, *The* Conseil d'Etat *in Modern Times* (New York: Columbia University Press, 1961), p. 4. See also Jean-Paul Negrin, *Le Conseil d'Etat et la vie politique en France depuis 1958* (Paris: PUF, 1968), pp. 30–37, 44–45, 140–141; and Margherita Rendel, *The Administrative Functions of the French Conseil d'Etat* (London: Weidenfeld & Nicolson, 1970), pp. 28–40.

37. Most of the work of the Council of State concerns *excès du pouvoir* (i.e., overstepping of responsibilities by an official in such a way as to damage a private citizen's interest). There are actually four grounds of challenge to bureaucratic action: (1) lack of authority (*ultra vires*), (2) failure to observe procedures called for by an existing law, (3) abuse of power (*détournement de pouvoir*), and (4) violation of the law.

38. The number of cases brought before the Council of State averaged about 4,000 annually from 1973 to 1976 but grew to 8,580 in 1982–1983 and to more than 10,000 in 1992. Blandine Barret-Kriegel, *L'Etat de la démocratie: Rapport à François Mitterrand* (Paris: Documentation Française, 1985), p. 202. See also *Le Monde*, 8 October 1987 and 9 September 1993.

39. In its annual report of 1992, the Council of State mentions 7,500 laws, 82,000 decrees, 20,000 European Community regulations, and more than 10,000 *circulaires* for the enforcement of which it is theoretically responsible. See Thierry Bréhier, "Le Conseil d'Etat critique la 'logorrhée législative et réglementaire,'" *Le Monde*, 21 May 1992; and Guy Braibant, "Qui fait la loi," *Pouvoirs* 64 (1993), 47.

40. See *Le Monde*, 8 October 1987; and Jacques Robert, "Désencombrer le Conseil d'Etat," *Le Monde*, 10 November 1987.

41. Gérard Soulier, *Nos Droits face à l'Etat* (Paris: Seuil, 1981), p. 33.

42. Ibid., pp. 33, 88–90, 124. In 1962, when the Council of State challenged the legality of an ordinance creating a military court of justice, de Gaulle was so enraged that he briefly thought of curtailing the power of the council.

43. The recruitment of members of the Council of State is complicated, involving competitive examinations given by ENA (for auditors), promotion from below, based on seniority (for *maîtres de requêtes*), and pure discretion of the government (for a third of the councilors).

44. The bill to provide for a mediator was introduced in 1972 by Premier Pierre Messmer; however, the idea can be traced to Michel Poniatowski (an intimate friend of Giscard), who, in 1970 (as an Independent Republican deputy), introduced a bill in 1970 to create a "High Commission for the Defense of the Rights of Man" (composed of members of the Council of State and the Court of Cassation [see Chapter 9]). See Bernard Maligner, *Les Fonctions du médiateur* (Paris: PUF, 1979), p. 13.

45. Pinay was replaced after only one year by a civil servant (André Paquet), who served a full six-year term and who was in turn replaced in 1980 by Robert Fabre, a pro-Giscard Left-Radical politician, who was replaced by Paul Legatte in 1986.

46. See Jean-Claude Masclet, *Nouveaux droits des administrés*, Documents d'Etudes, no. 4.03 (Paris: Documentation Française, December 1986), pp. 3–10. In addition to the

national staff, there are also departmental delegates, who deal with the public at the prefectures.

47. See Louis-Jérôme Chapuisat, "Le Médiateur français ou l'ombudsman sacrifié," *IRAS* 40:2 (1974), 109-129, and Masclet, *Nouveaux Droits*, pp. 5-7.

48. CNIL is composed of 17 members, of whom 3 are named by the government, 2 by the speakers of the two chambers of Parliament, 6 by the members of the chambers, and 6 by various national judicial bodies. CADA is named by the premier, and composed of 19 people, including (in 1988) 4 deputies, 2 municipal councilors, 2 university professors, and higher civil servants. Cf. J. Robert, "Le Giscardisme et les libertés," *Pouvoirs* 9 (1979), 95. See also J. Lemasurier, "Vers une démocratie administrative: Du refus d'informer au droit d'être informé," *Revue du droit public* 5 (1980), 1239ff; and *L'Accès au documents administratifs*, 5th Report of CADA (Paris: Documentation Française, 1988).

49. See J. Robert, "Le Giscardisme et les libertés," *Pouvoirs* 9 (1979), 95.

50. Cf. Victor Silvera, "Incompatibilité, fonction publique, et affairisme," *Revue administrative*, November-December 1971, pp. 642-647.

51. In 1946, civil servants obtained the right to join unions. Their right to strike has remained unclear; striking is not forbidden, but neither is it specifically permitted by law.

52. For example, in April 1975 the interior minister, Poniatowski, suspended a prefect because he had lacked the requisite "coolness" in negotiations with a group of kidnappers. *Le Monde*, 8 April 1975.

53. See Pierre Richard and Michel Cotten, *Les Communes françaises d'aujourd'hui* (Paris: PUF, 1986), pp. 12-14.

54. It was done, for example, in November 1970 in the case of the mayor of Saint-Laurent-du-Pont (Isère) after 145 young people were killed when a dance hall caught fire.

55. Mark Kesselman, *The Ambiguous Consensus* (New York: Knopf, 1967), p. 8. See Appendix B of that work (pp. 171-184) for a description (now somewhat dated) of the legal powers of communes.

56. Sidney Tarrow, "Local Constraints and Regional Reform: A Comparison of France and Italy," *Comparative Politics* 7:1 (October 1974), 1-36.

57. Sidney Tarrow, *Between Center and Periphery: Grassroots Politicians in Italy and France* (New Haven, CT: Yale University Press, 1977), pp. 111-141.

58. Edgar Morin, *Commune en France* (Paris: Fayard, 1967).

59. Philippe Garrard, "Le Recrutement des maires en milieu urbain," *Pouvoirs* 24 (January 1983), 29-43. See also Yves Mény, "Le Maire, ici et ailleurs," *Pouvoirs*, same issue, pp. 19-27, who argues that because of his local popularity, the mayor in effect "chooses" the city council and dominates whatever agent the national government might send.

60. Gabriel Mignot and Philippe d'Orsay, *La Machine administrative* (Paris: Seuil, 1977), p. 48. Cf. Jean de Savigny, *L'Etat contre les communes?* (Paris: Seuil, 1971), p. 64, which cites 8 percent for departments and 20 percent for communes.

61. Pierre Gaudez, "La Réforme des collectivités locales," *Le Monde*, 4 June 1975.

62. Odon Vallet, "D'abord, entre dans la vie des communes," *Projet* 142 (February 1980), 149-155.

63. See "La Décentralisation en marche," *Le Monde, Dossiers et Documents* 164 (March 1989), for conflicting comparative statistics.

64. *Le Monde*, 8 April 1970.

65. An example of such inequality: At the end of the 1960s the department of Basses-Alpes had 83,354 inhabitants, and the department of Nord, 1,917,452.

66. For a history of decentralization attempts, see Michel Phlipponeau, *Décentralisation et régionalisation* (Paris: Calmann-Lévy, 1981). For an excellent comprehensive work, see Vivien A. Schmidt, *Democratizing France: The Political and Administrative History of Decentralization* (Cambridge, MA, and New York: Cambridge University Press, 1991).

67. See Tarrow, "Local Constraints on Regional Reform." It has also been argued that the following prevailing ideologies (shared by local politicians) have militated against meaningful decentralization: individualism (which does not tolerate geographical intermediaries between citizen and state); the "logic of capitalism" and the "ethnocentrism of the bourgeoisie" (both of which have justified the traditional suppression of the provinces). Claude de Vos, "La Région: A la recherche d'un sens," in *Annales de la Faculté des Lettres et Sciences Humaines de Nice* (issue on "Urbanisation, développement régional, et pouvoir public"), no. 26 (1975), 137-151. See also Club Moulin, *Les Citoyens au pouvoir* (Paris: Seuil, 1968).

68. "L'Allègement de la tutelle administrative," *Revue administrative*, July 1971, pp. 459-462. See also Yves Madiot, *Fusions et regroupements de communes* (Paris: LGDJ, 1973). The commune associations—*syndicats intercommunaux à vocation unique* (SIVU), which are concerned with specialized services (e.g., water supply), or *syndicats intercommunaux à vocation multiple* (SIVOM), which deal with several types of service—are not "interest groups" in the proper sense; rather, they are gatherings of municipal councilors whose recommendations must still be approved by the national government. Elisabeth Zoller, "La Création des syndicats de communes: Une décision des communes ou de l'Etat?" *Revue du droit public* 92 (July–August 1976), 985-994.

69. P. B. M. Jones, "The Organisation of Regional Economic Planning in France," *Public Administration* (London) 45 (Winter 1967), 358. For a more detailed treatment, see François Damiette, *Le Territoire français et son aménagement* (Paris: Editions Sociales, 1969).

70. Jacques Baguenard, "L'Organisation régionale (loi du 5 juillet 1972)," *Revue du droit public* 89 (November–December 1973), 1405-1465. See also Dominique Henry, "La Région et l'aménagement du territoire," *Revue administrative*, January–February 1976, pp. 73-75; and for a general treatment, Jérôme Monod and Philippe de Castelbajac, *L'Aménagement du territoire* (Paris: PUF, 1971); and (on regional reform) William G. Andrews, "The Politics of Regionalization in France," in Martin Heisler, ed., *Politics in Europe* (New York: David McKay, 1974), pp. 293-322.

71. François Grosrichard, "Renouvellement politique et ouverture régionale," *Le Monde*, 28 March 1973. See also same author, "Le Crépuscule des régions," *Le Monde*, 28 November 1975.

72. See "Enfin, la décentralisation," *Regards sur l'Actualité* 74 (September–October 1981), 22-23; and "La Décentralisation," *Cahiers français* 204 (January–February 1982), 44-45.

73. *Le Monde*, 26 November 1975. See also Alain Peyrefitte, "Régionalisation ou décentralisation?" *Le Monde*, 22 November 1975; and Mark O. Rousseau, "President Valéry Giscard d'Estaing and Decentralization," *French Review* 54:6 (May 1981), 827-835.

74. As Premier Mauroy put it, the reforms were intended to lead to a selective "degovernmentalization" (*désétatisation*) of decision making by "[strengthening] the

structures of civil society . . . [building] a new citizenship . . . [and giving] the state back to the citizen." "La Décentralisation," p. 52.

75. Article I of the law of 2 March 1982, cited and discussed in Paul Bernard, *L'Etat et la décentralisation*, Notes et Etudes Documentaires, nos. 4711–4712 (Paris: Documentation Française, 1983), pp. 121ff.

76. Eventually, the elections of general councilors were to take place simultaneously with those of municipal councilors.

77. If the commissioner felt that local governments violated the laws or exceeded their budgetary authorities, she would no longer be able *herself* to nullify these local acts; instead, she would be empowered to submit them for a judgment to an administrative tribunal or to a newly constituted regional fiscal control tribunal, or "court of accounts."

78. For a fairly balanced analysis of decentralization, that is, as neither meaningless nor revolutionary but rather as a gradual process—with local government still effectively controlled by central government and by elements of the old "political class"—see Jean-Claude Thoenig, "La Décentralisation dix ans après," *Pouvoirs* 60 (1992), 5–16.

79. Ibid. See also Jean-Michel Linfort and Jean-Claude Closset, "Elus locaux: origine socio-professionnelle et fonctionnarisation croissante," *Revue politique et parlementaire* 91:941 (May–June 1989), 49–56; and Richard and Cotten, *Les Communes françaises*, pp. 17f.

80. See Jean-Michel Gaillard and Catherin Rambert, *La Fête des maires* (Paris: Lattès, 1993); and André Chandernagor, *Les Maires de France* (Paris: Fayard 1993). Examples frequently mentioned are Georges Frêche of Montpellier, Michel Noir of Lyons, and Catherine Trautmann of Strasbourg.

81. Gérard Fayolle, *Des Elus locaux sous la Ve République* (Paris: Hachette, 1989), p. 52. On the increasing pressure on mayors to initiate projects and seek funds, see Paul J. Godt, "Decentralization in France: Plus ça Change . . . ?" *Tocqueville Review* 7 (1985/86), 191–203.

82. See Patrick Coquidé, "Il y a trop de communes en France," *Le Point*, 1 May 1989, pp. 50–54.

83. See "Contrats clochemerlesques," *Le Monde (Heures Locales)*, 5–6 September 1993, which discusses the financial dilemmas of "Podunks."

84. See "L'état de la décentralisation," *Cahiers français* 256 (May–June 1992), 87ff. See also Marie-Christine Bernard-Gélabert and Patrick Labia, *Intercommunalités—Mode d'Emploi* (Paris: Economica, 1992).

85. Françoise Chirot, "Les Elus se font conseiller," *Le Monde (Heures Locales)*, 10–11 October 1993. See also "Regards sur dix années de réformes," *Le Monde, Dossiers et Documents* 202 (September 1992), 1.

86. From 1978 to 1985, total local revenues and expenditures grew by only 29 percent; in the latter year the proportion of local spending in France was only 8 percent of the gross national product and 16 percent of public expenditures, compared to 19 percent of GNP (and 37 percent of public expenditures) in the United States and 13 percent (and 26 percent) in Britain. Figures from Vincent Hoffmann-Martinot and Jean-Yves Nevers, "French Local Policy Change in a Period of Austerity: A Silent Revolution," in Susan Clarke, ed., *Urban Innovation and Autonomy: The Political Implications of Policy Change* (Newbury Park, CA: Sage, 1989).

87. According to SOFRES polls, in 1990, 22 percent of respondents thought of the state as being close to them (compared to 41 percent in 1970), while 74 percent thought of the state as being distant (compared to 51 percent in 1970). Thierry Bréhier,

"L'Opinion des Français," in *Dix Ans de décentralisation, Le Monde, Dossiers et Documents* 202 (September 1992), 4.

88. See Stéphane Dion, *La Politisation des mairies* (Paris: Economica, 1986), pp. 202-207 et passim.

89. "La Nouvelle vie locale," *Le Monde, Dossiers et Documents*, March 1989, p. 2.

90. On the "relocalization" of the political orientations of politicians, see Pierre Sadran, "La Décentralisation à l'âge de raison," *Regards sur l'actualité* 152 (June 1989), 36-46.

91. See Jean-Pierre Chevènement, "Dangers et limites," *ENA mensuel* 214: La Décentralisation (August 1991), 13.

92. The total budget for all 20 *arrondissements* in 1984, for example, was 300 million francs (i.e., roughly $35 million, or less than $2 million per *arrondissement*). This figure constituted only 4 percent of the total municipal-service budget for Paris—in effect little more than a "maintenance budget." See *Le Monde*, 31 March 1983.

93. "Le Nouveau statut de la Corse," *Regards sur l'actualité* 88 (February 1983), 47-56. The Corsican Assembly was expected to work closely with two advisory councils—a social and economic council and a council for culture, education, and the quality of life—each composed of representatives of interest groups.

94. Albert Lanza, *Les Projets de réforme administrative en France de 1919 à nos jours* (Paris: PUF, 1968), pp. 22, 30, 76, and 97ff. In 1975, civil servants formed the *Association pour l'amélioration des rapports entre administration et le public*, the task of which was to be the simplification of procedures and language, the sensitizing of officials to the needs of the public, and the improvement of the public image of officialdom.

95. "Gouverner autrement: La Circulaire Rocard du 25 mai 1988," *Regards sur l'actualité* 143 (July-August 1988), 15-18.

96. Practice may be different, especially for the higher and more responsible echelons, as pointed out above.

97. Stephen S. Cohen, *Modern Capitalist Planning: The French Model* (Cambridge, MA: Harvard University Press, 1969), pp. 35, 39, 52, 163.

chapter 9

Law, Justice, and Civil Liberties

THE JUDICIAL SYSTEM

The French judicial system shares many features with those of Britain and the United States: the belief in procedural due process, the principle that no action is punishable except on the basis of law (*nulla poena sine lege*), the rejection of ex post facto law, the presumption of the innocence of the accused, and the independence of the judiciary. Some of these principles were articulated in the Declaration of the Rights of Man and the Citizen proclaimed in 1789, and they have become part of republican constitutions; others have become part of political practice through legislation and judicial interpretation. The French system of legal norms is based on abstract principles (code law) as compared with the Anglo-American tradition of judicial precedents (common law or case law). However, this distinction has in reality become somewhat obscured. Much common law in Anglo-American democracies has been superseded by statute law; conversely, French code law allows for rules of custom and precedent in cases where codes are insufficient as guides for judicial decisions.

French civil and criminal codes date back to the Romans, but they were revised by the Napoleonic Civil Code of 1804, followed by the Criminal Code of 1810. Code law, in principle, has the merit of providing uniformity, of ensuring that in a given case the same principles apply throughout the country and that decisions are not dependent on diverse judicial temperaments. In practice, however, there is a great regional diversity of sentencing patterns.[1] Nevertheless, code law may be regarded as more rigid than common law, and its assumptions might quickly become antiquated. The French Parliament began to modernize the Criminal Code in 1959 and continued that process by fits and starts. Early in 1994, after 18 years of effort, the first thorough overhauling of the Criminal Code since

277

Napoleon was completed. Under this reform, new delicts were added, among them sexual harassment, crimes against humanity, and computer crimes.

The French judicial system has been widely imitated because it has many admirable features. There is a wide geographical distribution of courts at various levels and therefore easy accessibility to justice for most of the population. Courts of first instance are found in every *arrondissement*, and there are many higher courts (see Figure 9.1). In addition to the civil and criminal courts, a network of functionally specialized tribunals exist. The best known are the administrative courts, in which citizens can bring a suit against civil servants for violations of laws and regulations and for arbitrary behavior (see Chapter 8). There are also separate regional tribunals for labor relations (*conseils de prud'hommes*), social security matters, commercial disputes, and conflicts between tenant farmers and landlords (*baux ruraux*).[2] Some of these specialized tribunals date back to the First Empire and even to the *ancien régime*, but they are especially relevant for highly technical disputes engendered by the administration of the contemporary welfare state. Traditionally, these regional tribunals were structurally separate from the civil and criminal courts. In 1970, legislation was passed to bring these tribunals into the ordinary appellate court system. The law provided for setting up,

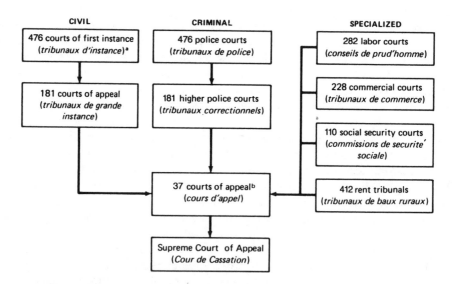

FIGURE 9.1 The French court structure

[a]Until 1958, there were about 3,000 justices of the peace—one for each canton—whose functions have since been taken over by the courts of first stance.
[b]There are also *cours d'assises* (one for each *département*) which are convoked for serious crimes subject to severe penalties (e.g., long imprisonment or confiscation of property).
NOTE: The figures, which are for 1986, include the overseas *départements*.
SOURCE: Ambassade de France, Service de Presse et d'Information, *France*, June 1974, pp. 5–8, and subsequent issues; and Daniel Rondi, "L'organisation de la justice en France," *Après-Demain* 122 (March 1970), 20–21 (adapted, simplified, updated).

within every court of appeal, "social chambers" to deal with labor relations and collective contracts. These chambers are each of composed of one judge and four lay assessors, two from trade unions and two representing employers, chosen by the government from lists submitted by the appropriate associations. (This method differs from that of the *conseils de prud'hommes*, where the assessors are elected by trade unions and employers' associations.)

The corps of judges in France represents a distinct segment of the legal profession. A privately practicing attorney cannot, after he or she is well established, decide to become a judge. A person who is interested in a judicial career must, after completing studies at a faculty of law, enter a special law school, the Ecole Nationale de la Magistrature (ENM), which was set up in Bordeaux in 1958 and which in terms of its study program and its social selectivity is patterned somewhat on the ENA.[3] Before completing studies at the ENM, students must opt for a specific part of the national judiciary—either the *magistrature* or the *parquet*, the former comprising the judges, and the latter, the prosecuting attorneys (*avocats généraux* or *procureurs*) working on behalf of the Ministry of Justice. By 1992, 4,700 of France's 6,000 sitting judges were graduates of ENM.

Career judges are technically part of the civil service, at least in terms of their security of tenure, pay, promotions, and retirement benefits. Original appointments of judges are made not by the minister of justice but by the president on the basis of recommendations by the High Council of the Magistrature. This body consists of the president of the republic, the minister of justice, and nine others who are appointed by the president; of these nine, two are chosen at his discretion, six are nominees of the Court of Cassation, and one is a nominee of the Council of State.

The organization of the French legal profession appears inordinately complex when compared to the American one with its single class of lawyers, or the British one, with its two categories, barristers and solicitors. The French have several types of legal professionals in addition to judges: (1) *avocats*, attorneys who can plead in most trial courts; (2) *notaires* (notaries public), whose main responsibility is the preparation of contracts, wills, and property settlements;[4] and (3) *fiduciaires*, who are concerned with tax matters. There used to be another type of juridical profession, that of *conseiller juridique*, who gave general legal advice (and who was often employed by corporations), but in 1992 this category was fused with that of *avocat*.[5]

At the top of the legal profession's hierarchy are the *avocats aux conseils*, of whom there are about sixty, who may appear before the Court of Cassation (*Cour de cassation*)—the highest court of appeal for civil, criminal, and socioeconomic cases—or the Council of State, its counterpart for administrative cases. The Court of Cassation is divided into six "chambers" or panels—five civil and one criminal[6]—each composed of at least seven judges and deciding by majority vote. (Unlike U.S. courts, neither the *Cour de cassation* nor other French courts publish dissenting opinions.)[7] This court does not determine the facts in the case, but rather the legality of the decision rendered by a lower court.[8] At the bottom of the judicial ladder are the *greffiers* (court clerks) and the *huissiers* (bailiffs).

This functional differentiation goes back several centuries. The "medieval" aspects of the profession are manifested in the special gowns the *avocats* are required to wear in court, the hereditary nature of some of the categories (e.g., *greffiers* and *huissiers*), and the retention of the practice of setting fees by law for all but the *avocats*.

The judicial procedure itself differs in some important respects from Anglo-American patterns. There is the "inquisitorial" system of trial procedure whereby the presiding judge intervenes actively in the trial by questioning the defendant, the witnesses, and the lawyers on both sides (in contrast with the "adversary" system common in the United States and Britain, where the judge's primary duty is to ensure the orderly progress of the trial). Most verdicts in the lower courts are decided by a panel of judges. The number of judges needed to decide a case varies according to the level of the court and the nature of the charges. However, trial by jury is becoming more common, particularly in courts of appeal (where, typically, nine jurors and three judges sit together to decide a case and a two-thirds majority is needed to uphold a conviction).

There is a much greater tendency in French courts than in Anglo-American courts to convict a defendant, a phenomenon that has given rise to the notion that in France the innocence of the accused is not safeguarded so well as it is in the Anglo-Saxon democracies, and that in a criminal trial, procedures favor the state. But not all cases go to a full trial; there is a lengthy pretrial investigation by police magistrates, in which the various due process guarantees are applied and the suspect may be able to use council.

The pretrial investigation of a crime has two stages: The second stage, the *instruction par le juge*, follows the police inquiry, which is often so protracted that an accused is held for a long time in pretrial detention. There is no writ of habeas corpus; nevertheless, the Constitution of 1958 (Article 66) provides that "no person may be detained arbitrarily," and there have been a series of piece-meal reforms to bring France closer to de facto habeas corpus protections. Thus the Penal Code Reform of 1959 specified that "preventive detention is an exceptional measure"; and in 1970, 1974, and 1980, bills were passed that gradually limited preventive detention to four months. The culmination of this gradual approach was the Habeas Corpus Act of 1984, which provided that no one could be placed in temporary detention without argument by a state attorney, evidence by the accused, and challenge by defense counsel.[9] Today, preindictment detention (*garde à vue*) is limited to 24 hours, unless extended to 48 hours with a warrant issued by an examining magistrate (*juge d'instruction*). A reform of 1993 confirmed the right of a defendant to an attorney after 20 hours of police custody even in serious cases (e.g., suspected terrorism or drug-related crimes) where such custody is extended;[10] and provided further that the Ministry of Justice be informed of any extension of police custody. Furthermore, a large proportion of those detained are ultimately not brought to trial because of lack of sufficient presumption of guilt.[11]

There has been a continuing debate about whether judges in France, who influence the course of a trial so strongly, render justice democratically—whether their formal position predisposes them to favor the state against the citizen and whether their bourgeois background prejudices them against the lower classes. Since in rendering justice, judges not only apply the law but also have a responsibility to reflect "the general will," it is widely believed that they tend to favor the government as the repository of that will against the individual.[12] However, in recent years, judges have increasingly asserted their independence in pronouncing judgment in the name of the French *people* (as distinct from the government) and following "general principles of rights" in order to take into account individual cases.[13] Moreover, French judges have become more sympathetic to the ordinary citizen as their own self-image as members of an elite has been blurred. Owing in part to an expansion of the judiciary and insufficient appropriations for the magistrature,[14] there has been an increase in the unionization of judges; most of them are members of the *Syndicat de la magistrature*. The judges' and lawyers' associations since the late 1960s have not only agitated for better pay but have also expressed concern for a liberalization of the penal code; the overhauling of the labyrinthine court structure; and the simplification of the legal language, which is often incomprehensible to the average citizen.[15]

There is no doubt that in France, as in most highly stratified societies where legal counsel costs money and the judiciary tends to be recruited from the bourgeoisie, the judicial system favors the existing regime and the established classes (although the members of the judiciary deny this charge[16]). This was reflected in the fact that before 1978, juries were highly selective—for the most part they included mayors, city councilors, and other "respectable" citizens and excluded manual and domestic workers. Since that time, however, juries have been drawn by lot from lists of registered voters.[17] There is an increasing number of magistrates whose leftist ideologies have predisposed them to proworker decisions,[18] and there are indications that the appointment and promotion of such magistrates was encouraged under recent Socialist governments. Yet discrimination against the underprivileged will undoubtedly continue, despite a reform in the early 1970s that provides for free legal counsel for indigent defendants and despite the dramatic increase in budgetary allocations for such counsel.[19] There is the additional problem of increased crime and overloaded dockets, which (because of the absence of plea bargaining) cannot be effectively disposed of by the relatively small number of state attorneys and defense lawyers.[20] This has resulted in the development of a sort of judicial rationing during the appeals process; for example, the various chambers of the Court of Cassation reject about 60 percent of the cases for "lack of interest."[21] Among the measures to relieve the burden on the courts were laws, enacted between 1991 and 1993, to increase the number of judges and court clerks, simplify the legal profession (see above), and computerize certain operational aspects of the judiciary.[22]

One approach to make access to justice speedier and less expensive (and, incidentally, to relieve the dockets of ordinary courts) was the creation in 1978 of a system of *conciliateurs*. These nonsalaried "conciliators," appointed for one-year terms, are not professional judges but laypersons—members of the liberal professions, educators, sociologists, and officials of private associations. They attempt to settle by "amicable means" a variety of disputes, such as conflicts between landlords and tenants, breaches of contract, neighborhood quarrels, and interracial or interethnic conflicts. By 1981 the number of conciliators had grown to 1,200, but—owing to the hostility of Robert Badinter, the Socialist minister of justice, who did not want to "deprofessionalize" the judicial process—the appointments of many of them were not renewed, and their number fell to 400 in 1986. Albin Chalandon, Chirac's (Gaullist) minister of justice, proposed to revive the system and bring the number of conciliators up to 3,800 (roughly one for each canton) by 1989,[23] but with the return of Socialist rule this ambitious scheme was scaled back.

Measures such as these were not enough to solve the problem of unequal justice, which was particularly apparent in the imposition of what Anglo-Americans might call "cruel and unusual punishment." The death penalty (by guillotine) was imposed mainly on members of the lower classes. Since the end of the Third Republic there have been no public executions, and presidents have exercised with increasing frequency their right of pardon in capital crimes.[24] In 1982, capital punishment was abolished (despite the fact that, in the face of an increasing incidence of violent crimes, a large proportion of the public favored its retention).

Three decades ago, the laws concerning abortion appeared to be much more discriminatory against the poor than the well-to-do. Abortion was considered a crime for which the patient was punished by a heavy fine; the physician was subjected to a fine, a prison sentence, or the loss of his or her license. However, in the early 1970s, sentences were suspended because of a public outcry and the issuance of a manifesto signed by several hundred physicians confessing to having performed abortions. As a result, in 1974, the government, in one of the first steps undertaken by the Giscard presidency to liberalize aspects of French society, successfully put forward a bill to legalize abortion. The government under President Pompidou had already promoted two other liberal measures: the introduction of sex education in public schools and the granting of equal rights of inheritance to illegitimate children.[25] These reforms were extended by Socialist governments to cover the equal protection under law of women, homosexuals, and the handicapped.

One set of reforms that touched on the question of equal justice was the "Security and Liberty" bill introduced by the Giscard regime in 1980 and passed (with modifications) early in 1981. Under the provisions of this legislation, criminal procedure was simplified, and the maximum allowable period of pretrial detention was reduced. The legislation also provided for mandatory minimum sentences for a number of crimes, especially crimes of violence, and thereby diminished the discretion of judges. This provision led to protest demonstrations, media publicity, and heavy lobbying by magistrates' and lawyers' associations and by university professors. An equally controversial feature of the reform provided that certain criminals (e.g., pimps, drug pushers, and selected white-collar transgressors) could have their prison sentences reduced if they quickly paid compensation to their victims—a provision that was interpreted by some as instituting a preferred system of justice for those with money.[26] Finally, the reform provided that the police could ask any person on the street to show his or her identification and detain those unable to furnish it—ostensibly in response to the growing number of illegal aliens. In 1982 most of the illiberal provisions of the "Security and Liberty" law were rescinded by Parliament.[27]

A persistent problem has been the overcrowding of prisons, which was aggravated by a variety of factors contributing to a growth of criminality: population growth, the rapid urbanization of society, the spread of drugs, and, with the modernization of the French economy, a steep increase in white-collar infractions and felonies involving property.[28] The Socialist government (basing itself on the recommendations of a committee of experts[29]) enacted a variety of measures, among them the improvement of prison conditions and the selective use of alternatives to prison, such as probation, fines, or community service. The Chirac government of 1986 in turn proposed to solve the problem by recommending the decriminalization of a number of acts usually leading to jail sentences and even toyed with the idea of setting up privately run prisons, but, under pressure from conservative Gaullists, the government abandoned these ideas.[30]

THE LEGAL PROTECTION OF ALIENS AND MINORITIES

The French legal system has reflected an ambivalence between widespread xenophobia and a tradition of welcoming immigrants. The 4 million foreign workers and their families, while contributing to the labor force, have also contributed their share to the growth of crime. (According to one estimate, 25 percent of the 1982 prison population consisted of foreigners.[31]) In response to this problem a law was passed in 1979 (the *loi Bonnet*) that permitted the minister of the interior, without resorting to the customary legal procedures, to expel foreigners not only for illegal entry and lack of proper documents but also for violating public order—a provision that had a chilling effect on the foreigners' freedom to join unions and participate in public demonstrations. In 1981 this law was rescinded; somewhat later, bills were passed granting foreigners the right to participate in elections to labor tribunals, giving them access to official documents pertaining to themselves, and providing for punishment of employers who underpaid them. In 1983, another bill gave naturalized citizens the same political rights as native-born citizens: They obtained the right to form associations, and they were permitted to run for political office, including the presidency of the republic, without having to wait ten years.

Ambivalence is shown also in the still-unsettled conflict between the right to political asylum and the extradition of criminals. Under the Socialists, the right of asylum (implicitly guaranteed by the Constitution[32]) was reaffirmed; but when the RPR and UDF returned to power in 1993, that right was challenged. Charles Pasqua, the tough-minded Gaullist who was again appointed minister of interior, introduced a bill to restrict the right of asylum. Before this bill could pass, it was necessary to amend the Constitution (see Art. 53) to reconcile it with the Schengen Accords of 1990, which provide for the free circulation of people within the European Community. Another "Pasqua bill" (passed after much parliamentary debate) toughened the conditions of entry for immigrants and the acquisition of citizenship and gave the police increased power to make random identity checks.[33]

Many French citizens, especially on the Left, have opposed these measures as discriminatory. At the same time, there has been a growing demand to deal with the many terrorist organizations that seemed to have made France a major theater of operations. So far, the problem has been handled in an ad hoc fashion: In 1977, the French government, under pressure from Arab countries, refrained from prosecuting a PLO terrorist implicated in the murder of Israelis;[34] but in 1982, the government issued a decree making it a punishable offense to belong to *Action directe*, an extreme-leftist group that was held responsible for several bombings throughout France, and eventually (in 1987) convicted a number of its members. In the interest of good neighborly relations, the Socialist governments extradited Spanish Basque separatists who had fled to France. In 1986 and 1987, the Chirac government had laws passed (the *lois Pasqua*, so named after the Gaullist minister of the interior) that made it more difficult for foreigners to enter France and obtain residence permits and easier for the Ministry of the Interior to expel them without judicial recourse. At the same time, laws were passed that lengthened the pretrial detention of suspected terrorists and that abolished popular juries in terrorist trials. However, during the trial of an Arab terrorist in 1987, the Chirac government was widely accused of sacrificing due process in the national interest (i.e., maintaining good relations with Arab states) and of having pressured the prosecuting attorney to ask for a light sentence. (The court, however, showed its independence by imposing a life sentence.) In 1992, the judicial authorities, under pressure from the Foreign Ministry, refused to indict or extradite a well-known Arab terrorist who was implicated in the killing of civilians.[35] During the final days of 1993, the French government, again invoking reasons of state, released two Iranian assassins from prison and permitted them to return to their homeland in defiance of a Swiss request for extradition.

"Political justice" sometimes results from a combination of government action (or inaction) and ideologically conditioned judicial arbitrariness, as in the case of Paul Touvier, a Vichy official whose case was temporarily thrown out in 1992 by a reactionary court of appeals.[36] More often, however, such justice results from the tendency of a government to protect its own members and political friends against embarrassing judicial proceedings.[37] The apparent immunity of politicians to the application of ordinary criminal law has provoked increasing public protests; it was partly in response to these protests that in 1993 the Constitution was amended to create a new tribunal, the Court of Justice of the Republic, in which members of the government could be judged (see Art. 68).

THE POLICE

The poor are particularly exposed to the vagaries of the police, who have significant power in the judicial process. There have been many reports of police brutality, especially against workers, farmers, and leftists. These categories of people not only form the class most likely to clash with the police force, which is recruited primarily from the petite bourgeoisie, but they are also the most likely to confront the police in situations judged by the latter to be provocative—in demonstrations and strikes.[38] In addition, the police must take orders from the government, the Ministry of the Interior, and the prefectures, which have been very concerned about threats to internal security.

The French obsession with law and order, which is understandable in a society until recently given to periodic challenges to the régime, is reflected in the size and complexity of the police system. All the French police forces combined comprised more than 200,000 members in 1992—1 for 275 inhabitants (compared to 1 for 454 inhabitants in Britain and 1 per 322 inhabitants in Germany). Approximately 60 percent of them—that is, 125,000—are in the National Police, of whom some 90,000 are in uniform. About half of the National Police are organized in the Urban Police, which operates in cities with more than 10,000 inhabitants; the rest are divided between the *Compagnies républicaines de sécurité* (CRS) and smaller specialized security services. The CRS maintains ten regional centers mobile units, and detachments for highways, beaches, and mountain areas, as well as several functional subdivisions (for intelligence, counter-espionage, judicial business, and border surveillance). In addition, there is the Paris police, a specially organized force of some 25,000 men and women, about 16,000 of whom are under the immediate direction of the prefect of police. Finally, there is the *gendarmerie nationale*, which is technically a component of the armed forces. The *gendarmerie* (with about 90,000) has at least one company in each *arrondissement* and includes maritime, civil air, and riot police as well as the *Garde républicaine*, a group of honor guards and bodyguards of prominent politicians.[39]

This impressive police establishment has not transformed France into a police state: The structural subdivisions, the jurisdictional competition between the Ministry of the Interior and the Ministry of Defense, the possibility of redress in administrative tribunals, and the watchful eye of the French Left, the intellectuals, and other sectors have all contributed to moderating the power of the police.

Moreover, the police has become concerned about its public image. Several years ago, the *Fédération autonome des syndicats de police* (FASP), the largest (and most leftist) of the four police officers' unions, held public interviews and protest demonstrations to counter the police's unpopularity and to inform the public about inadequate pay and working conditions. A spokesperson for the *Fédération* declared that "policemen wish to be neither the footmen of power nor the garbagemen of society."[40] The sensitivity of police officers to being the "unbeloved" of society has occasionally affected their performance, and once, in 1970, prompted the minister of the interior to initiate libel actions against several newspapers of the extreme Left that had been particularly critical of the police.[41] During the events of May–June 1968, there was evidence of fraternization between the police and the striking workers, and in 1971 the prefect of police was dismissed for not being tough enough on leftist demonstrators.

Governments under both Giscard and Mitterrand have been torn by the conflict between demands by segments of the population (especially workers and immigrants) for a curbing of excessive police powers and the need to equip the police with adequate means to do their job. In the late 1970s, police forces were increased and their operational budget was raised by 60 percent. Although Socialist governments were more sympathetic to the idea of restraining the police, they also had to be aware of both the increase in violent crimes and corresponding increases in gun ownership and vigilantism.[42] In 1982, a disagreement arose between Interior Minister Defferre, who controlled the police, and Justice Minister Badinter over the question of the police's right to demand of any person that he or she produce identity papers—with Badinter arguing that the police should not do so without prior judicial authorization. Whereas Badinter was concerned about due process and about protecting the rights of citizens, Defferre favored a freer use by police of their weapons beyond "legitimate defense," as current rules stipulated.[43] Under the pressure of events (including terrorist attacks), Socialist governments (both before 1986 and after 1988) shifted from a concern with sensitizing the police to democratic values toward an interest in making it more efficient—by providing higher pay, better training, more up-to-date weaponry, and the use of computerized data files.[44] The emphasis on strengthening the police, which continued with the return of the RPR-UDF to power in 1993, has evoked mixed public reactions. On the one hand, there is widespread belief that the police misbehave;[45] on the other hand, there are those who sympathize with the growing feeling among police officers that they are given insufficient means to deal with criminals, a feeling that has accounted for the growth of the influence of the National Front among police officers.[46]

FREEDOM OF ASSEMBLY, SPEECH, AND PRESS

Many of the infringements of a citizen's substantive rights are caused not so much by the police as by existing legislative provisions and the governmental attitudes that give rise to them. Although France is committed in its revolutionary principles and its statute law to freedom of speech, French regimes have found it necessary to infringe upon this freedom occasionally. Such infringement occurred especially after the Liberation, when the government had to deal with World War II collaborators, and during the Algerian crisis, when it was confronted with seditious elements. Between 1960 and 1962, a number of French military officers plotting against the regime, who had been arrested without warrant, were tried by special tribunals rather than by ordinary courts, and the usual rights of the defendants (including protection against self-incrimination) were severely restricted. In 1963 such an approach was institutionalized with the creation of the controversial State Security Court for cases of conspiracy and treason. Any case that involved persons accused of subversion could be transferred, by decision of the minister of justice, from the ordinary courts to the State Security Court. This power was used in more than 200 instances—at first to prosecute Maoists and other revolutionary leftists and later, leaders of Breton and other autonomist movements (but not international terrorists). In 1970 the Anti-Breakers' Law was enacted, under which participants in public disorders, members of organizations instigating them, and even innocent bystanders could be punished. Under this law, the government was able to ban public meetings of leftists, to suspend radical teachers, and to censor publications. During the first year of the Mitterrand presidency, the Socialist government abolished the State Security Court (as well as the military tribunals) and rescinded the Anti-Breakers' Law.

Freedom of the press was guaranteed by a law passed in 1881, but the same law made it a felony to publish statements damaging to the president of the republic (*lèse-majesté*) or to public authorities in general. This law seemed in desuetude for many years, but the Gaullists revived it. In the Third Republic the law was applied fewer than ten times; in the Fourth Republic, three times; but in the Fifth Republic (more exactly, between 1958 and 1970) about 100 times.[47] As if this law were not enough, Article 30 of the Penal Code of 1959 gave departmental prefects (and the prefect of police in Paris) the right to "undertake all acts necessary with a view to preventing crimes and violations of the . . . security of the state."[48] These laws were used as the basis for seizures of newspapers and occasionally even the harassment and temporary detention of newspaper vendors. An illustrative case of governmental interference concerned *Le Canard Enchaîné*, a mass-circulation weekly of political satire. Early in 1974, following a typical "revelation" by the paper of scandals involving Gaullists, the journal's offices were raided and its staff phones wiretapped by government agents.[49] In 1980, the minister of justice instituted criminal proceedings against the editor of *Le Monde*, the most respected French daily newspaper, for having published a series of articles alleging a mishandling of some cases by the judiciary. The government based its case on an article of the Penal Code that made it a punishable offense for "any person who publicly tries in deeds, words, or writings to discredit a judicial act or decision in circumstances likely to affect the judiciary and its independence."[50] The government's wrath against *Le Monde* had been fed by that paper's strong criticism of Giscard's entanglement in a number of scandals.[51] When the government was taken over by the Socialists, the proceedings against the paper were dropped.

Another challenge to the free press occurred in 1987, when Interior Minister Pasqua issued an order forbidding the sale of several pornographic magazines to minors. The order was based on a law enacted in 1949, and previous governments (including Socialist ones) had invoked it to stop the distribution of numerous issues of periodicals;[52] however, Pasqua's action was regarded as heavy-handed by several of his cabinet colleagues (especially the more liberal Giscardists).

Despite these instances, the French press has remained relatively free and unobstructed.[53] There is a great diversity and independence of opinion, and there are a number of highly respected newspapers (see Table 9.1). Most of the important newspapers are published in Paris, although there are some distinguished provincial newspapers. Journals are not the forums of expression of ordinary people they are ideally presumed to be in the United States. Letters to the editor are not so common in French newspapers as in American ones. The average person can contribute to weekly news magazines, such as *L'Express* and *Le Point*, but *Le Monde*, which is noted for the regular commentaries written by France's foremost intellectuals (and for its general excellence), accepts letters or responses largely from "established" individuals.

Theoretically, there are certain limits to a newspaper's independence since newspapers depend for many of their news sources on a government-controlled news agency (*Agence France-Presse*) and, more important, depend on the government's indirect financial subsidies. These subsidies involve reduced postal and railroad-transport charges and reduced tax rates (including a waiver of value-added tax). Such reductions may amount to 10 to 15 percent of the total budget of a typical newspaper and may make the difference between the continuation or termination of publication.

However, there is little concrete evidence that the government has used its fiscal powers to control the content of newspaper articles. Two of the top Parisian bourgeois dailies, *Le Figaro* and *France-Soir*, have generally been critical of Socialist governments, and a third, *L'Humanité*, has frequently been acerbic in

TABLE 9.1 Important Parisian newspapers

Newspaper	Circulation in 1989 (rounded off)	Orientation
Le Figaro	428,700	Conservative
Le Parisien	405,200	Conservative (lower middle class)
Le Monde	381,500	Liberal
France-Soir	301,700	Conservative
L'Equipe	268,300	Sports
International Herald Tribune	193,300	English language
Libération	178,200	Leftist
Paris Turf/Sport	126,600	Racing sport
Les Echos	104,500	Economic and financial
La Croix–L'Evénement	104,300	Catholic
L'Humanité	95,400	Organ of Communist Party
Quotidien de Paris	80,000	Conservative
Quotidien du Médecin	62,000	Physicians
Tribune de l'Expansion	57,000	Economic and financial

SOURCES: *Quid 1993* (Paris: Laffont, 1992), p. 1138; and *Europa Yearbook 1993* (London: Europa Publications, 1993), p. 119.

its treatment of the domestic policies of both right- and left-wing governments. *Le Monde*, although often critical of selected positions of the government, has tended in most cases to endorse it on foreign policy and other crucial issues.[54]

Several important newspapers have ceased publication in the past few decades, including the Gaullist-oriented *La Nation* and, in 1988, the pro-Socialist *Le Matin*. Newspapers are beset by rising costs of newsprint (much of it imported) and rising wages of reporters and printers. The decline in the number of dailies in France has been significant: from 414 in 1892 to 203 in 1946 to 73 in 1991. The number has since stabilized, but circulation has continued to decrease.

The typical French newspapers—with such notable exceptions as *L'Humanité*, which has Communist Party backing (though that party has been considerably impoverished), and *Le Monde*, which has an international and elite sub-scribership—cannot depend any longer on newsstand sales or on support by a political party because the latter's resources are limited. The increasing concentration of ownership or control of newspapers, including *Le Figaro*, *France-Soir*, and numerous provincial dailies and magazines, in the hands of a group led by industrialist Robert Hersant caused the government in 1983 to introduce a bill forcing the Hersant group to divest itself of some of its papers.[55] The bill attempted to guarantee "pluralism" by providing that no group could own more than one daily newspaper or more than three periodicals dealing with political affairs. Although the opposition claimed that the bill was motivated by a desire to muzzle a generally antigovernment press, the government asserted that the bill was inspired by the recommendations of a report adopted several years earlier by the Economic and Social Council.[56]

In recent years the relationship between the concentration of newspaper ownership and univocal (especially conservative) political opinion has become increasingly unclear. In 1986, the center-leftist editors of the near-bankrupt *Progrès de Lyon* agreed to the purchase of their paper by Hersant, who promised not to interfere with the paper's editorial positions. In 1988, Franz-Olivier Giesbert, an editor of the leftist *Nouvel Observateur* (and a biographer of Mitterrand) was appointed editor-in-chief of the conservative *Figaro*. This was symptomatic of the gradual evolution of many newspapers—of the Right and the Left—toward more moderate and centrist orientations. One of the most recent examples of that evolution was the inauguration, early in 1994, of *Infomatin*, a daily paper modeled after *USA Today* and providing only bare-bones news reports and selling at half the price of ordinary dailies.

The electronic media have been much more sensitive politically. For many years, the radio and television networks were government monopolies in France, as in many other countries. But whereas in Germany they are regionalized, in France they were centralized; whereas in Britain the BBC is an autonomous corporation rarely subject to government interference, in France all broadcasting was until two decades ago controlled by the *Office pour la télévision et la radiodiffusion françaises* (ORTF), which was never free of intervention by the ruling authorities. Cabinet control over radio and television during the Fourth Republic did not materially infringe on the independence and diversity of these media because there were so many cabinet reshuffles and several political parties were in a position to exert influence over broadcasts. Although technically an autonomous agency, ORTF in the Fifth Republic was a mouthpiece of the Gaullist regime and the president in particular. TV and radio news broadcasts were highly selective and one-sided—except for the limited time made available to opposition candidates during election campaigns and the occasional TV and radio programs in which political differences were aired by means of a dialogue (e.g., *Aux armes égales*). News was frequently doctored by distortion or omission, and the government was almost always presented in a favorable light. In 1964, the role of the government was strengthened when ORTF was put under the control of an interministerial committee including the premier and assisted by an advisory committee composed mainly of Gaullists. During the May events of 1968, the failure to provide full and accurate information led to resentment by the public and the reporting staff of ORTF. Many of the latter struck and were dismissed from their jobs. Periodic attempts by Parliament (especially by the Senate) to provide a truer measure of independence for radio and television failed.

This is not to say the ORTF was monolithic; in fact, several "fiefdoms" tried to make their influence felt and to provide input in broadcasting: the Ministry of Posts and Telecommunications, which collects the annual subscribers' fees; the Foreign Ministry, whose views must be taken into account in the presentation of international news; the ENA; big business (which pays for advertising); and the Ministry of Culture. But in the opinion of some observers, this diversity did not lead to real independence; rather, it introduced internal blockages.

In 1972, a bill providing for the reorganization of ORTF was passed. The network was divided, with the television channels and radio networks granted separate budgets and their own authority over finances. The system was to be "advised" by a board composed of representatives of viewers and listeners, the press, and the state, the last element (appointed by the cabinet) constituting a majority and with the director under the close control of the government. Under Giscard, further reforms were undertaken, ostensibly to provide for more meaningful autonomy. In 1975, ORTF was replaced by a number of independent units, each with its own budget. These measures were intended to facilitate technical innovation and internetwork competition, but since the state continued to maintain a monopoly over broadcasting, the reforms did not result in the media's gaining genuine freedom to criticize the government.[57] Partly for this reason, several private "pirate" stations broadcast between 1977 and 1981. One of these, *Radio Riposte*, was set up by the Socialist party; in 1979, when that station's criticisms of the government became unbearable to him, Giscard had the Paris police raid the PS headquarters. In the case of other stations, the government resorted to jamming, arrests, and the confiscation of equipment.

When the Socialists assumed office, they replaced the directors of two television networks and other television officials who were thought to have been dedicated Giscardists. Since then, the staffs have been given greater autonomy in programming and have not been subjected to direct government interference in news coverage. Furthermore, the government authorized the establishment of private radio stations; these must function on a nonprofit basis, limit their commercials, and confine their broadcasts to an area within a 20-mile radius. (In 1990 more than 1,700 private radio stations were in existence.) In 1982, a High Authority for Audiovisual Communication was created that would guarantee the independence of broadcasting, the "respect for pluralism, the promotion of [different] languages," and the "right to reply" to government pronouncements.[58] In 1983, the government set up a fourth TV channel, to be financed by monthly viewer subscription fees.

The Chirac government repoliticized the electronic media when it replaced the High Authority with the *Commission nationale de la communication de les libertés* (CNCL). This body was to be an autonomous agency, but it soon became a "transmission belt" for government (i.e., Gaullist) preferences—for example, in the matter of deciding who would be awarded contracts for the purchase of two television channels that were to be privatized.[59] Upon regaining power, the Socialists (in 1989) replaced the CNCL with a new body, the *Conseil supérieur de l'audiovisuel* (CSA), which was to be an autonomous administrative body less obedient to governmental wishes and subject to control by the Council of State.[60]

In the past several years, there has been a progressive privatization of television broadcasting;[61] four of the six television channels were privatized.[62] In addition, regional cable television channels were gradually set up in several large cities. These innovations have led to a relentless commercialization of the media (and the "Americanization" of their programs).[63] Moreover, the competition between the various private television channels has led them to hire "superstar" anchorpersons at astronomic salaries.[64] At the same time, these developments have contributed to a more genuine pluralism of the media, a pluralism reflected in the growing popularity of programs of political satire[65] as well as in the growth of investigative reporting, which has done much to expose the questionable behavior of public officials.[66]

NOTES

1. A recent inquiry revealed that judges in the Paris region, for example, are harsher in their sentencing for theft and drug dealing than provincial judges, but more lenient than a number of smaller towns in homicide cases. See "Le Tour de France des sanctions pénales," *Le Point*, 5 February 1994, pp. 44–51.
2. For a description of the competences of these various tribunals, see Hubert Pinsseau, *L'Organisation judiciaire de la France*, Notes et Etudes documentaires, no. 4777 (Paris: Documentation Française, 1985), esp. pp. 45–46.
3. In 1963, 24 percent of the entrants to the ENM (then known as the *Centre national d'études judiciaires*) had fathers who were magistrates or members of other legal professions; 24 percent were descended from civil servants, and only 3.5 percent from the working class. Charles Laroche-Flavin, "Le Magistrat, la justice, et l'Etat," *Après-Demain* 122 (March 1970), 11. In a typical year, ENM admits 200 to 230 students.

4. The *notaire* is the typical "village lawyer" who in more traditional times used to be one of the chief liaisons between the often illiterate peasant and the legal authorities, and he was, therefore, together with parish priest *(curé)*, village teacher, and prefect, a part of the rural elite.

5. There were other types of legal professionals, e.g., the *avoué* (who was largely concerned with the preparation of legal briefs) and the *agréé* (who specialized in pleading before certain commercial tribunals), but these were abolished in 1972.

6. More specifically, the civil chambers include one for commercial and one for social security and labor conflicts.

7. Laurent Cohen-Tanugi, *Le Droit sans l'Etat: Sur la démocratie en France et en Amérique* (Paris: PUF, 1985), p. 53.

8. If the legality of the lower court decision is in question, the case is sent back. The full complement of 25 *Cour de cassation* judges meets only on rare occasions.

9. See William Safran, "Rights and Liberties under the Mitterrand Presidency: Socialist Innovations and Post-Socialist Revisions," *Contemporary French Civilization* 12:1 (Winter/Spring 1988), 1–35. The 1984 law also obliged the judge to inform the accused of his right to counsel of his choice (or to counsel supplied to him) and of the right of counsel to examine the dossier against the accused.

10. This reform brought French procedure in line with European Community norms.

11. In 1980, of over 686,000 individuals against whom preliminary panel investigations were started, fewer than 89,000 were sentenced to prison. See Ministry of Interior statistics, cited in *Après-Demain* 254–255 (May–June 1983), 28.

12. See Georges Dupuis and Marie-Josée Guédon, *Institutions administratives et droit administratif* (Paris: Colin, 1986), and Cohen-Tanugi, *Le Droit sans l'Etat*. Both books emphasize the influence of the statist philosophy on the French legal system and exaggerate the weakness of the citizen's legal remedies against the state. There are persistent complaints that examining judges tend to keep suspects in pretrial detention not because of the gravity of the infraction but because the suspect is prejudged to be a danger to public order. See Antoine Garapon, "L'Evolution du rôle du juge," *Cahiers français* 251 (May–June 1991), 75–76.

13. Jacques Robert, "De l'indépendance des juges," *Revue du droit public et de la science politique* 1 (1988), 3–38.

14. In 1992 the judicial establishment employed 56,000, a figure that includes state attorneys, judges, and court clerks *(greffiers)*. The last category (85 percent of whom are women) is particularly underpaid.

15. *New York Times*, 15 December 1971. See also Raoul Dargent, "La Crise judiciaire en France," *Le Monde*, 17 September 1969; and *Le Monde*, 13 April 1973.

16. In a poll of judges in 1990, 61 percent insisted that rich and poor are treated equally. "La Justice déboussolée," *Le Monde, Dossiers et Documents* 215 (November 1993), 1.

17. *Faut-il avoir confiance en la justice de son pays?* (Paris: Les Dossiers du Canard, April 1992), pp. 64–65.

18. A director of a large firm interviewed a few years ago provided examples of leftist judges who have been active in the *Syndicat de la magistrature* (which is said to be close to the CFDT) and who have shown a clear antibusiness bias in their decisions. See André Harris and Alain de Sédouy, *Les Patrons* (Paris: Seuil, 1977), pp. 169–195.

19. A budget bill passed in 1991 allocated 1 billion francs for public defenders for 1992 (an increase from 414 million francs in 1990) and 1.5 billion for 1993. *Faut-il avoir confiance*, p. 32.

20. In 1992 there were only 550 *juges d'instruction* in France; moreover, that country had only one lawyer per 2,000 people as compared to 1 per 500 in the United States.
21. *Faut-il avoir confiance*, p. 35.
22. "Du Code Napoléon au Code Mitterrand," *Le Monde*, 10 May 1989.
23. François Koch, "Dix Fois plus de conciliateurs," *Le Monde*, 10 March 1987.
24. There were 17 executions between 1956 and 1967, 1 between 1968 and 1971, and 5 between 1972 and 1981.
25. "L'Oeuvre législative de l'Assemblée Nationale," *Le Monde*, 22 December 1972. For a somewhat pessimistic discussion of penal-code reforms since the early 1970s, see Roger Errera, *Les Libertés à l'abandon*, 3rd ed. (Paris: Seuil, 1975).
26. See Jean Foyer, "Le Projet de loi 'sécurité-liberté' devant l'Assemblée Nationale," *La Nouvelle Revue des deux mondes*, November 1980, pp. 276-286. The government, in resorting to the "blocked-vote" procedure to get the bill passed, was seemingly inspired by an increase in crimes of violence and by a perception of a growing public sentiment in favor of a tough "law-and-order" approach.
27. For a catalogue of the reforms of the penal code under the Socialist government between 1981 and 1986, see Blandine Barret-Kriegel, *L'Etat de la démocratie: Rapport à François Mitterrand* (Paris: Documentation Française, 1986), pp. 54-62.
28. See Annie Kensey, "Le Temps compté," *Travaux et documents* 43 (March 1992). According to this source, the number of people sentenced to more than 10 years imprisonment increased by 83 percent between 1980 and 1991. For more detailed statistics, see Anne Chemin, "L'Inflation carcérale," *Le Monde*, 13-14 September 1992.
29. Commission des maires sur la sécurité (the Bonnemaison Commission), *Face à la délinquance: Prévention, répression, solidarité* (Paris: Documentation Française, 1982).
30. Safran, "Rights and Liberties," pp. 9-10.
31. Gilbert Bonnemaison, "Prévention, repression, et solidarité," *Après-Demain* 254-255 (May-June 1983), 6.
32. The preamble of the Fifth Republic Constitution (which is held to have operative validity) embodies the catalogue of rights of the Fourth Republic Constitution, which stipulated in *its* preamble that "anyone persecuted because of his activities in the cause of freedom has the right of asylum within the territories of the Republic."
33. See *Le Monde*, 20-21 June, 12 and 15-16 August 1993. See also Chap. 2, n. 34.
34. Abu Daoud, who had been a ringleader in the murder of Israeli athletes at the Munich Olympics in 1972.
35. George Habbash, a "retired" member of the Palestine Liberation Front, had been secretly flown to France for medical treatment in January 1992. After his presence was revealed by the media, he was briefly put under police surveillance but subsequently spirited out of the country. Although the ministers of foreign affairs and interior were politically responsible, their directors-general had to resign.
36. Paul Touvier had been a high militia official of the Pétain regime in Lyons and had been responsible for the killing of Jewish hostages. Condemned to death in absentia during the purges in 1945 for war crimes, he was hidden by the Catholic church but reappeared in 1967 and was pardoned by President Pompidou in 1971. Fearful that he would be prosecuted again, he hid in a Catholic convent but was rearrested in 1989 and indicted for crimes against humanity. His trial began in 1991, but a year later the appeals court, in attempting to quash the indictment, rendered a lengthy opinion that contained a virtual whitewash of the Vichy regime and of Marshal Pétain. In the wake of considerable public agitation, the *Cour de Cassation* (upon request of the government) restored the indictment and ordered a new trial. See J. D. Bredin,

"Affaire Touvier: L'Histoire et la justice malmenés," *Libération*, 23 April 1992; and Bertrand Poirot-Delpech, "Les Juges entre responsabilité et immunité," *Le Monde*, 10 June 1992.

37. This is illustrated by reluctance to indict the principals in the Urba affair, involving the financing of the Socialist party, and the long delays in the prosecution of high officials implicated in the blood transfusion scandal.

38. See Jean Claude Monet, "Police et inégalités sociales," *Regards sur l'actualité* 117 (January 1986), 3–18.

39. An additional force that deserves mention is the *police municipale*, which operates in small towns and is subject to a certain amount of local control. This force includes about 15,000 full-time and several thousand part-time constables and guards. See Georges Carrot, *Histoire de la police française* (Paris: Tallandier, 1992), which deals with changes in the structure of various police forces. For recent details about the different police forces and their responsibilities and budgets, see Jean-Loup Reverier, "La Police au scanner," *Le Point*, 30 April 1993, pp. 24–29.

40. *Le Monde*, 23 January 1973.

41. An exposition of antipolice attitudes ("racisme anti-flic") is found in Rémy Halbwax and Jean-Charles Reix, *La Police assassinée* (Paris: La Table Ronde, 1983). Another book suggests a counter-theme: that there are numerous policemen who have little use for the democratically elected authorities that control them. See Alain Hamon and Jean-Charles Marchand, *P . . . comme police* (Paris: Editions Alain Moreau, 1983). A middle position is taken by Bernard Deleplace, *Une Vie de flic* (Paris: Gallimard, 1987). Deleplace is the general secretary of the FASP.

42. Gun ownership was estimated (in 1981) at about 5 million. Permits for firearms are granted for five-year periods, after a thorough check of the applicant's record. See French Embassy, Press and Information Service, *News and Comments from France* (New York, 4 August 1983), pp. 2–3.

43. *Année politique, 1982*, pp. 45–46. In 1983, two police unions organized a massive demonstration in Paris against the Socialist government's alleged hostility to the police and indulgent attitude toward criminals. The demonstration, sparked by the death in action of two police officers, led to the resignation of the prefect of the Paris police and the dismissal of the national police director.

44. See "Une Police au service des citoyens," *Après-Demain* 292 (March 1987), especially the articles by Pierre Joxe and Jean-Michel Belorgey.

45. According to an IFOP poll of March 1993, 20 percent fear the police; a majority believe that the police consider themselves above the law, and 57 percent, that they misbehave. *Antenne 2*, 13 April 1993.

46. The influence of the *Fédération professionnelle indépendante de la police*, a pro–Le Pen organization, has grown particularly in the Paris region.

47. In 1965 a right-wing author, Jacques Laurent, was sentenced to prison by a criminal court for having written a book, *Mauriac sous de Gaulle* (Paris: Table Ronde, 1965), that was critical of the general. The publisher too was fined. Between 1965 and 1970, the law was applied "only" three or four times a year. See François Sarda, "Offenses aux chef d'état," *Le Monde*, 8–9 March 1970.

48. Frede Castberg, *Freedom of Speech in the West* (Oslo: Oslo University Press, 1960), p. 47.

49. According to a law of 1970, wiretaps (generally placed by security services or interministerial committees) can be used, with the premier's approval, only for reasons of national security. But the law was widely abused during the presidencies of

de Gaulle and Pompidou, when the Paris telephones of union leaders, journalists, and left-wing politicians were bugged. See *Nouvel Observateur*, 7 March 1973. In the late 1980s and early 1990s, there were frequent press reports alluding to illegal wiretapping by the Mitterrand presidency as well. See Hervé Gattegno, "L'Elysée, les gendarmes et le journaliste," *Nouvel Observateur*, 11-17 March 1993, pp. 46-48. In 1991, a special committee (the *Commission nationale de contrôle des interceptions de sécurité*) was created to investigate and monitor wiretapping.

50. *Le Monde*, 9-10 November 1980.
51. One of the scandals revolved around the allegation that Giscard had accepted diamonds from ex-Emperor Bokassa of the Central African Empire.
52. See the series of articles by Jacques Sauvageot, "La Presse et le changement," *Le Monde*, 30 and 31 July and 1 August 1981.
53. However, during the Gulf War, journals were asked by the Ministry of Defense to refrain from publishing information tending to endanger the security of military operations. This was paralleled by a directive asking TV commentators to behave similarly. Jean-Marie Charon, "Le Malaise des médias," *Regards sur l'actualité* 173 (August 1991), 16-27.
54. See Michel Legris, Le Monde *tel qu'il est* (Paris: Plon, 1976), for a sharp (and now rather dated) critique of that newspaper's excessively pro-establishment position.
55. See "Le Groupe Hersant: Dix-neuf quotidiens," *Le Monde*, 24 November 1983, and Yves Agnès, "Le Dossier piégé," *Le Monde*, 16 December 1983. According to the latter source, the majority of journalists (and their associations) were in favor of the bill.
56. The Vedel Commission, which prepared that report, had been set up at the behest of Giscard's premier, Raymond Barre.
57. In 1974, a few months after his election, Giscard announced liberalization measures for the networks. In the same month, the government dismissed the director-general of Europe No. 1 because in his broadcasts he had not been "obsequious" enough to the government. *Figaro*, 25 October 1974. Europe No. 1 is technically a "private" station in which the government has 37 percent of the shares.
58. *Année politique 1982*, pp. 115-116.
59. See Jean-Jack Queyranne, "Télévision: Heure de vérité," *Nouvelle Revue socialiste*, nouvelle série, 2 (July 1987), 60.
60. See Jacques Chevallier, "Les Instances de régulation de l'audiovisuel," *Regards sur l'actualité* 149 (March 1989), 39-55; on the CSA, see esp. 51ff.
61. For a detailed discussion of this process, see Douglas J. Daniels, "Publicité, Politics, and Public Service TV: Crisis at the Crossroads," *Contemporary French Civilization* 12:1 (Winter/Spring 1988), 36-63.
62. One of these, the 5th channel (*La Cinq*) went bankrupt in 1992, and the government refused to respond to the demands of the staff to take it over.
63. The fear of the growing American influence on the audiovisual media has led the French government to limit the importing of U.S.-produced films and to require a minimum "European" content in TV programming. See Dominique Wolton, "L'Impatience de l'Europe et les langueurs de la communication," *Le Débat* 71 (September-October 1992), 114-129.
64. In order to keep their audiences, the remaining public-television channels (e.g., *Antenne 2*) have been under pressure to hire anchorpersons with equally large salaries that have far exceeded the established ceilings for public employees, annoyed the ministers of finance, and raised questions of legality. See "La Reine Christine met le feu aux poudres," *Le Point*, 26 September 1988, pp. 32-34.

65. These include *La Bébète Show* and *Le Guignol*, in which public figures (including the president of the republic) are portrayed as animal puppets.

66. The media have sometimes been accused of abusing their freedom. Thus, former premier Bérégovoy (while in office) was made the object of repeated criticism for irregular financial dealings, a criticism that was said to have contribued to his suicide shortly after the Socialists' electoral defeat in 1993. See Alain Rollat, "La Machine infernale," *Le Monde*, 5 May 1993; and "Qui lynche qui?" *Le Canard Enchaîné*, 5 May 1993.

chapter 10

Political Changes and Public Policies

An oft-repeated theme among both American and French observers, in particular during the 1950s and 1960s, was that many institutional arrangements and behavior patterns of the French polity produced instability and policy deadlocks. To some, the conflicting ideological orientations of various French subcommunities made it difficult for practical compromises to occur;[1] to others, the excessive bureaucratization of public life and the "overinstitutionalization" of public relationships created a series of bottlenecks in the governmental machinery that impeded necessary reforms.[2]

The streamlining of institutional relationships that the installation of the Fifth Republic brought about helped to unblock the decision-making process and, if judged in terms of policy outputs, transformed the French political system into a relatively efficacious and responsive one. Policies that had been inaugurated during the Fourth Republic were elaborated and reinforced and others were initiated. This success has been particularly apparent in the production of public goods: comprehensive medical and unemployment coverage, retirement benefits, family income supplements, subsidies for university students, paid vacations, low-cost housing, a constantly modernizing mass transport system, and the protection of the interests of the small-scale farmers and businesspersons. In terms of idealized (socialist, egalitarian, or Catholic) expectations, many of these policies have been judged inadequate, yet if measured against U.S. policies, they may be considered successful. French policies, at least since the end of World War II, have reflected a convergence of the demands of sectors with mass memberships, powerful organizations, and electoral weight: labor, big business, schoolteachers, war veterans, small business, and family agriculture—although as the numbers of the latter three categories have decreased, so has the attention paid to them by policy makers.

As suggested in Chapter 5, French policy making does not correspond to the American model of pluralism, which sees conflicting demands as articulated mainly in the marketplace by private "countervailing powers," with the state acting as a registration agent; nor does it conform to what has been put up as a countermodel, that of "corporatism." Rather, it is the result of an interplay of private-market decisions, inputs by socioeconomic sectors, and autonomous governmental preferences—these last sometimes influenced by considerations of political partisanship and sometimes by the "rationality" of professional planners' cost-benefit criteria. The traditional ideology of Colbertism[3] has influenced the tendency of the public authorities to control a large part of the credit machinery; socialism has been reflected in minimum-wage, nationalization, and educational policies; Catholic social doctrine is at least in part embodied in the benefits accorded to large families; and the "expertocratic" orientation has revealed itself in the French approach to planning.

ECONOMIC POLICY FROM THE LIBERATION
TO THE GISCARD PRESIDENCY

French economic after the Liberation was concerned primarily with the following objectives: the reconstruction of a war-ravaged economy; the modernization of the railroads; the consolidation of farms and the mechanization of agriculture; the gradual replacement of small firms by larger and more competitive ones; the rationalization of industrial production; general economic growth; and the division of the economic pie in a more egalitarian fashion. By the early 1970s, many of these goals had been achieved: For two decades, the growth of the gross national product was truly impressive, averaging about 6 percent annually; the food supply was plentiful, the franc was relatively stable, unemployment was low, and the real income of workers had risen steadily.

In pursuing their policies, governments were helped by a growing consensus among political parties about the desirability of government intervention and about the need to maintain and build upon the welfare-state legislation enacted by the Popular Front government of 1936, which included statutory medical coverage, old-age insurance, and minimum wages. There was also considerable popular support for the maintenance and expansion of the public sector by means of the nationalization of industries. These policies culminated in the public or semipublic ownership of railroads, gas and electric companies, seaports and airfields, urban transport, civil aviation, mines, several banks and insurance companies, and oil prospecting and marketing. Some of the nationalizations had been ideologically motivated; during the Popular Front regime, munitions manufacturing had been nationalized because it was hoped, naively, that war would become less likely once the profit-oriented "merchants of death" were expropriated. During the period of tripartite rule by Socialists, Christian Democrats, and Communists (1944–1947), the left-oriented parties had applied pressure to bring the major sectors of production under public control. Some nationalization was externally conditioned, episodic, or punitive. After World War II, the Renault auto works were taken over by the government because the firm's private owners had collaborated with the Nazi regime; the railroads in Alsace were nationalized when that area reverted to France after World War I; and the railroads in central France were bought by the government because under private ownership they had become unprofitable. A number of industries were acquired by the government because of their monopolistic character, such as gas and electricity. Whatever its origin, the nationalized sector in France is one of the most important among industrial democracies, accounting for a large proportion of investment and employment.

CAPITALIST PLANNING

Many economic policies were pursued in the context of an overall national plan, the first of which was unfolded in 1946. In arriving at such a plan, the government had rejected the Soviet planning model, which was "imperative" (i.e., based on central government directives and depending on a totally nationalized economy). However, in accordance with their interventionist traditions and in the interest of accommodating left-wing demands for welfare statism and social justice, the French authorities had also rejected the pure free-market model. They compromised by devising an economic plan that is "indicative" or "voluntaristic" in that it tries to combine governmental fiscal intervention and official policy preferences with the decisions, commitments, and projections of the private sector.

Economic planning in France has been based on several assumptions and processes: (1) the notion of a total set of goals for society, (2) a rational and empirical approach to problem solving, (3) a process of information gathering, (4) a matching of information on available resources with a number of "options," (5) the supply of information about projected government policies to private firms to help them make their own plans, and (6) the belief that the self-interest of the private sector can be reconciled with a common interest promoted by the public authorities. On the basis of a complex system of stocktaking and forecasting, the government makes long-range decisions affecting employment, production, consumption, the allocation of resources, growth, social security, public-works projects, and the like. These decisions are not absolutely binding upon all private sectors; rather, they are guidelines, based on economic data, that enable the government to coordinate, or "concert," its own decisions with those of private firms, the agricultural sector, and the trade unions.

Planning has involved a variety of governmental, quasi-public, and private institutions (see Figure 10.1). At the apex is the General Commission on Planning (*Commissariat général du plan*—CGP), which is staffed by economists, statisticians, sociologists, and other specialists, and is normally attached to the premier's office. (An exception was the period between mid-1981 and the spring of 1983, when the CGP was under the authority of Michel Rocard, then minister of planning.) The government provides a catalogue of general objectives or aims

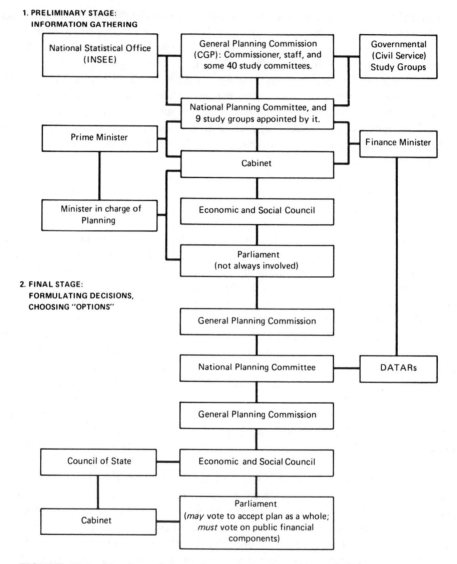

1. PRELIMINARY STAGE:
   INFORMATION GATHERING

FIGURE 10.1   The formulation of economic plans (simplified)

to the CGP, which in turn produces several alternative blueprints containing basic economic data, short- and long-range projections, and recommendations for resource allocation. These preliminary blueprints are then submitted to subnational and functional units for discussion and for additional inputs. In the course of time, many participating units or agencies have been set up; annually, more than 2,000 technocrats, local and regional politicians, industrialists, trade unionists, representatives of agricultural and other interests, and independent experts have provided to these agencies information supplementary to that already obtained by the CGP.

The oldest and most complex of these bodies of functional representation were the economic development (or "modernization") commissions. The number of these commission ranged from 25 to 30, depending on the plan. The commissions were functionally divided among several policy sectors; in addition, after France was divided into 22 economic-development regions, each of these regions was equipped with a Committee for Regional Economic Development (CODER). The CODERs, which existed from 1961 to 1974, consisted half of interest-group representatives, one-quarter of local and regional politicians, and one-quarter of experts and "personalities" chosen by the premier. The CODERs were concerned with geographically deconcentrating French industry, whereas the modernization commissions (comprising representatives of the government and the private sector) were concerned with aggregating the conflicting demands of business, labor, and the "public."

This consultative structure has been retained, except that, since 1982, new or, rather, relabeled, institutions have replaced some of the older ones. A National Planning Committee (*Commission nationale de planification*—CNP) now exists, whose large membership includes the presidents of regional councils; officials of trade unions; employers' and professional associations; spokespersons of public corporations and nationalized industries; representatives of cooperative and mutual-aid societies; delegates of the Economic and Social Council; and finally, independent persons chosen for their expertise in economics. The CNP in turn appoints nine working committees (*commissions de travail*), which work closely with (and obtain reports from) some 40 subcommittees or "working groups"; these groups, which have been set up by the CGP and are composed of civil servants and/or interest group officials, deal with such diverse matters as industrial strategy, agriculture, monetary policy, social policy, energy, housing, education and research, and nationalized industries. A further aggregative process takes place during the final phases of the planning enterprise, when the economic plan is discussed in the Economic and Social Council before it is approved by the cabinet.

The public authorities have been involved in the planning process at virtually every stage. During the first stage, the information-gathering one, there are ongoing consultations with the Finance Ministry, the nationally controlled credit institutions, and the National Statistical Office (*Institut national de la statistique et des études économiques*—INSEE). During the subsequent consultative phases, the Finance Ministry continues to be involved, while in addition there are the Delegations for Spatial Planning and Regional Action (DATARs), set up in 1963, which are composed of civil servants assigned by the premier's office to the various economic regions (see Chapter 8). The DATARs have worked closely with regional bodies—the (elected) regional councils and a variety of socioeconomic advisory committees. Technically, the DATARs are under the authority of the premier;[4] in practice, however, space planning, which embraces land-use and urban planning and environmental policies, has heavily involved the finance minister, who has had strong influence or control over a variety of funds for economic and social development, urban improvements, and industrial development projects.

The planning methods of the governmental authorities are (1) the traditional "Keynesian" methods of fiscal intervention: the manipulation of interest rates; the use of government contracts; the granting of tax concessions, export guarantees, and import licenses; the imposition of tariffs; and the determination of wage and price levels; (2) the allocation of investment loans and grants; and (3) the use of nationalized industries in order to influence the price structure of private industry. The question of whether the fiscal methods of the public authorities have been conservative or progressive is not easy to answer. On the one hand, some of the officials working for the CGP and the Finance Ministry have been suspicious of private-sector activities and have been striving to "direct" them on behalf of the state's purposes and on behalf of official notions of the public interest.[5] On the other hand, numerous higher civil servants have been inordinately receptive to the business viewpoint.

The initial fears of the business community that the economic plan might become a socialistic device were overcome with the appointment in 1946 of the first planner, Jean Monnet, himself a businessman, who convinced the business community that French-style planning would help save capitalism and stave off further nationalizations of industries.[6] Since then, most chief planners have been chosen either because of their affinity for capitalist management or their ideological acceptability to business-oriented presidents, premiers, or finance ministers.[7] The industrial outlook of these planning directors has accorded well with the composite objectives of each of France's development plans. The First Plan (1946-1952) concentrated on reconstruction and quantitative growth; the Second Plan (1953-1957), on the modernization of industrial and agricultural production; the Third Plan (1958-1961), on fiscal stability and the improvement of the balance of payments; the Fourth Plan (1962-1965), on regional development and the creation of a million new jobs; the Fifth Plan (1966-1970), on a rise in productivity; the Sixth Plan (1971-1975), on a strong annual growth rate, the raising of the level of foreign currency reserves, and an improved highway system. Subsequent plans—the Seventh (1976-1979), Eighth (1980-1983), Ninth (1984-1988), and Tenth (1989-1992)—were all concerned with problems that began with the oil crisis of the mid-1970s: unemployment, inflation, and the loss of world markets.

All these plans contained a number of social elements, such as vocational training and increased social benefits. But in view of the closeness of the planners to the business community, the trade unions have had doubts whether the social features of the plans would be actively promoted. To the trade unionist or the traditional socialist, whose ideal plan is more imperative and less voluntarist and is primarily an instrument of a redistributive policy, the capitalist nature of the plans is marked not only by its stress on productivity but also by the chronic underrepresentation of trade unions and farmers' organizations in the various discussion committees. In confronting the government and business sectors, unions have also been at a disadvantage because of their relative impecunious-ness, their lack of technical expertise and industrial information, and their con-flicting attitudes toward the plans. The CGT has been most consistently negative about the plans because they have been designed to preserve the capitalist struc-ture; the attitude of the CFDT has been reserved because in its view, the plan-ning process has not provided for genuine industrial democracy; the FO, however, has tended to be favorably inclined and has shown what its rivals have consid-ered an excessively "collaborationist" attitude.

For these reasons unions, and to a lesser extent small farmers and small business, have unsuccessfully presented counterplans, have periodically boycotted the planning bodies, or have tried to appeal to Parliament to "rectify" the plans. The parliamentary involvement in the plans has been selective and uneven. Tech-nically, parliamentary legitimation is required only for the "carrot-and-stick" as-pects of economic policy contained in the plans (i.e., those involving taxing and spending); nevertheless, most plans have been debated in Parliament. During periods of domination by Gaullists and Giscardists, the Assembly was reluctant to disapprove the plans. In any case, the plans were periodically subjected to de facto modifications or additions by acts of Parliament, by executive decrees, and by central accords between government and the "social partners" in response to outside pressures (as, for example, the Grenelle Agreement of 1968 between the government, industry, and labor, as a result of which workers' wages were raised by some 30 percent). Some of these measures were incorporated into sub-sequent plans.

The relevance and success of French economic plans have depended on a variety of factors: the realism and internal consistency of the plan; the thrust of supplementary policies (which might redound to the credit of the plan); exter-nal events (such as the disturbances of 1968, which upset the Fifth Plan almost completely); the degree of collaboration of the private sector; and the attitudes of presidents. De Gaulle had viewed planning as "an ardent obligation," not only because of his faith in the guiding hand of a wise state, but also because of his disdain for political parties and his distrust of Parliament as an economic deci-sion maker.

Since de Gaulle's departure, there has been an avalanche of publications dealing with the decline or death of planning. What is meant by decline is not the absence of a four- or five-year plan but the tendency of decision makers to follow its detailed recommendations less seriously (if at all), to be guided by political rather than "objective" criteria, and to produce policies that are increas-ingly short term rather than long term. It has been widely suggested that Pompidou and Giscard were hostile to planning because of their neoliberal ide-ologies or their personal connections with big business. For Giscard specifically, "advanced liberalism" meant that instead of *directing* the economy, the state would limit its role to *facilitating* economic concentration, respecting competi-tion, and helping to conquer foreign markets.[8] In conformity with this orienta-tion, price controls on consumer goods were gradually abolished, as were licenses for the import of raw materials; unions were encouraged to secure improvements in wages and fringe benefits by means of collective bargaining (*contrats de progrès*); private business was encouraged to consolidate and expand by means of tax concessions; and the public sector (e.g., electricity, railroads, and the medical care system) was urged to strive toward financial self-reliance by raising rates.

Giscard's neoliberalism had its limits: Electoral pressures, the threat of violence by workers, farmers, and shopkeepers, the growing insolvency of social security funds, and the scarcity of private investment capital forced Giscard and his premier, Barre, to raise the minimum wage, to grant selective subsidies to nationalized and private firms, and to impose surtaxes on excess profits. Tax concessions, low-interest loans, and outright subsidies were to be awarded in particular to certain "champion" (or "sunrise") industries: electronics, aeronautics, sophisticated office machinery, food processing, and transport and communications equipment. These industries were considered to have global marketing potential on the basis of such criteria as existing knowhow, available manpower and energy resources, and hard-currency earning capacity. To some extent, these policies had been embodied in the Seventh Plan (1976–1979), but neither reliance on a single multiannual plan nor confidence in market forces proved to be realistic with the onset of the worldwide economic crisis. What followed were the "Barre plans," a series of short-term emergency measures that included surtaxes on high incomes and excess profits that were not plowed back into investment, a freeze on high salaries, selective price controls, and supplementary government outlays for social security and unemployment payments and other welfare benefits—all of which increased the government's deficit and aggravated the pressure on the franc.

ECONOMIC POLICIES UNDER MITTERRAND

The Socialists assumed their governmental functions in 1981 full of optimism and committed to promoting truly "socialist" rather than "social-democratic" policies. They wished to make up for what they perceived to be the failure of their predecessors in redistribution. It was expected not only that planning would be revived but that its processes and nature would change. The plan would be made in a more democratic fashion, on the basis of more equitable participation of trade unions, local authorities, and Parliament; and the final plan would pay at least as much attention to social justice as to growth.[9]

In their first year in office, the Socialists raised minimum wages by 10 percent, imposed surtaxes on the rich, enlarged social security benefits, increased total social spending by 20 percent, raised corporate taxes, and extended the fifth week of paid vacations to all remaining workers who had not yet been entitled to it. In an effort to reduce unemployment, the new government raised interest rates (hoping that this measure would attract investment capital), made available low-interest loans to private business in the amount of about $700 million, reimbursed private firms for a large proportion of their expenditures for hiring and training young people, and created 50,000 additional public-service jobs. Further-more, the government pushed through a series of bills (the Auroux laws) that strengthened the union presence in factories and obliged employers to negoti-ate annually with factory union representatives about wages and workplace de-mocracy. Perhaps the most controversial policy was the nationalization of about a dozen industrial groups (including steel, electronics, chemical, textile, and aeronautics firms) and 36 banks.

The Politics of Austerity

By the fall of 1982, the government had begun to shift its economic-policy orientation in response to a deepening crisis. The number of unemployed was rapidly approaching 2 million (about 9 percent of the workforce) and threatened to surpass that figure, as nearly 20,000 firms were going bankrupt. The rate of inflation was still 14 percent, and deficits in both the national budget and the balance of trade were increasing at dangerous rates. To some extent, the eco-nomic situation was the consequence of chronic problems in the French economy and the failure of previous governments to deal with them. These problems in-cluded a loss of global markets for French goods, insufficiently aggressive sales techniques, and inadequate investments by private firms—which could in turn be attributed to the habit of reliance on the state to provide capital and to excessive private consumption. Between 1974 and 1981, nearly 700,000 indus-trial jobs had been lost, the number of unemployed had risen from 340,000 to about 1.7 million (from 2.3 percent to 7.5 percent), and prices had nearly doubled; at the same time, despite grandiose rhetoric about the "restructuring" of industries, and selective government allocations for this purpose, many anti-quated industries (such as steel) could neither be consolidated nor left to their own devices lest the ranks of the unemployed be expanded even further.

The Socialist government compounded the problem by a policy of national-ization that was soon perceived as hasty and ill advised. When they took office, some Socialist politicians thought that the firms intended for nationalization had a great deal of money and that once the government took them over, it would use the profits for public purposes. But the amount of money the government had to pay the expropriated shareholders, originally calculated at $6.7 billion (spread over 15 to 20 years), had to be increased to $10 billion as a consequence of a ruling by the Constitutional Council. More important, several newly nation-alized firms turned out to be bankrupt, or close to it,[10] and the government had to pay considerable sums to keep these firms afloat, sums that came in part from loans squeezed out of the nationalized banks, and in part from the Treasury.

The government policy shift entailed a reorientation from a policy of redis-tribution, job creation, and deficit financing to a policy of wage and price restraints, forced savings, limits on consumption, curbs on deficit spending, and the fight against inflation. The extension of public-sector jobs was to be limited; native workers were encouraged to retire early, and foreign workers were encouraged (by the payment of a lump sum) to return to their countries of origin. The implementation of the 35 hour workweek, which was to have occurred in 1982, was delayed until 1985; the franc was devalued; wage deductions for social security were permitted to go up, but not benefits; and when business and the unions failed to cooperate in a voluntary approach to price and wage restraint, a temporary freeze on wages and prices was imposed.

In March 1983, after these measures had proved inadequate, the government inaugurated a "policy of rigor." This policy embraced a reduction of credit allocations to industries and of loans to local communities, a levy of 1 percent on all incomes, and the imposition of a forced loan on upper-income groups; supplementary taxes on large fortunes and new surtaxes on alcohol and tobacco—to be used to replenish the social security funds; an increase in patient fees for hospital stays and increases in charges on gas, electricity, telephones, and train tickets; a limit in the amount of currency French citizens could take out of the country; and cuts in public-sector spending for roads and other projects.[11] The innovative and systematic nature of these measures was underscored by a reordering of the cabinet. The most leftist Socialist minister (Chevènement) was replaced, and a conservative Socialist, Jacques Delors, was put in charge of a "superministry" of Economics, Finance, and the Budget and given primary responsibility for implementing the new policies.

In 1984, Premier Mauroy presented a new set of proposals to the cabinet for a "restructuring" of French industry. Under these proposals, obsolescent plants would be gradually phased out, and more dynamic and internationally competitive industries would be encouraged by means of tax concessions and subsidies. These measures would apply to the "champion" industries mentioned earlier and would entail government investment of more than $500 million. To some critics, these proposals were hardly distinguishable from the policies of Giscard and Barre and constituted a virtual abandonment of the "social" commitments (if not the socialism) with which the government had come into office.[12] But that characterization was not entirely fair. Although the proposals would not correspond to the demand of Henri Krasucki, then president of the CGT, for "modernization without unemployment," they did contain a number of measures designed to render economic modernization policy more humane: the encouragement of early retirement; the granting of long leaves of absence to workers in steel, shipbuilding, and coal mines, so that they could be retrained, and the payment of two-thirds of their salaries by the government; and loans to artisans.

Some of these proposals had been embodied in the Ninth Plan, which was to go into effect in 1984. This plan had called for measures to foster industrial and educational modernization, the reduction of inequalities, the improvement of the regional equilibrium, the streamlining of the public services, and the expansion of scientific-industrial research.[13] In fact, 60 billion francs had been budgeted for these measures in 1984 alone, and it was envisaged that 350 billion francs would be spent for them by 1988. Yet one could argue that the multiannual plan had been more or less sidetracked and replaced by interim "adjustment" policies in which interest groups, political parties, and Parliament were heavily involved. On the one hand, the government wished to make policies in an orderly and objective fashion, and thus leaned heavily on the reports of "study commissions" (*comités de sages*, e.g., on labor relations, immigrant workers, and social security); on the other hand, it tried to shift responsibility for generating employment, increasing productivity, and controlling inflation to the "social partners," labor and management, which would, the government hoped, show some understanding for one another and solidarity with the government.[14]

At the same time, the government's interim plans had to be modified constantly because of pressures from business, farmers, and workers, and ultimately because of general political considerations. Thus in 1983–1984, in response to the violence of hog farmers (who sacked a subprefecture in Brittany) in protest against a decline in hog prices, the government imposed restrictions on imports of foreign meat. When the shipbuilding industry threatened to lay off too many workers, the government responded by refusing to grant an import license to a firm that had ordered several foreign-built ships and pressured that firm to order more expensive ships built in French shipyards (while undertaking to pay the price difference—in this instance, more than $100 million). When the management of a Peugeot automobile plant near Paris decided to dismiss 3,000 workers, provoking a strike and confrontations between strikers and scabs, the firm threatened to close down, but the government (which had earlier acknowledged that there were 10,000 excess jobs at the plant) persuaded the factory to stay open by providing an emergency subvention for paying the wages of redundant workers. The government had been pressured into this response by the attitudes of two trade unions, the CFDT and the CGT, which competed with each other in radical rhetoric and, if not appeased, had the potential of mobilizing large numbers of voters against the government in future elections.

The Chirac Government and the Politics of Neoliberalism

What had been a matter of pragmatic adaptation for the Socialists had become a matter of ideology for Chirac. As a relatively new convert to the principles of the free market, he promised to limit the amount of government interference in the economy by lowering taxes, reining in public spending, abolishing controls on prices, rents, and currency transactions, and denationalizing selected industries. Laws were enacted to privatize 13 public industrial groups, to permit employers to lay off redundant workers, and to allow firms to set up variable (and flexible) work schedules for their employees. Surtaxes on great wealth were annulled, value-added taxes on certain durable goods (e.g., cars) were lowered, income and corporate taxes were reduced, and tax allowances were provided for the start of new businesses and the (job-creating) expansion of old businesses. Furthermore, a bill was passed to reduce the social security contributions by firms that undertook to employ and train young people.

Yet none of these measures constituted a dramatic departure from the policies to which the outgoing Socialist government had gradually become converted.

Moreover, the Chirac government embraced policies that were a far cry from the supply-side economics associated with the Ronald Reagan presidency in the United States. Thus, the existing system of family income supplements was retained, subsidies to farmers were increased, and a significant sum of money was allocated to promote the integration of "repatriates" into the French economy. Yet despite his embrace of the private market and his disdain for state economic planning, Chirac could not bring himself to abolish the planning machinery.

The Governments of Rocard, Cresson, and Bérégovoy: Prospects and Constraints

The installation of a new government under Socialist Rocard in 1988 was greeted with optimism by those elements (the industrial workers, the poor, and the unemployed) that had felt neglected under Chirac. However, by the end of 1989 there had been no drastic departures from preceding policies because fiscal realities and external influences (e.g., the world market and the European Community) had limited Premier Rocard's options and because the fact that his party had only minority representation in the Assembly had limited his political power. Rocard's policies were to be based not on grand designs but on a series of dialogues—between socialists and nonsocialists, the state and the local authorities, the "political class" and the citizens, and the employers and workers. His policies would reflect the needs of "everyday democracy": practical and relatively modest steps to improve education, housing, and the environment, and—consistent with the imperative of growth and productivity—measures to foster greater social justice. The budget for 1990 contained a number of traditionally "socialist" features: a surtax on high incomes, a reduction of taxes on rents, the creation of several thousand new civil-service posts, and supplementary budgetary allocations to support the long-term unemployed. However, the budget did not call for a renationalization of privatized industries.[15]

Both the content and the methods of Rocard's policies were in some measure reflected in the Tenth Plan (1989–1992). This "medium-term program of action," which was oriented heavily toward the modernization of French industry, confined the role of the state to taxation and selected subsidies (e.g., for retraining, research, and education), the improvement of infrastructures (such as the railroads), and the enforcement of rules of competition.[16] The plan could be considered more a series of intellectual exercises than a "socialist" program of action, because both economic growth and wage increases were expected to be the consequence not of government action but of collective negotiations (*pactes de croissance*) between business and (weakened) trade unions, negotiations in which both sides promise to behave responsibly (i.e., postpone immediate gratification). The trade unions, middle-level public-service workers, the Communists, and many of the more traditional Socialist politicians (the latter occasionally encouraged by Mitterrand) wanted a more activist and a more clearly redistributive policy, but they had little power and few realistic alternatives.

This applied equally to the governments that succeeded Rocard. The priorities of Edith Cresson were to make French industry more competitive while at the same time safeguarding and expanding the achievements of the welfare state. The first priority, embraced under pressure of competition generated by the European Community, was incompatible with the second priority, formulated in order to recapture the support of workers and other traditional supporters of the PS who had been alienated by Rocard's "centrist" moderation. One of the concrete measures enacted in the spring of 1992 was the *revenu minimum d'insertion*, a minimum total income (which had been introduced earlier on an experimental basis). Another measure was a subsidy to small business for the training of apprentices, destined primarily for small business. Under Pierre Bérégovoy, Cresson's successor, there were no major departures from that policy, except for an emphasis on protecting the stability of the franc. Confronted with a series of scandals, charges of government corruption, increased urban violence, and clear indications of a continuing loss of support for the PS (signaled by the party's steep losses in the regional elections of March 1992 and polls predicting defeat in the forthcoming Assembly elections), Bérégovoy had little time to develop new economic policy approaches.

The Balladur Government:
Redressement and *Rigueur*

When he assumed office, Premier Balladur was faced with several major challenges: unemployment, nearly empty social-security funds, a continuing flight of industries, and the pressures of competition generated by the European Community—it became the *European Union* in November 1993—and the negotiations under GATT, which required a reduction of subsidies to farmers. Balladur's program of recovery (*redressement*), which he presented to Parliament soon after assuming the premiership, was in essence a hybrid of the policies of Chirac's cohabitation government and the continuation of existing "social" measures. (It was also reminiscent of Chaban-Delmas's "new society" program of more than 20 years earlier.) Measures were introduced to provide for a reduction of social security charges on small businesses; funds were allocated for retraining; limited attempts were made to bail out farmers (and reduce their opposition to the GATT talks); greater cost-sharing for hospital care was mandated, accompanied by a reduction in social security benefits; and laws were enacted to increase taxes on tobacco, alcohol, and gasoline. A major policy component related to privatization; and bills were passed to denationalize 21 large companies, embracing aerospace, maritime transport, electronics, automobiles (Renault), insurance, and banks. Some of these (including Crédit Lyonnais) had been offered for privatization in 1986–1988 but had not been sold before the Socialists recaptured control of the government. The privatization policy not only was in accord with the government's conservative ideology but it also promised to bring in over $7 billion in 1993 alone and help to reduce the budget deficit, estimated at $64 billion that year.[17]

There was a "stimulus" element in Balladur's policy as well: a program to spend $2.5 billion on construction and environment projects, intended mainly to create jobs for youth.[18] Some of the reform proposals, such as the reduction of the workweek to 32 hours, were met with skepticism on the part of employers; others, such as the hiring of young people at 80 percent of the minimum wage, were met with fierce opposition by the trade unions.[19] Still other reforms were symbolic, including a 10 percent cut in the salaries of ministers (who earned about $100,000 a year) and a ban on ministers' official use of luxury cars. Although pressed by Gaullist hard-liners to reduce taxes on business, Balladur had to listen to more "socially oriented" Gaullists (like Séguin) and Giscardists (like Veil) to preserve the achievements of the welfare state.

Balladur's popularity, based on his image as a pragmatic moderate, would serve him in good stead as he attempted to balance these conflicting aims. Some of these aims were envisaged by the Eleventh Plan (1993–1997), which stressed the encouragement of competitive industries, contracts with regions, and the retraining of redundant labor. The various policies (subsumed under a "five-year recovery plan") would have to be adjusted in an ad hoc fashion to the global pressures and the evolving policies of the European Union.

EDUCATION, RESEARCH, AND CULTURE

As was pointed out in Chapter 2, the reforms of education began more than two decades ago in the face of popular demands and the changing labor market. In 1981 the pace of reform had quickened: The number of nursery schools was enlarged; many new teaching positions were been created, especially for science and mathematics courses in the middle schools (*collèges*); class sizes were reduced; and the salaries of lycée and university professors were raised substantially. These reforms must be attributed in part to the fact that a third of the Socialist deputies elected in 1981, and a large proportion of the politicians in the executive branch, were educators; but many of the reform proposals that Parliament embraced originated with several study commissions dealing with education that were set up at the behest of the Socialist government: The Bernard Schwartz Report advocated an expansion of vocational education; the Laurent Schwartz Report recommended greater attention to scientific studies; the Peretti Report pointed to the need for an improvement in teacher training; the Soubré Report proposed more meaningful decentralization of school administration and curriculum planning; and the Legrand Report suggested that admission to, and tracking within, the *collèges* be made more democratic and that "tutorials" be provided for students having difficulties.

In addition, the minister of education, Alain Savary, made his own proposals, some of which provoked unexpected resistance. In mid-1983, he proposed that the academic year for universities be extended and that the professors' teaching load be raised. Another controversial matter was the place of parochial schools in the French educational system. When the Socialists came to power, they signaled their intention (largely as a result of pressure from the more dogmatic officials of the FEN) virtually to integrate the private, largely Catholic, schools[20] into the public system by tightening government controls over the use of public funds, making public financial support received by them subject to more stringent curriculum controls by the state, and granting the private-school teachers a more official status.[21] This issue has been difficult to resolve, as it has involved a clash of two conflicting but strongly held values: that of uniform national education, and that of freedom of choice. Although only one-fifth of French pupils are enrolled in private schools, recent polls have indicated that more than two-thirds of the French population favored the retention of the dual school system. In any case, public opposition was such that in 1984 the government withdrew this proposal (which had already been passed by the Assembly).

The controversy over the relationship between public and private schools was renewed in the fall of 1993, when the Balladur government introduced legislation to reform the Falloux laws of 1850. Under these laws, local authorities were permitted to subsidize up to 10 percent of the cost of maintaining the physical plant of private secondary, but not primary, schools. However, since many of these schools were in such precarious physical condition that they proved unsafe and the local communities (which under decentralization were given the responsibility to maintain school buildings) were unable to solve this problem, the government was forced to step in. A bill introduced in the Assembly by a Gaullist deputy and subsequently incorporated in a government bill provided that parts of the budgetary grants to departments and localities could be allocated to private elementary as well as secondary schools. Government support of private schools was not new; since the Debré Law of 1959 (see Chapter 2) subsidies had been gradually extended, so that by 1992 they covered private schoolteachers and their training; moreover, the total proportion of the proposed allocation was not expected to be significant.[22] But to the defenders of public secular education, the legislation reflected bad timing, especially in view of the budgetary stringencies that public schools were enduring and the periodic challenges to secular education posed by Muslim fundamentalists.[23] The FEN (still representing 100,000 members) and the SNES (62,000), supported by Socialist opposition politicians (some of whom had children enrolled in private schools), protested energetically;[24] as a result, the bill was dropped, to be replaced by the promise of a sustained "dialogue" between the government and the interested parties—teachers' unions, associations of parents, and local authorities.[25]

Related to both economic and educational policy was the Socialist government's approach to science and technology. Prompted in part by the ambitions of Chevènement, the minister of science and technology, the government committed itself to large increases in public funding for basic research.[26] Several hundred million dollars would be spent annually for selected research projects, among them robotics, electronics, biotechnology, and energy conservation. The aim of these projects, which constituted a revival of efforts initiated by de Gaulle, was to make France the third global science center (after the United States and Japan). The global orientations of Socialist research-and-development policy were moderated by several interesting government proposals. One was to "democratize" research by giving labor a greater role in research councils; another was to "regionalize" research by dispersing research activities in a kind of pork-barrel fashion; and the third (which occasioned some resistance) was to have French scientists use French, not English, in writing up the results of their government-supported research. The emphasis on regionalization and globalization has not been regarded as addressing the problems of the majority of university students, namely, overcrowded lecture halls, underequipped laboratories, inadequate financial support, and insufficient job opportunities for graduates.

Since the mid-1980s there have been few policy departures in the area of science policy, except that governments have attempted, with limited success, to encourage universities to make research contracts with private industries and with foreign institutions. An interesting symptom of the increasingly global orientation of French science (and of culture in general) was the governmental acquiescence in the decision of the prestigious Pasteur Institute in the spring of 1989 to publish its proceedings on biological research henceforth in English instead of French. Such acquiescence is not likely to be reversed despite the intention of the government to introduce a bill providing for the exclusive use of French by civil servants and others representing France in international forums.

French governments have long taken an interest not only in enhancing the prestige of the French language and guarding its purity but also in promoting the arts, music, theater, and literature. Since the time of the monarchs, most French citizens have accepted it as entirely proper that governments have a set of cultural policies. As we have seen, under de Gaulle, arts centers were set up in various cities, centers in which films and concerts were to be presented. Although the working class did not take much advantage of these facilities, the Socialists continued their efforts at subsidizing theaters and the cinema; in fact, subsidies to the film industry alone increased by 600 percent from 1981 to 1983. In deference to France's economic problems, the 1984 budget for culture and the arts represented an increase of only 15 percent over the previous year, but it still amounted to nearly $1 billion. By the end of 1992, the budget for the arts had more than doubled, and the amount allocated to the Ministry of Culture for 1993 was $2.8 billion, or 1 percent of the total state budget.[27] This money has been used to subsidize theaters, opera, museums, art education, libraries, the maintenance of historic monuments, and films.

For many years, French culture was xenophobic, and its purveyors (artists, writers, and professors, who were predominantly leftist) tended to complain about American cultural imperialism. Shortly after his appointment in 1981 as Mitterrand's minister of culture, such a complaint emanated from Jack Lang, who tried to put French art and literature on the world map and to prevent them from being "polluted" by un-French and antisocialist influences. Since then, the French establishment view of culture has become more open (even under Lang, who was reappointed to his old post in 1988), for, paradoxically, just as the Left was gaining ground politically, there was a simultaneous tendency on the part of many intellectuals to question Marxist assumptions about economics, politics, and culture.

An important innovation in cultural policy related to the legitimation of the claims of France's ethnic minorities. Between 1981 and 1986 the government not only legalized the teaching of Breton, Basque, and other "peripheral" languages in elementary and secondary schools but also allocated money for the training of teachers of these languages. Two landmark government reports[28] recommended a more comprehensive "decentralization" of cultural policy, under which ethnically oriented museums, social studies, theater, and literature would be actively promoted.

Under the Chirac government, and to a lesser extent under the succeeding Rocard government, French cultural policy was pulled in several directions: On the one hand, there was a lessening of interest in the culture of minorities; on the other hand, a kind of cultural pluralism was to emerge as culture was to be increasingly privatized, the funding of a number of cultural institutions (e.g., the National Library and the *Comédie Française*) was to be reduced, and private corporations and individuals were encouraged to support libraries and museums and to "sponsor" musical, theatrical, and athletic events. At the same time, it was expected that French culture would become increasingly Europeanized as a result of developments in European integration[29] and "Americanized" as a result of the success of U.S. enterprises in appealing to the tastes of the French public.[30] But there were limits; indeed, the protection of the French cultural patrimony was an issue that went beyond the confines of party ideology. One of the issues that held up the GATT negotiations in 1993 was the insistence of the Balladur government (which in this instance was supported by Mitterrand) that the import of American films be restricted and continue to be subjected to heavy tariffs.

ASPECTS OF FOREIGN POLICY

The role of international diplomacy in France's political development may be adduced from the list of foreign policy misadventures that led to the change of regimes. The Napoleonic defeat in the war with Prussia in 1870 was instrumental in the collapse of the Second Empire; the French defeat in 1940 resulted in the Vichy regime; the "victory" of France on the side of the Allies in 1945 permitted that country to restore its parliamentary republic; and the humiliation of France in Southeast Asia in 1954, at Suez in 1956, and in Algeria in the late 1950s undermined the credibility of the Fourth Republic and led to the establishment of the Fifth Republic.

The affective relationship of the citizen to the regime has been heavily influenced by France's position in the international system, its domestic self-image having depended on the image it could project to the world. To the extent that average French citizens view the *ancien régime* in a favorable light, they do so mainly because under the Bourbon kings, and notably under Louis XIV, France had become one of the foremost nation-states; French culture had been imitated in foreign lands; and the French language had become the lingua franca of international diplomacy. It was also during the *ancien régime* that France began to lay the foundations for a policy that, by the beginning of the twentieth century, was to make it the second largest colonial empire in the world.

During the nineteenth century, France's foreign policy was concerned primarily with retaining its role as one the most important diplomatic powers in Europe. From 1815 to 1914, France pursued, often together with Britain, a policy of alliances to keep the Germans, the Austrians, the Russians, and the Ottoman Turks from gaining undue strength and upsetting the European balance. This Eurocentric foreign policy was frustrated by the rise of Germany, which undermined the dominance of France in Europe: France could not match Germany's rapid industrialization and population increase, and consequently could put up no effective resistance in the Franco-Prussian War. France defeated Germany in World War I (and regained the province of Alsace, which it had lost to Germany in 1870) but only with the help of its allies. France then attempted, by means of the Treaty of Versailles and the Little Entente, to keep Germany in check, but the attempt ended in failure.

The collapse of the Little Entente and Locarno Treaty systems and the rise of Hitler proved that France had lost its capacity to preserve the European status quo. Defeat by Germany in 1940 confirmed France's military weakness, which the Gaullists were later to attribute to the weakness of parliamentarism. Similarly, France's liberation by the Americans in 1944 underscored its renewed dependence on the United States. After World War II, Europe as a whole had become a political and military vacuum, and the "European system" had been effectively replaced by a bipolar balance in which the two main actors, the United States and the Soviet Union, were extra-European, continental giants. France was permitted the appearance of great-power status by winning a permanent seat on the United Nations Security Council, securing an occupation zone in Germany, and regaining control over its colonies. But such prestige proved ephemeral because the United Nations was immobilized, the occupation of Germany ended, and France, like Britain and the Low Countries, was unable to retain its colonies.

In the mid-1950s, France began the slow process of decolonization. Under the leadership of Pierre Mendès-France, it granted independence to Morocco and Tunisia and at the same time disengaged itself from Indochina. Algeria was a different matter because about 1.5 million settlers in that territory regarded themselves as fully French and wished to retain a permanent political tie with the mainland. These settlers and the French military were embroiled in a protracted war against the indigenous Algerian population, and this conflict was the proximate cause of the collapse of the Fourth Republic in 1958.

When de Gaulle returned to power as first president of the Fifth Republic, he set out to achieve two main goals: the solution of the Algerian problem and the restoration of France to a position of importance in the international system. Under the Evian Accords of 1962, Algeria was granted independence. As for its sub-Saharan colonies, France in 1958 asked them to elect one of several options: to remain dependencies of France, to become provinces (or overseas departments), to acquire membership in a "French Community" (somewhat analogous to the British Commonwealth), or to become completely independent. Although virtually all ultimately chose independence (and the French Community therefore never developed in a meaningful sense), France's former African colonies retain a degree of economic dependence on their former protector.

The problem of enhancing France's global role was a more complex one. At the end of World War II, a condition of inequality existed between France and the other two major Western powers, a condition that de Gaulle felt the Americans and the British wished to perpetuate. During the Fourth Republic, France had been content with its role as client state of the United States; the need for aid under the Marshall Plan and military weakness in the face of potential Soviet aggression made France a willing junior partner in the North Atlantic alliance inaugurated in 1949. Moreover, France's recognition of its economic weakness made it amenable to European integration.

By 1958, France was well on the way to economic recovery and had made a start toward the development of a nuclear weapons system. It is possible that the Atlantic collaborative spirit might have been maintained if de Gaulle had felt that his country's national ego had been accommodated by changes in the structure of NATO—specifically, the establishment of a military leadership triumvirate consisting of the United States, Britain, and France. But the United States rejected that idea because it was not willing to slight a revived West Germany.

Because the Atlantic alliance frustrated French aspirations of prestige, de Gaulle increasingly pursued a policy of independence from the two blocs. In 1966, he withdrew French military forces from the integrated command of NATO and expelled the European NATO headquarters from French soil. At the same time, he sought rapprochement with Communist regimes, in particular the Soviet Union (while simultaneously warning his compatriots of the danger of communism within France). In a further attempt to free France, and Europe, from American domination, he twice vetoed the British application for membership in the Common Market because he considered Britain a potential American "Trojan horse" in Europe and feared that Anglo-American influences would undermine a traditional French linguistic hegemony. De Gaulle's visits to Latin America, Romania, and Canada (where, to the dismay of many Canadians, he proclaimed the slogan "Long Live Free Quebec") must have been inspired by pan-Gallic pretensions to capitalize on a common Latin heritage.

De Gaulle was convinced that a nation's diplomatic independence was predicated on its ability to defend itself. He was not satisfied by the fact that the nuclear umbrella over the NATO countries was controlled solely by the United States, not only because there was no assurance that nuclear weapons would be used to protect primarily European interests but also because there was imperfect consultation on a joint Western policy. He therefore expended much effort on building France's own nuclear deterrent. France's *force de frappe* was frequently criticized, by both Americans and Frenchmen, as an expensive toy that cut too deeply into the domestic budget while providing neither adequate defense nor significant spillover for nonmilitary technology. The nuclear deterrent might bring France prestige as a member of the then more exclusive nuclear club; and it might even be usable as a last-ditch weapon for self-defense in case a neighboring power (Germany?) should think of attacking France; but it was doubtful whether French stockpiles or delivery systems, even after considerable expansion by de Gaulle's successors, would be sufficient for inflicting unacceptable damage on the Soviet Union.

While the likelihood of a new world war was receding, de Gaulle pursued a strictly "national" foreign policy. This policy was reflected in France's refusal to sign the test ban and nonproliferation agreements and (until 1981) the European Human Rights Convention. The policy expressed itself also in a pronounced hostility to the United Nations and in a reluctance to foster the evolution of the European Community toward greater supranationality.

Despite de Gaulle's abhorrence of nonpragmatic, purely ideological considerations in the conduct of foreign policy, his actual foreign policy approach was subject to intrusions of ideologism (and even irrationalism) that cannot be clearly related to the promotion of national interest. Thus, in the late 1960s de Gaulle demonstrated a rather surprising friendship for nondemocratic regimes. He declined to endorse the Council of Europe's denunciation of Greece's military dictatorship, refused to join a United Nations condemnation of South Africa's apartheid policy, and advocated the membership of then-fascist Spain in the Common Market.

Four great achievements in foreign policy have been ascribed to de Gaulle or Gaullism: the liberation and economic revival of France; decolonization; a reconciliation with Germany; and the attempt to find an alternative to the bipolar conflict and to moderate it by the creation of a "third force." But it can be argued that these were not achievements of Gaullism at all or, at best, phantom achievements; that France was liberated by the Anglo-Americans rather than by its own efforts; and that the economic rehabilitation of France, for which the foundations were laid in the Fourth Republic, was made possible by American aid. Decolonization was begun in the Fourth Republic and was pursued by de Gaulle because he had little choice: Continued involvement in Algeria proved an unbearable economic and psychological strain on the French people. Reconciliation with Germany, too, was begun when France committed itself to the Schuman Plan and signed the Treaty of Rome that set up the Common Market; the Franco-German Treaty of Friendship of 1963, which formally ratified this reconciliation, was in a sense made necessary by de Gaulle's exclusion of Britain from the Common Market.

De Gaulle's reminder that Europe consisted of separate nations and national interests that could not be easily submerged into an Atlantic civilization was realistic, but his evocation of a Europe "from the Atlantic to the Urals"—embracing Western and Eastern European countries—ignored the postwar satellization of Eastern Europe (whose partial reversal in our own day could not have been predicted). The attempt to find an alternative to the bipolar conflict and to create an atmosphere of détente in Europe was a worthy one, but it is doubtful that the attempt succeeded, if at all, by means of French efforts. It is ironic that to the extent that there was an East-West rapprochement in Europe, it was brought about not by French efforts but by Germany's *Ostpolitik* in the late 1960s on the one hand, and Soviet-American bilateral efforts and the domestic needs of the Soviet Union on the other; that the problems in U.S.-Canadian relations have been a consequence not of Gaullist policy but of disagreements over trade and the control of scarce natural resources; that the war in Vietnam, against which de Gaulle had railed so vehemently, was ended not through French diplomacy but by a concatenation of domestic developments in the United States; that the loss of American power in the United Nations was occasioned not by French efforts at building a "third force" but by the skillful use of the oil weapon by Middle Eastern countries of which France, too, had been a victim; and that the Middle East crisis was, by turns, encouraged and "controlled" by the two super-powers, despite the long-held French illusion that the crisis would be resolved by a four-party agreement in which France would have a prominent role. Yet in spite of doubts regarding the long-range significance of de Gaulle's foreign policy, there is no question that he restored the pride of the French and left an imprint on the world scene by dint of his personality.

What is left of Gaullism in contemporary French foreign policy? To the extent that Gaullist foreign policy was based on the position of the United States as a *bête noire*, it has been undermined by a number of developments: the receding memory of the McCarthyism of the 1950s; the end of the war in Vietnam, an event that showed the United States as a less than omnipotent and therefore less threatening giant; the weakness of the dollar and the vulnerability of the U.S. economy to oil embargoes by Middle East countries and trade pressures by Japan, which put in question old assumptions about American economic imperialism. Furthermore, the rapid modernization of French society and economy have had the effect of "Americanizing" many aspects of French social life and culture.

Nevertheless, the essentials of de Gaulle's foreign policies were continued by Pompidou and Giscard, except that they were less stridently anti-American, more actively interested in promoting intra-European cooperation, more acutely aware of France's limited power, and more responsive to global economic pressures than de Gaulle had been.

It is doubtful whether French citizens expected dramatic departures in foreign policy with the election of Mitterrand. Some commentators have argued that one could detect distinctly "socialist" foreign policy aims, which included the promotion of peace and disarmament, support for international organizations, a more circumspect approach to arms sales, expanded economic aid to poor Third World countries, and a refusal to join a military bloc led by any superpower.[31] The policies thus far pursued under the Socialists and under both cohabitation governments have in part corresponded to these aims; but, more important, they have reflected a degree of continuity and a readiness to adapt to current realities.

The Gaullist features that were retained included the promotion of *francophonie* (the spread of the French language by means of a network of French schools and cultural activities abroad), the refusal to rejoin the NATO integrated command, and the maintenance of a national nuclear strike force (as well as the intermittent testing of nuclear weapons). At the same time, there was a more vocal condemnation of Soviet actions in Afghanistan and Poland, and of the Soviet deployment of SS-20 missiles in Eastern Europe; a greater sympathy for a strong American military presence and, more specifically, for the deployment of Pershing missiles in Western Europe; and a greater interest in selective Atlantic military collaboration. There were clear signs of a rapprochement between France and the United States, although this was dampened by occasional controversies over economic issues—for example, French resentment of American opposition to Western European sales of pipeline equipment to the Soviet Union, American monetary policy (including high interest rates of the dollar) and the occasional articulation of anti-American sentiments by intellectuals and cabinet officials.[32]

With respect to the Middle East, the substantive elements of French policy have remained more or less the same: the continuation of Israel's existence but in the context of a recognition of the legitimacy of the PLO's claims to a Palestinian state on the West Bank of the Jordan river. At the same time, France has been playing a less active role in the Arab-Israeli conflict; this change has been accompanied by the cessation of criticism of the Camp David agreements, a less acerbic and less moralizing critique of Israel (at least until the invasion of Lebanon by that country), and several official visits by Mitterrand to Israel.

It has been said that intellectuals have played a significant role in the shaping of French foreign policy.[33] To the extent that that has been the case, this circumstance was once an obstacle to good Franco-American relations, but in recent years relations have been better because of the gradual displacement of the traditional humanistic (and nationally oriented) elite by a more technocratic and often English-speaking elite and the decline of Marxism and the banalization of Gaullism, two important anti-American ideologies.

However, the changes in French foreign policy have had less to do with ideology than with evolving realities. The greater sympathy to the United States and the Atlantic alliance could be attributed to a variety of factors: discomfort over a growing German neutralism, the fact that the old fear of American economic domination has been partly displaced by a concern over Japanese inroads into European markets, and a diminished concern about the critical reaction of the now greatly weakened French Communist Party. Similarly, the fact that French policy in the Middle East became less obsequiously pro-Arab than before was not merely a matter of sentiment: Mitterrand's personal sympathies for Israel were balanced by the continued anti-Israel attitudes of officials in the Foreign Ministry and of a significant number of ideologues on the left fringes of the Socialist party. Rather, the change had to do with the oil glut, the reduced power of OPEC, a growing perception of the Jewish community in France as an electoral factor,[34] and finally, French manpower losses in Lebanon, a country to which France had sent a peacekeeping force in 1982, and the transformation of that country into a virtual protectorate of Syria.

In regard to Third World countries, the Giscardian idea of establishing a "trialogue" among OPEC countries, poor African states, and France, in which the last would play a dominant role, was given up by the Socialists as a delusion. Instead, France's relationships were determined by treaty commitments—as in the case of its continued, though reluctant, military intervention in Chad—and by hard-nosed economic considerations: Opposition in principle notwithstanding, France has continued to sell arms and military technology to a number of dictatorial and unstable Third World regimes.

The response of France to the collapse of the Communist system in Eastern Europe and of the Soviet Union itself has been ambiguous. On the one hand, that collapse has vindicated de Gaulle's convictions about the *national features of Russia* (as opposed to the transitory nature of *Soviet ideology*) and his notions of a Europe embracing East and West. On the other hand, the reunification of Germany (which the French government tried vainly to prevent or delay) has enhanced the status of that country and made it more assertive. This assertiveness, reflected in demands for a permanent seat on the UN Security Council and for an enlarged political role in the European Union, and in Germany's role in the disintegration of Yugoslavia, has revived the traditional French fears of Germany. Whether such fears are realistic is open to question; nevertheless, the perception that these developments have diminished the relative global status of France explains why France, while proclaiming the solidity of the Franco-German partnership, began to express greater interest in NATO and in a continuing U.S. involvement in Europe.[35] In fact, France played a crucial role in "activating" the involvement of NATO (and of the United States) in Bosnia.

As if to compensate for their reduced weight in Europe, the French have explored various opportunities for participation in global affairs, whether military (as in their contribution to peacekeeping forces in Bosnia, Cambodia, and Somalia), economic (aid to Russia), humanitarian (the missions of the French "Doctors without Borders" [*Médecins sans frontières*]), or symbolic (the French involvement in the Gulf War in 1991).[36] The growing power of Germany also explains why nearly half of the French citizens voted against the creation of the European Union.

FRANCE AND EUROPE

It is increasingly difficult to deal with the French polity in isolation from the European regional context. France was a crucial and often dominant partner in European integration efforts, from the inauguration of the Coal and Steel Community (the Schuman Plan) between 1950 and 1952 to the signing of the Treaty of European Union in 1992. It was due to France's insistence that a Common Agricultural Policy (CAP) was put in place in the late 1960s. With the progressive development of supranational institutions and European Community laws, many decisions taken in Paris are no longer entirely national. This is particularly true in economic policy; legislation on agriculture, social security, education, investment, value-added taxation, transport, and interest rates enacted in Paris must follow the guidelines and parameters set in Brussels.

These developments have had institutional and constitutional implications. French politicians and civil servants have played prominent roles in European institutions. Simone Veil, a prominent member of Balladur's government, once served as the president of the European Parliament; Giscard d'Estaing, until recently a member of that body, long harbored the ambition to become "president" of the European Union. A Frenchman, Jacques Delors, is president of the European Commission; another, Jacques Larosière, directs the European Bank for Reconstruction and Development.[37] Within the French state, too, new agencies and positions have been created to deal with the European Union: an ambassador to the European Union, assisted by several high officials; a ministerial portfolio (the deputy minister for European affairs under the foreign minister); a specialist in the premier's office; a presidential advisor; and an interministerial committee for problems of European economic cooperation.[38] The French Constitution has had to be amended (Art. 53) in order to make it conform to supranational norms on political asylum, and the role of the French Parliament will be enhanced (Art. 88) in conformity to the stipulations of the Maastricht Treaty on European Union. An important institutional adaptation was the creation, at the end of 1993, of an autonomous French National Bank. Modeled on the German Federal Bank (*Bundesbank*), this institution is expected to safeguard the stability of the French franc and to make monetary policy without direct interference by the government.

As we have seen (Chapter 4), conflicts over Europe have contributed to the factionalism within the mainstream parties of the Right and the Left, and one small party (Hunting, Fishing, Nature, and Traditions) was formed specifically in protest against European Union directives affecting hunting and gained considerable support during the elections to the European Parliament in 1989. To be sure, the French party divisions or voting patterns relating to European Parliament elections (and party organization within that body) do not correspond exactly to those obtaining for national contests;[39] nevertheless, such elections function as preliminary indicators of the popularity of national parties.

Despite the Gaullist emphasis on nationalism, most of the French did not object to the growth of European supranationalism and the corresponding sacrifice of state sovereignty as long as they gained symbolic as well as concrete benefits. The symbolic benefits were reflected in the location of the European Parliament in Strasbourg, the Alsatian capital; in the use of French as the major "working language" of the European Community (at least until the entry of Britain in the Community in the early 1970s); and in France's leading role in the Community's political relations with the outside. The concrete benefits were embodied in the fact that under the external tariff wall for agricultural imports, a cornerstone of CAP, the French farming sector enjoyed a privileged position in the Community's agricultural markets.

But as European integration proceeded, many French citizens worried about a growing loss of control over their own fate. Under pressure from the Commission of the European Union, the French government was forced to end its subsidies to the steel industry; the growth of multinational corporations (in part capitalized by France's European partners) reduced the possibilities of an "autonomous" national industrial policy; the raising of the interest rate on the German mark in 1992 contributed to the flight of French capital; and lower costs of production in neighboring countries—in Britain, for example—led to the transfer of industries and aggravated France's unemployment.

The question of European integration became a matter of serious controversy with the signing of the Treaty of Maastricht. The extended debate before the referendum on the ratification of the treaty revealed a cleavage that overlapped the various political parties. The pro-Maastricht forces insisted that France's economic well-being and European stability could best be safeguarded in the context of a united Europe. They also contended that the treaty contributed to democracy insofar as it called for an enlargement of the involvement of national legislatures in policy decisions taken by the European Union. Opponents of the treaty, especially on the Left, argued that the European Union was an essentially capitalist enterprise concerned more with profits than employment and that the decision makers in Brussels were too far removed from local needs. Other opponents, especially on the Right, warned that the European Union spelled the end of French independence and therefore constituted "a crime against the nation" (as Le Pen put it).[40] They pointed to various threats to the French way of life and to the country's environment[41] and to a possible disruption of traditional French political patterns.[42]

There was substance to both arguments: On the one hand, the European Community has, inter alia, helped to expand the market for French agricultural goods, protect French culture by reducing the influx of American audiovisual products, and encapsulate Germany in the Western European democratic system. On the other hand, the European Community has not been helpful in compensating for the loss of jobs in France or in guaranteeing the achievements of the welfare state (despite the European "Social Charter," which stipulates minimum supranational norms of social protection). More seriously, it has done little to enhance French military security. The Western European Union (formed in 1948 in a feeble attempt to produce a strictly European defense policy) has so far been unable to function as a substitute for NATO (although the utility of the latter organization has itself been put in question with the end of the Cold War); the creation of a joint Franco-German military contingent of 30,000 soldiers has been little more than symbolic; and the European Union provides no guarantee either against its political domination by Germany or against future attempts by that country to engage in adventures tending to destabilize Europe. In the meantime, however, the French have been forced to think in increasingly European terms and to redefine their notions of citizenship on the basis of less Jacobin and less "national" criteria.[43]

CONSTITUTIONAL AND INSTITUTIONAL ISSUES: CONCLUSIONS

In contrast to the continuing arguments about socioeconomic and educational policy, there has been a growing consensus about "system" issues. The major developments in the past decade have been the end of the legitimacy crisis, the weakening of extremist ideological thinking, and the gradual abandonment of the traditional Jacobin approach to defining French politics and society.

The first change is reflected in public opinion polls. In a poll conducted in 1983, the majority of respondents (57 percent) expressed the view that Fifth Republic institutions *as a whole* have functioned well (as against 25 percent who held a contrary view); in a 1985 poll, the results were similar,[44] and subsequent polls (specifically, for 1988 and 1991) show an overall predominance of positive views (see Table 10.1). Moreover, the negative views were often a reflection of dissatisfaction with the behavior of politicians and the policies pursued by the government rather than of a desire to change the institutions.[45] A significant exception has been the length of the presidential term of office, which a majority would like to see reduced to five years.[46]

TABLE 10.1 Confidence in political institutions

	1988			1991			1993		
	Yes	*No*	*No Opinion*	*Yes*	*No*	*No Opinion*	*Yes*	*No*	*No Opinion*
President of the Republic	77	14	9	73	18	9	56	35	9
Mayors	77	14	9	67	21	12	73	19	8
Prime Minister	66	22	12	65	26	9	56	34	10
Municipal councils	70	18	12	64	24	12	73	19	8
The institutions of the Fifth Republic	63	13	24	63	21	16	58	20	22
The general councils	58	18	24	59	22	19	61	23	16
The National Assembly				56	29	15	53*	36*	11*
The Constitutional Council	58	14	28	52	20	28	53	21	26
The civil service	59	29	12	49	42	9	53	39	8
The ministers	53	28	19	47	36	17	45	41	14
The deputies	52	29	19	46	38	16	51	36	13
Politicians in general	32	51	17	28	60	12	27	62	11
Political parties in general	24	58	18	19	69	12	21	69	10

*Parliament as a whole.
SOURCE: Poll conducted by *Nouvel Observateur* in March 1991. Adapted and abbreviated from *SOFRES, L'Etat de l'opinion 1992*, p. 33 and *1994*, pp. 221, 236. © Editions du Seuil, 1992, 1994.

Attitudes are even more positive toward certain specific aspects of the political system, such as the direct election of the president, the role of the Constitutional Council, and the use of popular referenda (see Table 10.2). With respect to the direct election of the president, the statistics represent a steadily positive evolution: In 1962, only 46 percent of French citizens were favorable to it; in 1969, 74 percent, and in 1978, 85 percent. In some cases, there has been a differential perspective, depending on whether the party with which a respondent identified belonged to the majority or the opposition. Thus, in 1978 only a minority of Communists and Socialists were favorably inclined toward the presidential dissolution power; in 1983, a majority of about 60 percent were so inclined.[47]

These attitudinal changes are inevitably mirrored in the acceptance of Fifth Republic institutions by the leaders of all the major parties to the extent that they entertain serious electoral ambitions. This is particularly noticeable among the Socialists, who have shown that they too can gain and maintain power in the context of the system established by and for de Gaulle. On the basis of the Communist Party's systematic electoral participation, its official commitment to such bourgeois values as competitive elections and civil liberties, its tacit acceptance of the patterns of presidential decision making, and its willingness to serve as a coalition partner of the Socialists, it may be argued that the PCF, too, has accepted the Fifth Republic. This change suggests a departure from the traditional extremism of that party, a departure that is also associated with the growing questioning of Marxism by France's intellectuals (and more recently with the disintegration of the Soviet Union). The National Front, although more critical than the other parties of the political roles assigned to the president and the prime minister, accepts, or pretends to accept, the overall institutional arrangements of the Fifth Republic. The Gaullist party was, of course, the party most

TABLE 10.2 Attitudes toward constitutional features (in percent of respondents)

Feature	Favorable	Unfavorable	No Opinion
Popular referendum	91	6	3
Popular election of president	89	7	4
Annulment of unconstitutional bills by Constitutional Council	72	14	14
Use of censure by National Assembly to oust government	71	18	11
Right of president to appoint prime minister of his or her choice	69	24	7
Right of president to dissolve National Assembly	59	30	11
President's use of emergency power (Art. 16)	54	37	9
Right of Assembly to override Senate	44	30	26
Government's power to adopt a bill without vote by deputies unless they vote for censure (Art. 49.3)	28	54	18

SOURCE: SOFRES poll, cited in *Le Monde*, 19 November 1992.

closely identified with the Fifth Republic. However, apart from having lost its monopoly as the defender of Fifth Republic institutions, the RPR has come to be identified with themes not specifically associated with Gaullism, such as neoliberalism, Europeanism, international cooperation, and a growing pro-American orientation.

These developments do not imply that political disagreements have been eliminated. There are still significant differences of opinion about the extent, speed, and desirability of decentralization policies, about the question of whether the systems of national and subnational elections should be retained or modified, and (as we have seen) about the length of the presidential term of office. There are also those who favor the simultaneous holding of presidential and parliamentary elections, in order to eliminate (or at least reduce) the likelihood of a president's being confronted with a hostile Assembly. Furthermore, although most of the French seem to favor an institutional balance of power, they are not necessarily in favor of "cohabitation" experiments and they have differences of opinion about what balance should exist between the rights of citizens and the rights of the state and what kind of diffusion of power there ought to be between the state and the local authorities and between the legislative and executive branches. Among the reforms that appear to enjoy wide support and are likely to be enacted are those proposed by a recent blue ribbon commission;[48] they include the abolition of Article 16, the right of ordinary citizens to appeal to the Constitutional Council, and the enhancement of the powers of Parliament.

Despite occasional arguments to the contrary,[49] presidential succession has proved to be quite orderly and has not provoked institutional crises thus far because the policy consequences of the shifts from one president to another have not been so drastic as one might have feared. This was true even of the shift from Giscard to Mitterrand, regardless of all the rhetoric about "revolutionary" changes: Many of Mitterrand's reforms—decentralization, the penal code, the organization of the media, and steps to consolidate and modernize industry— had been conceived or launched by Giscard, if not earlier. Succession crises have been avoided in part by the exercise of the dissolution power, in part by the continuities of bureaucratic structures, and in part by a "*decrispation*" (loosening) of interparty discourse on matters of social, economic, and institutional policies.

The growing consensus about political issues, which is one of the symptoms of the end of French "exceptionalism," was reflected in the reelection of Mitterrand—less as a Socialist than as a figure who has been both an architect and a beneficiary of the decline of ideology. An indication of this is the fact that public-opinion polls from 1986 on gave Mitterrand high marks, not for pursuing specific economic policies, but for maintaining social peace, safeguarding individual liberties, and ensuring the smooth functioning of political institutions.[50] French consensus has been reflected above all in a widespread feeling that France is becoming "dull and banalized."[51] The people's relative lethargy on political issues has allowed Mitterrand to occupy himself with matters that, during more difficult and divisive periods, would be considered trivial: glittering international festivities, pronouncements about art and literature, and a series of grandiose building projects in Paris.

Problems still persist. Some of them are transitory and likely to be resolved with the passage of time. This would be true of the periodic discoveries and trials of French war criminals, events that serve as reminders that the issue of French collaboration during World War II remains a sensitive one. It would also be true of the presence of a large number of foreigners, a problem that serves as a reminder of France's erstwhile colonial involvements, but one that is likely to be settled as the children of many of the immigrants become integrated into French society.

Other problems are older and likely to be more persistent, either because they are by nature more intractable or because their solutions are not voiced with sufficient clarity or conviction. For example, the political role of the bureaucracy has been a factor of continuity and stability, but even if the civil service were perceived as too powerful or too partisan, attempts at "depoliticizing" it and at weakening its decision-making role would be resisted by the beneficiaries of the status quo. Decentralization has been viewed positively, both as a principle and as a process, but old habits and expectations as well as the uncertain resources of local communities make it difficult to determine the ideal balance between national and local responsibilities. Many of the French are convinced that the judicial system is too partisan, too class-oriented, and too dependent on the political executive, but reforms of this system will be slow and piecemeal because the problem is not serious and because alternatives (such as those found in Anglo-American judicial processes) are not coherently articulated.

Whether the acceptance of institutions and the emerging pragmatism on a variety of policy issues have become permanent features on the French political scene—whether, in short, the "post-Gaullist" era inaugurated by Giscard's election and the "post-Socialist" era heralded by Mitterrand's reelection in 1988 will continue—is difficult to predict. It is possible that if current policies fail, ideologically extremist thinking might be renewed more significantly than it has been in the recent past or that economic frustrations might lead to the revival of a xenophobia that might threaten the fragile patterns of pluralism. One can only hope that the resilience, genius, and democratic spirit of the French will enable the political system to survive such challenges and to flourish.

NOTES

1. Gabriel A. Almond and G. Bingham Powell, *Comparative Politics: A Developmental Approach* (Boston: Little, Brown, 1966), pp. 263–266.
2. See Michel Crozier, *The Stalled Society* (New York: Viking Press, 1974); Mark Kesselman, "Overinstitutionalization and Political Constraint: The Case of France," *Comparative Politics* 3:1 (October 1970), 21–44; and Alain Peyrefitte, *Le Mal français* (Paris: Plon, 1976), especially Chapters 9, 10, and 23.
3. So named after Jean-Baptiste Colbert, the chief financial advisor (or "finance minister") of Louis XIV (seventeenth century). Colbert was a mercantilist under whose direction the state promoted industrialization and economic self-sufficiency by means of protective tariffs, taxes, subsidies, and price controls.

4. Except in 1981–1983, when Planning Minister Rocard was given authority over them.
5. Crozier, *The Stalled Society*, p. 97. Gaullist ministers (at least until the mid-1980s) generally endorsed the notion of the primacy of the public authorities over the private sector in economic affairs. However, as Ezra Suleiman points out in *Politics, Power, and Bureaucracy in France* (Princeton, NJ: Princeton University Press, 1974), pp. 173–177, certain ministers have felt that the hold of the higher civil service over the business community was excessive and favored a more rapid devolution of economic initiatives to the private sector.
6. Stephen S. Cohen, *Modern Capitalist Planning: The French Model* (Cambridge, MA: Harvard University Press, 1969), p. 4. Though dated, this work remains one of the most detailed on the subject.
7. For example, Etienne Hirsch (1952–1959), who had once been director of a private chemical firm; Pierre Massé (1959–1966), a director of the French Electricity Board; François-Xavier Ortoli (1966–1967) and Pierre Monjoie (1967–1974), both friends of Pompidou; and Jean Riper (1974–1978), an agricultural engineer, an official with the CGP, and subsequently director of INSEE. The director of the CGP for the 10th Plan, Pierre-Yves Cossé (appointed in 1988), had once been a major advisor of Jacques Delors, a conservative Socialist who had been Mitterrand's first finance minister. However, Cossé had also worked closely with Rocard in 1981–1982, when the latter was minister of planning.
8. Pierre Birnbaum, *Les Sommets de l'Etat* (Paris: Seuil, 1977), p. 123.
9. In mid-1981, the government set up an ad hoc study committee on the reform of planning, consisting of deputies, civil servants, academics, businesspersons, party leaders, and local politicians. Its report, submitted to Planning Minister Rocard and to Parliament, recommended greater administrative centralization, greater regional involvement in planning, and a more "social" orientation of the plan. See *Commission de réforme de la planification* (Paris: Documentation Française, June 1982). For a discussion of what planning came to mean under the Socialists, see Howard Machin, "Economic planning: Policy-making or policy-preparation?" in Paul Godt, ed., *Policy-Making in France: From de Gaulle to Mitterrand* (London: Pinter, 1989), pp. 127–141.
10. One commentator referred to these industries as "a row of lemons." Paul Lewis, "French Socialism Stubs Its Toe," *New York Times*, 31 July 1983. Another source, the *Economist* (16 July 1983, pp. 83–85), suggests that the Socialists "nationalized the Gaullists' mistakes."
11. See William Safran, "The Socialist Alternative in France: Mitterrand's Economic Policies," in Norman J. Vig and Steven E. Schier, eds., *Political Economy in Western Democracies* (New York: Holmes & Meier, 1985), pp. 200–227.
12. There was a pronounced shift from rhetoric about social responsibility to slogans about individual responsibility, productivity, and creativity.
13. See *Document d'orientation pour la préparation du IXe Plan* (Paris: Documentation Française, 1982); and Michel Ozenda and Omar Senhaji, "Le 9e Plan pour 1984–1988," *Regards sur l'actualité* 98 (February 1984), esp. 9–24.
14. See Pierre Bérégovoy, "Emploi, solidarité, dialogue social: un projet pour l'avenir," *Le Monde*, 14 December 1983; and George Ross, "Socialists v. Workers," *New Republic*, 17 February 1984, which refers (p. 15) to "multilevel backroom dealings among government, employers, and unions."
15. See "Rentrée sociale: Les Cinq Grands Dossiers de Rocard," *Le Point*, 28 August 1989, p. 34; and *Le Monde*, 5 September 1989.
16. See "Xe Plan: Ambition et modestie," *Regards sur l'actualité* 152 (June 1989), 3–35. Still, the plan entailed a projected state expenditure of 55 billion francs annually.

17. However, the government planned to retain ownership of the telephone system, the railroads, and gas and electrity.
18. Alan Riding, "French Leader Proposes Tax Rises and Stimulus," *New York Times*, 11 May 1993.
19. Under pressure from unemployed sectors of the lower-middle class, the Balladur government subsequently modified this proposal (the *"SMIC jeunes"*) by suggesting that young diploma holders be hired at 80 percent of the *average wage*.
20. There are also non-Catholic schools, including about 50 Jewish schools and a number of Protestant and nonsectarian private schools.
21. For a detailed analysis of this issue, see Frank R. Baumgartner, *Conflict and Rhetoric in French Policymaking* (Pittsburgh: University of Pittsburgh Press, 1989), pp. 178–183. On various postwar attempts to weaken the secular character of the French school system, see Philippe Raynaud and Paul Thibaud, *La Fin de l'école républicaine* (Paris: Calmann-Lévy, 1990), esp. Chapter 2.
22. The total outlay was expected to be about 5 billion francs. See François Dufay, "Loi Falloux: Chahut en perspective," *Le Point*, 3 July 1993, pp. 31–33.
23. In December 1993 (as four years earlier) several schoolgirls were expelled from a provincial junior high school for wearing Islamic headscarves to class.
24. A protest march in Paris in January 1994, involved more than 300,000 participants, including the leaders of the major trade unions and of all the left-wing parties.
25. Christine Garin, "Le Report de la discussion sur la révision de la loi Falloux," *Le Monde*, 7 September 1993. See also *Le Monde*, 29 June, 2 July, 2 August, and 6 November 1993. In an initial attempt to appease the defenders of laic education, the government had promised an extra 500 million francs, spread over a five-year period, to communes to repair public school buildings. Subsequently, it decided to create 2,500 new jobs in public elementary and secondary schools.
26. At least a third of the total allocations for research were earmarked for the *Centre national de recherche scientifique* (CNRS), a governmental institution employing more than 20,000 scholars in the natural and social sciences as well as the humanities.
27. This compares to the combined outlay for 1993 of $363 million by the National Endowment for the Arts and the National Endowment for the Humanities. It is estimated that the per capita expenditure for culture in France is $41, compared to $1.43 in the United States. See John Rockwell, "French Culture under Socialism: Egotism or a Sense of History?" *New York Times*, 24 March 1993.
28. Henri Giordan, *Démocratie culturelle et droit à la différence: Rapport au ministre de la culture* (Paris: Documentation Française, 1982); and Jean-Jack Queyranne, *Les Régions et la décentralisation culturelle: Rapport au ministre de la culture* (Paris: Documentation Française, 1982). See also W. Safran, "The French State and Ethnic Minority Cultures: Policy Dimensions and Problems," in J. R. Rudolph, Jr., and R. J. Thompson, eds., *Ethnoterritorial Politics, Policy, and the Western World* (Boulder, CO, and London: Lynne Rienner, 1989), pp. 115–157.
29. For example, the ERASMUS program, which provides for the exchange of students and teachers among members of the European Community, the support of multinational research projects, and the equivalence of diplomas.
30. An illustration is the opening of Disneyland east of Paris in 1991.
31. See *Changer la vie: Programme de gouvernement du parti socialiste* (Paris: Flammarion, 1971), pp. 183–207; *Projet socialiste* (Paris: Club Socialiste du Livre, 1980), pp. 337–360. See also "Le Vrai Programme de Mitterrand," *Nouvel Observateur*, 15 June 1981, pp. 22–23. For less recent but more comprehensive treatments, see Edward Kolodziej, *French International Policy under de Gaulle and Pompidou: The*

Politics of Grandeur (Ithaca, NY: Cornell University Press, 1974); and Michael M. Harrison, *The Reluctant Ally: France and Atlantic Security* (Baltimore, MD: Johns Hopkins University Press, 1981). For more recent analyses, see the critical Gabriel Robin, *La Diplomatie de Mitterrand ou le triomphe des apparences* (Paris: Editions de la Bièvre, 1985); and Stanley Hoffmann, "Mitterrand's Foreign Policy, or Gaullism by any other Name," in George Ross et al., *The Mitterrand Experiment* (New York: Oxford University Press, 1987), pp. 294–305.

32. For example, statements by Michel Jobert, minister of foreign trade in the first Mauroy government; Pierre Chevènement, former minister of technology; Jack Lang, the minister of culture; and Claude Cheysson, the foreign minister.

33. See Dominique Moïsi, "Franco-Soviet Relations and French Foreign Policy," in Godt, *Policy-Making in France*, pp. 211–225.

34. In 1981, an estimated 80 percent of the Jewish electorate voted for Mitterrand.

35. See Michel Drain, "La Sécurité européenne," *Regards sur l'actualité* 179 (March 1992), 3–32. For a well-reasoned study of post–Cold War French foreign policy, see Philip H. Gordon, *A Certain Idea of France: French Security Policy and the Gaullist Legacy* (Princeton, NJ: Princeton University Press, 1993). The recent foreign policy adaptations can be called "Gaullism" if one considers it a generic term for French foreign policy as such, and if one believes that de Gaulle, were he alive, would have pursued the policies currently pursued.

36. See Pia Christina Wood, "François Mitterrand and the Persian Gulf War: The Search for Influence," *French Politics and Society* 10:3 (Summer 1992), 44–62.

37. The first president of the bank (whom Larosière replaced) was Jacques Attali, who had been for many years a close political advisor to President Mitterrand.

38. See Christian Lequesne, *Paris-Bruxelles: Comment se fait la politique européenne de la France* (Paris: Presses de la Fondation Nationale des Sciences Politiques, 1993).

39. In the European Parliament elections of 1989, the Center-Right, united nationally in the UDF, was split between the Liberals (headed by Giscard d'Estaing) and the much larger Christian Democrats.

40. Robert Ladrech, "France in the European Community: Implications for Domestic Politics and Institutions," paper presented at the annual meeting of the American Political Science Association, Chicago, 1992, p. 9. See also Daniel Carton, "A la recherche de la dimension européenne," *Le Monde*, 8–9 March 1992, p. 7; Hughes Portelli, "Le référendum sur l'Union européenne," *Regards sur l'actualité* 184 (September–October 1992), 3–12; Elisabeth Guigou, "Les Français et l'Europe, regard d'une pro-Maastricht," and Philippe Séguin, "Les Français et l'Europe, regard d'un anti-Maastricht," in SOFRES, *L'Etat de l'opinion 1993*, pp. 87–97.

41. For example, in 1991, a European Commission ruling banning the use of unpasteurized milk in cheese, which would have made the production of Camembert illegal; and in 1992, the shipment of German industrial waste to France. The first problem was resolved when the Commission reversed itself, and the second was dealt with by bilateral negotiations.

42. For instance, the right of residents of France who are citizens of other European Union countries to vote in municipal elections (Art. 88, sec. 2) enables them to influence the outcome of national (i.e., Senate) elections.

43. See William Safran, "State, Nation, National Identity, and Citizenship: France as a Test Case," *International Political Science Review* 12:3 (July 1991), esp. 235–236.

44. A poll conducted in December 1985 revealed that 56 percent of the respondents had confidence in the institutions of the Fifth Republic, 14 percent had no confidence,

and 30 percent did not express an opinion. SOFRES poll, cited in SOFRES, *L'Etat de l'opinion 1987* (Paris: Seuil, 1987), p. 162.

45. SOFRES, *L'Etat de l'opinion 1993*, p. 225. The distinction the French often make between the state and the institutions as such and the people who run them is reflected in a poll of November 1992 showing that a majority of the respondents think the institutions function well but that democracy does not. See *Le Monde*, 19 November 1992, p. 13.
46. According to a poll of January 1992, 57 percent favored a five-year term, 18 percent a four-year term, and only 17 percent the existing seven-year term. Furthermore, 78 percent would favor a two-term limit. SOFRES, *L'Etat de l'opinion*, pp. 228–229. In one of his books (*2 Français sur 3* [Paris: Flammarion, 1984]), Giscard d'Estaing came out in favor of a six-year term.
47. *Le Monde*, 4 October 1983.
48. The Commission Vedel, appointed by Mitterrand in 1992.
49. For example, Douglas Ashford, *Politics and Policy in France: Living with Uncertainty* (Philadelphia: Temple University Press, 1982), p. 310.
50. See SOFRES poll of April 1987 on "Mitterrand six ans après," SOFRES, *L'Etat de l'opinion 1988*, p. 23, in which 66 percent gave Mitterrand a positive evaluation of his performance (since 1981) with respect to civil liberties; 65 percent, with regard to social peace; 55 percent, with regard to the smooth functioning of institutions; 48 percent, information and television policies, and 40 percent, the reduction of inequalities.
51. Olivier Duhamel and Jérôme Jaffré, "Dix Leçons de 1988," in SOFRES, *L'Etat de l'opinion 1989* (Paris: Seuil, 1989), p. 240.

appendix

The French Constitution of 1958

[This is an abridged version, containing the most important provisions, and including all parts mentioned in the book.][1]

PREAMBLE

The French people hereby solemnly proclaim their attachment to the Rights of Man and the principles of national sovereignty as defined by the Declaration of 1789, reaffirmed and completed by the Preamble to the Constitution of 1946.

[Article 1, which follows this preamble, deals with the establishment of the French Community (meant to be the equivalent of the British Commonwealth of former colonies). The Community has been defunct since 1960.]

TITLE I—ON SOVEREIGNTY

Article 2. France is a Republic, indivisible, secular, democratic, and social. It shall ensure the equality of all citizens before the law, without distinction of origin, race, or religion. It shall respect all beliefs.

The language of the Republic is French.
The national emblem is the tricolor flag, blue, white, and red.
The national anthem is the "Marseillaise."
The motto of the Republic is "Liberty, Equality, Fraternity."
Its principle is government of the people, by the people, and for the people.

Article 3.   National sovereignty belongs to the people, which shall exercise it through their representatives and by means of the referendum.

No section of the people, nor any individual, may attribute to themselves or himself the exercise thereof.

Suffrage may be direct or indirect under the conditions stipulated by the Constitution. It shall always be universal, equal, and secret.

All French citizens of both sexes who are of age and who enjoy civil and political rights may vote under the conditions to be determined by law.

Article 4.   Political parties and groups shall play a part in the exercise of the right to vote. They shall be formed freely and shall carry on their activities freely. They must respect the principles of national sovereignty and of democracy.

TITLE II—THE PRESIDENT OF THE REPUBLIC

Article 5.   The President of the Republic shall see that the Constitution is respected. He shall ensure, by his arbitration, the regular functioning of the governmental authorities, as well as the continuity of the State.

He shall be the guarantor of national independence, of the integrity of the territory, and of respect for Community agreements and treaties.

Article 6.[2]   The President of the Republic shall be elected for seven years by direct universal suffrage.

The procedures implementing the present article shall be determined by an organic law.

Article 7.[3]   The President of the Republic shall be elected by an absolute majority of the votes cast. If no such majority obtains on the first ballot, a second ballot shall take place on the second Sunday following the first ballot. Then only the two candidates who have received the greatest number of votes on the first ballot, after taking into account, if need be, better placed candidates who have withdrawn, may present themselves.

The voting shall begin at the formal summons of the Government.

The election of the new President shall take place twenty days at the least and thirty-five days at the most before the expiration of the powers of the President in office.

In the case of vacancy of the Presidential office for any reason whatsoever, or if the President is declared incapable of exercising his functions by the Constitutional Council, the question having been referred to the latter by the Government and the decision being taken by an absolute majority of the members of the Council, the functions of the President, with the exception of those listed in Articles 11 and 12, shall be temporarily exercised by the President of the Senate, or, if the latter is in turn prevented from functioning, by the Government.

In case of vacancy or when the Constitutional Council declares the President permanently incapable of exercising his function, the ballot for the election of the new President shall take place, except in case of *force majeure* officially noted by the Constitutional Council, at least twenty days and not more than thirty-five days after the beginning of the vacancy or the declaration of the permanent character of the incapability.

If, within seven days before the deadline for the registration of candidacies, a person who, less than thirty days before this date, had publicly announced his decision to be a candidate should die or encounter an impediment, the Constitutional Council may decide to postpone the election.[4]

If, before the first ballot, one of the candidates should die or encounter an impediment, the Constitutional Council shall order postponement of the election.

In the event that one of the two candidates who had received the greatest number of votes before any eventual withdrawals should die or encounter an impediment, the Constitutional Council shall declare that the whole electoral process should be started again; the same rule applies when one of the two candidates running for the second ballot dies or becomes impeded.

All cases are submitted to the Constitutional Council according to conditions set out in Article 61, paragraph 2, below or to those required for candidacy by the organic law referred to in Article 6 above.

The Constitutional Council may extend the deadlines included in the third and fifth paragraphs, provided that the ballot is held not later than thirty-five days after the date of the Constitutional Council's decision. If implementation of this paragraph results in postponing the election to a date subsequent to the expiration of the mandate of the President in charge, then the President remains in office until his successor is proclaimed.

There may by no application of either Articles 49, 50, or 89 of the Constitution during the vacancy of the Presidency of the Republic or during the period that elapses between the declaration of the definitive character of the impediment of the President of the Republic and the election of his successor.

Article 8. The President of the Republic shall appoint the Prime Minister. He shall terminate the functions of the Prime Minister when the latter presents the resignation of the Government.

On the proposal of the Prime Minister, he shall appoint and dismiss the other members of the Government.

Article 9. The President of the Republic shall preside over the Council of Ministers.

Article 10. The President of the Republic shall promulgate the laws within fifteen days following their final adoption and transmission to the Government.

Before the end of this period he may ask Parliament for a reconsideration of the law or of certain of its articles. This reconsideration cannot be refused.

Article 11. The President of the Republic, on the proposal of the Government during Parliamentary sessions, or on joint motion of the two Assemblies, published in the *Journal Officiel,* may submit to a referendum any bill dealing with the organization of the public authorities, entailing approval of a Community agreement, or authorizing the ratification of a treaty that, without being contrary to the Constitution, might affect the functioning of the institutions.

When the referendum decides in favor of the bill, the President of the Republic shall promulgate it within the time limit stipulated in the preceding article.

Article 12. The President of the Republic may, after consultation with the Prime Minister and the Presidents of the Assemblies, declare the dissolution of the National Assembly.

General elections shall take place twenty days at the least and forty days at the most after the dissolution.

The National Assembly shall convene by right on the second Thursday following its election. If this meeting takes place between the periods provided for ordinary sessions, a session shall, by right, be held for a fifteen-day period.

There may be no further dissolution within a year following these elections.

Article 13. The President of the Republic shall sign the ordinances and decrees decided upon in the Council of Ministers.

He shall make appointments to the civil and military posts of the State.

Councilors of State, the Grand Chancellor of the Legion of Honor, Ambassadors and envoys extraordinary, Master Councilors of the court of Accounts, prefects, representatives of the Government in the Overseas Territories, general officers, rectors of academies [regional divisions of the educational system], and directors of central administrations shall be appointed in meeting of the Council of Ministers.

An organic law shall determine the other posts to be filled in meeting of the Council of Ministers, as well as the conditions under which the power of the President of the Republic to make appointments to office may be delegated by him and exercised in his name.

Article 14. The President of the Republic shall accredit Ambassadors and envoys extraordinary to foreign powers; foreign Ambassadors and envoys extraordinary shall be accredited to him.

Article 15. The President of the Republic shall be commander of the armed forces. He shall preside over the higher councils and committees of national defense.

Article 16. When the institutions of the Republic, the independence of the Nation, the integrity of its territory, or the fulfillment of its international commitments are threatened in a grave and immediate manner and when the regular functioning of the constitutional public authorities is interrupted, the President of the Republic shall take the measures required by these circumstances, after official consultation with the Prime Minister, the Presidents of the Assemblies, and the Constitutional Council.

He shall inform the nation of these measures by message.

These measures must be inspired by the desire to ensure to the constitutional public authorities, in the shortest possible time, the means of fulfilling their assigned functions. The Constitutional Council shall be consulted about such measures.

Parliament shall meet by right.

The National Assembly may not be dissolved during the exercise of emergency powers [by the President].

Article 17. The President of the Republic shall have the right of pardon.

Article 18. The President of the Republic shall communicate with the two assemblies of Parliament by means of messages, which he shall cause to be read and which shall not be followed by any debate.

Article 19. The acts of the President of the Republic, other than those provided for under Articles 8 (first paragraph), 11, 12, 16, 18, 54, 56, and 61, shall be countersigned by the Premier and, should circumstances so require, by the appropriate ministers.

TITLE III—THE GOVERNMENT

Article 20. The Government shall determine and direct the policy of the nation. It shall have at its disposal the administration and the armed forces.

It shall be responsible to Parliament under the conditions and according to the procedures stipulated in Articles 49 and 50.

Article 21. The Prime Minister shall direct the operation of the Government. He shall be responsible for national defense. He shall ensure the execution of the laws. Subject to the provisions of Article 13, he shall have regulatory powers and shall make appointments to civil and military posts.

He may delegate certain of his powers to the ministers.

He shall replace, should the occasion arise, the President of the Republic as chairman of the councils and committees provided for under Article 15.

He may, in exceptional instances, replace him as chairman of a meeting of the Council of Ministers by virtue of an explicit delegation for a specific agenda.

Article 22. The acts of the Prime Minister shall be countersigned, when circumstances so require, by the ministers responsible for their execution.

Article 23. Membership in the Government shall be incompatible with the exercise of any Parliamentary mandate; with the holding of any office at the national level in business, professional, or labor organizations; and with any public employment or professional activity.

An organic law shall determine the conditions under which the holders of such mandates, functions, or employments shall be replaced.

The replacement of members of Parliament shall take place in accordance with the provisions of Article 25.

TITLE IV—THE PARLIAMENT

Article 24. The Parliament shall comprise the National Assembly and the Senate.

The deputies to the National Assembly shall be elected by direct suffrage.

The Senate shall be elected by indirect suffrage. It shall ensure the representation of the territorial units of the Republic. Frenchmen living outside France shall be represented in the Senate.

Article 25. An organic law shall determine the term for which each assembly is elected, the number of its members, their indemnities, the conditions of eligibility, and the offices incompatible with membership in the assemblies.

It shall likewise determine the conditions under which, in case of a vacancy in either assembly, persons shall be elected to replace the deputy or senator whose seat has been vacated until the holding of new complete or by-elections to the assembly concerned.

Article 26. No member of Parliament may be prosecuted, pursued, arrested, detained, or tried as a result of the opinions or votes expressed by him in the exercise of his functions.

No member of Parliament may, during Parliamentary sessions, be prosecuted or arrested for criminal or minor offenses without the authorization of the assembly of which he is a member except in the case of *flagrante delicto.*

When Parliament is not in session, no member of Parliament may be arrested without the authorization of the Secretariat of the assembly of which he is a member, except in the case of *flagrante delicto,* of authorized prosecution, or of final conviction.

The detention or prosecution of a member of Parliament shall be suspended if the assembly of which he is a member so demands.

Article 27.   All binding instructions [upon members of Parliament] shall be null and void.

The right to vote of the members of Parliament shall be personal.

An organic law may, under exceptional circumstances, authorize the delegation of a vote. In this case, no member may be delegated more than one vote.

Article 28.   Parliament shall convene by right in two ordinary sessions each year. The first session shall begin on October 2 and last eighty days.

The second session shall begin on April 2 and may not last longer than ninety days.

If October 2 or April 2 is a holiday, the session shall begin on the first working day following.

Article 29.   Parliament shall convene in extraordinary session at the request of the Prime Minister, or of the majority of the members of the National Assembly, to consider a specific agenda.

When an extraordinary session is held at the request of the members of the National Assembly, the closure decree shall take effect as soon as the Parliament has exhausted the agenda for which it was called, and at the latest twelve days from the date of its meeting.

Only the Prime Minister may ask for a new session before the end of the month following the closure decree.

Article 30.   Apart from cases in which Parliament meets by right, extraordinary sessions shall be opened and closed by decree of the President of the Republic.

Article 31.   The members of the Government shall have access to the two assemblies. They shall be heard when they so request.

They may call for the assistance of commissioners of the government.

Article 32.   The President of the National Assembly shall be elected for the duration of the legislature. The President of the Senate shall be elected after each partial election [of the Senate].

Article 33.   The meetings of the two assemblies shall be public. An *in extenso* report of the debates shall be published in the *Journal Officiel.*

Each assembly may sit in secret committee at the request of the Prime Minister or of one-tenth of its members.

TITLE V—RELATIONS BETWEEN PARLIAMENT AND THE GOVERNMENT

Article 34.   All laws shall be voted by Parliament.
Laws shall establish the regulations concerning:

- civil rights and the fundamental guarantees granted to the citizens for the exercise of civil liberties; the obligations imposed by national defense upon the persons and property of citizens;

- nationality, status, and legal capacity of persons, marriage contracts, inheritance, and gifts;
- definitions of crimes and misdemeanors as well as the penalties applicable to them; criminal procedure; amnesty; the creation of new types of jurisdictions and the statute of the judiciary;
- the basis, the rate, and the methods of collecting taxes of all types; the currency system.

Laws shall likewise determine the rules concerning:

- the electoral system for the Parliamentary and local assemblies;
- the creation of categories of public corporations;
- the fundamental guarantees granted to civil and military personnel employed by the State;
- the nationalization of enterprises and the transfer of property from the public to the private sector.

Laws shall determine the fundamental principles of:

- the general organization of national defense;
- the free administration of local communities, the extent of their jurisdiction, and their resources;
- education;
- property rights, civil and commercial obligations;
- labor law, trade-union law, and social security.

Finance laws shall determine the resources and obligations of the State under the conditions and with the reservations to be provided for by an organic law.

Laws pertaining to national planning shall determine the objectives of the economic and social action of the State.

The provisions of the present article may be developed in detail and completed by an organic law.

Article 35. Parliament shall authorize the declaration of war.

Article 36. Martial law shall be decreed in a meeting of the Council of Ministers. Its prolongation beyond twelve days may be authorized only by Parliament.

Article 37. Matters other than those that fall within the domain of law shall be subject to rule-making.

Legislative texts concerning these matters may be modified by decrees issued after consultation with the Council of State. Those legislative texts which may be passed after the present Constitution has become operative shall be modified by decree only if the Constitutional Council has stated that they have a regulatory character as defined in the preceding paragraph.

Article 38. The Government may, for the implementation of its program, ask Parliament to authorize it, for a limited period, to take through ordinances measures that are normally within the domain of law.

The ordinances shall be enacted in meetings of the Council of Ministers after consultation with the Council of State. They shall come into force upon their publication, but shall become null and void if the bill for their ratification is not submitted to Parliament before the date set by the enabling act.

At the expiration of the time limit referred to in the first paragraph of the present article, the ordinances may be modified only by law in those matters which are within the legislative domain.

Article 39. The Premier and the members of Parliament alike shall have the right to initiate legislation.

Government bills shall be discussed in the Council of Ministers after consultation with the Council of State and shall be filed with the Secretariat of one of the two assemblies. Finance bills shall be submitted first to the National Assembly.

Article 40. Bills and amendments introduced by members of Parliament shall not be considered when their adoption would have as a consequence either a diminution of public revenues, or the creation or increase of public expenditures.

Article 41. If it appears in the course of legislative procedure that a parliamentary bill or an amendment is not within the domain of law or is contrary to a delegation of authority granted by virtue of Article 38, the Government may request that it be ruled out of order.

In case of disagreement between the Government and the President of the assembly concerned, the Constitutional Council, upon the request of either party, shall rule within a time limit of eight days.

Article 42. The discussion of Government bills shall pertain, in the first assembly to which they have been referred, to the text presented by the Government.

An assembly, given a text passed by the other assembly, shall deliberate on the text that is transmitted to it.

Article 43. Government and Parliamentary bills shall, at the request of the Government or of the assembly concerned, be sent for study to committees especially designated for this purpose.

Government and Parliamentary bills for which such a request has not been made shall be sent to one of the permanent committees, the number of which shall be limited to six in each assembly.

Article 44. Members of Parliament and of the Government shall have the right of amendment.

After the opening of the debate, the Government may oppose the examination of any amendment which has not previously been submitted to a committee.

If the Government so requests, the assembly concerned shall decide, by a single vote, on all or part of the bill under discussion, retaining only the amendments proposed or accepted by the Government.

Article 45. Every bill is discussed successively in the two assemblies with a view to agreement on identical versions.

When, as a result of disagreement between the two assemblies, a bill has not been passed after two readings in each assembly, or, if the Government has declared the bill urgent, after a single reading by each assembly, the Prime Minister is entitled to have the bill sent to a joint committee composed of equal numbers from the two assemblies, with the task of finding agreed versions of the provisions in dispute.

The version prepared by the joint committee may be submitted by the Government to the two assemblies for their approval. No amendment may be accepted without the agreement of the Government.

If the joint committee does not produce an agreed version, or if the version agreed is not approved as provided for in the preceding paragraph, the Government may ask the National Assembly, after one more reading by the National Assembly and by the Senate, to decide the matter. In this case, the National Assembly may adopt either the version prepared by the joint committee or the last version passed by itself, modified, if necessary, by one or any of the amendments passed by the Senate.

Article 46. The laws that the Constitution characterizes as organic shall be passed and amended under the following conditions.

A Government or Parliamentary bill shall be submitted to the deliberation and to the vote of the first assembly to which it is submitted no more than fifteen days following its introduction.

The procedure of Article 45 shall be applicable. Nevertheless, lacking an agreement between the two assemblies, the text may be adopted by the National Assembly on final reading only by an absolute majority of its members.

The organic laws relative to the Senate must be passed in the same manner by the two assemblies.

Organic laws may be promulgated only after a declaration by the Constitutional Council on their constitutionality.

Article 47. Parliament shall pass finance bills under conditions to be stipulated by an organic law.

Should the National Assembly fail to reach a decision on first reading within a time limit of forty days after a bill has been introduced, the Government shall refer to the Senate, which must rule within a time limit of fifteen days. The procedure set forth in Article 45 shall then be followed.

Should Parliament fail to reach a decision within a time limit of seventy days, the provisions of the bill may be put into effect by ordinance.

Should the finance bill establishing the revenues and expenditures of a fiscal year not be filed in time for it to be promulgated before the beginning of that fiscal year, the Government shall immediately request from Parliament the authorization to levy the taxes and shall make available by decree the funds needed to meet the Government commitments already voted.

The time limits provided for in the present article shall be suspended when Parliament is not in session.

The Court of Accounts shall assess Parliament and the Government in supervising the implementation of the finance laws.

Article 48. The discussion of the bills submitted or agreed upon by the Government shall have priority on the agenda of the assemblies in the order determined by the Government.

One meeting each week shall be reserved, by priority, for questions asked by members of Parliament and for answers by the Government.

Article 49.   The Prime Minister, after deliberation in the Council of Ministers, may pledge the responsibility of the Government before the National Assembly with regard to the program of the Government, or if it be so decided with regard to a declaration of general policy.

The National Assembly may call into question the responsibility of the Government by the vote of a motion of censure. Such a motion shall be in order only if it is signed by at least one-tenth of the members of the National Assembly. The vote may only take place forty-eight hours after the motion has been introduced. Only votes favorable to the motion shall be counted. It shall be considered adopted only if supported by a majority of the members of the Assembly. Should the motion of censure be rejected, its signatories may not introduce another motion in the course of the same session, except in the case provided for in the next paragraph.

The Prime Minister may, after deliberation in the Council of Minister, pledge the Government's responsibility before the National Assembly on the vote of all or part of a bill or motion. In that case, the text shall be considered as adopted, unless a motion of censure, filed in the succeeding twenty-four hours, is voted under the conditions laid down in the previous paragraph.

The Prime Minister shall be entitled to ask the Senate for the approval of a general policy declaration.

Article 50.   When the National Assembly adopts a motion of censure, or rejects the program or a declaration of general policy of the Government, the Prime Minister must submit the resignation of the Government to the President of the Republic.

Article 51.   The closure of ordinary or extraordinary sessions shall by right be delayed, should the occasion arise, in order to permit the application of the provisions of Article 49.

Article 52.   The President of the Republic shall negotiate and ratify treaties.

He shall be informed of all negotiations leading to the conclusion of an international agreement not subject to ratification.

TITLE VI

Article 53.   The Republic may conclude, with the European states with which it is linked by commitments identical with its own with respect to asylum and the protection of human rights and fundamental liberties, agreements establishing their respective competences to examine the demands for asylum presented to them. Nonetheless, even if the demand does not come under their competence by virtue of these agreements, the authorities of the Republic continue to maintain the right to grant asylum to any foreigner persecuted because of his activities in the cause of freedom, or who asks for the protection of France for another reason.[5]

Peace treaties, commercial treaties, treaties or agreements relative to international organization, those that imply a commitment for the finances of the State, those that modify provisions of a legislative nature, those relative to the status of persons, and those that call for the cession, exchange or addition of territory may be ratified or approved only by a law.

They shall go into effect only after having been ratified or approved.

No cession, no exchange, no addition of territory shall be valid without the consent of the populations concerned.

Article 54. If the Constitutional Council, the matter having been referred to it by the President of the Republic, by the Premier, or by the president of one or the other assembly, or by sixty deputies or sixty senators, shall declare that an international commitment contains a clause contrary to the Constitution, the authorization to ratify or approve the international commitment in question may be given only after amendment to the Constitution.[6]

Article 55. Treaties or agreements duly ratified or approved shall, upon their publication, have an authority superior to that of laws, subject, for each agreement or treaty, to its application by the other party.

TITLE VII—THE CONSTITUTIONAL COUNCIL

Article 56. The Constitutional Council shall consist of nine members, whose term of office shall last nine years and shall not be renewable. One-third of the membership of the Constitutional Council shall be renewed every three years. Three of its members shall be appointed by the President of the Republic, three by the President of the National Assembly, three by the President of the Senate.

In addition to the nine members provided for above, former Presidents of the Republic shall be ex officio for life of the Constitutional Council.

The President shall be appointed by the President of the Republic. He shall have the deciding vote in case of a tie.

Article 57. The office of member of the Constitutional Council shall be incompatible with that of minister or member of Parliament. Other incompatibilities shall be determined by an organic law.

Article 58. The Constitutional Council shall ensure the regularity of the election of the president of the Republic.

It shall examine complaints and shall announce the results of the vote [for president].

Article 59. The Constitutional Council shall rule, in the case of disagreement, on the regularity of the election of deputies and senators.

Article 60. The Constitutional Council shall ensure the regularity of referendum procedures and announce the results thereof.

Article 61. Organic laws, before their promulgation, and the rules of procedure of the Parliamentary assemblies, before they come into application, must be submitted to the Constitutional Council, which shall decide whether they conform to the Constitution.

To the same end, laws may be submitted to the Constitutional Council, before their promulgation, by the President of the Republic, the Prime Minister, the President of either assembly, sixty deputies, or sixty senators.[7]

In the cases provided for by the two preceding paragraphs, the Constitutional Council must make its ruling within a time limit of one month. Nevertheless, at the request of the Government, in case of emergency, this period shall be reduced to eight days.

In these same cases, referral to the Constitutional Council shall suspend the time limit for promulgation.

Article 62. A provision declared unconstitutional may not be promulgated or implemented.

The decisions of the Constitutional Council are not subject to appeal. They are binding on public authorities and on all administrative and judicial authorities.

Article 63. An organic law shall determine the rules of organization and functioning of the Constitutional Council, the procedure to be followed before it, and in particular the periods of time allowed for bringing disputes before it.

TITLE VIII—ON JUDICIAL AUTHORITY

Article 64. The President of the Republic shall be the guarantor of the independence of the judicial authority.

He shall be assisted by the High Council of the Judiciary.

An organic law shall determine the status of magistrates.

Magistrates may not be removed from office.

Article 65. The High Council of the Judiciary shall be presided over by the President of the Republic. The Minister of Justice shall be its Vice President ex officio. He may preside in place of the President of the Republic.

The High Council of the Judiciary shall comprise two sections, one of them having competence regarding judges and the other, regarding state attorneys.

The section having competence regarding judges shall include, in addition to the President of the Republic and the Minister of Justice, five judges and one state attorney, one State councilor nominated by the Council of State, and three individuals belonging neither to Parliament nor to the judiciary, nominated, respectively, by the President of the Republic, the Speaker of the National Assembly, and the Speaker of the Senate.

The section competent with regard to state attorneys shall include, in addition to the President of the Republic and the Minister of Justice, five state attorneys and one judge, the Councilor of State and three of the individuals mentioned in the preceding paragraph.

The section of the High Council of the Judiciary competent with regard to judges shall present nominations for judges of the Court of Cassation, for First Presidents of Courts of Appeal, and for presidents of lower courts of appeal.

The High Council shall act as a disciplinary council for judges. In such cases, it shall be presided over by the First President of the Court of Cassation.

The section of the High Council of the Judiciary competent with regard to state attorneys shall give its opinion on proposals for nomination of state attorneys. It shall be consulted on disciplinary sanctions concerning state attorneys.

An organic law shall determine the procedures implementing the present article.

Article 66. No one may be arbitrarily detained. The judicial authority, guardian of individual liberty, shall ensure respect for this principle under the conditions stipulated by law.

TITLE IX—THE HIGH COURT OF JUSTICE

Article 67. A High Court of Justice shall be instituted.

It shall be composed of members [of Parliament] elected, in equal number, by the National Assembly and the Senate after each general or partial election to these assemblies. It shall elect its President from among its members.

An organic law shall determine the composition of the High Court, its rules and the procedure to be followed before it.

The President of the Republic shall not be held accountable for actions performed in the exercise of his office except in the case of high treason. He may be indicted only by the two assemblies ruling by identical vote in open balloting and by an absolute majority of the members of said assemblies. He shall be tried by the High Court of Justice.

TITLE X—ON THE PENAL RESPONSIBILITY OF MEMBERS OF THE GOVERNMENT[8]

Article 68.[9] The members of the government shall be held criminally liable for actions performed in the exercise of their office and deemed to be crimes or misdemeanors at the time they were committed.

They shall be judged by a Court of Justice of the Republic.

The Court of Justice of the Republic shall be bound by the definition of crimes and misdemeanors as well as by the determination of penalties as they are established by the criminal laws [in force when the acts were committed].

The Court of Justice of the Republic includes fifteen judges; twelve members of Parliament elected, in equal numbers, by the National Assembly and the Senate after each general or partial election of these chambers; and three judges of the Court of Cassation, one of whom shall preside over the Court of Justice of the Republic.

Every person who deems himself to have been injured by a crime or misdemeanor [committed by] a member of the government in the exercise of his functions may lodge a complaint with an appeals commission.

This commission either ends the procedure or transmits it to the state prosecutor attached to the Court of Cassation in order that the Court of Justice of the Republic may be convoked.

An organic law shall determine the procedures implementing the present article.

TITLE XI—THE ECONOMIC AND SOCIAL COUNCIL

Article 69. The Economic and Social Council, at the request of the Government, shall give its opinion on such Government bills, ordinances, and decrees, as well as on the private members' bills that have been submitted to it.

A member of the Economic and Social Council may be designated by the latter to present, before the Parliamentary assemblies, the opinion of the Council on the Government or Parliamentary bills that have been submitted to it.

Article 70. The Economic and Social Council may likewise be consulted by the Government on any problem of an economic or social character of interest to the Republic or the Community. Any plan, or any program-bill of an economic or social character, shall be submitted to it for its advice.

Article 71. The Composition of the Economic and Social Council and its rules of procedure shall be determined by an organic law.

TITLE XII—ON TERRITORIAL UNITS

Article 72. The territorial units of the Republic are the communes, the Departments, the Overseas Territories. Other territorial units may be created by law.

These units shall be free to govern themselves through elected councils and under the conditions stipulated by law.

In the departments and the territories, the Delegate of the Government shall be responsible for the national interests, for administrative supervision, and for seeing that the laws are respected.

Article 73. Measures of adjustment required by the particular situation of the Overseas Departments may be taken with regard to their legislative system and administrative organization.

Article 74. The Overseas Territories of the Republic shall have a special organization, which takes into account their own interests within the general interests of the Republic.

The statutes of the Overseas Territories are determined by organic laws which define in particular the competencies of their own institutions and are modified in the same form after consultation with the Territorial Assembly concerned.

The other modalities of their special organization are defined and modified by law after consultation with the Territorial Assembly concerned.

Article 75. Citizens of the Republic who do not have ordinary civil status, the only status referred to in Article 34, may keep their personal status as long as they have not renounced it.

Article 76. The Overseas Territories may retain their status within the Republic.

TITLE XV—ON THE EUROPEAN COMMUNITIES AND THE EUROPEAN UNION[10]

Article 88. The Republic participates in the European Communities and the European Union, composed of the States that have chosen, freely and in accordance with the treaties they have adopted, to exercise certain of their competencies in common.

Subject to reciprocity and according to the methods provided by the Treaty of European Union signed on 7 February 1992, France agrees to the transfer of the competencies necessary for the establishment of the European Economic and Monetary Union as well as for the determination of rules and regarding the crossing of the frontiers outside the member countries of the European Community.

Subject to reciprocity and according to the methods provided by the Treaty of European Union signed on 7 February 1992, the right to vote and eligibility to candidacy in municipal elections may be granted only to citizens of the Union residing in France. The citizens may not exercise the functions of mayor or deputy mayor nor participate in the selection of senatorial electors or in the election of the Senate. An organic law, voted in identical terms by the two chambers [of Parliament], shall determine the procedures implementing the present article.

TITLE XVI

Article 89.   The initiative for amending the Constitution shall belong to the President of the Republic on the proposal of the Prime Minister and to the members of Parliament.

The proposed amendment must be passed by the two assemblies in identical terms. The amendment shall become effective after approval by a referendum.

However, the proposed amendment shall not be submitted to a referendum when the President of the Republic decides to submit it to Parliament convened in Congress; in this case, the proposed amendment shall be approved only if it is accepted by a three-fifths majority of the votes cast. The Bureau of the Congress shall be that of the National Assembly.

No amendment procedure may be initiated or pursued when the integrity of the territory is in jeopardy.

The Republican form of government shall not be subject to amendment.

[Title XVII (Articles 90-92) contains temporary provisions that deal with the initial phases of effectuating the Constitution. Since they are no longer applicable, this title has been eliminated.]

NOTES

1. Based on English translation furnished by the French Embassy, Press and Information Division, Washington, D.C.
2. Adopted by referendum of October 28, 1962.
3. Adopted by referendum of October 28, 1962.
4. This and the following four paragraphs were adopted as an amendment on June 14, 1976.
5. Amendment by Congress, 19 November 1993.
6. Amendment by Congress, 19 July 1993.
7. This paragraph was modified by a constitutional amendment adopted on 29 October 1974.
8. (old) Title X (The Economic and Social Council) becomes Title XI.
9. Amendment by Congress, 19 July 1993.
10. Amendment by Congress, 26 June 1992.

Select Bibliography

The following list includes a sampling of books that have been consulted by the author as well as a number of additional works of interest to the student of French politics. The periodical literature cited in the footnotes is not listed separately, nor are a number of French-language titles that are of use primarily to the specialist. However, the reader's attention is directed to the following periodicals that have been found most useful: French Embassy Press and Information Service, *News from France* (monthly and irregular bulletins); *Année politique; Contemporary French Civilization;* Documentation Française, *Documents d'études; French Politics and Society; Le Monde* (daily and [occasionally] weekly editions, and *Dossiers et Documents); Pouvoirs; Regards sur l'Actualité; Revue administrative; Revue française de science politique; Revue française de sociologie; Revue politique et parlementaire; SOFRES; Sondages; Tocqueville Review;* and the weekly news magazines *L'Express, Le Nouvel Observateur,* and *Le Point.*

The Historical and Constitutional Background and General Treatments

Andrews, William G., and Hoffmann, Stanley, eds. *The Fifth Republic at Twenty.* Albany: SUNY Press, 1981.

Avril, Pierre. *La Ve République: Histoire politique et constitutionnelle.* Paris: Presses Universitaires de France, 1987.

Beaucé, Thierry de. *La République de France.* Paris: Grasset, 1991.

Becker, Jean-Jacques. *Histoire politique de la France depuis 1945.* Paris: Armand Colin, 1988.

Bell, John. *French Constitutional Law.* Oxford: Clarendon Press, 1992.

Brogan, Denis W., *The Development of Modern France.* London: Hamish Hamilton, 1940.

Debré, Jean-Louis. *La Constitution de la Ve République.* Paris: Presses Universitaires de France, 1975.

De Gaulle, Charles, *The Complete War Memoirs,* 3 vols. New York: Simon and Schuster, 1972.

————. *Major Addresses, Statements, and Press Conferences of General de Gaulle, May 19, 1958–January 31, 1964.* New York: French Embassy, Press and Information Division, 1964.

Denquin, Jean-Marie. *1958: La Genèse de la Ve République.* Paris: Presses Universitaires de France, 1988.

Duhamel, Olivier, and Parodi, Jean-Luc, eds. *La Constitution de la Cinquième République.* Paris: Presses de la Fondation Nationale des Sciences Politiques, 1985.

Hall, Peter, Hayward, Jack, and Machin, Howard, eds. *Developments in French Politics.* New York: St. Martin's Press, 1990.

Hoffman, Stanley. *Decline or Renewal? France Since the 1930s.* New York: Viking Press, 1974.

Hughes, H. Stuart. *The Obstructed Path: French Social Thought in the Years of Desperation, 1930–1960.* New York: Harper & Row, 1968.

Jones, H. S. *The French State in Question.* Cambridge, England: Cambridge University Press, 1993.

Maier, Charles S., and White, Dan S., eds. *The Thirteenth of May: The Advent of de Gaulle's Republic.* New York: Oxford University Press, 1968.

Rohr, John A. *To Write a Constitution.* Lawrence: University of Kansas Press, 1994.

Shirer, William L. *The Collapse of the Third Republic.* New York: Simon & Schuster, 1969.

Thomson, David. *Democracy in France Since 1870,* 5th ed. New York: Oxford University Press, 1969.

Society, Economy, and Political Culture

Ardagh, John. *France Today.* London and New York: Penguin, 1987.

Borne, Dominique. *Histoire de la société française depuis 1945.* Paris: Armand Colin, 1988.

Crozier, Michel. *The Stalled Society.* New York: Viking Press, 1973.

————. *Strategies of Change: The Future of French Society.* Cambridge, MA: MIT Press, 1982.

Duhamel, Alain. *Le Complexe d'Astérix.* Paris: Gallimard, 1985.

Fourastié, Jean. *Les Trente glorieuses ou la révolution invisible.* Paris: Fayard, 1979.

Hough, J. R. *The French Economy.* New York: Holmes & Meier, 1982.

Mendras, Henri, ed. *La Sagesse et le désordre.* Paris: Gallimard, 1980.

Mendras, Henri, and Cole, Alistair. *Social Change in France: Towards a Cultural Anthropology of the Fifth Republic.* Cambridge, U.K.: Cambridge University Press, 1991.

Michelat, Guy, Potel, Julien, Sutter, Jacques, and Maître, Jacques. *Les Français sont-ils encore Catholiques?* Paris: Cerf, 1991.

Noiriel, Gérard. *Le Creuset français.* Paris: Seuil, 1988.

Peyrefitte, Alain. *The Trouble with France.* New York: Knopf, 1981.

Tilly, Charles. *The Contentious French: Four Centuries of Popular Struggle.* Cambridge, MA: Harvard University Press, 1986.

Todd, Emmanuel. *La Nouvelle France.* Paris: Seuil, 1988.

Weber, Eugen. *Peasants into Frenchmen.* Stanford, CA: Stanford University Press, 1976.

Wylie, Laurence. *Chanzeaux: A Village in Anjou.* Cambridge, MA: Harvard University Press, 1967.

———. *Village in the Vaucluse,* 2nd ed. New York: Harper & Row, 1964.

Zeldin, Theodore. *The French.* New York: Pantheon, 1982.

Political Parties and Elections

Bell, David S. *Contemporary French Political Parties.* New York: St. Martin's Press, 1982.

Bell, David, and Criddle, Byron. *The French Socialist Party: The Emergence of a Party of Government,* 2nd ed. Oxford: Clarendon Press, 1988.

Birenbaum, Guy. *Le Front national en politique.* Paris: Balland, 1992.

Cayrol, Roland. *La Nouvelle Communication politique.* Paris: Larousse, 1986.

Charlot, Jean. *The Gaullist Phenomenon.* New York: Praeger, 1971.

Cole, Alistair, and Campbell, Peter. *French Electoral Systems and Elections Since 1789,* 3rd ed. Brookfield, VT: Gower, 1989.

Converse, Philip, and Pierce, Roy. *Political Representation in France.* Cambridge, MA: Harvard University Press, 1986.

Dreyfus, Michel. *PCF: Crises et dissidences de 1920 à nos jours.* Paris: Editions Complexe, 1990.

Dupoirier, Elisabeth, and Grunberg, Gérard. *Mars 1986: La Drôle défaite de la gauche.* Paris: Presses Universitaires de France, 1986.

Furet, François, Julliard, Jacques, and Rosanvallon, Pierre. *La République du centre.* Paris: Calmann-Lévy, 1988.

Gaffney, John. *The French Left and the Republic.* New York: St. Martin's Press, 1989.

Gaxie, Daniel, ed. *Explication du vote.* Paris: Presses de la Fondation Nationale des Sciences Politiques, 1985.

Johnson, R. W. *The Long March of the French Left.* New York: St. Martin's Press, 1981.

Lancelot, Alain, ed. *1981: Les Elections de l'alternance.* Paris: Presses de la Fondation Nationale des Sciences Politiques, 1986.

Mayer, Nonna, and Perrineau, Pascal, eds. *Le Front national à découvert.* Paris: Presses de la Fondation Nationale des Sciences Politiques, 1989.

Penniman, Howard, ed. *France at the Polls: 1981 and 1986: Three National Elections.* Durham, NC: Duke University Press, 1988.

Poniatowski, Michel. *La Catastrophe socialiste.* Paris: Editions du Rocher, 1991.

Rémond, René. *Les Droites en France.* Paris: Aubier, 1982.

Robrieux, Pierre. *Histoire intérieure du parti communiste.* 2 vols. Paris: Fayard, 1980–1983.

Schain, Martin. *French Communism and Local Power.* London: Pinter, 1985.

Wilson, Frank L. *French Political Parties under the Fifth Republic.* New York: Praeger, 1982.

Ysmal, Colette. *Le Comportement électoral en France.* Paris: La Découverte, 1986.

Interest Groups

Baumgartner, Frank R. *Conflict and Rhetoric in French Policymaking.* Pittsburgh, PA: University of Pittsburgh Press, 1989.

Berger, Suzanne D., ed. *Organizing Interests in Western Europe.* Cambridge, U.K.: Cambridge University Press, 1981.

Cerny, Philip G., ed. *Social Movements and Protests in France.* New York: St. Martin's Press, 1982.

Keeler, John T. S. *The Politics of Neocorporatism in France.* New York and Oxford: Oxford University Press, 1987.

Labbé, Dominique, and Croisat, Maurice. *La Fin des syndicats?* Paris: L'Harmattan, 1992.

Mouriaux, René. *La CGT.* Paris: Seuil, 1982.

————. *Le Syndicalisme face à la crise.* Paris: Armand Colin, 1988.

Rosanvallon, Pierre. *La Question syndicale.* Paris: Presses Calmann-Lévy, 1988.

Smith, W. Rand. *Crisis in the French Labor Movement.* New York: St. Martin's Press, 1987.

Stasi, Bernard. *Vie associative et démocratie nouvelle.* Paris: Presses Universitaires de France, 1979.

Weber, Henri. *Le Parti des patrons: Le CNPF, 1946-1986.* Paris: Seuil, 1986.

Wilson, Frank L. *Interest-Group Politics in France.* Cambridge, MA: Cambridge University Press, 1987.

The Executive and the Legislature

Andrews, Williams G. *Presidential Government in Gaullist France: A Study of Executive-Legislative Relations, 1958-1974.* Albany, NY: SUNY Press, 1982.

Antoni, Jean-Dominique, and Pascale. *Les Ministres de la Cinquième République.* Paris: Presses Universitaires de France, 1976.

Auger, Véronique. *Trois Hommes qui comptent.* Paris: Pluriel, 1993.

Colombani, Jean-Marie. *Le Mariage blanc.* Paris: Gallimard, 1986.

————. *Portrait d'un président.* Paris: Gallimard, 1985.

Conte, Arthur. *Les Premiers ministres de la Ve République.* Paris: Le Pré aux Clercs, 1986.

Derfler, Leslie. *President and Parliament.* Boca Raton: University Presses of Florida, 1983.

Duverger, Maurice. *Bréviaire de la cohabitation.* Paris: Presses Universitaires de France, 1986.

Elgie, Robert. *The Role of the Prime Minister in France, 1981-1989.* New York: St. Martin's Press, 1993.

Frémy, Dominique. *Quid de présidents de la République et des candidats.* Paris: Laffont, 1987.

Hollifield, James, and Ross, George, eds. *Searching for the New France.* New York and London: Routledge, 1991.

Laurens, André. *Le Métier politique ou la conquête du pouvoir.* Paris: Alain Moreau, 1980.

Massot, Jean. *La Présidence de la République en France.* Paris: Documentation Française, 1986.

Maus, Didier, ed. *Les Grandes Textes de la pratique institutionnelle de la Ve République.* Paris: Documentation Française, 1988.

Nay, Catherine. *Les Sept Mitterrand.* Paris: Grasset, 1988.

Northcott, Wayne. *Mitterrand: A Political Biography.* New York: Holmes & Meier, 1992.

Pfister, Thierry. *Dans les coulisses du pouvoir.* Paris: Albin Michel, 1986.

Rémond, René, et al. *Quarante Ans de cabinets ministériels: De Léon Blum à Georges Pompidou.* Paris: Fondation Nationale des Sciences Politiques, 1982.

Ross, George, Hoffmann, Stanley, and Malzacher, Sylvia, eds. *The Mitterrand Experiment.* New York: Oxford University Press, 1987.

Stone, Alec. *The Birth of Judicial Politics in France: The Constitutional Council in Comparative Perspective.* New York: Oxford University Press, 1992.

Thody, Philip. *French Caesarism from Napoleon I to Charles de Gaulle.* New York: St Martin's Press, 1989.

Administration and the Judicial Process

Bernard, Paul. *L'Etat et la décentralisation: Notes et Documents.* Paris: Documentation Française, 1983.

Birnbaum, Pierre. *Les Elites socialistes au pouvoir, 1981-1985.* Paris: Presses Universitaires de France, 1985.

Cohen-Tanugi, Laurent. *Le Droit sans l'Etat.* Paris: Presses Universitaires de France, 1985.

Dion, Stéphane. *La Politisation des maires.* Paris: Economica, 1986.

Fayolle, Gérard. *Des Elus locaux sous la Ve République.* Paris: Hachette, 1989.

Pfister, Thierry. *La République des fonctionnaires.* Paris: Albin Michel, 1988.

Pinsseau, Hubert. *L'Organisation judiciaire de la France.* Paris: Documentation Française, 1985.

Schmidt, Vivien A. *Democratizing France: The Political and Administrative History of Decentralization.* Cambridge and New York: Cambridge University Press, 1991.

Suleiman, Ezra. *Elites in French Society.* Princeton, NJ: Princeton University Press, 1978.

_____. *Private Power and Centralization in France.* Princeton, NJ: Princeton University Press, 1987.

Tarrow, Sidney. *Between Center and Periphery: Grassroots Politicians in Italy and France.* New Haven, CT: Yale University Press, 1977.

Economic, Social, and Foreign Policies

Aldrich, Robert, and Connell, John, eds. *France in World Politics.* London and New York: Routledge, 1989.

Ambler, John S., ed. *France Under Socialist Leadership.* Philadelphia: Institute for the Study of Human Issues, 1983.

Ashford, Douglas E., ed. *Policy and Politics in France: Living with Uncertainty.* Philadelphia: Temple University Press, 1982.

Cerny, Philip G., and Schain, Martin A., eds. *French Politics and Public Policy.* New York: St. Martin's Press, 1980.

Christofferson, Thomas R. *The French Socialists in Power: From Autogestion to Cohabitation.* Newark: University of Delaware Press, 1991.

Friend, Julius W. *Seven Years in France: François Mitterrand and the Unintended Revolution, 1981–1988*. Boulder, CO: Westview Press, 1989.

Godt, Paul, ed. *Policy-Making in France from de Gaulle to Mitterrand*. London: Pinter, 1989.

Gordon, Philip H. *A Certain Idea of France: French Security Policy and the Gaullist Legacy*. Princeton, NJ: Princeton University Press, 1993.

Hall, Peter. *Governing the Economy: The Politics of State Intervention in Britain and France*. New York: Oxford University Press, 1986.

Hayward, Jack. *The State and the Market Economy*. New York: New York University Press, 1986.

Kolodziej, Edward A. *French International Policy under de Gaulle and Pompidou*. Ithaca, NY: Cornell University Press, 1974.

Machin, Howard, and Wright, Vincent, eds. *Economic Policy and Policy-Making under the Mitterrand Presidency*. New York: St. Martin's Press, 1985.

Robin, Gabriel. *La Diplomatie de Mitterrand ou le triomphe des apparences*. Paris: Editions de la Bièvre, 1985.

Wilsford, David. *Doctors and the State: The Politics of Health Care in France and the United States*. Durham, NC: Duke University Press, 1991.

Index